MA

Reconstruction in Post-War Germany

British Occupation Policy and the Western Zones, 1945–55

GERMANY UNDER ALLIED OCCUPATION

Reconstruction in Post-War Germany

British Occupation Policy and the Western Zones,
1945–55

Edited by
Ian D. Turner

BERG
Oxford / New York / Munich
Distributed exclusively in the US and Canada by
St. Martin's Press, New York

First published in 1989 by
Berg Publishers Limited
Editorial Offices:
77 Morrell Avenue, Oxford OX4 INQ, UK
105 Taber Avenue, Providence R.I. 02906, USA
Westermühlstraße 26, 8000 München 5, FRG

British Library Cataloguing in Publication Data
Reconstruction in post-war Germany : British
    occupation policy and the Western Zones, 1945–55
    1. Germany. Occupation by British Military
    forces, 1945–1959
    I. Turner, Ian D.
    943.087'4
    ISBN 0–85496–096–1

Library of Congress Cataloging-in-Publication Data
Reconstruction in post-war Germany : British occupation policy and the Western
    Zones, 1945–55 / edited by Ian D. Turner.
        p.   cm.
        Bibliography: p.
        Includes index.
        ISBN 0–85496–096–1   : $45.00 (U.S. : est.)
        1.   Reconstruction (1939–1951)—Germany.   2. World War, 1939–1945–
    Occupied territories.   3.   Great Britain—Foreign relations–
    Germany.   4.   Germany—Foreign relations—Great Britain.
    I.   Turner, Ian D., 1955– .
    D829.G3R38 1989
    940.53'41—dc19   88–23452

Printed in Great Britain by Billing & Sons Ltd, Worcester

Contents

Tables

Figures

Foreword

With the opening of the archives, post-war German history has become a major area of research, and this volume of essays seems to me to be a particularly good example of the impressive work currently being done by a younger generation of historians in Britain. It also neatly reflects a shift of emphasis towards economic and social history, after political themes, and above all the reconstruction of constitutional government and parliamentary parties, had provided the main focus of research during the 1970s. In a curious way, this shift has led to a revaluation of the British role in Allied occupation policy. As Ian Turner points out in his Introduction, the debate on the origins of the Cold War and the conflict between the United States and the Soviet Union in Europe has tended to divert attention from the British contribution to occupation policy. What recent work now seems to demonstrate is that Britain moved into defeated Germany with a comparatively much more coherent view of what was to be done than did the United States. In Washington the Treasury and Justice Departments had developed concepts of what to do with Germany which were very different from those of the War and State Departments. In these circumstances it took some time for the views of the War and State Departments, which were less radical and punitive, to assert themselves within the Administration and the US occupation authorities on the ground.

This difference between Britain and America may in itself be very telling of the character of Whitehall and Westminster where there tends to exist a greater homogeneity of outlook than in the executive and legislative branches of government in Washington. The implication for early post-war occupation policy in Germany is that the more prolonged bureaucratic infighting that continued in the US Administration provided Britain for a relatively brief, but clearly identifiable period with considerable opportunities on a

Volker Berghahn

broad front to shape the development of her zone of occupation. Only after Washington had resolved its interdepartmental conflicts and a clear line had emerged both with regard to the treatment of the Soviet Union and on what was to be done with the western zones of occupation, did the Americans begin to assert their greater weight and to use their considerable economic leverage against those British policies with which they disagreed. This change is embodied by the creation of the Bizone in January 1947—the result of both the American determination to play the first fiddle and of the growing realisation in London that Britain did not have the material resources to support its own policies of reconstruction of Germany. Thus the wealthier Americans were brought in and particularly into the Ruhr, the industrial centre of western Germany. What remained thereafter was a British capacity to retard, though not to stop, those economic policies of which London disapproved. What also remained was the British determination to put through at least those *non*-economic reconstruction policies which they had always seen as inseparable from industrial reconstruction.

While it is worthwhile studying these later phases of British occupation policy, the most fascinating period, it seems to me, is the very early post-war phase, when the United States had not yet become the dominant actor on the western stage. To be sure, there were at this point the Vansittartists who held that there was no hope of redemption for the Germans. This view was succinctly put by A. J. P. Taylor in his widely read *The Course of German History*, published in July 1945:

> The history of the Germans is a history of extremes. It contains everything except moderation, and in the course of a thousand years the Germans have experienced everything except normality. . . . One looks in vain in their history for a *juste mileu*, for common sense—the two qualities which have distinguished France and England. Nothing is normal in German history except violent oscillations.

And to a later edition of the book which appeared in 1961 he added:

> There was a great pother after the war about how we should educate the Germans in democracy. I never understood how this should be done. Democracy is learned by practice, not by sitting on forms at a political finishing school. Our only contribution should have been to ensure that the Germans did not 'solve' their problem at the expense of others.

x

But as this last sentence also indicates this view of defeated Germany never achieved the weight it sometimes looked like having gained in the eyes of contemporaries. From the start, the dominant approach was a more constructive and 'reasonable' one. It aimed at the reintegration of the Germans into the community of European nations once their capacity to wage war had been destroyed.

This British approach is discernible across the whole range of policies. It informed the efforts to get the economy going as quickly as possible; it also guided British efforts to rebuild the administrative infrastructure and the Civil Service. To be sure, in each area of activity there was also the immediate and pragmatic calculation of reducing the costs of the occupation to Britain by enabling the Germans to help themselves. However, behind this there was always the long-term objective of creating institutions which were not only stable, but also structurally compatible with those of western Europe and of Britain in particular. Not surprisingly perhaps, the British way of organising and of doing things was invariably the yardstick to be applied to the German case. In no other area was this more tangible than in the field of education and political education. Those who were involved in designing school curricula, press licensing instructions or broadcasting reforms appreciated that it was not enough to restructure and recast institutional arrangements. Attitudes and mentalities also had to be changed, and being educators, as many of them were, they believed that people's minds could and should be shaped and moulded just as decisively as organisational structures.

If, in tackling these tasks, the British underestimated one thing—though not as badly as the Americans—it was that mentalities of an entire society and national culture, even of a country as thoroughly defeated and shaken as Germany, cannot be recast within a few years. In terms of the speed of change, occupied western Germany may be compared with a big ocean-liner, subjected to a sharp movement of its rudder. For a while this liner will continue to move straight on, and the response to the change of direction will not be immediately visible. This inertia of West German society has led those historians who chose to study the immediate effects of, say, re-education to feel that the whole British effort had been largely futile. However, in order to judge the success or failure of this effort, it may be advisable to take a more long-term view; for in the long run Germany's reintegration into the western community of nations, which Britain had been aiming at since 1945, appears to have been successful at all levels. If this is so, it was to no small degree also due to British policies in their zone of occupation. If, on the other hand, some authors in this volume tend to take a more critical view of the British impact, their contributions will promote lively debate, and indeed have already done so. What, apart from this important point, I found particularly valuable about this volume is chapter 12. Clearly, this overview of current research in the field will not merely help interested readers to orientate themselves, but will perhaps also encourage others to move into it.

Volker Berghahn
June 1988

Acknowledgements

This work is more than usually a cooperative effort. Apart from the direct participation of the contributors, I have also been able to draw on the knowledge and information of what has become an international community of scholars interested in this period in German history. Indeed, the response of these individuals to a questionnaire I sent out on current research provided much of the raw data for the survey and the bibliography.

Some of the contributions to this book were originally written for a German History Society Conference held at St Antony's College, Oxford University, in March 1987. I should like to thank the Society's then chairman, Professor Volker Berghahn, for his advice and support in the preparation and conception of the conference. We are also grateful to the Stiftung Volkswagenwerk whose generous funding made the project possible.

Lastly, I should like to thank Carol Crosbie for the hard work she did on the typescript and the bibliography.

Ian Turner
Henley-on-Thames, June 1988

Abbreviations

ACA	Allied Control Authority
ACC	Allied Control Council
ADGB	Allgemeiner Deutscher Gewerkschaftsbund
AFL	American Federation of Labour
AHC	Allied High Commission
AN	Archives Nationales
APW	Armistice and Post-war Committee (of Cabinet)
ATCA	Armistice Terms and Civil Affairs Committee
AVB	Akten zur Vorgeschichte der Bundesrepublik
AZG	Archiv der Zeche Gneisenau
BAK	Bundesarchiv, Koblenz
BA–ZWA	Bundesarchiv-Zwischenarchiv Hangelar
BBA	Bergbau-Archiv
BBC	British Broadcasting Corporation
BDA	Bundesvereinigung deutscher Arbeitgeberverbände
BDI	Bundesverband der Deutschen Industrie
BHE	Bund der Heimatvertriebenen und Entrechteten
BHStA	Bayerisches Hauptstaatsarchiv
BICO	Bipartite Control Office
BLA	Bayerisches Landtagsarchiv
BPA	British Purchasing Agency
BSL	Bayerisches Statistisches Landesamt
CCG	Control Commission for Germany
CCG(BE)	Control Commission for Germany (British Element)
CDU	Christlich-Demokratische Union
CCS	Combined Chiefs of Staff (US–UK)
CFM	Council of Foreign Ministers
COGA	Control Office for Germany and Austria
CSG	Combined Steel Group
CSU	Christlich-Soziale Union
DGB	Deutscher Gewerkschaftsbund
DIW	Deutsches Institut für Wirtschaft
DKBL	Deutsche Kohlenbergbau-Leitung

DKU	Deutsche Kohlenverkauf
DMG	Deputy Military Governor
DNVP	Deutsch-nationale Volkspartei
ECOSC	Economics Sub-Commission, CCG
ECSC	European Coal and Steel Community
EIPS	Economic and Industrial Planning Staff (Foreign Office)
EMPC	Economics and Movement Planning Committee (CCG)
EPC	Economic Planning Committee (21 Army Gp)
ERP	European Recovery Program
FDP	Freie Demokratische Partei
FDGB	Freier Deutscher Gewerkschaftsbund
FO	Foreign Office
FOGS	Foreign Office (German Section)
FRUS	Foreign Relations of the United States
GMSO	German Mines Supplies Office
GOVSC	Governmental Sub-Commission, CCG
H and HT	Highways and Highway Transport
HSta Düsseldorf	Nordrhein-Westfälisches Hauptstaatsarchiv
HStA Hanover	Niedersächisches Hauptstaatsarchiv
IAR	International Authority for the Ruhr
IARA	Inter-Allied Reparation Agency
I A and C	Internal Affairs and Communications Division (CCG)
IHK	Industrie- und Handelskammer
ISK	Internationaler Sozialistischer Kampfbund
IVB	Industrieverband Bergbau
JCS	Joint Chiefs of Staff (US)
JEIA	Joint Export–Import Agency
KPD	Kommunistische Partei Deutschlands
KRO	Kreis Resident Officer
LAA	Landesarbeitsamt
LSH	Landesarchiv Schleswig-Holstein
MR	Monthly Report
NATO	North Atlantic Treaty Organisation
NdsLA	Niedersächsisches Landtagsarchiv
NGCC	North German Coal Control
NGISC	North German Iron and Steel Control
NRCs	Nominated Representative Councils
NRW	Nordrhein-Westfalen (North Rhine-Westphalia)
NSDAP	Nationalsozialistische Deutsche Arbeiter-Partei
NWDR	Nordwestdeutscher Rundfunk
ObaD	Oberbergamt Dortmund
OBADA	Archive of the Landesoberbergamt Dortmund

OKD	Oberkreisdirektor
OMGUS	Office of Military Government (US)
ORC	Overseas Reconstruction Committee (of the British Cabinet)
PORO	Public Opinion Research Office
PPC	Post-Hostilities Planning Committee
PR/ISC	Public Relations and Information Services Control
PRO	Public Record Office, Kew
PS	Public Safety (CCG)
PSSB	Public Safety (Special Branch)
PWD	Psychological Warfare Division
PWE	Political Warfare Executive
RB	Regierungsbezirk
RC	Regional Commissioner
RD	Rural District
REO	Regional Economics Officer
RGO	Regional Governmental Officer
RP	Regierungspräsident
SAP	Sozialistische Arbeiterpartei
SCD	Standing Committee on Denazification
SCDP	Standing Committee on Denazification Policy
SED	Sozialistische Einheitspartei Deutschlands
SHAEF	Supreme Headquarters Allied Expeditionary Forces
SPD	Sozialdemokratische Partei Deutschlands
StA	Staatsarchiv Munich
STA	Steel Trustee Association
STAM	Staatsarchiv Münster
SVR	Siedlungsverband Ruhrkohlenbezirk
TUC	Trades Union Congress
TV	Treuhandverwaltung
UK/US	
CCG	UK/US Combined Coal Group
VFW	Verwaltung für Wirtschaft
WAM	Wiederaufbau-Ministerium NRW
WAV	Wirtschaftliche Aufbau-Vereinigung
WFTU	World Federation of Trade Unions
WWA	Westfälisches Wirtschaftsarchiv
WWI	Wirtschaftswissenschaftliches Institut
ZAC	Zonal Advisory Council
ZdKw	Zahlen der Kohlenwirtschaft
ZEI	Zonal Executive Instruction
ZEO	Zonal Executive Offices
ZFA	Zentralamt für Arbeit
ZPI	Zonal Policy Instruction

PART I

Setting the Scene

Introduction

The British Occupation and its Impact on Germany
Ian Turner

This volume has a threefold purpose. It is intended first of all to produce in an accessible form and in the English language a work which deals with the most important and interesting aspects of Germany's immediate post-war history and in particular with the role played by Britain as an occupying power. Secondly, it is designed to act as a showcase for recent research in the area by British scholars. Together, the findings reproduced here constitute, if not a unified view, a distinctive perspective on a subject which has hitherto been dominated by West German historians. Finally, and most importantly, through the stimulus of the individual contributions and by the overview which the book seeks to provide of what already has been achieved and what still needs to be done, it is hoped that this anthology will encourage further research in the area.

It would not betray any secret to reveal that this book has its origins in an academic conference.[1] Chapters 2, 3, 4, 6, 10 and 12 were originally delivered as papers. However, from the beginning the selection and treatment of the topics was intended to ensure a high degree of internal coherence. These papers have since been revised for publication and chapters have been commissioned from specialists to fill the more obvious gaps.

The British occupation has never achieved the same sort of attention from historians as has been devoted to US rule in Germany. In part, the early availability of US records is responsible for this. But mainly it can be attributed to the preoccupation of historians with the breakdown of Soviet–American relations as the main

1. 'British Occupation and the Reconstruction of Western Germany' German History Society Regional Conference, St Antony's College, Oxford, March 1987.

cause of the Cold War and a tendency to relegate Britain to the level of a faded imperial power living on past glories. Nobody can deny the eventual preponderance of the United States in West Germany. But in many ways the most significant aspects of West Germany's post-war development have their seeds in the British Zone. This was the area of greatest industrial significance and it was also the area where the most influential political leaders of the period built their power bases: Adenauer in the CDU, Schumacher in the SPD and Böckler in the DGB. For these reasons alone the policy of the British in Germany and its impact on the British Zone deserve examination.

Whilst no volume of this nature can claim to be in any way comprehensive or 'definitive', the range of work represented here affords an opportunity for at least an interim assessment or *Zwischenbilanz* of the nature and impact of the British occupation on German society. This introduction draws on the material presented here to sketch answers to three questions: what were the British trying to achieve in Germany; what did the occupation actually achieve; and what forces were at work to produce this result?

The Aims of British Occupation Policy

There is a school of thought which insists that British aims in Germany can be encapsulated in the words 'responsible government, federation of Germany and European partnership'.[2] Each of these goals had their place in British policy, though not all had equal weight or necessarily applied all the time. As a description of the essence British policy, however, they are at the very least misleading. The overriding purpose of Britain's involvement in the occupation of Germany was to ensure that after two world wars, both provoked in British eyes by German aggression, the German nation would never again be in a position to wage war against Britain and her allies. Security was the prime concern but the threat was not just a revival of Nazism. The perceived danger stemmed rather from a deep-seated flaw in the German 'national character': the inherent bellicosity of Germans through the ages, the teutonic lust for conquest and domination. These views, propounded most forcefully by Lord Vansittart, were widely held right across the political

2. See K. Jürgensen, 'British Occupation Policy after 1945 and the Problem of Re-educating Germany', *History*, Vol. 68, No. 223, June 1983, pp. 225–44.

spectrum in wartime Britain[3] and informed much of British policy-making towards Germany. Unlike his American counterpart, Morgenthau, whose prejudices gave a radical, restrictive orientation towards early US policy in Germany, Vansittart's chief legacy was a cynical view of all Germans, irrespective of past history or political convictions, which in its effect proved deeply conservative. Thus, Barbara Marshall in her contribution on democratisation reveals British mistrust of the radical anti-fascist elements in post-war German society. David Welch shows how mobilising the collective guilt of all the German people for wartime atrocities was one of the dominant themes of British re-education policy and my own chapter on denazification describes how Vansittartism made British officials sceptical of the value of replacing one set of elites with another which might be equally tainted with unsound Germanic ideas.

Not that Vansittartism was uncontested within the British policy establishment. As the contributions in part III make clear, other views, more enlightened by present standards perhaps, were represented in the Foreign Office and in some divisions of the Control Commission. Moreover, British preoccupation with security and the tendency to view the Germans as being congenitally predisposed towards acts of aggression did not, as might be expected, produce draconian plans for dismemberment or de-industrialisation. As Alan Kramer shows in his chapter on dismantling, industry which existed for military purposes and which was surplus to peacetime requirements was removed even at the risk of upsetting powerful allies or alienating the Germans. But policy towards German industry as a whole (see chapter 3) was largely constructive. The British had learnt from the aftermath of the First World War the difficulties of sustaining punitive restrictions on Germany over an extended period and the corrosive consequences such a policy could have on relations between occupier and occupied. Moreover, the process of establishing an effective democratic system of government in Germany depended upon preventing a collapse of the economy with the danger that the Germans might succumb once again to the siren call of extremism.

The scepticism harboured by the British policy-making establishment about the amenability of the Germans to democratic ideals did not prevent the British from conceiving wide-ranging and far-

3. See H. Fromm, *Deutschland in der öffentlichen Kriegszieldiskussion Grossbritanniens 1939–1945* (Lang, Frankfurt on Main, 1982).

Ian Turner

reaching reforms to democratise German society. Indeed it was recognised that British security depended ultimately on the establishment of a stable, popularly elected government. But to British eyes German society had been tried and found grievously wanting. The traditional pillars of German society were unsound. They were either overtly anti-democratic and authoritarian or else guilty of complicity and capitulation. The only way to ensure that democracy in Germany would be built on firm foundations was to replace discredited institutions and structures with a new model, one with impeccable credentials: British liberal democracy. As the preamble to a key British policy document expresses it: 'Our democracy, the strongest in the world, is the result of our character and our country. It flourishes best in British soil, but we export it and, carefully tended, it blossoms and blooms in different lands.'[4]

In retrospect, of course, it is easy to be scornful of such statements. But victory in the Second World War had imbued Britain's elites with a new confidence in the superiority of British institutions. Who could deny that British democracy, for all its weaknesses, had triumphed over European dictatorship? If only British structures and ideals could be transplanted to German soil, so the thinking went, then it might be possible to divert the disastrous course of German history. Nor it seems did policy-makers question whether Britain still had the wherewithal to force such policies through. There was no sensation that 1940 had exposed the limitations of Britain's great power status, no perception of the British Empire slipping slowly and quietly beneath the waves. Britain was not shorn of its power. It was just short of cash. The 'export of English democracy'[5] therefore figures prominently in the policies discussed here: in local government, the civil service and the electoral system (see chapter 8), in the British attitude towards worker participation in industry (see chapter 10), in broadcasting and the press (see chapter 9), and in many other areas.

The wholesale rejection of German and in particular Prussian traditions as unsound and illiberal, and an unshakeable belief bordering at times on arrogance in the manifest superiority of British

4. Preamble to the 'Directive on Administration, Local and Regional Government and the Public Services' September 1945, quoted by, amongst others, Peter Hüttenberger in *Nordrhein-Westfalen und die Entstehung seiner parlamentarischen Demokratie* (Respublica Verlag, Siegburg, 1973), p. 43. (My retranslation.)
5. See W. Rudzio, 'Export englischer Demokratie?' *Vierteljahreshefte für Zeitgeschichte*, Vol. 17, No. 2, 1969, pp. 219–36.

6

institutions were the cornerstones upon which British reforms in Germany were laid. Despite these common elements it would be an exaggeration to talk of a coherent British 'plan' for Germany. The constraints on developing independent policy, discussed below, prevented that. Moreover, there were some areas, for example, policy towards the Churches,[6] where the British had apparently no considered policy at all. On balance, however, the historian cannot fail to be impressed by the scope of British occupation policy, particularly in view of the limitations on personnel and time. This was to be a very different occupation from those that had come before, altogether more ambitious in its attempts to reshape a conquered nation.

The Impact of the British Occupation

The International Dimension

Arguably, Britain's most momentous contribution to the development of post-war Germany was geopolitical. The British decision, taken in April 1946, not to relinquish control of the Ruhr or to countenance Soviet participation at a time when other Allies were calling for internationalisation of the area was a critical decision which ensured that a future West German state would be politically and economically viable. Of course, there is such a thing as a self-fulfilling prophecy. Anne Deighton, in her contribution to this book, takes this logic a stage further and argues that the British 'spearheaded' the division of Germany from early 1946 onwards. I believe there is room here for different interpretations of British aims and indeed of the Soviet intentions upon which they were based. What seems clear is that the British perceived the Soviet threat earlier and more clearly than their US counterparts. According to what is fast becoming the new orthodoxy, a definite 'turning point' was reached in the spring and summer of 1946. Thereafter, unity in Germany was neither feasible nor desirable from Britain's point of view and all public declarations of support for a united Germany were merely subterfuge designed to avoid the odium of responsibility for forcing the break.[7]

6. See, for example, the forthcoming thesis on this subject by Fionualla Corry, Oxford University.
7. Apart from Deighton's contribution, the 'turning point' thesis is associated

My own view is that this interpretation exaggerates the significance of this juncture. There was nothing intrinsically irrevocable about the 1946 *Wende*, as subsequent events were to prove.[8] Nor can it be claimed that it represented the start of the division of Germany which can be traced according to preference to the Potsdam Conference,[9] the zonal 'carve-up'[10] or even Hitler's attack against the Soviet Union in 1941. What I think can be stated is that suspicions of Soviet intentions, fuelled by events in the Soviet Zone and eastern Europe, made the British increasingly wary of conceding 'a bird in the hand for two in the bush'. But by the same token the shift to acceptance of the division of Germany proceeded in a manner which was tentative, incremental and often just confused.[11]

The Management of the Economy

Turning to the economy, the British record is positive but not without blemish. The initial task of restoring the economy in a makeshift way was accomplished remarkably quickly and efficiently. Alone amongst the occupying powers, Britain insisted from the beginning that Germany's peacetime economy would have to be revived (see chapter 3). Considering the strategic significance of the great Ruhr industries situated in the British Zone, the importance of the commitment should not be overlooked. Of course, good intentions alone are not enough. Running a command economy of such complexity in the conditions then prevailing proved to be a Herculean task. As Mark Roseman points out in chapter 4, British Military Government had none of the dictatorial powers of the Hitler regime, but nor were they willing to discriminate sufficiently in favour of key workers like the miners to aid economic recovery. Moreover, the British were also constrained in their promotion of the German economy by the demands of other European countries, above all France, whose moral claims to Ruhr coal were undeniable. The realities of economic life under British rule are described vividly in Wendy Carlin's contribution, below. In

with the works of Rolf Steininger and Falk Pingel referred to in chapter 12.

8. See, for example, R. Steininger, 'Wie die Teilung Deutschlands verhindert werden sollte. Der Robertson-Plan aus dem Jahre 1948', *Militärgeschichtliche Mitteilungen*, Vol. 33, No. 1, 1983, pp. 49–90.

9. See, for example, C. L. Mee, *Meeting at Potsdam* (Deutsch, London, 1975).

10. See T. Sharp, *The Wartime Alliance and the Zonal Division of Germany* (Clarendon Press, Oxford, 1975).

11. See, for example, I. D. Turner, 'Great Britain and the Post-War German Currency Reform', *Historical Journal*, Vol. 30, No. 3, 1987, pp. 685–708.

contrast to some recent West German historians, Carlin attributes a key role in Germany's recovery to the currency reform and its associated measures of economic liberalisation. By this point, however, British influence over economic policy in Germany had dwindled. The creation of the Bizone, the announcement of the Marshall Plan and the Bizonal financial agreement of November 1947 had formalised US predominance in western Germany.

The rapid change in US policy in 1947, from restricting Germany's economic potential to pushing for all-out reconstruction, caught British policy-makers 'on the hop' and forced a protracted and bitter quarrel between the two Allies over dismantling. British policy consisted of playing off the new-found US enthusiasm for reconstruction against French fears of their traditional enemy. But, by the end of 1948, one of the assumptions upon which this balancing act was based had started to change. French government officials had reassessed their position in the light of the new realities: West German economic recovery with US assistance was now viewed as inevitable. If France were to regain the initiative, policy would have to embrace these facts of life. The result was the Schuman Plan. It is a tribute to French ingenuity that they succeeded in clothing what was in effect a mutual accommodation of national interests in the elegant garb of European unification.[12] So much the worse for Great Britain. At this crucial moment British policy-makers turned away from a European commitment. Whatever the economic logic of Britain's position,[13] the decision betrayed a lack of vision that was to cost her dear. The effects were soon apparent. As Isabel Warner's contribution makes clear, the speed and skilfulness of French diplomacy and the surefootedness of Konrad Adenauer marginalised British influence in German economic affairs. The British government had either to swallow its reservations about the degree of concentration still prevailing in the German steel industry or accept the blame for torpedoing the Schuman Plan.

Developments in German Society and Political Life

British influence on the social order of West Germany was limited. Although the practice of British economic management was based

12. See A. S. Milward, *The Reconstruction of Western Europe 1945–51* (Methuen, London, 1984).
13. Ibid.

on central intervention and planning this was conditioned more by the imperatives of the situation and the influence of the military than by any desire to promote socialism in Germany. The British disapproved of the free-market line taken by Ludwig Erhard and his patrons in US Military Government. The objection, however, was not to capitalism *per se* but to the anticipated hardship and social tension which, as Ian Connor shows, accompanied the sudden economic liberalisation after the currency reform. The British could have moved quickly to take the 'commanding heights' of the economy into public ownership. Instead, the disposition of the Ruhr coal and steel industries was left to an elected West German government. Similarly, despite substantial German support, the British authorities declined to replace the Bismarckian health insurance system with a unitary state-funded service.[14] Overall, through reluctance to intervene in matters which either due to principle or expediency were deemed the prerogative of a future German national government, the British strengthened the elements of continuity in German society.

The impact of the British occupation on political life was profound even if the outcome was not always what was intended. The specifically British model of democracy, which the occupying authorities had hoped would take root in Germany, for the most part quickly withered and died. A few shoots flourished in the alien soil: the system of local government in parts of northern Germany and a public broadcasting system which adheres, albeit imperfectly, to the principles of the British Broadcasting Corporation, but not much else. By the same token, many features of German society which the British had been at pains to eradicate reasserted themselves quickly as the Germans regained sovereignty. Thus, as we see in chapter 8, the status of the public official as a privileged servant of the state with party affiliations was restored and in the field of industrial relations the German trade unions' attachment to codetermination proved too strong for British objections. In other areas, like the Länder constitutions, the British were either constrained in what they could achieve or, as in the field of education, they made a virtue out of liberal non-intervention. There was one aspect of political life that was simply not amenable to change in such a short time: the values and thought-processes of the Germans. Re-

14. See H. G. Hockerts, *Sozialpolitische Entscheidungen in Nachkriegsdeutschland. Alliierte und deutsche Sozialversicherungspolitik 1945 bis 1947* (Klett-Cotta, Stuttgart, 1980).

education failed to have any broad impact on political culture. Opinion polls conducted at the time in the British and US Zones confirm the conditional attachment of the populace to democratic ideals. Ian Connor's contribution also shows how those alienated from society, like the refugees, were particularly susceptible to political extremism.

It would be a mistake, however, to conclude that post-war West Germany was simply a continuation of previous German states. In the first place the division of Germany and the radical transformation of the Soviet Zone meant the Bonn Republic had different social parameters. Gone were the Social Democratic strongholds in the east, but gone too were the Prussian *Junker* as a pillar of German society.[15] Militarism had in any case lost its appeal. Post-war West Germany would be a nation of reluctant warriors.

Whilst this book concentrates on the impact of the occupiers, the Germans themselves were, of course, by no means passive subjects. The founding of a single 'catch-all' bourgeois party, the CDU, or the drafting of the Federal Republic's 'Constitution', the Basic Law, for example, were essentially German initiatives. Occasionally, imaginative German ventures were sponsored by perceptive British officers. The twinning of German and British towns and the starting up of weekly magazines like *Der Spiegel* are examples of this. But the lasting contribution of the British to West Germany's political development is broader and less easy to quantify than such isolated acts. In the first place, British efforts ensured that the Federal Republic inherited, if not the desired two-party system, then at least the basis for stable alternating governments centred around the two major moderate political parties. The emergence of the CDU and SPD should not be taken for granted. As Barbara Marshall remarks in her contribution, one of the greatest services the British performed for German democracy was to shoulder public criticism during the turbulent years of the occupation and draw fire away from the major parties. Above all, the British, like their American and French allies, ensured that democracy became respectable again. This is not to gainsay the efforts of German democrats or to minimise the effect of war and defeat, particularly upon the German elites. But the occupying powers provided an alternative set of ideals which the new state could embrace and which became the formal norms of political behaviour in the Federal Republic. West

15. Jürgen Kocka quoted by U. Schneider, 'Britische Besatzungspolitik 1945', PhD thesis, University of Hanover, 1980, pp. 229–30.

Germany did not become a democracy overnight. It took sustained growth, an authoritarian *Kanzlerdemokratie* and a generational change in the 1960s to complete the process. But at least a start had been made in those early post-war years.

The Constraints on British Occupation Policy

That developments in Germany did not turn out as planned must by now be evident. In reality, the scope which Britain possessed for shaping Germany's future was limited. Consideration for the other Allies was a major constraint. Initially, this meant adhering, at least in principle, to the bipartisan policy worked out with the Americans under the auspices of SHAEF. In the long term Britain was committed to four-power rule in Germany. (For a description of the apparatus of occupational rule, see the appendix to this volume.) The principles of quadripartite policy were laid down at Potsdam and the details were supposed to be agreed in the Allied Control Council (ACC). It soon became apparent to the British, however, that the reality of quadripartite control was singularly unattractive from their point of view. In the Control Council they found their pragmatic constructive plans for Germany at odds with the more restrictive punitive policies of the other Allies. And whilst four-power rule was seen as hamstringing British policy it seemed to Whitehall that it failed to exercise similar constraints upon the Soviet Union. The British authorities found their master plan for a gradual rebuilding of democracy rapidly overtaken by events in the Soviet Zone where the Russians were forcing the pace of political reconstruction. It was not even as if four-power rule gave them any influence over such developments. The British were powerless, for example, to prevent the enforced fusion of the SPD and KPD in the Soviet Zone.

The problem for the British government was that even if it was prepared to draw the logical conclusion from its pessimistic analyses of the realities of Allied rule in Germany, zonal autonomy was not a realistic option. True, the British Zone had the greatest concentration of heavy industry in Germany, but given the state of the economy in 1945–6 this was scarcely a realisable asset. The more pressing problem was food, and in this area the British Zone was simply not capable of producing sufficient goods to support an increased population for any length of time at a level which would permit economic activity. Food had to be imported and paid for in dollars by the British taxpayer. This had two immediate consequences. First, the Treasury became a powerful ally of the CCG in promoting German recovery to a level at which the British Zone would become self-supporting. Secondly, the British became dependent upon the US because North America was the only substantial accessible source of grain. As John Farquharson has made clear the Americans exacted a political price for this dependency.[16] Fortunately for the British, however, US policy was also moving into a more constructive phase.

The other power which British policy sought to assuage was France. Apart from the moral duty of supporting a former wartime ally, Britain had a strong interest in bolstering French power on the Continent as a counterweight to a revived Germany, but more realistically, to the spectre of Soviet communism. Prior to September 1946 when the US formally committed itself to remain in Europe, this was a matter of vital importance to Britain and, as Mark Roseman shows (chapter 4), the British authorities had to tread a fine line between promoting West German recovery and exporting fuel for France and other former occupied territories in western Europe.

Finally, a major obstacle to the achievement of British aims was represented by the Germans themselves. Consolidation and integration in western Germany and the continuing pressures to reduce the administrative costs of the occupation meant executive power was increasingly transferred to the Germans. Ordinance 57, which came into force in January 1947, meant the phase when the British could dispose at will of the German political system was abruptly ended. Advice, support and persuasion, with the ultimate threat of veto, was the new policy style and the Germans were quick to perceive the opportunities which 'non-intervention' offered.

Conclusion

Contemplating developments in occupied Germany from the vantage point of 1949, British policy-makers may still have had some lingering doubts about the way things had evolved. Would the new state be viable or would it succumb to extremism of the right or left?

16. J. Farquharson, *The Western Allies and the Politics of Food* (Berg, Leamington Spa, 1985).

Could the astonishing recovery of the economy since the currency reform be sustained and Germany become once again the engine of western European growth? Six years later, when the occupation formally came to an end, most of these doubts had been stilled. West Germany at least was no longer a threat to British security. On the contrary, the Federal Republic was a stalwart ally in the defence of the west against Soviet communism and would soon be a member of NATO. Support for the main democratic parties in West Germany was high and the Federal government was stable and popular. On the economic side, the crisis precipitated by the Korean War had been successfully weathered and the scarcity and privations of the early post-war period were now distant memories. West Germany hummed to the tune of busy factories and the seemingly endless vista of economic growth and prosperity stretched out ahead of it. Beneath the aura of self-congratulation in Whitehall and the professions of Anglo-German friendship, only the nagging doubt remained: would competition from industry revived under British control end up conquering the former occupier's markets?

1

Cold-War Diplomacy: British Policy Towards Germany's Role in Europe, 1945–9
Anne Deighton

Introduction

This chapter, based mainly on British official archives, argues that, to the extent that the Cold War is characterised by the dividing of Germany between east and west, Britain carries the responsibility for that division as much as the Soviet Union or the United States.[1] By the end of 1947 it had become publicly clear that agreement would not be reached within the framework of the 1945 Potsdam Agreement over what to do about Germany. In that intervening period Britain played a major diplomatic role, helping to convince the Americans that in the short run a united Germany would threaten both Germany itself, and western Europe, with communism. For despite public declarations of four-power cooperation in Germany, Ernest Bevin, the British Foreign Secretary, and his leading officials in Whitehall realised very early after the war that the united Germany envisaged at Potsdam was too risky an enterprise to be pursued wholeheartedly. This realisation was not simply the result of fear felt by a country which had been economically devastated and now found itself wedged between two increasingly antagonistic powers. It was a policy actively and successfully pursued during the preliminary four-power negotiations which were intended to pave the way for a peace treaty and a settlement with Germany.

Britain's relations with Germany in the early post-war period were therefore not only important in the bilateral but also in the inter-

---

1. An earlier version of this article appeared as 'The "frozen front": the Labour Government, the Division of Germany and the Origins of the Cold War, 1945–1947', *International Affairs*, Vol. 63, No. 3, Summer 1987, pp. 449–65.

national context. It was not until 1948 and after that the familiar lines of a bipolar confrontation were publicly drawn, symbolised by the European Recovery Programme, the Berlin crisis and the formation of NATO. But in the early post-war diplomatic negotiations about Germany, negotiations which themselves helped to shape the subsequent superpower confrontation, Britain played a leading part.

Potsdam and the Hopes for a United Germany

As the war ended, a major preoccupation of the Allies was the future of Germany. Their wartime decision that Germany should surrender unconditionally left a power vacuum in the centre of Europe. For very practical reasons, something had to be done with Germany. It was at the centre of Europe, straddling east and west and holding the key to the balance of power there. France and the Soviet Union both knew, to their cost, of Germany's ability to threaten their borders. Historically and psychologically, Germany represented a threat. The lessons both of the Versailles settlement and of appeasement were not forgotten.

At the Potsdam Conference of July–August 1945, the Allies confirmed the military occupation of Germany through the British, US, Soviet and French Zones. Each zone had a measure of autonomy, but the Allied Control Council (ACC) was charged to make unanimous decisions about the major questions affecting Germany's future, in particular the re-establishment of economic and political unity. The responsibility for the future shape of Germany was placed in the hands of the Allies.

But Potsdam was a flawed and ambiguous agreement. It set the parameters of that conflict which so dogged subsequent Anglo-Soviet relations over Germany—whether reparations should take precedence over economic unity. Moreover, the French were to refuse to be bound by the Potsdam Agreement as they had not been represented at the Conference.[2]

2. On the Potsdam Conference, see R. Butler and M. E. Pelly (eds.), *Documents on British Policy Overseas. The Potsdam Conference*, Series 1, Vol. 1 (HMSO, London, 1984), pp. 920–1258; A. Cairncross, *The Price of War. British Policy on German Reparations 1941 to 1949* (Blackwell, Oxford, 1986), pp. 93–9; R. Edmonds, 'Yalta and Potsdam, Forty Years Afterwards', *International Affairs*, Vol. 62, No. 2, 1986, pp. 197–296. For a study of France's reaction to the Potsdam Agreement and the German problem, J. W. Young, 'The Foreign Office, the French and the Postwar Division of Germany, 1945–46', *Review of International Studies*, Vol. 12, 1986, pp. 223–34.

Germany's industrial and economic power was a major focus of Allied interest. The Ruhr area, now in the British Zone, had been the powerhouse for the civilian and military might of Germany throughout the twentieth century. Although the economy now appeared to be in ruins and large quantities of food were being imported to prevent starvation, the Allies knew Germany's potential for recovery. In Britain, its latent economic wealth was viewed with great ambivalence. It was already clear that Germany's economic recovery would underpin that of western Europe. But too-prosperous a Germany could become a rival for Britain as well as a potential military threat once again. Thus, Germany was the major international problem of the 1940's as it had been throughout the twentieth century. No resolution of this problem could be divorced from the interests and aims of the great powers.[3]

The Framework for Negotiations

The diplomatic negotiations of 1945–7 towards a peace settlement were the bridge from the wartime alliance to the Cold War. At Potsdam the Allies had agreed to set up a Council of Foreign Ministers(CFM).[4] The Council met five times between 1945 and 1947, in London, Paris, New York and Moscow, each time for several weeks. The United States was represented by Secretaries of State James Byrnes and later George C. Marshall. The Soviet Union's Foreign Minister was the experienced negotiator Viacheslav Molotov, Foreign Minister since 1939 and veteran of the Teheran, Yalta, and Potsdam Conferences. France, the weakest of the powers, was represented by the diplomat Georges Bidault. Lastly, Ernest Bevin, a skilled trade-union leader and one of the most powerful figures in the Labour government of 1945–51, negotiated at the Council on behalf of Britain. A man of immensely strong personality and an instinctive and emotional politician, he inspired affection and loyalty in those who worked closely with him and advised him during these arduous diplomatic encounters.

3. Public Record Office (PRO)FO942/515 and 516. Subsequent PRO references are to the Cabinet Series (CAB), the Prime Minister's Operational Papers (PREM), Treasury (T), Foreign Office (FO371), Control Office (FO942) and the Control Commission (FO1034, 1049). All quotations appear by permission of the Controller, HMSO.
4. *Foreign Relations of the United States* (FRUS) (US Government Printing Office, Washington, DC) Vol. 2, 1945, p. 615; PRO/CAB66/67, Protocol of Proceedings of Berlin Conference.

17

The stakes were very high. The Council meetings were widely covered by the press and aroused great international interest. Each minister used them to communicate intentions and policies to the other powers, to their domestic constituencies and, increasingly, to the Germans. They were a catalyst for British policy-making, as well as giving British diplomats the opportunity to exercise the skills at which they traditionally excelled—diplomacy and persuasion. As Bevin was to comment at Moscow, 'we have only leadership to sell'. Britain used the face-to-face contact that the Councils gave with great deftness; through them the British established a close peacetime relationship with the Americans and edged the western powers towards the public rift with the Soviet Union, which came in Europe to be symbolised by a divided Germany.

The Roots of British Post-War Policy

What were the formative influences on the making of British foreign policy after the Labour Party swept to power with its unexpected majority in the election of July 1945? Of the many influences, four were crucial: first, the inheritance of wartime thinking about the post-war world; secondly, British fears about the Soviet Union; thirdly, British perceptions of the US; and lastly, the practical problems that the responsibility for the British Zone represented.

In the first place, a steady trend had developed at ministerial and official level in British wartime thinking, away from preoccupation with Germany as the enemy and toward anxiety about the Soviet Union. This emerges most clearly among the Chiefs of Staff, who produced a series of reports during the second half of the war about future security problems. Their primary concern was with the altered balance of power that the Soviet Union created in Europe. Their worst nightmare was a future alliance between Germany and the Soviet Union. They proposed that a strategy of defence in depth against the Soviet Union should be considered, and that any future western bloc would have to include the western part of dismembered Germany, as well as having the backing of America. The Armistice and Post-War Commitee and the Post-Hostilities Planning Committee both reflected these same preoccupations: the short-term problem was Germany, but the long-term threat was the Soviet Union. At the same time the Foreign Office was wrestling with US plans for the future United Nations Organization, which

18

was intended to police the world in a cooperative mannner between the four great powers—the USA, the Soviet Union, Britain and China.

But, because of the war, British planning still had to be very tentative. However much the Soviet Union was distrusted, the war was not yet won. Foreign Secretary Anthony Eden, refused to allow the anti-Soviet ideas of the Chiefs of Staff to be widely circulated or to allow the creation of any impression that an anti-Soviet security bloc was being contemplated. Moreover, US policy was still very uncertain, and the British were most anxious not to create the impression that the post-war cooperation favoured by Roosevelt was viewed with any scepticism in Britain. However, the wartime coalition government included leading members of the future Labour government. There can be no doubt that they were much influenced by the discussions that took place during 1944 and 1945. Both Bevin's wartime enthusiasm for dismembering Germany and his suspicions about Soviet intentions in Europe are particularly striking.[5]

A second formative influence on Labour post-war foreign policy was the British establishment's deeply held suspicion of communism. The nature of Soviet foreign policy was widely discussed. Was ideology the main motivating force? Would the Soviet Union continue to press for advantage in Europe after the war, or would it act like a satiated power, anxious to secure its borders but otherwise content to follow a conservative path in foreign policy? These were dilemmas that encompassed an economic and political threat as well as a military one: for it 'should be borne in mind that Russia can absorb countries without spending money on them, but we cannot. The Western way of life demands a minimum of material well-being.'[6]

But the Soviet Union was still widely popular in the public mind. The heroism of the Russians during the war and the benevolent image of 'Uncle Joe' Stalin, as well as a strong sense among many in

5. PRO/CAB81/PHP (44) 27 (0) Final, November 1944; J. Baylis, 'British War-time Thinking about a Post-War European Security Group', *Review of International Studies*, Vol. 9, 1983, pp. 265–81, and *idem*, 'Britain, the Brussels Pact and the Continental Commitment', *International Affairs*, Vol. 60, No. 4, 1984, pp. 615–29; K Sainsbury, 'British Policy and German Unity at the End of the Second World War', *English Historical Review*, Vol. 94, No. 373, 1979, pp. 786–804; F. Williams, *Ernest Bevin* (Hutchinson, London, 1952), p. 241; K. Harris, *Attlee* (Weidenfeld and Nicolson, London, 1982), pp. 209–13; T. D. Burridge, *British Labour and Hitler's War* (Deutsch, London, 1976), ch. 11.
6. PRO/CAB129/9, CP(46)186, 3 May 1946.

the Labour Party that left could talk to left, continued to prevail. Public opinion had to be let down slowly. 'If there is to be a break [over Germany],' Bevin told the Cabinet as early as May 1946, 'the Russians must be seen to be responsible for it.'[7] Bevin therefore publicly emphasised the need to control German nationalism and militarism in his speeches to the House of Commons.[8]

The third factor that influenced post-war policy was Britain's perception of the United States. She was viewed with great ambivalence during these years. It was clear that aid, and a lot of aid, was needed, especially after the sudden ending of Lend–Lease in August 1945. Negotiations with the Americans for another loan began in September. But her policy was unclear. Could Roosevelt's idealistic attitude actually be sustained? Might not the Americans once more retreat into isolationism as they had done after the First World War? They had spoken at Yalta of a two-year military commitment to Europe. In the USA Britain was viewed, it was well known, with distrust; and there was a fear that the Americans might try to deal directly with the Russians over the heads of the British. But perhaps the greatest fear was the inconsistency of US policy. 'The Americans are a mercurial people unduly swayed by sentiment and prejudice', the writers of a Foreign Office 'stocktaking' memorandum concluded in January 1947.[9] Many British policy-makers felt that the Americans wavered between hesitancy and overreaction, and that they did not really understand Europe.

Despite these worries, the overriding aim of the British government quickly emerged: to secure a continuing US commitment to the recovery of Germany and to a balance of power in Europe that would not favour communist influence. This concern emerges dramatically in the CFM meetings of 1946 and 1947. It was not that the British wanted to hand over power to the Americans. Far from it, Britain still insisted upon her great-power status and this underpinned her diplomacy. But she wanted US military and economic support to help to carry out a British policy of recovery and security at least for the western part of Germany.

The fourth formative influence on Labour foreign policy was the

---

7. Ibid.
8. For example, on 27 February 1947; House of Commons Debates, cols. 2296–305.
9. PRO/FO371/66546, Stocktaking memorandum, January 1947. On Anglo-American relations in the early post-war years see, for example, R. M. Hathaway, *Ambigous Partnership: Britain and America, 1944–47* (Columbia University Press, New York, 1981).

actual situation in the British Zone of Germany itself. The Zone was heavily populated, had a damaged industrial base and very little agricultural output. The Russians were not supplying the western zones from their more agricultural zone and probably had very little agricultural surplus anyway. The British Zone was extremely expensive; the estimated bill for 1946 was £80 million (roughly £800 million in today's prices). Nevertheless the Zone represented the sweetest prize in Germany, with its potential for industrial recovery and wealth. It needed US aid to feed its population and to bring recovery. To the democratic west, the industrial potential of the British Zone seemed to offer a way of ensuring that communism, which thrived upon 'hunger, chaos and poverty', would not take hold there.

Between 1945 and 1947 the Labour government stated publicly its desire for a united Germany: a Germany that was democratic, economically self-sufficient, but militarily disarmed. This stance was essential for Labour Party supporters, for British public opinion and for the Americans. But privately the priorities of Bevin and his senior officials were very different. By 1946 the principal postwar threat was felt to be the Soviet Union. It was not expected that there would be another European war for at least five years, as the extent of the devastation in the Soviet Union was well known, so any struggle over Germany would be economic and ideological. If Germany prospered, it would be less prone to communism—so Germany had to be revived. If Britain could not secure a united Germany on her own terms, then the risks of communist infiltration into Germany would be too great; and a Germany divided, with the wealthy Ruhr looking westwards, was a safer bet for the west than a united Germany that might fall under communist influence. From 1946 onwards British diplomats took every opportunity to convince the Americans both that the Soviet Union could not be trusted and that at least the western zones of Germany had to be revived, and revived quickly despite the risks, to prevent the spread of communism across Europe.

The Paris Council

It was at the Paris meeting of the CFM in the summer of 1946 (25 April–12 July) that this British attitude first became clear, although the Council's agenda was dominated by the proposed peace treaties for the east European states and Italy.[10] By now it was also obvious that Germany would not be the passive object of four-power politics indefinitely. The German problem had become increasingly acute. In February 1946 the Social Democrats in the Soviet Zone agreed, under pressure, to merge their party with the German Communist Party (KPD) to form a new party, the Socialist Unity Party (SED). Bevin reported to the Cabinet that they 'must proceed on the assumption that the Soviet Government will continue to do all it can to ensure that the future German government will be Communist and Soviet-controlled. This is the attitude they have adopted in other border countries; their methods in Germany are true to type.'[11] Within the Foreign Office, it was reported gloomily that, as a result of the creation of the SED, Britain could 'kiss goodbye to democracy on the western pattern for what is practically half of pre-war Germany . . . A German puppet regime for the Soviet Zone will soon be an accomplished fact.'[12] It was clear that the lack of economic recovery in Germany also threatened the creation of a democratic, westward-looking country. Industrial recovery was still a pipedream of the future, and levels of output were far below those allowed for in the Four-Power Level of Industry Agreement, concluded in March 1946 with the aim of establishing how much plant would be available for reparations. Montgomery warned Bevin that:

> the whole country is in such a mess that the only way to put it right is to get the Germans 'in on it' themselves. We must tell the German people what is going to happen to them and their country. If we do not do these things, we shall drift towards possible failure. That 'drift' will take the form of an increasingly hostile population, which will eventually begin to look east. Such a Germany would be a menace to the security of the British Empire.[13]

Bevin therefore warned the Cabinet that '[d]elay in reaching a settlement is to Russia's advantage but it is to our serious disadvantage, and the sooner we take positive action, the better'. The danger of Russia in Europe was 'certainly as great as, and possibly even

10. For the Paris Council see PRO/FO371/57265-83; FRUS, Vol. 2, 1946, CFM; P. D. Ward, *The Threat of Peace* (Kent State University Press, Kent City, Ohio, 1979).
11. PRO/CAB129/9, CP(46)186, 3 May 1946.
12. PRO/FO371/55586, Franklin minute, 8 February 1946.
13. PRO/PREM8/216, Montgomery memorandum, 1 May 1946.

greater than, that of a revived Germany'.[14] The Soviets' preoccupation with their war claims and with security against renewed German aggression was perceived in Whitehall as 'a catchword which was being used to support something very like aggression', characterised by 'economic and ideological infiltration'. This could only be halted by unmasking Soviet intentions to the world.[15]

It is quite clear that this determination, although intensified by the crippling costs of the Zone, was motivated primarily by the instinctive sense of a great power (albeit a temporarily impoverished one) acting positively to secure its interests in Europe. There was much private discussion in the Foreign Office about the possibility of breaking with the Potsdam Agreement. In the Cabinet paper of May 1946 some of the arguments for this were spelt out. To break with Potsdam and follow a 'western' policy would, it was admitted, be dangerous. It would mean that the 'whole of eastern Germany and indeed of eastern Europe would be *irretrievably* lost to Russia' (emphasis added). Western Germany would have to be defended from the infection of political and economic influences from the east, which would mean creating a western bloc. The support of the continental Europeans could not yet be guaranteed, as this policy would involve a '"forgive and forget" policy towards the western Germans'. But of most importance, the 'Americans are probably not ready for this. Certainly their leading representatives in Germany would oppose it tooth and nail. In any case one could not count on continued American support even if they came to agree to it. But full American support would be essential.'[16]

These were arguments for caution, but not for dropping the 'western' policy, which held formidable advantages—not least, a show of determination to resist the expansion of communism, which would in itself attract the support of many Germans. The end of the Level of Industry plan and the limiting of reparations would further encourage German support. But such a policy had to be conditional on two things: one was the economic recovery of Germany, and the other was 'full and continued support from the United States'. Whitehall's major preoccupation was now to alert the Americans to the dangers that the Soviet Union presented: 'the key to our external policy was the closest co-operation with the US'.[17]

14. PRO/CAB129/9, CP(46)186, 3 May 1946.
15. PRO/FO371/55588, ORC(46)56, Revise, 19 June 1946.
16. PRO/CAB129/9, CP(46)186, 3 May 1946.
17. Ibid.

But there was as yet no encouraging sign from the Americans as to their policy for Europe, although the British knew that the tide might be about to turn. George Kennan's celebrated long telegram alerting the US goverment to the nature of the Soviet threat was sent from Moscow in March 1946 and caused a great stir in Washington. But on US insistence, there had been no joint preparation for the Paris Council. The British had a clear anti-Soviet strategy, but they realised that without the Americans they were impotent in Europe. Moreover, they feared that Byrnes, the unpredictable US Secretary of State, might 'off the top of his head' go soft on the Russians and try to secure a deal with them, as the British had seen him try to do in Moscow the previous Christmas.[18]

When Germany came up for discussion at the Paris Council, it became clear that the conflict between the two priorities of economic unity and reparations was not going to be resolved quickly. The Soviet Union insisted that its claim at Yalta for $10 billion of reparations must be settled before the Potsdam Agreement on economic unity and self-sufficiency could be implemented.[19] The British were particularly anxious that these problems should be treated the other way round: that plans for the future of Germany should be laid *before* old scores were settled. Furthermore, the British team insisted that the restrictions imposed on them by the Level of Industry Agreement should be conditional upon creating economic unity in Germany. The Ruhr, moreover, was the British team's one negotiating asset: they were determined to use it as effectively as possible, both by refusing to discuss four-power control there and by creating a new, large province which would eventually involve more Germans in the administration of their country and which would in turn help to 'keep Communism beyond the Elbe'.[20] On 10 July, both Bevin and Molotov showed their hands. Bevin argued forcefully and bitterly that Germany's lack of economic unity was contributing to a hefty bill for the British taxpayer. 'I must formally state,' he threatened,

> that the United Kingdom will co-operate on a fully reciprocal basis with the other zones, but in so far as there is no reciprocity from any particular zone or agreement to carry out the whole of the Potsdam

18. D. Yergin, *Shattered Peace: The Origins of the Cold War and The National Security State* (Houghton Mifflin, Boston, Mass, 1977), ch. 9; G. F. Kennan, *Memoirs, 1925–50* (Hutchinson, London, 1968), ch. 11 and Annex C.
19. 'Billion' means a thousand million.
20. PRO/FO371/55843, Harvey note, 24 May 1946.

Protocol, my Government will be compelled to organise the British Zone of Occupation in Germany in such a way that no further liability shall fall on the British taxpayer.

In other words, the British were prepared to go it alone in Germany. This was the first public move towards the division of Germany and, with it, the European Cold War.[21]

The impact of this speech was dramatic. It raised the level of debate from verbal gymnastics to a serious threat to dispense with the quadripartite settlement of Potsdam. Molotov responded to Bevin's threat by going on to the attack himself. Like the British, the Russians realised that the battle to win the support of the Germans themselves had been opened in Paris. It was incorrect, Molotov said, 'to identify Hitler with the German people'. The Soviet Union would be prepared to accept an increase in Germany's peaceful production levels beyond that recommended in the Level of Industry Agreement, central administrations should be introduced, and plebiscites should be held to determine the real wishes of the German people. But, far from building upon any of the tentative suggestions in Molotov's speech, Bevin retaliated by attacking the Soviet Union over reparations. He was all too aware that the Russians could not afford to retreat publicly from their demands for high reparations as compensation.

The next day, Byrnes, who was reluctant to face a showdown, tried to get agreement to refer the whole German question to Special Deputies. When he failed to do so, he responded to Bevin's threat formally, stating that the US was prepared to cooperate with any zone to create economic unity in Germany. Bevin reminded the Council that it was he who had already suggested breaking out of the Potsdam impasse.[22]

Thus the so-called Bizone in Germany was first publicly mooted. The economic unification of the British and American Zones was to herald the division of Germany and Europe. Bevin himself remarked that 'at last [we] have come to a turning point, and on a long view it is no bad thing to have done'.[23]

British officials worked ferociously hard over the next six months

21. For Bevin's speech, FRUS, Vol. 2, 1946, pp. 860–77, 10 July 1946.
22. FRUS, Vol. 2, 1946, pp. 843–920; PRO/FO371/57281, meetings of 10, 11 July 1946.
23. PRO/FO371/55844, telegram 351, Paris to London, 11 July 1946.

to assure the success of the Bizone and to convince Bevin that the right steps had been taken at Paris. He had serious second thoughts about the project, not least because he had hoped that if the Potsdam Agreement was to be the cast aside, it would be the Russians who did the casting. That the Bizone represented a breach of Potsdam by the west was in fact to be argued publicly and repeatedly by the Soviet Union. Bevin also doubted whether the Americans would stick with the scheme. To his officials, though, the Bizone represented the lifeline that would enable the British Zone to recover and to ward off the threat of communist infiltration that poverty encouraged. It would also ensure continued US interest and investment in the economic recovery of Germany, and with it western Europe.[24] Despite their diplomatic breakthrough, however, the British had no intention of handing over their control of the battlefield of the Cold War: they hoped, unsuccessfully, to get the Americans to pay 70% of the costs of the Bizone while sharing executive responsibilities equally, and it was only by December 1947 that the Americans agreed to shoulder the greatest burden —nearly a year after the Bizone had been agreed.[25]

'New Potsdam': British Diplomacy and the Moscow Council

The Moscow Council of 10 March to 25 April 1947 was heralded at the time, and has since been accepted, as a benchmark in early post-war European history.[26] It was as he returned from Moscow that the new US Secretary of State, Marshall, set in train the studies that were to lead to the European Recovery Programme. The tide of public opinion in the west began to shift away from sympathy with the Soviet Union, although in Britain the 'Keep Left' group proposed a more subtle response than simple anti-communism. In Moscow, the British team succeeded in a remarkable display of leadership and played a major role in contributing to the change of

24. PRO/FO371/55589, Departmental meetings of 22 and 23 July 1946; for Bizone negotiations see PRO/T236/994–9.
25. Text of Bizone Agreement, *Keesings Contemporary Archives*, 1946, p. 8297.
26. For example see, Kennan, *Memoirs*, pp. 325–6; W. Bedell Smith, *Moscow Mission, 1946–49* (Heinemann, London, 1950), p. 208; J. Gimbel, *The American Occupation of Germany. Politics and the Military 1945–49* (Stanford University Press, Stanford, Cal., 1968) p. 121; A. Bullock, *Ernest Bevin: Foreign Secretary 1945–1951* (Heinemann, London, 1984) pp. 392–4; Yergin, *Shattered Peace*, pp. 301–2. For proceedings of Moscow Council see PRO/FO371/64206 and FRUS, Vol. 2, 1947, pp. 234–391.

tone in US policy towards Europe as well as binding the United States ever more closely to the success of the Bizone in Germany. By the time the Council ended the Soviet Union had been completely outflanked, failing to secure any commitment to current reparations, losing the public backing even of the French, and finding itself isolated from the west.

The British were well prepared for any confrontation in Moscow; indeed they wanted to bring matters to a head, fearing that the Russians might instead 'put them in the dock'. The international climate had also changed. In September 1946, Byrnes had publicly commited the US to not withdrawing troops from Germany. Moreover, British appraisal of events in Germany had increased British anxiety about Soviet influence there. As a Foreign Office brief for the Moscow Council expressed it:

> If a German Government in Berlin fairly reproduced the outlook of the country it would be neither wholly eastward looking nor wholly westward looking. The question would then turn on whether the western democracies or the Soviet Union would exercise the stronger pull. On the whole the balance of advantage seems to lie with the Russians . . . Communism has its addicts in Western Germany . . . and the prevailing material conditions would give them excellent ground.[27]

For four months before the Moscow meeting British officials had been drawing up what became known as the New Potsdam, nicknamed in the Foreign Office the Bevin Plan. This was a unilateral updating and revision of the Potsdam Agreement of August 1945. It was intended as a statement of British principles, not as a basis for negotiation as 'the principles at stake are too important for compromise'. The Bevin Plan has received very little scholarly attention, but it is most revealing about British policy intentions over Germany.[28] It was a masterly device for forcing the Russians to exclude themselves from western Germany and to leave Germany divided, at the very least in the short term, thus enabling western Germany to play its part in the restoration of a healthy Europe. It stated that before Germany could be reunited, Russia would have to make a statement of the reparations it had already taken from the Soviet Zone, and pay at least part of them back to meet Anglo-

27. PRO/FO944/762, brief for Moscow, 6 February 1947.
28. The 'New Potsdam' appears in PRO/CAB129/17, CP (47)68, 27 February 1947, Appendix 2, although it was marginally revised at Moscow.

American deficits; further, it would have to contribute to the bills of the western powers. It was to have no reparations in the form of steel or coal until Germany was self-sufficient again. These conditions had now been taken far beyond the reparations question: they betray Britain's refusal to deal constructively with the Soviet Union over Germany.[29]

The British knew that the Russians could not accept all these conditions; and they did not want them to. 'If, as is very possible,' Bevin explained, 'we fail to agree, we could proceed without difficulty to implement the conclusions recommended in this memorandum [regarding constitutional changes] in respect of the British, American, and if possible, the French zones only.' So the British would secure a continued division of Germany and the exclusion of the Soviet Union from the west under the cover of an updated Potsdam Agreement. Soviet rejection of the plan would enable the west to claim that 'the responsibility for failure of Potsdam and quadripartite agreement should be placed fairly and squarely on the Russians', in spite of knowing that the conditions were well-nigh impossible for the Russians to meet.[30]

Like the British and the Americans, the Russians were consolidating gains in their zone, and their resolve to compromise was not strong. This the British knew. The problem, still, was the United States. General Marshall, the new Secretary of State, was 'wobbly' on German problems, and had to go to Moscow before he had fully come to grips with the complexities of the issues involved. He also took with him a team that reflected all too clearly the deep divisions of opinion within the American foreign-policy elite. In a revealing memo, Sir Edmund Hall Patch, who went to Moscow with the British team, saw US policy as comprising three options:

(a) a firm policy vis-à-vis Russia, which involved backing Western Europe (on the lines of Greece and Turkey) at what might prove to be considerable expense; (b) doing a deal with the Russians and staying in Europe on terms which would involve more expense in Germany (e.g. on current reparations) but might make it unnecessary to give such full financial support to Europe; and (c) pulling right out of Europe.[31]

29. PRO/CAB129/17, CP(47)68, 27 February 1947.
30. PRO/FO371/64244, Dean minute, 11 February 1947; PRO/FO371/64244, ORC (47) 16, 24 February 1947, para. 20; PRO/CAB129/9, CP(46)186, 3 May 1946.
31. PRO/T236/999, Hall Patch to Eady, 2 May 1947.

He thought Marshall was wavering very much between the first two options.

Before the Council opened, the Foreign Office managed to secure two meetings with the Americans in London which gave officials a chance to assess US thinking and express their fears. Although common ground existed, based upon the Robertson–Clay Agreement of December 1946 on the principles to be followed in Germany, there still existed little mutual confidence. The Bevin Plan was not very well received by the American team, whose 'first reaction was that the idea of changing the Potsdam text would cause great difficulties with the Russians and provide them with a useful propaganda weapon'. The best that Bevin could do was to emphasise the link between economic disarray and communism and stress the need to rebuild Germany within an integrated European structure, a theme that had interested him since 1945. He then alerted the Americans that the British 'could never again contemplate holding out alone against an enemy for a year or two until others came to our help . . . We must keep very close to the United States.' This was as close as he could come to a warning about present and future threats to western Europe.[32]

The principal thrust of British diplomacy in Moscow was to ensure that the Americans would come around to Hall Patch's option (a), by supporting New Potsdam. The most serious threat to the British position at Moscow came when the Americans began seriously to explore the possibility of striking a deal which would enable the Russians to take some reparations from current production—in particular, coal and steel—and thus ease the path to economic unity in Germany. British diplomatic machinery went into top gear to head off these proposals. Bevin wrote to Marshall personally to try and dissuade him. The Americans would be feeding the German cow in the west while it was being milked in the east, he suggested. Liberated Europe's problems, the British argued, began and ended with Germany. If Germany could recover economically, so would the rest of Europe. If Germany played hostage to the needs of the Soviet economy, it would fester and become a cesspool, attractive only to the ideas of communism. He realised that the Americans were under domestic pressure to resolve the dilemmas that Germany presented, but reiterated that current reparations could only be contemplated when the conditions of the

32. PRO/FO371/64244, Anglo-American meeting, 28 February 1947.

Bevin Plan were met and when Germany and Europe were economically sound once again.[33]

The British team persuaded the Americans to focus not on current reparations but on the restoration of the western German economy. In three private meetings Bevin offered the Americans practical suggestions for increasing the prosperity of the Bizone by raising substantially the agreed levels of industrial capacity and production. He proposed to improve the efficiency of the Bizonal machinery within the framework of the Bevin Plan, with a view (as some officials hoped) to eventual political unity.

These initiatives flew in the face of the Potsdam Agreement. But powerful sections of the American negotiating team were now also convinced of the importance of West German rehabilitation. A long and unproductive meeting between Marshall and Stalin on 15 April finally convinced Marshall that the Russians were not seriously interested either in a quadripartite settlement for Germany or in the economic recovery of Europe. On his way back to the US, he stopped in Berlin to instruct General Clay to proceed with the rehabilitation of the Bizone on the lines agreed with the British in Moscow.[34]

On his return to America Marshall pronounced that in Europe the patient was dying while the doctors deliberated. On 5 June his offer of aid to Europe was made. It was this offer that provided the real substance for what had been a sweeping declaration of policy by Truman in his celebrated speech of 12 March 1947. Whereas the Truman Doctrine came to represent the military arm of containment, the Marshall Plan was the economic arm; they were, as Truman himself once put it, 'two halves of the same walnut'.[35]

33. FRUS, Vol. 2, 1947, pp. 273–5; PRO/PREM8/702, telegram 302, Moscow to Foreign Office, 23 March 1947; Dixon Diary, 23 March 1947. I am grateful to Mr Piers Dixon for permission to read his father's diaries and notes for the Council sessions. PRO/FO1030/4, undated brief; PRO/FO942/516, Bevin memorandum, 16 December 1945; PRO/FO371/64197, Foreign Ministers meeting, 1 April 1947. See also J. H. Backer, *The Decision to Divide Germany. American Foreign Policy in Transition* (Duke University Press, Durham, NC, 1978), p. 177.
34. For Bevin–Marshall meeting of 5 April see FRUS, Vol. 2, 1947, pp. 309–10, PRO/FO371/65052, Hall Patch to Makin, 5 April 1947. For Bevin–Marshall meeting of 8 April, see FRUS, Vol. 2, 1947, pp. 315–17, PRO/FO371/64203, and Dixon Diary, 8 April 1947. For Bevin–Marshall meeting of 18 April see FRUS, Vol. 2, 1947, pp. 356–8, PRO/FO1049/743, telegram 855, Moscow to Foreign Office, 19 April 1947. See also FRUS, Vol. 2, 1947, pp. 337–44 for Marshall–Stalin meeting, 15 April 1947; and Bedell Smith, *Moscow Mission*, pp. 212–13.
35. Quoted in W. LaFeber, *America, Russia and the Cold War 1945–1975* (John Wiley, New York, 1976), p. 64.

With the inauguration of the Marshall Plan, the pattern of inter-national politics was to be dramatically altered and Bevin took the lead in coordinating Europe's response. It was critical that the Soviet Union should not be allowed to sabotage the US offer. Bevin, Bidault and Molotov met in Paris to plan a response to Marshall's offer. On 2 July, Molotov withdrew from the discussions. Bevin had forced the pace, insisting that a 'shopping list' of European needs such as the Russians were proposing would not convince the Americans that Europe seriously intended to make a positive con-tribution to its own recovery.[36]

The British never lost sight of the fact that Marshall Aid, despite its implications for western Europe as a whole, was essentially a response to the German problem, that 'vital center' as Marshall called it.[37] Throughout the summer of 1947 Britain continued to negotiate for an upward revision of the level of industry in the Bizone. The inclusion of Germany in the Marshall Aid programme was also a priority: Germany had to be helped to recover so that it too could play its part in the recovery of western Europe. Molotov's decision not to participate in the response to Marshall's offer was therefore doubly significant, reinforcing the divide between east and west both in Germany and in Europe as a whole. Not only did it mean that the Soviet Union and eastern Europe would not receive aid, but it also meant that the Soviet Zone of Germany was excluded as well. Only the Bizone (later the Trizone) was to be helped to return to economic self-sufficiency. The prospect of political reuni-fication was appearing increasingly remote.

It was therefore perhaps inevitable that the fifth Council of Foreign Ministers, held in London in November 1947, would make no progress at all, and it was adjourned *sine die*. The London meeting was used by the western powers as final proof that the Soviet Union was not prepared to do business on their terms. Before the Council opened, the British and Americans decided jointly to use the meeting to test for one last time whether the Russians were prepared to concede to the provisions of the Bevin

36. On the diplomacy of Marshall Aid see, in particular, A. S. Milward, *The Reconstruction of Western Europe 1945–51* (Methuen, London, 1984), ch. 11; Bullock, *Ernest Bevin*, ch. 10; W. C. Cromwell, 'The Marshall Plan, Britain and the Cold War', *Review of International Studies*, Vol. 8, No. 4, 1982, pp. 233–50; PRO/FO371/62386, Washington to Foreign Office, weekly political summary, 26 May 1947; PRO/T236/782, notes for Departmental meeting on 9 June 1947; PRO/CAB21/1759, passim.
37. Department of State Bulletin, 22 May 1947, pp. 919–24.

Plan as Marshall remained more anxious than Bevin to give the Soviet Union one more chance to escape a 'frozen front' in Europe. Bevin, on the other hand, declared that he had 'no intention of uttering an unnecessary word' at the Council.[38] But the Council's usefulness had run out. The bridge between wartime alliance and Cold-War confrontation had been crossed. Public opinion was swinging round behind the Labour government's policies, and that Council was accepted as the last of a round of negotiations.

After the Council, a crisis atmosphere permeated both British and US policies towards Germany. The Soviet Union's reaction to the Marshall Plan and its propaganda efforts in the west only heightened this sense of crisis. Bevin warned Cabinet and Commons that the public contours of British policy towards Germany now had to change. Britain was charged with the moral leadership of the west against communism.[39] As the Council ended he had held secret meetings with the US and French Foreign Secretaries.[40] German questions were discussed in some detail with the Americans. The British Military Governor, Sir Brian Robertson, was at this point keen to proceed quickly with reforming the currency in the western zones, despite the risks involved and the psychological significance that such a reform would have upon east–west relations.

In the new year, the Americans launched an initiative in the Control Council to secure a four-power currency reform on their own terms, but this failed and by late February 1948 both British and US authorities had concluded that quadripartite action in this field was neither possible nor desirable.[41] It was therefore something of a relief when the Soviet delegation stalked out of the Control Council meeting of 20 March 1948, openly signalling the end of four-power control in Germany.

The Prague coup of February 1948 served to confirm western suspicions of Soviet aims. Preparations for a western zone currency reform had already been made, and a new currency was issued on 20 June 1948. Partly in response to this measure, the Soviet Union

38. PRO/FO371/64250, Bevin–Marshall conversations, 17 and 18 December 1947; PRO/FO371/64629, note to Strang, 3 November 1947.
39. PRO/CAB129/23, CP(48), 5 January 1948, House of Commons Debates, cols. 1874–82, 18 December 1947.
40. PRO/FO371/64250, Anglo-French and Anglo-American meetings, 17 and 18 December 1947.
41. For the most recent assessment of Britain's role in the German currency reform, see I. D. Turner, 'Great Britain and the Post-War Currency Reform', *Historical Journal*, Vol. 30, No. 3, 1987, pp. 685–708. See also P. Windsor, *German Reunification* (Elek Books, London, 1969), pp. 34–6.

retaliated by closing land communications to Berlin, which lay deep inside the Soviet Zone. A land blockade was thus imposed, and the ensuing crisis lasted until May 1949. Although the US was by now the principal western actor, Bevin continued to hold a firm line.[42] He rejected proposals made by Robertson that Germany should be united but neutralised.[43] He encouraged the toughest of American responses to the blockade and agreed to the stationing on British soil of American B29 bombers. Aeroplanes of this design were technically capable of being converted to hold nuclear bombs, and it was not known at the time whether in fact they had a nuclear capability.[44]

Less than two months after the western zonal currency reform, negotiations began with the heads of the western Länder on the creation of a western German state. These negotiations culminated in the founding of the Federal Republic in May 1949 as the blockade of Berlin foundered. Thus the blockade had further cemented western relations over Germany's political future, as well as over western security arrangements.[45] Although Bevin had already sounded out US opinion about an Atlantic security system, the Berlin blockade hastened both the establishment of the Federal Republic and of the unique and far-reaching commitment of the Americans to western Europe's security through NATO.[46] By 1949, therefore, after these uncertain but decisive years, the Americans had made both an economic and military commitment to the restoration and defence of western Europe.

42. A. Shlaim, *The United States and the Berlin Blockade, 1948–1949* (University of California Press, Berkeley, Cal., 1983), reveals both the political drama of the Berlin blockade and analyses it within the framework of a crisis-management study. See also M. Bell, 'Die Blockade Berlins—Konfrontationen der Alliierten in Deutschland' in J. Foschepoth (ed.), *Kalter Krieg und deutsche Frage* (Vandenhoeck and Ruprecht, Göttingen and Zurich, 1985), pp. 217–39.
43. PRO/FO371/70501, 'Appreciation of the Present Situation in Berlin and the Effect on our Policy for Germany as a Whole', 12 July 1948. For Robertson's initiative, see also R. Steininger, 'Wie die Teilung Deutschlands verhindert werden sollte. Der Robertson-Plan aus dem Jahre 1948', *Militärgeschichtliche Mitteilungen*, Vol. 33, No. 1, 1983, pp. 49–90.
44. A. Shlaim, 'Britain, the Berlin Blockade and the Cold War', *International Affairs*, Vol. 60, No. 1, 1984, pp. 1–14.
45. Bullock, *Ernest Bevin*, pp. 698–9.
46. E. Barker, *The British Between the Superpowers, 1945–50* (Macmillan, London, 1984), pp. 147–8.

Conclusion

This outline of the British Labour government's intentions in its policy towards Germany suggests two emendations to more traditional views on the origins of the Cold War. First, Britain was not a minor, but a major actor, particularly in the 1945–47 period, when the lines of the Cold War were drawn. This factor has to be brought into any adequate account of the origins of this minutely researched yet persistently elusive international conflict. In the second place, traditionalists portray the Cold War as a western response to the Soviet challenge. In Germany—a fundamental cause and the principal battlefield of the Cold War in Europe—the reality was more complex. Both the Soviet Union and the western powers viewed each other's motives with considerable apprehension and thought they were responding to a threat from the other. In the CFM proceedings of 1945–7[47] and in the dramatic events in Germany of 1948–9, Britain clearly acted as a pacesetter in a policy that was to lead inexorably towards a divided Germany. She helped to encourage the Americans as partners in a strategy that turned western Germany from a defeated and devastated enemy into a potential loyal partner of the western powers.

47. For a fuller account see A. Deighton, *The Impossible Peace: Britain, the German Problem and the Origins of the Cold War* (Clarendon, Oxford, forthcoming).

PART II

British Policy and the Economy of the Western Zones

2

Economic Reconstruction in Western Germany, 1945–55: The Displacement of 'Vegetative Control'
Wendy Carlin

Introduction

Historical research over the past decade has enabled a much more detailed picture to be drawn of social and economic conditions in the western zones of Germany after 1945.[1] The extent and constraints on production, the policies of the occupying authorities, and the development and reformation of the labour movement, business associations and political parties have all been addressed. For an economist, the period raises fascinating questions on which new historical research can be brought to bear. Three such questions will be posed in this chapter.

First, how should economic activity in the period following the military collapse in 1945 be conceptualised? In particular, what was the nature of the incentive structures facing producers, consumers and workers? The second question relates to the currency reform and associated measures of decontrol in 1948. How can the economic importance of the reform be assessed? Did it mark a 'change of regime' in the form of economic activity or was it simply a continuation and acceleration of the incremental changes already occurring from the spring of 1947? The third problem is to identify the key policy decisions in the post-reform period which provided the preconditions for the successful growth of the 1950s. What was the economic logic of those choices and, in the context of the

1. For helpful comments on an earlier draft, I thank Werner Abelshauser, Andrea Boltho, Andrew Glyn, Alan Kramer, Hans-Jürgen Schröder, David Soskice, Ian Turner and participants at the German History Society Conference, St Antony's College, Oxford, March 1987.

Korean War boom, did it matter which way policy moved in 1949?

In response to the first question, it will be argued that it was not physical constraints which blocked the emergence of a self-sustaining growth process in the immediate post-collapse years. Rather, institutional constraints in the form of an inappropriate incentive structure for the promotion of long-term decision-making by enterprises blocked recovery. Western Germany's industrial base in terms of capital and labour was fundamentally intact in 1945. The missing physical prerequisites of recovery were highly visible but of a short-term nature: transport, raw materials, food. However, the policies and practices of the occupying powers and the discrediting and demoralisation of German business combined to prevent either a planned rebuilding of the economy or a propitious environment for private enterprise to reconstruct a market economy.

The aim of this chapter is to use the concept of 'vegetative control' developed by Janos Kornai[2] to provide an explanation for the form of economic activity which characterised the economy in the western zones between 1945 and 1948, and in turn for the change of regime which, it will be argued, occurred in 1948. Between 1945 and 1948, large parts of the economy were characterised by quantity rather than price adjustments to changes in economic conditions. Allocation occurred through some combination of administrative rationing, queuing by consumers, barter and the black market. The notion of vegetative control can help to explain how it was possible for production to increase over these years and yet for the scope of economic growth to be strictly limited. Only when a coherent set of incentives had been created by the decisive shift toward a free-market economy (reflected in the reforms of June 1948) were the conditions created for rapid capital formation.

The gradual move toward restoring a market economy paralleled the growing dominance of the United States amongst the occupying powers, the shift in the balance of domestic influence toward the Christian Democrats and the growing confidence and organisation of German business as the labour movement became weaker and more fragmented.

It became apparent in the months following the currency reform that further measures would be necessary to secure the successful displacement of vegetative control. Increased demand for both investment and consumption goods together with the liberalisation

2. J. Kornai, *The Economics of Shortage*, Vols. A and B, (North Holland, Amsterdam, 1980).

of prices provided the opportunity for businesses to build up their profit margins. Prices increased rapidly and barter transactions, a key symptom of vegetative control, reappeared as confidence in money fell.

Attention is focused below on the subsequent policy choices made by the German authorities to break this pattern of behaviour—in particular on the deflationary measures of spring 1949. Generalised deflationary measures were introduced to contain the open inflation, labour unrest and collusive practices of business which were threatening the successful re-establishment of a market economy. These were widely criticised at the time by Keynesians within and outside Germany. Their success in forcing firms to concentrate on cost reductions and on seeking foreign markets is traced.

Finally, it is argued that the Korean War provided an essential demand boost which enabled the West German economy to move on to a rapid growth path. In a sense, the deflationary measures were a necessary but not a sufficient condition for the consolidation of export-led growth. Export-orientation and investment financed largely through retentions were promoted in the 1950s through an undervalued exchange rate, tax incentives and by the maintenance of high profitability.

Physical Preconditions for Production

Capital

The size of the industrial gross capital stock at the end of the war relative to its size in 1938 was the outcome both of the level of investment during the course of the war and of the extent to which the capital stock had been destroyed in the war. The net effect of these factors was a growth of the capital stock in the western zones from 1938 to 1945 of 14%.[3] Real gross investment peaked in 1942 at a level nearly two-and-a-half times the level in 1936, a year of approximately full capacity utilisation and before the shift of the economy to a war footing.[4]

3. R. Krengel, *Anlagevermögen, Produktion und Beschäftigung der Industrie im Gebiet der Bundesrepublik Deutschland von 1924 zu 1958* (DIW, Berlin, 1958), p. 94.
4. Krengel, *Anlagevermögen*, p. 98.

In addition, the conditions of war provided opportunities in Germany for the introduction of new technology, especially in the application of mass-production techniques. This shift in technology was aided by reductions in the specialisation of product ranges during the war. Kaldor reports spectacular increases in productivity in the vehicle industry due to the standardisation of types where, by reducing the number of types of lorry from 76 to 9, 'output per manhour, over the industry as a whole, was more than doubled (in certain cases more than trebled) despite the fact that the proportion of skilled workmen in the total labour force was cut in half'.[5]

Turning to the second determinant of the post-war capital stock—namely, war damage—we find a broad spectrum of estimates. Recent historical research suggests that the findings of the US Strategic Bombing Survey are the most reliable and shows that the collapse of the economy was due entirely to the paralysis of the transport system.[6] The Strategic Bombing Survey estimated that not more than 6.5% of all machine tools were destroyed or damaged (and most of the latter had been repaired). Even in the vital ball-bearing industry only 16% of all machine tools were destroyed. Krengel estimates war damage for 1943 (the first year of the bombing war) at 2% of the 1942 gross capital stock; in 1944 at 10% and for the first four months of 1945 at 7.5% of the respective previous year's capital stock.[7] This adds up to a reduction of the capital stock by 23% as compared with its 1939 level, a loss as noted above more than compensated for by the new investment carried out during the war.

The conclusion to be drawn is that the industrial capital stock in the western zones of Germany was considerably larger and probably at a higher technical level in 1945 than it was before the war. To complete the picture it is necessary to examine the changes to the capital stock through investment and reparations that occurred in the years after the end of hostilities in 1945. For institutional reasons discussed below, with a low level of capacity utilisation went a low level of investment. Gross investment was less than depreciation in each year from 1945 to 1948, much of it being repairs carried out by workers in their own plants, the so-called

5. N. Kaldor, 'The German War Economy', *Review of Economic Studies*, Vol. 13, No. 2, 1945–46, p. 51.
6. W. Abelshauser, *Wirtschaft in Westdeutschland, 1945–1948* (Deutsche Verlags-Anstalt, Stuttgart, 1975), p. 117.
7. Krengel, *Anlagevermögen*, p. 76.

'self-installed plant'. The inclusion of plant lost through reparations and dismantling (which amounted to much less than originally proposed) meant a fall in the gross capital stock between 1945 and 1948 of just under 7%.[8]

On balance, although war damage and dismantling may have resulted in specific shortages of industrial capacity, it seems that the quantity and quality of investment during the early years of the war was more than sufficient to offset the losses, leaving the gross capital stock through the 1945 to 1948 period just larger than it was before the war (1939) with a more favourable age structure and technically more advanced.

Labour

The population of the three western zones increased by over 5 million or 13% between 1939 and 1946.[9] The movement of people in and out of Germany in the immediate post-war years was massive. There was the emigration of some of the 7.5 million foreign workers who had been brought to Germany during the war[10] and the immigration of 6 million refugees and expellees to the British and US Zones alone between mid-1945 and 1946.[11] Well over 100% of the increase in population was attributable to net migration.

The registered labour force fell by 12.9% between 1939 and 1946, but this reflected reduced participation rates from 81.2% to 65.9%[12] and disguised unemployment in a situation of extreme economic dislocation. Bearing in mind the fall in the male working population, the effective labour supply was probably unchanged. This was also true of its quality. If anything, it is likely that the 'sum of knowledge and experience was higher in 1946 than in 1939'.[13] Abelshauser supports this view by pointing, for example, to efforts during the war to increase the qualifications of labour through

8. Ibid., p. 94.
9. W. Bauer, 'Der allgemeine wirtschaftliche Charakter der Zonen', in Deutsches Institut für Wirtschaft (DIW) (ed.), *Wirtschaftsprobleme der Besatzungszonen* (DIW, Berlin, 1948), p. 11.
10. United Nations Economic Commission for Europe (UNECE), *Economic Survey of Europe since the War: A Reappraisal of Problems and Prospects* (UN, Geneva, 1953), p. 2.
11. K. Häuser, 'The Partition of Germany' in W. Stolper *et al.*, *The German Economy 1870 to the Present* (Weidenfeld & Nicolson, London, 1967).
12. Abelshauser, *Wirtschaft in Westdeutschland*, pp. 103, 109, tables 19, 22. Participation rate is defined as the proportion of the population of working age which is in the labour force (employed or registered unemployed).
13. Ibid., p. 105.

accelerated training of those who went from other sectors of the economy into industry as a consequence of recruitment for the armed forces.

However, a short-run problem immediately after the war was the considerable mismatch between potential workers and jobs because of the direction of inflow of refugees and expellees, the uneven destruction of dwellings by area and the general disorganisation prevalent in the country. The locational maldistribution of the population is reflected in the unemployment and vacancy figures. In June 1946, there were 329,000 registered unemployed and 369,000 registered vacancies.[14] By way of contrast with the capital stock, between 1946 and 1948 the changes in the potential labour supply were all in a favourable direction. The inflow of labour continued and reallocation occurred between the regions.

Materials, Food and Transport

Also necessary to production are raw material inputs to the industrial sector including food, and transportation. A vivid example of the interdependencies affecting production refers to the low production of coal because of a lack of wood to shore up the coal mines. But the foresters refused to work in the rain because they lacked clothes or shoes, which in turn were in short supply in part because of low coal supplies to consumer-goods industries.[15]

The materials most frequently cited in accounts of the constraints on production are food, coal and iron and steel. There seems little doubt that the limited level of food supply reduced productivity in the post-war years.[16] Over an extended period, food deprivation is directly correlated with reduced labour output: '[S]ome areas reported urban consumer rations to be as low as 700 calories per day, a ration "decidedly below the minimum necessary to health and muscular activity essential to productive labour".'[17] Despite a flourishing black market in food, it is unlikely that any but a tiny minority benefited from such supplements to the rations. General

14. C. Arnold, 'Der Arbeitsmarkt in den Besatzungszonen', in DIW (ed.), *Wirtschaftsprobleme*, p. 53.
15. Abelshauser, *Wirtschaft in Westdeutschland*, p. 130.
16. See G. J. Trittel, 'Die westlichen Besatzungsmächte und der Kampf gegen den Mangel 1945–1949', *Aus Politik und Zeitgeschichte*, B22/86, May 1986, pp. 20–1, 27–8.
17. J. Gimbel, *The American Occupation of Germany. Politics and the Military 1945–49* (Stanford University Press, Stanford, Cal., 1968), p. 35.

Clay, the Military Governor of the US Zone, suggested that on-average supplementary food, including that from the black market, did not exceed 200 calories per person per day.[18]

It is not difficult to point to the reasons for the shortage of food. First of all, the increase in population reduced the potential feeding capacity of the agricultural areas of the western zones.[19] Secondly, there was a chronic shortage of fertiliser as a result both of the zonal division which prevented the movement of raw materials to processing plants and of the embargo on the production of chemical fertilisers for military reasons. Actual production in the British Zone was about two-thirds of the pre-war level.[20]

A solution to the problem of inadequate supplies of food was conditional on a change in the policies of the military occupation to permit increased production of manufactures so that exports could rise and thus generate the foreign exchange with which to purchase imports. A necessary implication of the economic separation of the western zones (from the food-surplus Soviet Zone and eastern territories) was a new pattern of trade involving new and larger export markets to support the volume of food and raw-materials imports necessary for a level of activity comparable to that before the war.

Coal production was actively supported by the military authorities because of the needs of the rest of European industry for coal. Production rose rapidly from mid-1945 with only a seasonal fall in the winter of 1945–6 and a second downturn in spring 1947 due to the food crisis on the Ruhr.[21] Yet output had only risen to a half of the 1936 level by 1947 and was generally unavailable to large users like the iron and steel industry.[22]

The dislocation of economic activity caused by the destruction of the transport system was considerable. The bombing campaign from September 1944 had little effect on the industrial capital stock but its strategic success lay in isolating the Ruhr from the rest of Germany through the total paralysis of the transport network.[23]

18. L. D. Clay, *Decision in Germany*, (Doubleday, Garden City, NY 1950), p. 266.
19. The number of standardized hectares per 100 inhabitants fell by nearly 20% in the US Zone, 13% in the British Zone, and by 4% in the French between 1938 and 1946 (Bauer, 'Allgemeine Wirtschaftliche Charakter', p. 12).
20. Abelshauser, *Wirtschaft in Westdeutschland*, p. 135, table 34. For a comprehensive account of food policy in western Germany see J. Farquharson, *The Western Allies and the Politics of Food* (Berg, Leamington Spa, 1985).
21. Abelshauser, *Wirtschaft in Westdeutschland*, p. 139, table 36.
22. For a fascinating analysis of the inadequacies of British coal policy see chapter 4.
23. Abelshauser, *Wirtschaft in Westdeutschland*, p. 152, table 48.

Railways carried two-thirds of pre-war goods traffic and were completely immobilised. For example, in the British Zone in May 1945, of 13,000 km of track, only 1,000 were open; there was not a single permanent bridge left over the Rhine; and all waterways were blocked by wreckage.[24] Over 60% of locomotives were not functioning and a third of the rest of the rolling stock was damaged.

Although the destruction of the transport system paralysed the economy, it was repaired remarkably quickly. For instance, by the end of June 1946, 93% of railway tracks and 800 bridges were open, including two Rhine bridges. At a superficial level, transport was not a binding constraint on economic activity by the summer of 1946. However, serious weaknesses in rolling stock emerged in the winter of 1946–7 when additional strain was put on the railways because of the severe weather conditions which left canals and waterways frozen. In January 1947, only 65% of demands for transporting food, coal and other products could be met. It was the vulnerability of the transport system which meant that despite the priority assigned to coal production, coal supplies constrained output in other sectors until mid-1947.

In response to the crisis, the military authorities directed all efforts to the improvement of transport and by August 1947 the situation was improving. In January 1948, the rail network, rolling stock and waterways were in a satisfactory state—no longer a constraint on the growth of economic activity.[25]

To summarise, from the evidence available it seems that the capital stock and the labour supply were at least at the pre-war level but the economy was hampered by short-run bottlenecks, regional dislocation and restrictions on international trade. To identify the reasons for the persistence of bottlenecks and shortages it is necessary to move beyond the level of physical inputs and outputs to the uncertainties which dominated economic activity in the first years after the collapse.

Institutional Preconditions for Economic Growth

For the successful mobilisation of the economic resources which were available in western Germany from 1945, clarity was required at a political level. In 1945, there was no grand plan on the part of

24. Ibid., p. 152.
25. Ibid., pp. 155–6.

the Allies for the future of Germany as a political or economic entity. Apart from democratisation, what was to be done to Germany was expressed entirely in negative terms—disarm, deindustrialise, denazify, dismember, deconcentrate, decartelise. It was through the cumulative effect of a series of decisions by the US between 1945 and 1947, that it became clear that the economy in western Germany was to be rehabilitated along free-enterprise lines.

Yet initially, the question of the type of economic organisation appeared to be an open one. In the western zones, there was a divergence between the US and British authorities as to the balance between 'plan' and 'market' in their administration of the economy. The Americans eschewed all forms of planning and centralised administration in their own zone. There was only loose coordination of the production and distribution of raw materials: 'To an even greater extent than in the north German occupation zone [British Zone], a functioning control system was lacking.'[26]

The British, on the other hand, more for pragmatic than for ideological reasons[27] moved towards reinstating central planning of production and administered their zone in a much more centralised way. Indeed Germans working in the administration of British occupation policy had 'the feeling that England expected a completely planned economy'.[28] The plans were ambitious, purporting to provide a plan for total production and distribution, but were not accorded sufficient authority by the British, with the result that industrial production functioned largely outside effective controls.[29]

The uncertainty about property relations in the Ruhr and more generally was reflected in the positions of the political parties. The 1945 programme of the Christian Democratic Union–Christian

26. G. Ambrosius, 'Marktwirtschaft oder Planwirtschaft?', *Vierteljahresschrift für Sozial- und Wirtschaftsgeschichte*, Vol. 66, No. 1, 1979, p. 78.
27. See for example R. Steininger, 'Die Sozialisierung fand nicht statt' in J. Foschepoth and R. Steininger (eds.), *Britische Deutschland- und Besatzungspolitik 1945–1949*, (Schöningh, Paderborn, 1985), pp. 135–50. Plumpe provides some telling evidence that the planning and administration in the British Zone relied for its implementation on the structures of private business and did not provide the preconditions for a radical change in the economic system. Werner Plumpe, 'Wirtschaftsverwaltung und Kapitalinteresse im britischen Besatzungsgebiet 1945–46' in D. Petzina and W. Euchner (eds.), *Wirtschaftspolitik im britischen Besatzungsbiet 1945–1949* (Schwann, Düsseldorf, 1984) pp. 136–40.
28. Abelshauser, *Wirtschaft in Westdeutschland*, p. 76.
29. Ambrosius, 'Marktwirtschaft oder Planwirtschaft?', pp. 76–7. For a useful discussion of the scope and limitations of the so-called Spartan Plans see A. Drexler, W. Krumbein and F. Stratmann, 'Die britischen "Sparta-Pläne" 1946' in Foschepoth and Steininger (eds.), *Britische Deutschland- und Besatzungspolitik*, pp. 245–63.

Social Union (CDU–CSU) called for state ownership of natural resources and key monopoly industries and the elimination of large-scale capitalist enterprises. Although political activists were overwhelmingly in favour of socialist measures of some kind in the initial period of occupation, the mood amongst the general population was one of apathy toward political affairs.[30]

Major uncertainty also related to the level of industrial activity that was foreseen for Germany. At the Potsdam Conference in mid-1945, it was decided that the German economy should be capable of supporting a standard of living not higher than the European average. This formula implied German living standards at Great Depression level. Whatever industrial capacity was not deemed necessary to this standard of living was to be available for reparations, that is, to be dismantled and removed from Germany. A radical restructuring of the sectoral pattern of German industry away from its heavy industrial base was envisaged.

Through the course of 1946–8, these fundamental political and economic uncertainties were resolved. By early 1947, agreement was reached within and between the British and American authorities that their two zones would be merged for economic purposes. Economic recovery to at least a self-supporting level was to be fostered. The French were brought in by linking the Coal for Europe Plan[31] (which implied a strengthening of German industry so as to provide increased coal exports) with longer-run plans for European recovery financed by a continuation of US aid. Bit by bit, the Marshall Plan emerged along with conditions relating to private enterprise and free trade which made Soviet participation unthinkable.[32] The western zones of Germany were included as an econ-omic unit in the plan and steps were taken early in 1948 toward the political unification of western Germany.

The centre of gravity of domestic political opinion shifted right-ward and moved firmly in favour of the market and private enter-prise. A key landmark was the decision of the SPD to remain in opposition in the Bizonal Economic Council. This decision by the SPD was crucial and had the additional effect of weakening the

30. Ambrosius, 'Marktwirtschaft oder Planwirtschaft?', p. 38, n. 13.
31. A. S. Milward, *The Reconstruction of Western Europe 1945–51*, (Methuen, London, 1984), pp. 74–6, 88–9. See also Carsten Lüders, 'Die Regelung der Ruhrfrage in den Verhandlungen über die politische und ökonomischer Stabilisierung Westdeuschlands 1945–1949', in Petzina and Euchner (eds.), *Wirtschaftspolitik*, pp. 87–105.
32. J. Gimbel, *The Origins of the Marshall Plan* (Stanford University Press, Stanford, Cal., 1976), p. 269.

Christian Socialists within the CDU–CSU.[33]

Long-term decision-making by enterprises was further hampered by the initial policies of the occupation authorities toward business. The fact that little of a lasting nature was achieved through the policies of decartellisation and deconcentration does not nullify the effect that these commitments had in compounding uncertainty and despondency about business prospects in the first couple of years after the collapse. However, American businessmen stressed the need for re-establishing the economy on free-enterprise tracks and exerted pressure to make this a condition of US aid.[34] General Clay reflected this pressure when he argued that support for British plans to nationalise the coal industry: 'would not be acceptable to the American businessmen and bankers on whom we must depend in the final analysis for the success, not only of our export program, but for subsequent financing to enlarge the export program.'[35]

The gradual re-emergence of the employers' associations was an important measure of the growing confidence of business. Although initially, reorganisation lagged somewhat behind that of the unions, the business associations were organised on a supra-zonal level before the trade unions, with the formation of the BDI in 1948 and of the BDA in early 1949.[36]

The Nature of Economic Activity, 1945–8

Vegetative Control of Economic Activity

In order to account for the persistence and growth of economic activity in the industrial sector under conditions of such extreme uncertainty, Kornai's concept of vegetative control proves useful. It provides an explanation, first, for the extent of industrial produc-

33. J. Domes and M. Wolffsohn, 'Setting the Course for the FRG: Major Policy Decisions in the Bizonal Economic Council and Party Images, 1947–49', *Zeitschrift für die gesamte Staatswissenschaft*, Vol. 135, No. 3, 1979, p. 337.
34. W. Link, *Deutsche und amerikanische Gewerkschaften und Geschäftsleute 1945–75*, (Droste Verlag, Düsseldorf, 1978), pp. 101–121, E. Schmidt, *Die verhinderte Neuordnung 1945–52*, (Europäische Verlaganstalt, Cologne, 1970), pp. 55–6.
35. Quoted by Gimbel, *Origins*, p. 202.
36. HMSO, *Overseas Economic Surveys: The Federal Republic of Germany: Economic and Commercial Conditions in the Federal Republic of Germany and West Berlin* (HMSO, London, 1955) pp. 78, 280. See also D. Prowe, 'Unternehmer, Gewerkschaften und Staat in der Kammerneuordnung in der britischen Besatzungszone bis 1950', in Petzina and Euchner (eds.), *Wirtschaftspolitik*, pp. 235–54; Plumpe, 'Wirtschaftsverwaltung', pp. 131–6.

tion which actually occurred—its recovery to approximately a half the 1936 level by the end of 1947—and secondly, for the specific constraints on reconstruction which existed during those years. This in turn provides a key to understanding the significance of the currency reform.

The essence of the concept of vegetative control is that in a modern economy (i.e. characterised by a complex division of labour) there is a form of economic activity that operates independently of the political and ownership relations of the system. There are mechanisms based on decentralised quantity signals which control the 'most simple, elementary, and trivial adjustment of real economic processes'.[37] These are, for example, the increase in the purchase of inputs if production has increased; the increase in production if sales to other firms have increased, or if stocks of output have fallen. These simple behavioural rules are stronger when price signals have little or no influence.

Kornai argues that: '[a]utonomous [i.e. vegetative] function is based on the average diligence, conditioning, routine, identification with one's job of the people working within the system. Beyond that it also relies on the fact that, as in every material system, a certain inertia prevails also in economic systems.'[38] As a result, vegetative control mechanisms can only permit a very limited range of economic activities. They apply only to low-level repetition of production, the use of 'rules of thumb' for standard decision-making, simple adaptation such as building up stocks to afford protection from the risk of shortage, and forced substitution to enable production to carry on even in the presence of shortage.[39] But higher forms of control which are dependent on the particular incentive or authority structure of the politico-economic system are required for decisions regarding fixed investment (other than maintenance and simple replacement), major technical developments, the release of new products and radical changes in the volume and pattern of production.[40]

The criteria for a vegetative control mechanism are four-fold:
(i) In terms of organisation, in contrast to the centralised hierarchy of directive control or decentralised organisation resulting

37. Kornai, *Economics of Shortage*, p. 141.
38. J. Kornai, *Anti-Equilibrium: On Economic Systems Theory and the Tasks of Research*, (North Holland, Amsterdam, 1971), p. 178.
39. M. Cave and P. Hare, *Alternative Approaches to Economic Planning* (Macmillan, London, 1981), p. 147.
40. Kornai, *Anti-Equilibrium*, p. 181.

from the common activity of all buyers and sellers with price signals, vegetative control is organised exclusively between single pairs of buyers and sellers.

(ii) The information used is direct information on demand and supply possibilities (not instructions or prices).

(iii) Rules of behaviour are simple responses to stock signals or to the information gained directly from sellers/buyers/consumers (not fulfilment of instructions or responses to price signals).

(iv) The motivation of the producers is identification with the survival of the firm (not an interest in the fulfilment of instructions or increasing profits).[41]

These four criteria appear to provide an accurate characterisation of the form of much of economic activity in the western zones between 1945 and 1948. The bulk of the material used to illustrate this contention comes from descriptions of economic behaviour made at the time by a number of economists, several of whom were working for the occupying powers.

Between 1945 and mid-1948 resource allocation in the western zones occurred through means of barter in a large part of the economy, an active black market, and military-government direction in a few sectors. These mechanisms operated in the shadow of an edifice of controls inherited from the Nazi war economy and maintained by the military authorities. The military governments kept the bulk of the controls in place, including the general price and wage freeze introduced in 1936. As a result, relative prices remained virtually fixed for more than a decade and could play no role in reallocating resources in the economy.[42] But despite this apparent continuity, there was a significant change in economic life after the collapse because the degree of control exercised by the Nazis in operating the 'command' economy was never equalled by the occupation[43] and shortages of food and consumer goods became much more serious.

Just as the higher-level control system of the hierarchical command type inherited from the Nazi war economy was unable to provide a coherent framework for economic activity, so the black market was unable to provide decentralised market incentives for

41. J. Kornai and B. Martos, 'Autonomous control of the economic system', *Econometrica*, Vol. 41, No. 3, 1973, p. 513.
42. H. Mendershausen, 'Prices, Money and the Distribution of Goods in Post-War Germany', *American Economic Review*, Vol. 39, No. 4, 1949, pp. 647–8.
43. Abelshauser, *Wirtschaft in Westdeutschland*, p. 54.

the economy. It was confined to a narrow range of predominantly consumer goods.

The new form of economic activity that emerged during the occupation which conforms to the description of a low-level vegetative control mechanism was a complicated form of barter referred to as bilateral exchange. Goods generally changed hands at the official prices, and legal wages prevailed, but as Mendershausen (who was the Assistant Chief of Price Control for the US Military Government) put it 'the legal prices and rates did not represent the essence of the bargain'.[44] The role of money as a medium of exchange was restricted to the settlement of net balances in transactions in which barter was decisive. The Reichsmark had become useless as fully functional money, not because of the devaluation of the currency through open inflation, but because of the extreme shortage of goods available for purchase compared with the nominal purchasing power. In 1947, for example, currency in circulation in the four zones plus Berlin was estimated to be ten times the amount that circulated in 1936 when the price freeze was introduced, whereas real national income was put at roughly a half that of the Reich (1936).[45]

Bilateral exchange took several forms and represented the adaptation of producers and consumers to the prevailing conditions. Supplies were obtained through 'compensation trade', 'distributions in kind to workers' and through ordinary barter. Compensation trade refers to the typical form of exchange amongst industrial producers and wholesale traders in which a chain of barter deals was engaged in to secure raw materials for production. Although the compensation trade system was illegal and both costly and cumbersome, it acted to maintain a trading mechanism which prevented a complete breakdown of industrial activity in conditions of scarcity and trade prohibitions.[46]

44. Mendershausen, 'Prices, Money and the Distribution of Goods', p. 651.
45. Ibid., p. 649.
46. Christoph Buchheim develops an argument as to the importance of the 1948 Reforms which also draws on the work of Kornai. However, Buchheim uses Kornai's general theory of the shortage economy which is the characteristic state of a command-type planned economy to describe conditions prior to the reforms. My argument, by contrast, emphasizes that the pre-reforms economy is better described by vegetative control, that is, by the absence of *either* a coherent command structure *or* a functioning market. In particular, the concept of vegetative control can explain the severe limitations on the incentive to invest. See C. Buchheim, 'Die Währungsreform 1948 in Westdeutschland', *Vierteljahrshefte für Zeitgeschichte*, Vol. 36, No. 2, 1988, p. 197. Ritschl makes the same use of Kornai as Buchheim: A. Ritschl, 'Die Währungsreform von 1948 und der Wiederaufstieg der westdeutschen Industrie', *Vierteljah-*

Bilateral exchange also dominated relations between employer and worker. The payment of the legally prescribed wage was insufficient to secure a regular supply of labour from employees. The reason for this was obvious—the allotted rations of food could be purchased with part of a week's wages. There was little else to do with one's earnings since savings were already high and black-market prices were exhorbitant in terms of earnings. For example, a miner working three shifts a week would earn enough to buy just a pound of butter on the black market and in the process become hungrier and wear out clothing which could not be replaced. It was more worthwhile to spend some of the time going to the country-side to try to barter food or work on an allotment to grow food.[47]

To prevent or reduce absenteeism, employers provided payment in kind. They provided factory meals more substantial than warranted by the ration coupons handed in by the workers and also gave factory output to workers which they could barter directly with peasants for food. It seems from several estimates that in the British and US Zones at least half of commercial activity was transacted on a barter compensation basis.[48] The black market was of much less importance. Even in the Volkswagen factory under the direct control of the British Military Government, barter compensation trade played a significant role. *Der Spiegel* reported that some 5% of total Volkswagen production was allocated to compensation trade.[49]

For employers or producers, the basic aim was to buy as much and sell as little as possible. The accumulation of physical assets—particularly stocks—was the activity from which producers had most to gain.[50] An observer noted at the time that: '[t]he motives of the business man are to keep his business in being, to retain the

resheʃte für Zeitgeschichte, Vol. 33, No. 1, 1985, p. 160.
47. A. M. Stamp, 'Germany Without Incentive', *Lloyds Bank Review*, ns, Vol. 5, 1947, p. 18; H. C. Wallich, *Mainsprings of the German Revival* (Yale University Press, New Haven, Conn., 1955), p. 65; Häuser, 'Partition of Germany', pp. 204–7.
48. F. H. Klopstock, 'Monetary Reform in Western Germany', *Journal of Political Economy*, Vol. 57, No. 4, 1949, p. 279; Stamp, 'Germany Without Incentive', p. 23; Mendershausen, 'Prices, Money and the Distribution of Goods', p. 655.
49. *Der Spiegel*, 25 June 1948, quoted in I. D. Turner, 'British Occupation Policy and its Effects on the Town of Wolfsburg and the Volkswagenwerk 1945–1945', PhD thesis, Manchester University, 1984, p. 204. Turner also documents high levels of absenteeism from the Volkswagenwerk (pp. 207–8).
50. Wallich, *Mainsprings*, pp. 65. Buchheim provides further evidence, 'Die Währungsreform 1948', pp. 196–7.

goodwill of his customers and to maintain his stocks of raw materials in the hope that some day conditions may improve.'[51] Under the system of controlled prices and wages, in which legal prices were based on those determined in an unregulated price system in 1936, a cursory consideration of the level of unit costs in 1946 compared with 1936 makes it clear that firms would in many cases be unable to cover costs. The problem was exacerbated by the removal of numerous subsidies by the occupation authorities.[52] It was only because profit margins were very high in 1936 and throughout the war that not more than an estimated 30–40% of German industry was making a loss in 1946.[53]

In view of the unpropitious conditions for production, it is perhaps surprising that output was as high as it was in the years immediately after the collapse (reaching 50% of the 1936 level by the last quarter of 1947). In the absence of either a coherent incentive structure for decentralised production or effective planning, the economy was described as 'drifting without rudder or pilot'.[54] It was the inertia referred to by Kornai which resulted in continued production, albeit at a low level, and continued attendance at work.

The bilateral exchange economy in Germany described above would seem to be a rather pure form of vegetative control, existing in the presence of conflicting and confused elements of higher-level controls of both directive and price types. Mendershausen's assessment of the situation in post-war Germany hints at the notion of vegetative control: 'Where neither trading for money nor redistribution of goods by political authority, alone or in combination, can ensure a reliable division of labor, bilateral exchange seems to be the safest line of economic retreat.'[55] Economic reconstruction was hampered until a medium of exchange was re-established and rules decided by which commodities could be imported or exported. The better functioning of the vegetative mechanisms could provide a certain growth in production but such growth was strictly limited in the absence of coherent higher-level controls.

51. Stamp, 'Germany Without Incentive', p. 21.
52. Ibid.
53. F. A. Burchardt and K. Martin, 'Western Germany and Reconstruction', *Bulletin of Oxford Institute of Statistics*, Vol. 9, No. 12, 1947, p. 411.
54. Häuser, 'Partition of Germany', p. 208.
55. Mendershausen, 'Prices, Money and the Distribution of Goods', pp. 657–8.

The Limits to the Growth of Production

The extent to which industrial production grew in 1947 is still in dispute.[56] Nevertheless, even if Abelshauser's estimates lie closer to the truth, the argument here is that a qualitative change was required to displace vegetative control as the central economic mechanism. Such a change would be registered not in the growth of production within the capacity of the existing capital stock, but of *investment* and other higher-level decisions such as innovation, radical changes in the organisation of production, the introduction of new products, etc. In interpreting the revised output data, Abelshauser does not differentiate growth due to the easing of bottlenecks and the smoother functioning of the vegetative control mechanisms of the economy from a dynamic process of growth. The latter, as noted above, requires decision-making of a higher order and presupposes a longer-term view in which incentive structures have a certain stability. As table 2.1 shows, gross investment shot up in 1948 to a level just above the 1936 level. Indeed net investment was negative until 1948.

Currency Reform and Deflation, 1948–9

The Change of Regime with the Currency Reform

By 1948, there had been a progressive reduction in the level of uncertainty surrounding the West German economy. The business sector was largely rehabilitated, the labour movement firmly in the hands of moderates, and the inclusion of the western zones as an entity in the Marshall Plan meant that US aid would continue and that the US was committed to full industrial recovery. On the political side, although it was unclear whether the CDU–CSU or the SPD would win the general election and form a government some years hence, the CDU–CSU had the initiative through their control of the Bizonal Economic Council.

The notion of an economy operating primarily through the very limited mechanisms of vegetative control highlights the key role of

56. See the debate between Ritschl and Abelshauser, Ritschl, 'Die Währungs-reform', pp. 136–65; W. Abelshauser, 'Schopenhauer's Gesetz und die Währungsreform', *Vierteljahrshefte für Zeitgeschichte*, Vol. 33, No. 1, 1985, pp. 214–18.

Table 2.1 Indices of production and gross investment (industry), 1945–9 (1936 = 100)

Year	Quarter	Industrial Output Official quarterly	Industrial Output Estimated quarterly	Industrial Output annual	Gross Investment annual
1945	III		14		
	IV		21		
1946	I		30	36	36
	II		34		
	III		40		
	IV		41		
1947	I	31	34	43	46
	II	40	44		
	III	42	46		
	IV	45	50		
1948	I	48	54	63	104
	II	50	57		
	III	65	65		
	IV	76	76		
1949					156

Sources: Production indices calculated from Abelshauser (1975), pp. 80, 57, table 16. Gross investment indices from Krengel (1958), p. 94.

the currency reform in enabling more complicated economic decision-making with a longer time horizon, notably investment, to occur. The importance of the abolition of price controls which occurred at the same time as the currency reform was twofold: first, it released the constraints on an increase in the supply of labour and of output; secondly, it fostered favourable expectations about the profitability of production.

With nominal wages and prices fixed, the level of the real wage in conjunction with the limited availability of goods acted to constrain the supply of labour.[57] The constraint on the supply of labour meant in turn that the supply of goods was below what it would have been had firms been able to hire as much labour as they wanted

57. Thus the low level of labour productivity in the form of absenteeism and low effort at work prior to the reforms was not due simply to the food shortage but reflected the distorted incentives facing workers and employers. Trittel stresses the role of food in 'Die westlichen Besatzungsmächte', especially pp. 27–9). Buchheim notes the role of incentives in 'Die Währungsreform 1948', pp. 192–3.

at the fixed real wage.[58] The German case displayed the additional feature of side-payments made in kind by firms to workers which induced a supply of labour greater than would have been the case in a pure repressed inflation situation. Once the price and wage controls were lifted to release the rationing of goods to consumers and of labour to firms, and given the existence of stocks of finished goods and raw materials, the supply of labour and of output increased rapidly; barter and side-payments in kind vanished.[59]

The shape of the currency reform, price decontrol and tax changes which were introduced into western Germany, beginning on 20 June 1948, was 'strongly influenced by the desire of both the U.S. Military Government and the majority parties in the German Bizonal Economic Administration to reestablish money incentives and the free market mechanism as the decisive determinants of economic life'.[60] In the short run, this was achieved with startling effectiveness through the allocation of cash to each person in two instalments (on a one-for-one basis against savings of up to RM 600—savings above this amount were eventually exchanged in the ratio of approximately DM 6.5 for RM 100), the repudiation of the German national debt and the provision of only DM 60 per employee to employers for payroll purposes (DM 60 was about the equivalent of the average weekly wage of an industrial worker).

Because of their enforced illiquidity and with the incentive of higher prices and the availability of labour to raise production, businesses were induced to release their hoards of goods. And after the long years of commodity famine, exacerbated by speculative stock building in the months immediately before the currency reform, consumers spent their cash allocations freely on goods which had once more become available, literally overnight. Barter transactions disappeared, black-market prices tumbled and absenteeism dropped dramatically. The timing of the currency reform in mid-summer at the peak of agricultural production contributed to its short-run success. *The Economist* reported on 3 July 1948 that:

58. E. Malinvaud, *The Theory of Unemployment Reconsidered* (Blackwell, Oxford, 1977), pp. 44–53, 70–5.
59. Buchheim makes a very interesting comparison between the effects of the combined currency reform and price deregulation in the Bizone and the currency reform without thoroughgoing deregulation in the French Zone, 'Die Währungsreform 1948', pp. 226–7. My argument is that both were necessary to displace the vegetative control regime.
60. Klopstock, 'Monetary Reform', p. 281.

Table 2.2 Real wages, product wages and productivity (industry), 1948–52 (1938 = 100)

Year	Weekly earnings 1	Cost of living 2	Output prices 3	Input prices 4	Industrial productivity 5	Industrial employment 6
1948	126	168	197	193	61	103
1949	141	166	191	204	75	108
1950	157	156	186	230	94	114
1951	177	168	221	284	113	124
1952	191	171	226	294	122	129

Year	Real wages 1/2	Product wages 1/3	Productivity 5/6	Real input costs 4/3
1948	75	64	59	98
1949	85	74	69	107
1950	101	84	82	124
1951	105	80	91	129
1952	112	85	95	113

Sources: Bank deutscher Länder, *Monthly Reports* 1948–52 and *Annual Reports* 1948/9–1952. UNECE (1949), table 3; UNECE (1953), tables 1, 2; UNECE (1954), tables 1, 2.

[h]ousewives strolled down the streets gazing in astonishment at shop-windows—at shoes, leather handbags, tools, perambulators, bicycles, cherries in baskets, young carrots tied in neat bundles. In the early morning, farmers had been seen making their unaccustomed way into town with produce for sale, a little uncertain what were the legal channels for selling it.[61]

On the third working day after the currency reform, the report went on, 'manufacturers in Nuremberg said that absence from factories from all causes had fallen from 18 to 20% to 2 or 3%'.

Profits from the sale of stocks were high as price controls on all manufactures and many other goods were withdrawn. However, the lasting success of the 'change of regime' was dependent on the profitability of current production. In the second half of 1948, industrial productivity was 59% of the 1938 level, whilst product wages (the measure relevant to the profitability of production) were just higher at 64% of the 1938 level (see table 2.2). Given the very favourable situation for profits in 1938 it is clear that profits in 1948

61. *The Economist*, 3 July 1948, p. 11.

were satisfactory. The fact that real materials costs were just below the pre-war level would have offset the slightly less favourable balance for profits between productivity and product wages. The currency reform had favoured firms in another way by reducing their debts in the ratio 10:1 whilst leaving the real value of their assets unchanged. Furthermore the taxation reform shifted the burden of tax from property and profits to lower-income groups.[62]

As output rose, the volume of profits increased and along with the abolition of price controls generated favourable expectations and produced an investment boom.[63] As shown in table 2.1, fixed investment in 1948 was more than double the level of 1947 and the bulk of investment in 1948 occurred in the second half of the year. The source of the inflationary pressure which emerged in late 1948 as a threat to the monetary basis of the market economy lay in the failure of supply (both in quantity and composition) to keep up with the demand for goods. Consumption and investment demand remained high. With the boost to liquidity from the second instalment of blocked savings, and access to credit easy, there was a tendency towards building up stocks again as confidence in the value of monetary assets fell. Although production was rising fast, the initial process of destocking was over and imports were slow to come in to act as a deflationary factor.[64]

Businesses appeared to be taking advantage of the favourable demand conditions to rebuild their profit margins:

> Dr Erhard's hope that the removal of price controls would permit a normal competitive price structure to be formed has been brought to nothing by the activities of the business people in whom he has put his confidence. Rather than face price competition, they have banded together to enforce 'price discipline'—in other words, to ensure that profits are not reduced by outsiders who cut production costs.[65]

The movement of the price indices shown in table 2.2 understates the actual rise in prices. The direction of the pressure on prices is clear from the fact that the price index for luxuries had risen to four times the 1938 level, clothing from 200 to 272 (1938=100), whilst the

62. W. W. Heller, 'The Role of Fiscal–Monetary Policy in the German Economic Recovery', *American Economic Review Papers and Proceedings*, Vol. 40, No. 2, 1950, p. 543.
63. For example, Klopstock, 'Monetary Reform', p. 287.
64. Ibid., p. 288.
65. *The Economist*, 27 November 1948, p. 868.

food index remained relatively low at about 160.[66] Confidence in money fell and hoarding and barter transactions reappeared at the end of 1948.[67]

Policy Choices in 1949

There were two alternative courses of action open to the German authorities (in the Central Bank and on the Economic Council), faced, on the one hand, with the undermining through inflation of the monetary precondition for reconstruction, and on the other, with the threat of disruptive industrial action if real wages were kept down. The policy option favoured by the trade unions, the Social Democrats on the Economic Council and some elements of the occupation authorities was for the reintroduction of price controls and other physical controls over production and consumption to exert localised deflationary pressure on industry. The alternative policy was for a generalised deflation. The Central Bank decided on a sharp credit squeeze in November 1948. Their colleagues on the Bizonal Economic Authority concurred with the choice of general deflation. This choice signalled an approach to macro-economic policy which has dominated West Germany in the post-war period.

Because of the comfortable liquidity position of business, the restrictive credit measures took time to have an effect. However, against the usual seasonal pattern there was a sharp fall in the rate of growth of industrial production from 9.5% in the first quarter to 5.6% in the second. An additional deflationary element was the emergence of budget surpluses. Early in 1949, black-market prices and prices in free markets for non-essential goods dropped considerably and there was a sharp fall in sales of semi-luxuries. With the addition of half a million unemployed in the first half of 1949, unemployment rose rapidly to a level of 1.25 million by June 1949 (6.6% of the total labour force, 9.3% of the wage- and salary-earning labour force).

Employment in industry actually fell (from 6.44 to 6.34 million) in the first half of 1949 despite the substantial increase in output. The German authorities emphasised the structural nature of the

66. T. Balogh, 'Germany: An experiment in Planning by the "Free" Price Mechanism', *Banca Nazionale del Lavoro Quarterly Review*, Vol. 13, No. 3, 1950, p. 83.
67. Mendershausen, 'Prices, Money and the Distribution of Goods', p. 667, Klopstock, 'Monetary Reform', p. 289.

high unemployment but there is no doubt that a significant part (a half of total unemployment according to one estimate[68]) was due to the deflationary measures. A survey by the Manpower Division of the US Military Government concluded that to a considerable extent: 'unemployment centers around a lack of purchasing power on the part of individual consumers, which makes it difficult or impossible for businessmen at all levels to sell their goods at the prices asked.'[69]

Whilst Balogh attacks the deflationary policies pursued by the central banking and economic authorities on the basis that the leaders were pursuing obsolete monetary theories,[70] it seems more fruitful to see the choice of policies as the attempt to impose a discipline on business and labour to establish once and for all 'sound' money and high profits as the arbiters of economic life. The success of this policy is illustrated in a number of ways. If we consider first the disciplinary effect on business, deflation acted to increase the attention of firms to their costs. In the post-reform period, firms were 'banding together to prevent price cutting by competitors with lower costs' and along with easy access to credit, this 'made a broad sector of the economy entirely immune to changes in costs'.[71] Under the harsher climate of deflation, rationalisation 'involving reequipment, adoption of labour saving processes and machinery, and substitution of more for less efficient labor . . . [was] going on apace, not only releasing labor, but inhibiting reabsorption of those released'.[72] Rationalisation was also reported by the Bank deutscher Länder in its report on the situation in 1949 (see table 2.2, especially columns 5 and 6).

The slack in domestic demand not only served to curb price increases and wage demands but also exerted pressure on businessmen to seek foreign markets for their goods. The import dependence and loss of markets suffered by the new western Germany, as the result of the break-up of the highly complementary economic entity of the Reich was reflected in the fact that as late as 1949, a half of German imports were financed by Marshall Aid. This was obviously unsustainable and implied a requirement for strong exports and underlined the importance of avoiding inflationary tend-

68. Heller, 'The Role of Fiscal–Monetary Policy', p. 536, n. 15.
69. Quoted by Heller, 'The Role of Fiscal–Monetary Policy', p. 536.
70. Balogh, 'An Experiment in Planning', pp. 84–6.
71. Klopstock, 'Monetary Reform', p. 288.
72. Heller, 'The Role of Fiscal-Monetary Policy', p. 534.

encies at home. As Wallich put it: 'German businessmen, having so long been cut off from the outside world, would not willingly seek new markets abroad if selling was made easy for them at home.'[73]

With prices falling for well over a year, confidence in the currency was restored. The economic authorities, strengthened by the CDU–CSU win in the first election for the Bundestag in August 1949, resisted continued pressure from the Social Democrat opposition for the introduction of expansionary policies to utilise the economy's resources more fully.

Exports and Investment: The Sources of Growth, 1949–55

The period from the currency reform and deflation of 1948–9 to the achievement of full capacity utilisation in 1955 was a critical one for the West German economy since it was in these years that a pattern of rapid and sustainable growth was established. The basis of growth was high profits and an undervalued exchange rate but the Korean War played a key role.

Given the favourable physical and institutional preconditions outlined above, a crucial element in the successful establishment of rapid growth was the orientation of the economy toward the production of exports. Through a combination of design and good fortune, exports provided the solution to nascent problems on both the demand and supply sides of the economy. The element of design came, first, from the administration's deliberate policy of keeping domestic demand below potential, and secondly, from its foreign-trade policy. Evidence of the first was provided by the deflation of 1949 and by the frequent subsequent recourse to restrictive monetary policy with the economy still well below potential output. Budget surpluses contributed to the restraint on domestic demand in the mid-1950s but it is unclear the extent to which this was deliberate.[74] The restraint on domestic demand encouraged firms to seek export markets. In their foreign-trade policy, the German authorities sought to increase the competition faced by domestic firms from imports.

These policies were derided at the time both inside Germany (by the SPD and elements of the US and British occupying authorities)

73. Wallich, *Mainsprings*, p. 83.
74. W. Stolper and K. Roskamp, 'Planning a Free Economy: Germany 1945–60', *Zeitschrift für die gesamte Staatswissenschaft*, Vol. 135, No. 3, 1979, p. 399.

and outside. Indeed, given the developments in 1949 and early 1950 which forced Economics Minister Erhard to undertake a modest employment promotion programme, it is far from clear that even steady growth would have been re-established in Germany without the intervention of the boost to world aggregate demand provided by the Korean War rearmament.

The export boom which followed in West Germany meant that the strong bias in the factor distribution of income in favour of profits could be maintained without a consequent problem of inadequate demand. The high level of profitability provided much of the funds and, in the context of buoyant demand, the incentive for investment which transformed an export-led upturn into sustainable growth. A second element of good fortune for the German economy lay in the coincidence of the structure of its industrial base with the structure of export demand. Germany's industrial strength since the early period of industrialisation lay in the manufacture of capital goods and chemicals and it was in these areas of specialisation that demand was highest in the 1950s. Whilst world trade in manufactures grew by one-fifth between 1951 and 1955, trade in machinery and transport increased by one-third, a greater increase than for any other commodity group.[75]

In addition to the high-income elasticity of demand for the product bundle the Germans sought to export, available data suggests that in terms of labour costs and productivity, German export competitiveness was already high by the early 1950s.[76] The high level of competitiveness left the Deutschemark undervalued in spite of its small revaluation against the other European currencies in 1949.

Although in the simple Keynesian model, it is irrelevant in which sector the pump is primed, it seems clear that in an open economy with price-setting agents in both labour and product markets, an export-led upswing has the advantage of carrying with it some measure of price-and wage-setting restraint. By enforcing attention

75. *Board of Trade Journal*, 30 March 1957, p. 671.
76. The following indices of unit labour costs in manufacturing provide an indication of West German competitiveness vis-à-vis the UK and the US (WG = 100): UK 1951 (140), 1955 (138); US 1951 (106), 1955 (114). Total hourly labour costs/Output per employee, assumes that average hours remained constant across the countries. Sources: Total hourly labour costs: calculated from *National Institute Economic Review*, November 1962, table 22, p. 59 and OECD, *National Accounts 1950–68* (OECD, Paris, 1970), table 9.
Output per employee: from S. J. Prais, *Productivity and Industrial Structure* (Cambridge University Press, Cambridge, 1981), table A1, p. 279.

to competitiveness, if advantage is to be taken of this demand stimulus, export-led growth also does away with the disruptive effects of having to face a balance-of-payments constraint.

Along with exports, the basis for West Germany's rapid growth rate in the 1950s and for the continued expansion of its share of world markets was the rate of growth of the capital stock. The growth of the gross capital stock not only indicates expanding capacity for production but also the rate at which old equipment or plant is being replaced by new. The real gross capital stock in manufacturing grew at 7% p.a. between 1950 and 1955 (8% for the decade 1950 to 1960); such a rapid growth rate was not matched elsewhere. By the beginning of 1957, estimates suggest that in the key sectors of basic producer goods and investment goods more than 40% of plant and equipment was less than five years old.[77] West Germany's modern capital stock was the result, not of extensive wartime damage or reparations, but of the rapid growth of the capital stock due to high levels of investment once the incentives for long-term decision-making had been established.

With the exception of the basic and producers goods sector (especially coal, iron and steel and electricity), where uncertainty about property rights remained until the mid-1950s and where prices were still controlled, profitability in production was very high in the early 1950s. The share of profits in gross value added averaged 33.5% for business, 35.7% in manufacturing.[78] In the absence of a functioning capital market and with interest rates high, retained profits played a key role in investment financing. Between 1950 and 1954, in the private sector excluding house-building, 87% of gross investment (fixed plus stocks) was financed by retentions including depreciation. An indication of the fact that self-financing provided the bulk of investment funds whenever high profits were available comes from the sector which would be most able to secure external funds, *Aktiengesellschaften* in industry (excluding construction, energy, etc.) where retentions financed 90% of gross investment between 1950 and 1954.[79]

77. Krengel, *Anlagevermögen*, pp. 52–3.
78. For method of calculation and sources, see data appendix to chapter four of W. Carlin, 'The Development of the Factor Distribution of Income and Profitability in West Germany, 1945–1973', DPhil. thesis, Oxford University, 1987, pp. 144–50.
79. Calculated from E. Baumgart *et al.*, *Die Finanzierung der industriellen Expansion in der BRD während der Jahre des Wiederaufbaus*, (Duncker & Humblot, Berlin, 1960), pp. 82, 84–5.

The government played an important role in investment promotion both through its use of fiscal policy to reduce consumption and hence generate additional savings and through the use of tax incentives to ensure that such additional savings were invested. After the currency reform, firms were allowed wide scope to revalue their fixed assets. This provided the opportunity for very large tax deductible write-offs. Estimates of deductions from taxable income due to accelerated depreciation and other deductions and credits (non-housing) amount to 8.2% of total retentions of the enterprise sector, excluding housing, between 1950 and 1954.[80]

Whilst the government played a significant role in promoting business investment, its direct role was confined to two specific sectors: residential construction and the basic-goods sector. These were both sectors in which prices remained controlled. The rate of return on housing for 1950 and 1954 has been estimated at only 1.1% and 0.7%, respectively.[81] Government direct investment, loans and interest subsidies amounted to 54% of gross investment in house-building between 1950 and 1954.[82] This is pushed up to almost 60% if the government's contribution by way of tax deductions both to employers who provided housing and to individuals is included.[83]

The low profits in the basic industries meant that until 1952, Marshall Aid Counterpart funds played a critical role in these sectors, financing over 40% of investment in coal mining in 1949–50; over 20% in electricity between 1949 and 1951; and over 15% in the iron and steel industry between 1950 and 1951.[84] This device enabled vital investment projects to be supported by a government whose ideology was strongly opposed to direction of investment. Yet investment in basic and producer goods remained inadequate to provide for the increased output demanded. In a major survey of the German economy in the autumn of 1952, *The Economist* reported that the industrial leaders of the Ruhr were

80. Calculated from K. W. Roskamp, *Capital Formation in West Germany* (Wayne State University Press, Detroit, Mich., 1965), tables 22, 23 and E. Baumgart, 'Investitionen und ERP Finanzierung', *DIW Sonderhefte*, No. 56, 1961, p. 82.
81. K. D. Arndt, 'Wohnungsversorgung und Mietenniveau in der Bundesrepublik', *DIW Sonderhefte*, No. 35, 1955, p. 37.
82. Roskamp, *Capital Formation*, pp. 180–1, Baumgart *et al.*, *Die Finanzierung*, p. 82.
83. Calculated from Roskamp, *Capital Formation*, pp. 180–1, Wallich, *Mainsprings*, p. 161.
84. Baumgart, 'Investition und ERP Finanzierung', pp. 51, 71.

turning their energies toward the manufacturing ends of the reorganised heavy industrial combines because of concern about the implications for the basic industries of the Schuman plan, and the likely socialisation of the Ruhr if the Social Democrats won office.[85] The strong position of the works councils in the basic industries was also considered a disincentive to investment.

The relative backwardness of the basic sectors became of concern to the occupation authorities following the outbreak of the Korean War and the need to increase Germany's contribution to the western rearmament drive. US High Commissioner McCloy called for the reimposition of wartime control and planning measures to redirect resources to the basic industries. The West German government was not prepared to do this. Adenauer was provided with a means of dealing with the bottlenecks by the re-emergence of a traditional German institutional arrangement: the *Spitzenverbände* (leading industrial associations). Organised German business offered to lend over DM 1 billion of investment funds to basic industry by levying a tax on the consumer goods and services sector.[86] Although the intervention of the industry associations was viewed with dismay by Erhard, who had sought to shift the organisation of the German economy to an atomistic, competitive footing, he saw it as less of an evil than direct state intervention and reluctantly agreed to the plan.[87] In total, the investment aid and special depreciation allowances contributed some 18% toward gross fixed investment in coal, iron and steel and power between 1952 and 1956.[88]

To sum up, high profits, boosted somewhat by generous depreciation allowances, enabled private business to finance a high rate of investment in the early 1950s. The private sector also provided funds for basic sector investment under the investment aid scheme. The government's direct financial role was confined to housing and, through the allocation of counterpart funds, to the basic-goods sector.

The government successfully promoted high investment in the private sector through tax policies, but a prerequisite for this success

85. *The Economist*, 18 October 1952, p. 208.
86. W. Abelshauser, 'Ansätze korporativer Marktwirtschaft in der Koreakrise der frühen fünfziger Jahre', *Vierteljahrshefte für Zeitgeschichte*, Vol. 30, No. 4, 1982, p. 716.
87. H. R. Adamsen, *Investitionshilfe für die Ruhr* (Peter Hammer Verlag, Wuppertal, 1981), pp. 113–20.
88. Calculated from Roskamp, *Capital Formation*, pp. 128, 170, 172, 174.

was the existence of the strong incentive to invest provided by high profits and strong demand. Export demand played an important role in securing optimistic expectations about markets and exerted pressure on firms to invest in order to re-enter the world market.[89]

Conclusion

It has been argued in this chapter that until the political and institutional framework of the West German economy had been erected and had created the preconditions for a successful currency reform in 1948, the economy was stuck on a plateau, with the scope for growth largely constrained by the existing capital stock. The form of the currency reform and the subsequent deflation succeeded in sweeping away the regime of vegetative control. The authorities sought to sustain an adequate level of profitability and international competitiveness in German business by forcing firms to attend to their costs and by maintaining tight control over demand at home. The Korean War boom provided a critical external demand stimulus to the economy and began the period of export-led growth.

89. R. Krengel, 'Die Investitionstätigkeit der westdeutschen Industrie seit Mitte 1948 im konjunkturellen Verlauf', *Vierteljahrshefte zur Wirtschaftsforschung*, Vol. 1, 1957, p. 64.

3

British Policy Towards German Industry,
1945–9:
Reconstruction, Restriction or Exploitation?
Ian Turner

Introduction

This chapter deals with a question which crops up frequently in the
literature on the occupation of Germany but to my knowledge has
yet to be addressed squarely in any depth, namely the nature of
Britain's economic policy in Germany during the occupation period.

For the sake of clarity, the argument I intend to put forward can
be summarised as follows:

(i)   British policy sought to reconcile two, occasionally conflict-
      ing, aims: the maintenance of security against a potential
      resurgence of German military might and the restoration of a
      viable German economy.
(ii) From 1945 to 1947, in the period when British influence was at
      its highest, the accent of policy was firmly on reconstruction.
(iii) British policy had some short-run successes in reactivating the
      economy but reconstruction was hampered by unfavourable
      conditions and a makeshift planning system.
(iv) After 1947 with the United States increasingly pressing for
      unrestrained economic growth, Britain became concerned
      about the security aspect and looked to France to help counter
      US preponderance.
(v)   Considerations of eliminating German competition were never
      central to British policy and attempts to exploit the German
      economy were unsystematic and largely unsuccessful.

Ian Turner

Wartime Planning for the Treatment of Germany

The dilemma in British policy between the need for security and the necessity of the German economic recovery were apparent at an early stage in the wartime planning process. It emerged, for instance, over the question of dismemberment. In Whitehall, all serious studies of measures to divide Germany into several states led to the conclusion that dismemberment would be impractical.[1] Implementing the partition and maintaining the necessary controls over the newly created states to prevent reunification would have presented insurmountable practical difficulties. The dislocation to the economy resulting from dismemberment would have been so great as to wipe out any benefits to British commercial interests, would have reduced Germany's capacity to make reparations and would in any case be of uncertain value as a measure of security against a revival of German aggression at a later date. Fortunately, the spectre of dismemberment was removed in March 1945, when the Soviet Ambassador in London announced out of the blue, and much to the astonishment and relief of the Foreign Office, that the Soviet Union no longer regarded itself as committed to the policy.[2]

Consideration of controls on German industry as a means of maintaining security was another matter. A disarmament committee was set up at the Foreign Office by late 1942,[3] and soon after an Interdepartmental Committee on Reparations and Economic Security was established under the chairmanship of Sir William Malkin, which submitted a final report in August 1943.[4] Thereafter, the

1. PRO/FO1005/959, EIPS/P(44)30 (Final), 'Economic Aspects of the Proposal for the Dismemberment of Germany', Economic and Industrial Planning Staff (FO), August 1944. See also H.-J. Ruhl (ed.), *Neubeginn und Restauration. Dokumente zur Vorgeschichte der Bundesrepublik Deutschland 1945–1949* (Deutscher Taschenbuch Verlag, Munich, 1982), pp. 27–8. The dismemberment discussion has attracted the attention of scholars out of all proportion to its historical importance. The best work is R. G. Webb, 'Britain and the Future of Germany: British Planning for German Dismemberment and Reparations 1942–1945', PhD thesis, University of New York at Buffalo, 1979. See also L. Kettenacker 'Preussen in der alliierten Kriegszielplanung 1939–1947' in L. Kettenacker *et al.* (eds.), *Studien zur Geschichte Englands und der deutsch–britischen Beziehungen. Festschrift für Paul Kluke* (Fink, Munich, 1981), pp. 322–33; E. L. Woodward, *British Foreign Policy in the Second World War*, Vol. 5 (HMSO, London, 1976) and A. Cairncross, *The Price of War: British Policy on German Reparations 1941–1949* (Blackwell, Oxford, 1986), pp. 38–49.
2. Webb, 'Britain and the Future of Germany', p. 255; Woodward, *British Foreign Policy*, p. 335. Dismemberment, or rather partition of western Germany, was proposed by the Chiefs of Staff in 1945, however. See chapter 1.
3. V. Rothwell, *Britain and the Cold War 1941–1947*, (Cape, London, 1982), p. 30.
4. E. F. Penrose, *Economic Planning for Peace* (University Press, Princeton, NJ,

problem was examined by a number of Whitehall bodies including the Foreign Office's Economic and Industrial Planning Staff (EIPS), founded in January 1944 with the specific remit of studying in depth the economic aspects of the occupation of Germany.[5] The results of these investigations were then submitted either directly to the War Cabinet, as in the case of the Malkin report, or to the War Cabinet's Armistice and Post-War Committee (APW), the main ministerial clearing house for policy towards Germany.[6]

There is not space here to examine in detail the workings of these bodies but a common thread seems to have run through much of the thinking on industrial disarmament. With the exception of plans for some form of international control of German industry, and in particular of the Rhine–Ruhr industrial area,[7] the discussion revolved around the type of physical controls to be imposed on the German economy, that is to say, on the restriction or the prohibition of production of certain goods and processes regarded as constituting war potential. The British planners were acutely aware of the difficulties involved in carrying out such a policy. They recalled the ease with which the Germans had evaded the restrictions placed on rearmament after the First World War and the dwindling enthusiasm for such controls exhibited by British public opinion with the passage of time.[8] With this in mind, the planners believed that the most effective measures of economic security would be those, like the destruction or removal of plant, which could be carried out early in the period of direct control and would not involve a continued Allied presence within Germany to maintain supervision. Where such long-term controls or prohibitions were judged essential they should preferably be enforceable from

---

1953), pp. 217–24; Webb, 'Britain and the Future of Germany', pp. 273–9; Cairncross, *Price of War*, pp. 17–33.

5. F. S. V. Donnison, *Civil Affairs and Military Government. Central Organisation and Planning* (HMSO, London, 1966), pp. 92–3.

6. Donnison, *Civil Affairs . . . Planning*, pp. 41–2. Following the conclusion of hostilities the APW committee became the Overseas Reconstruction Committee (ORC).

7. The notion of international control was raised by Eden in a paper to the War Cabinet in September 1943. (Woodward, *British Foreign Policy*, p. 201.) The idea was resuscitated in March 1945 by a French proposal on the future of the Ruhr, but was later dropped in favour of socialisation. (See R. Steininger, 'Die britische Deutschlandpolitik 1945–6', *Aus Politik und Zeitgeschichte*, B1–2/82, January 1982, pp. 28–47.)

8. PRO/FO371/47560/UE 3236, EIPS/P(45)23, 'Industrial Disarmament of Germany', Economic and Industrial Planning Staff (FO), 26 July 1945. This paper, although not officially approved at ministerial level due to the change of government, represents a synthesis of all the various studies conducted since the Malkin Report and can be taken as the Foreign Office view at that time.

outside Germany and their breach should therefore be easily detectable. In general, measures of control should only be extended to those industries central to the needs of war since 'each additional German industry subjected to restriction or elimination tends after a certain point to give a diminishing return in terms of additional security provided'.[9]

Even accepting the need for restrictions on German industry there was still a balance to be struck 'between the value of economic measures as an effective means of maintaining world peace and their cost in reducing the contribution that German industry can make to the rehabilitation of Europe and ultimately to world prosperity'.[10]

Thus, as early as July 1941, Anthony Eden was stressing that any policy of industrial disarmament should not be pursued to the extent of bankrupting Germany as this 'would poison all of us who are her neighbours'.[11] The final EIPS paper on the subject, moreover, stressed the political consequences of a system of economic security so oppressive as to cause long-lasting unemployment and destitution in Germany, and in so doing give an opportunity to another dictator to seize power on a programme of national revenge.[12] This recognition of the key role of Germany in the European economy and its importance to Britain as a trading partner as well as the linkage between economic and political stability was, of course, not new. It had been a feature of much Foreign Office thinking in the 1930s and has since been characterised by historians as a component of so-called 'economic appeasement'.[13]

The conclusions of the deliberations in Whitehall were clear: the most promising approach would be to adopt 'a drastic policy over a selected field of German industry with a view to eliminating the basis of Germany's war potential'.[14] Removal of war plant and surplus capacity not needed in peacetime there would have to be, but 'any policy of excessive deindustrialisation would be likely to

---

9. PRO/FO1005/959, EIPS/P(44)23 (Final), 'Report on issues affecting the economic obligations to be imposed on Germany', 15 August 1944.
10. Ibid. See also Woodward, *British Foreign Policy*, p. 328.
11. Quoted in H. Fromm, *Deutschland in der öffentlichen Kriegszieldiskussion Grossbritanniens 1939–1945* (Lang, Frankfurt on Main, 1982), pp. 122–3.
12. See above note 8.
13. See B.-J. Wendt, *Economic Appeasement. Handel und Finanz in der britischen Deutschlandpolitik 1933–1939* (Bertelsmann, Düsseldorf, 1971) and G. Schmidt, *The Politics and Economics of Appeasement* (Berg, Leamington Spa, 1986).
14. See note 8.

defeat our own ends'.[15] Even so, the list of controls proposed by the British planners amounted to a substantial incursion into Germany's economic structure. Categories to be prohibited included the production and ownership of civil aircraft, the production of ammonia and methanol and the manufacture of synthetic oil. The production of machine tools except for peaceful internal needs and the manufacture of ball and roller bearings were to be banned for up to ten years. Maximum steel capacity was also to be kept to 11.5 million tons for that period. Merchant ship-building and repairs were to be prohibited 'until further notice'.[16] The newly created Control Commission for Germany (CCG) charged with carrying out occupation policy on the ground, whilst not contesting the basis of the proposals, was at pains to secure postponement of their full implementation in many cases.[17]

Hand-in-hand with a reduction in the capacity of war-related industries it was recognised that there would have to be an increase in the production of peaceful industries: even at the expense of encouraging competition with Germany.[18] Although protection of British commercial interests was listed as a policy aim by the Malkin committee there appears to have been no systematic attempt to apply it in the planning stage. The instructions issued to Military Government in Germany therefore listed a series of industries and economic sectors which were to have priority call on resources. These included fuel, transport, public utilities, medical and sanitation goods, materials for food production, building and construction material, textiles and timber. A rider stated that: 'Subject to the provisions of the preceding paragraphs, you should facilitate the resumption of peaceful activities for which plant, materials, power, fuel and labour are available and not required for purposes of higher priority.'[19]

It is therefore scarcely surprising that the Morgenthau Plan,

---

15. Ibid. See also PRO/FO371/45760/UE 3163, CSBZ/P(45)20, 'Interim Directive to the Commander-in-Chief on the Industrial Disarmament of Germany', 17 July 1945.
16. Ibid. See also Cairncross, *Price of War*, pp. 51, 58–9.
17. PRO/FO371/45760/UE 3236, 'Comments on Interim Directive to Commander-in-Chief . . . concerning Industrial Disarmament', 15 July 1945.
18. See note 8.
19. PRO/FO371/45695/UE3194, ACAO/P(45)52, 'German Industry: Draft General Directive', prepared by EIPS for consideration by the War Cabinet's Official Committee on Armistice Terms and Civil Administration, 16 June 1945. The terms of the directive were supported by the FO as the basis for discussion at the inter-Allied European Advisory Commission and for subsequent transmission to the Commander-in-Chief in Germany.

conceived by the US Treasury Secretary with the aim of reducing Germany to a basically pastoral economy, aroused such opposition in Whitehall and government circles when the news of Churchill's apparent acceptance of it at the Quebec Conference filtered back to London in September 1944,[20] nor that the British should subsequently distance themselves from the punitive elements of US policy contained in the US post-surrender directive JCS 1067.[21]

Post-War Policy-Making

During the war, inter-Allied discussions on policy towards German industry had reached no firm conclusions due to a lack of political will at a high level. This deficit was supposed to be remedied by the summit conferences, most notably by the Potsdam Conference in 1945. The agreements signed by the three major powers at Potsdam on 2 August dealt extensively with the measures to be adopted by the occupation authorities in Germany. However the clauses of the agreement were couched in such general terms and at such a high level of abstraction that they permitted a number of different interpretations. This weakness was exacerbated by the tendency of clauses to contradict one another in certain respects, as, for example, the provisions on reparations and economic policy. True, such differences could be resolved in the Allied Control Council (ACC), but as this body could only act unanimously, the seeds of later dissension were already sown in Potsdam.

The quadripartite experiment soon ran aground. By early 1946 it was clear that the French were determined to prevent any move towards a central German administration. Moreover, the British

20. Like dismemberment, the Morgenthau Plan has attracted an immense amount of attention from scholars. Best sources are Penrose, *Economic Planning*, pp. 243–57; Woodward, *British Foreign Policy*, pp. 222–7; Webb, 'Britain and the Future of Germany', pp. 167–202; O. Nübel, *Die amerikanische Reparationspolitik gegenüber Deutschland 1941–1945* (Metzner, Frankfurt, 1980), pp. 78–113; P. Y. Hammond, 'Directives for the Occupation of Germany: The Washington Controversy' in H. Stein (ed.), *American Civil–Military Decisions* (University of Alabama Press, Birmingham Ala., 1963), pp. 348–88. The 'plan' itself is described by Morgenthau, or rather his staff, in H. Morgenthau jr, *Germany is Our Problem* (Harper, New York, 1945). For an account of the genesis and fate of the plan, based on Morgenthau's own diaries, see J. M. Blum, *Roosevelt and Morgenthau* (Houghton, Boston, Mass., 1970), pp. 559–645. Morgenthau apparently believed until his death in 1967 that Germany still constituted the greatest danger to world peace.
21. M. Balfour and J. Mair, *Four-Power Control in Germany and Austria 1945–1946*, (Oxford University Press, London, 1956), pp. 23–4.

were at loggerheads with the Americans over economic policy. The US complained of British foot-dragging in implementing the agreed Allied policy and talked bitterly of Anglo-French sabotage.[22] In fact, there was more than a grain of truth in these allegations, for although Britain had its differences with France over policy, the British were compelled to cultivate good relations with the French to bolster British influence on the Continent, especially in view of a possible American return to isolationism in the near future.[23]

The rift with the Americans was perhaps most visible over the question of reparations and the post-war German level of industry. As Wendy Carlin's contribution in this volume explains, the Potsdam decisions had specified that Germany would make reparations to the Allies from industrial plant declared surplus to maintaining a standard of living in Germany not exceeding the average for Europe as a whole. What this meant in practice was left to the ACC to decide. The Level of Industry talks in the ACC revealed that Britain was alone among the occupying powers in calling for a reasonable level of industrial capacity to remain in Germany.[24] In fact, the levels of production in Germany at the time were so low that lack of capacity was never a constraint on recovery. But as Alan Kramer shows in chapter 5 on dismantling, the Level of Industry talks revealed the differences in approach to economic policy among the Allies. Agreement on the Level of Industry was eventually reached in March 1946, but only after the British had inserted a rider to the effect that the plan would be subject to revision if any of the assumptions upon which it was based changed.[25] In the meantime a British cabinet committee had already decided that no permanent limit would be imposed on German industry as a whole subject to prohibition and controls on war-important industries.[26]

22. A good insight is provided in W. W. Rostow, *The Division of Europe after World War II: 1946* (Gower, Aldershot, 1982), p. 146.
23. See, for example, PRO/FO371/55600/C2503, Franklin (FO) on a letter from Robertson, n.d.
24. B. U. Ratchford and W. D. Ross, *Berlin Reparations Assignment. Round One of the German Peace Settlement* (University of North Carolina Press, Chapel Hill, NC, 1947), pp. 108–13, 119–21 and Cairncross, *Price of War*, pp. 107–29.
25. Ratchford and Ross, *Reparations Assignment*, pp. 123–30, 145, 170–3; Cairncross, *Price of War*, pp. 131–6, 146; *Foreign Relations of the United States* (FRUS), Vol. 5, 1946 (State Department, Washington, 1969), pp. 482–99, 529–34; J. E. Smith (ed.), *The Papers of General Lucius D. Clay. Germany 1945–1949* (Indiana University Press, Bloomington, Ind. and London, 1974), Vol. 1, pp. 152–5; Minutes of the Level of Industry Committee and the Metals Sub-Committee of the Allied Control Council in PRO/FO1005/1219–21; Foreign Office and ministerial comments on Level of Industry talks in PRO/FO371/55599/C823/C1030; 55600/C3260; 55379/C7.
26. Cairncross, *Price of War*, p. 105.

Occupation Policy in Action: The Early Period

In the event, the Level of Industry agreement was of less importance at the time than the policy which the occupying powers were actually applying in their respective zones. In the period prior to the Potsdam Conference economic policy had of necessity been an *ad hoc* affair determined above all by the needs of the occupying forces in each locality. General instructions on the type of industrial activity to be promoted were contained in the Anglo-American pre-surrender directive CCS 551 (coal, public utilities, food and agriculture),[27] and in the Supreme Headquarters Allied Expeditionary Forces (SHAEF) Handbook (food products, medical and sanitation supplies, soap, solid and liquid fuels and fertilisers).[28] In the British area of occupation, Montgomery's Army Group was in any case in fundamental disagreement with the restrictive policy implied by SHAEF instructions, and the policy was widely ignored in practice.[29]

This 'constructive pragmatism' was officially sanctioned by the September Directive on Military Government which laid down that the extent to which industry could be reactivated was dependent on:
(i)   the amount of destruction to plants,
(ii) the availability of coal,
(iii) Allied policy on the future level of German industry as stipulated in the Potsdam Agreement.
The directive noted that unemployment was 'a very serious menace' and concluded that 'It is, therefore, essential that within the limitations mentioned above, industry should be restarted as quickly as possible.'[30]

With this in mind, and in the absence of a German planning apparatus at zonal level, Military Government was forced, initially at least, to abandon the cherished principle of indirect rule and establish Military Government control over the economy. In July

27. For CCS 551, see H. Holborn, *American Military Government* (Infantry Journal, Washington, 1947), p. 143.
28. SHAEF 'Handbook for Military Government in Germany' (Revised ed, December 1944), paras. 1016–27. See also F. S. V. Donnison, *Civil Affairs and Military Government. North West Europe 1944–1946* (HMSO, London, 1961), p. 197.
29. See, for example, the statement by General Templer, Montgomery's Chief of Staff responsible for the administration of the British Zone, in H. Balshaw, 'The British Occupation of Germany, 1945–1949 with Special Reference to Hamburg', D.Phil thesis, Oxford University, 1972, pp. 27–9.
30. PRO/FO371/46735/C5961, 'Directive on Military Government' issued by Chief of Staff (BZ), 10 September 1945.

1945, therefore, once the period of mobile occupation had come to an end, an Economic Planning Committee (EPC) was established at HQ 21 Army Group to coordinate economic activity and the allocation of scarce resources.[31] The activities of the committee were concentrated in the first instance on the granting of permits for certain factories whose reactivation was required by local Military Government formations. Once planning subcommittees had been created at Province level, the main committee intended to restrict its control to the basic industries—coal, steel, timber, etc.—whilst the subcommittees decided which factories to award permits to and how supplies of raw materials, fuel, labour and transport were to be allocated within each region.[32]

By December 1945 it had become clear that this 'federal' planning system was inadequate to the task.[33] There was insufficient coordination at the centre and no recognisable overall economic plan, sectors of the economy and individual regions were examined in isolation, and the Plans Branch of the CCG's Economic Division found it impossible to attend every meeting of the various subcommittees. A reorganisation was undertaken in an attempt to correct the situation: a central Economics and Movement Planning Committee (EMPC), chaired by the chief of Economics Division of CCG or his deputy and held not less than five days before the end of each month, was formed to decide the planned production for the month after next for each industry and to allot movement capacity for the transport of goods. The EMPC represented a conscious attempt to centralise decision-making at zonal level.[34] Meeting for the first time at the end of February 1946 its immediate task was to set levels of production for the first Spartan Plan, the quarterly production plan for the British Zone starting from April 1946.[35]

The Spartan Plan had been delayed by the necessity of incorporating the results of the Level of Industry discussions in Berlin and in particular the proposed export–import plan. The plan fully lived up to its name. As General Templer remarked in introducing it to German officials: 'It is called the Spartan Plan and promises, for reasons so overwhelming as to be unanswerable, nothing but a

31. PRO/FO1030/370, minutes of EPC meetings, 18 July–21 August 1945.
32. PRO/FO1030/370, minutes of 6th meeting of EPC, 21 August 1945.
33. PRO/FO1034/38, 'Economic and Movement Planning', Econ. 22(Mov.), Main HQ, 18 December 1945.
34. Ibid.
35. PRO/FO1034/38, Director General, Planning and Intelligence Branch, Minden, to Deputy Chief, Berlin, n.d.

Ian Turner

Spartan rigour.'[36]

The Spartan Plan constituted an attempt at comprehensive economic planning by sectors, based on the allocation of the most important raw materials, above all coal and steel, according to a series of priorities. Its main aims were the promotion of basic industries and the maintenance of the production apparatus, and the swift reduction of the costs of the occupation to the British Exchequer.[37] The aims were to change little following the fusion of the British and US Zones and were reiterated in an instruction sent to the German Bizonal authorities by the Bipartite Economic Control Group in July 1947.[38]

In practice, the British planning system suffered from a number of deficiencies most of which were probably inevitable. The plans, despite their claim to comprehensiveness, only dealt centrally with the allocation of coal and steel. They were essentially short-term, subject to sudden production changes and based on inadequate and inaccurate data.[39] Changes in the availability of factors of production at short notice necessitated a reallocation of resources which in turn set off a chain reaction through the planning system until, in practice, planning was reduced to a perpetual iterative process of readjustment and reconciliation of sectoral plans. Furthermore, the attempt to direct resources to the so-called 'basic industries' ignored the complexity of the industrial process and led inevitably to the emergence of a succession of bottleneck sectors. In response to these bottlenecks the authorities mounted a series of 'battles', 'campaigns' or 'emergency programmes' to overcome the shortages. Yet these special efforts were by definition extraneous to the plan and in effect amounted to overriding the plan without openly admitting it. Devolution of authority to German authorities or trade organisations only exacerbated the problems of control to produce the conditions described in chapter 2 of this volume.

36. PRO/FO1034/38, App. 'A' to ECSC/German Org./780/30, Annexure 'Speech by General Templer', 18 April 1946.
37. W. Abelshauser, *Wirtschaft in Westdeutschland 1945–1948*, (Deutsche Verlags-Anstalt, Stuttgart, 1975), pp. 74–8; G. Ambrosius, 'Marktwirtschaft oder Planwirtschaft? Planwirtschaftliche Ansätze der bizonalen deutschen Selbstverwaltung 1946–1949', *Vierteljahrschrift für Sozial- und Wirtschaftsgeschichte*, Vol. 66 No. 1, 1979, pp. 75–7 and O. Emminger, 'Wirtschaftsplanung in der Bizone' in Deutsches Institut für Wirtschaftsforschung (DIW), *Wirtschaftsprobleme der Besatzungszonen* (Duncker and Humblot, Berlin, 1948), pp. 146–7. A copy of the original plan can be found at PRO/FO1010/18.
38. Emminger, 'Wirtschaftsplanung', p. 157.
39. A. Drexler, *Planwirtschaft in Westdeutschland* (Steiner, Stuttgart and Wiesbaden, 1985).

The manifest defects of the British planning system notwithstanding, the occupying authorities saw no alternative to direct
economic controls at least in the short run. The Allies could not
hope to achieve even the most minimal aims of policy without them.
Industrial disarmament, the provision of essential goods and services for the occupying forces, the distribution of vital raw materials
to the liberated countries of Europe and the prevention of disease
and disorder: none of these requirements could be fulfilled with any
assurance unless Military Government were in a position to direct
the flow of resources.

To these reasons of policy were added the imperatives of the
situation confronting Military Government in Germany. The low
level of production and the destruction and disruption of the
German economy dictated a policy of direct administrative action,
at least until subsistence levels had been reached and quadripartite
action on financial reform had been taken to restore the relation
between money in circulation and goods produced. In the meantime, the fact that Great Britain was financing the import bill for the
British Zone was all the more reason for the Control Commission
to intervene vigorously.

All of this meant that the British authorities had to tackle the coal
problem. As chapter 4 below shows, the British made intense but
largely unsuccessful efforts to raise coal production by maintaining
and increasing the size of the workforce and improving its productivity. Production, however, was adversely affected by food shortages in March 1946 and April and May 1947 and delivery was
impeded by the collapse of the transport system in early 1946 and
again in late 1946 and early 1947. The British, moreover, were faced
with an additional problem in controlling the Ruhr coalfields: how
much of production was to be allocated for domestic consumption
and how much was to be exported?[40] Reducing the export quota
would leave more coal for Germany's internal needs and more
railway capacity for transporting it to factories within the Zone.
Both effects would be beneficial to German economic recovery and
bring it nearer to the stage where it would be self-supporting in
accordance with the aims of British policy in Germany. Yet the fuel
resources of the Ruhr were also urgently required to mend the

40. Donnison, *Civil Affairs . . . North West Europe*, pp. 395–405. W. Milert 'Die
verschenkte Kontrolle. Bestimmungsgründe und Grundzüge der britischen
Kohlenpolitik im Ruhrbergbau 1945–1948', in D. Petzina and W. Euchner
(eds.), *Wirtschaftspolitik im britischen Besatzungsgebiet 1945–1949* (Schwann,
Düsseldorf, 1984), pp. 105–7.

economies of the liberated countries of western Europe and repair the damage and neglect wrought by war and German occupation. The French government, in particular, was relying on German coke to achieve the ambitious targets for steel production set out in the Monnet Plan.[41] On the one hand, therefore, the British government was constantly being urged by German politicians[42] and senior Control Commission officials [43] to halt, or at the very least drastically reduce, coal exports, at least in the short term, whilst on the other hand being subjected to a continuous barrage of diplomatic pressure from the French, with the US State Department support, aimed at achieving an increase in the amount of coke and coal available for export.[44]

In practice, the reconciliation of these two opposing demands tended to favour the needs of the German economy, for the export quota did not rise appreciably above the proportion of coal exported in 1936.[45] Indeed, in autumn 1946, Bevin gave instructions for coal exports to be reduced, much to the chagrin of the French who had to be content in December with deliveries of only 12,055 tons compared with 194,000 tons in the previous January.[46]

The importance of the transport system to Germany's post-war economic situation has been clearly demonstrated by Werner Abelshauser.[47] To repair the massive damage inflicted by Allied bombing and the Nazis' last minute flurry of self-destruction, the

41. F. M. B. Lynch, 'The Political and Economic Reconstruction of France 1944–1947 in the International Context', PhD thesis, Manchester University, 1981.
42. Abelshauser, *Wirtschaft in Westdeutschland*, p. 146; *Akten zur Vorgeschichte der Bundesrepublik*, (Oldenbourg, Munich, 1976) Vol. 1, pp. 442–51, report by Viktor Agartz, 2 May 1946; ibid., p. 517, motion from Dr Lehr, 28–9 May 1946.
43. PRO/FO371/55483/C10921, 'Some Aspects of the Economic Situation in Germany as Affecting European Recovery', COGA, 12 September 1946; Donnison, *Civil Affairs . . . North West Europe*, p. 416. For opinions of CCG officials expressed to the Select Committee on Estimates of the House of Commons, see House of Commons, *Second Report from the Select Committee on Estimates. The Control Office for Germany and Austria (Expenditure in Germany)* (HMSO, London, 23 July 1946), pp. x–xi, 17–19. See also Lynch, 'Reconstruction of France', pp. 149–50.
44. Lynch, 'Reconstruction of France', pp. 157ff.
45. I. D. Turner 'British Occupation Policy and its Effects on the Town of Wolfsburg and the Volkswagenwerk 1945–1949', PhD thesis, Manchester University, 1984, p. 116.
46. Ibid., p. 193. See also Abelshauser, *Wirtschaft in Westdeutschland*, pp. 144, 146 and N. Balabkins, *Germany under Direct Controls* (Rutgers University Press, New Brunswick, 1964) p. 123. Agreement was finally reached in Moscow in April 1947 on a sliding scale for coal exports taking into account the level of production.
47. Abelshauser, *Wirtschaft in Westdeutschland*.

British Army achieved miracles of improvisation.[48] Even so the capacity of the system was severely limited. Overcoming the transport problem meant above all improving the freight capacity of the railways which in turn was conditioned by the supply of open wagons and locomotives. Yet, as General Robertson was to recognise,[49] the inability to repair rolling stock and locomotives was due to low steel production, caused by insufficient supplies of coal in 1946, which was ultimately attributable to the food shortage and the cut in rations in March of that year. Only in the last quarter of 1947 after special action had been mounted by the German Bizonal authorities to increase repairs could the transport situation improve sufficiently to withstand the winter months and begin to make an impression on the backlog of fuel and raw materials to be cleared.[50]

The limitations of Britain's influence as an occupying power were most cruelly exposed in the food sector. There is insufficient space here to discuss food policy in detail and a recent monograph by John Farquharson has covered the area comprehensively.[51] In order to reduce the financial burden of occupation, the British encouraged agricultural output in their zone. Production was limited, however, by shortages of fertiliser and other materials. Such food as was produced in the Zone in any case proved difficult to collect. As no appreciable supplies of food were forthcoming from the German *Ostgebiete* it rapidly became clear to the British authorities that grain would have to be imported from the US to prevent starvation in the Zone. Unfortunately, the United States did not initially prove very forthcoming and in March 1946 the ration had to be cut to 1,100 calories per day. The reality of the situation was that increasing grain shipments to Germany meant reducing supplies to Britain.[52] To its credit, the British government introduced bread rationing in July 1946. Ration levels were still considerably higher in the UK than in Germany, of course, but viewed realistically, few in Britain were prepared to share physical privation on equal terms with the defeated enemy—especially when the Americans were

48. Donnison, *Civil Affairs . . . North West Europe*, pp. 424ff.
49. In evidence to the Select Committee on Estimates on 22 September 1947. House of Commons 147/148(47), *8th Report from the Select Committee on Estimates together with the Minutes of Evidence taken before Sub-committee F. Session 1946–47. British Expenditure in Germany* (HMSO, London, 1947), p. 13.
50. Abelshauser, *Wirtschaft in Westdeutschland*, pp. 154–7.
51. J. E. Farquharson, *The Western Allies and the Politics of Food* (Berg, Leamington Spa, 1985).
52. Turner, 'British Occupation', pp. 129–31.

enjoying an unprecedentedly high standard of living.[53] Only in June 1947 could the British Military Governor, against the bitter opposition from the UK Ministry of Food, persuade his US counterpart to agree to a minimum ration level of 1,550 calories and a rise to 1,800 by the winter.[54]

In sum, then, the initial phase of the occupation from mid-1945 until mid-1947 was characterised by desperate attempts on the part of the British authorities to reinvigorate the economy. The early recognition amongst British officials of the need to maintain adequate levels of economic activity in Germany, the increasing concern within Whitehall at the costs of running the British Zone, and the pragmatism of the Military Government officers at the 'sharp end' were all contributory factors here. Moreover, the policies were not without success. The underlying economic trend was upwards, albeit from a very low base and with interruptions such as the winter of 1946–7.[55] Indeed, in some industries the progress made was creditable. In the iron and steel industry, for instance, investment during the first three years of the occupation effectively replaced the capacity lost during the war.[56] In the case of the Volkswagenwerk, to give another example, a German workforce under British control was manufacturing the first production Beetles at a rate of approximately 1,000 a month.[57]

The *ad hoc* actions of Military Government on the ground and the more conscious policies towards basic and essential industries therefore had some effect. Ultimately, however, the economic regime was not conducive to long-run economic growth. A currency reform with associated economic measures might have eased the problem and had been the subject of quadripartite discussion since 1945. A resolution of the issue, however, presumed an inter-Allied consensus on how Germany should be governed and what sort of society it would be. These conditions proved impossible to achieve.[58]

53. PRO/BT211/32, FO to British Embassy, Washington, 24 October 1946.
54. PRO/MAF83/2211, Berlin to FO, 28 June 1947.
55. See Abelshauser, *Wirtschaft in Westdeutschland*.
56. T. Horstmann 'Financing the Reconstruction of the German Iron and Steel Industry 1945–1951'. Unpublished conference paper, 1984, p. 6.
57. Turner, 'British Occupation', pp. 182ff and idem, 'Das Volkswagenwerk—ein deutsches Unternehmen unter britischer Kontrolle' in J. Foschepoth and R. Steininger (eds.), *Britische Deutschland- und Besatzungpolitik 1945–1949* (Schöningh, Paderborn, 1985), 281–300
58. See I. D. Turner, 'Great Britain and Post-War German Currency Reform', *Historical Journal*, Vol. 30, No. 3, 1987, pp. 685–708.

British Policy towards German Industry, 1947–9

Britain's economic policy in Germany has to be seen against the background of developments in the international arena. As we saw in chapter 1, above, from early 1946 onwards Foreign Office suspicions of Soviet intentions caused them increasingly to discount four-power rule as a basis for governing Germany. In July 1946 the Anglo-American response to perceived Soviet intransigence was to fuse zones. The United States had now abandoned its earlier flirtation with the Soviet Union and was moving closer towards the British perception of Russia. On economic policy, too, the Americans were now shifting towards the British position. Increasingly, the Americans began to see that European recovery was impossible without an economically stable Germany. Secretary of State Byrnes announced as much at the Paris Council of Foreign Ministers in July, and the sea change in US policy was reiterated in Byrnes' famous Stuttgart speech in September 1946.[59] The new-found harmony between Britain and the United States, however, also foreshadowed the decline of British influence in German affairs.

The decline was not coterminous with the creation of the Bizone in January 1947. It was already heralded by Britain's dependence on US food imports and, in any case, for the first year Britain shared the costs of maintaining the Bizone equally with the US. But as the UK's international financial position deteriorated drastically during 1947 the financial arrangements had to be renegotiated.[60] From the new agreement in December 1947 onwards, the Americans were paying the piper, so they naturally wanted to call the tune.

The shift in power was at first obscured by the apparent rapprochement of British and US economic policy. A new Bizonal Level of Industry Plan was agreed by the Military Governors in July 1947.[61] The British, however, for all their satisfaction at the increased industrial capacity specified by the plan, could not help feeling a little uneasy. For with the announcement of the Marshall Plan in June the American disposition to retain any form of economic control on Germany or to persist with the reparations pro-

59. H.-D. Kreikamp, 'Die amerikanische Deutschlandpolitik im Herbst 1946 und die Byrnes-Rede in Stuttgart', *Vierteljahrshefte für Zeitgeschichte*, Vol. 29, No. 2, 1981, p. 273.
60. J. Backer, *Priming the German Economy. American Occupational Policies 1945–1948* (Duke University Press, Durham, NC, 1971), p. 158; L. D. Clay, *Decision in Germany* (Doubleday, Garden City, NY, 1950), pp. 177–8.
61. FRUS, Vol. 2, 1947, pp. 986–1067; PRO/FO371/65191/64244/65192.

gramme appeared to wane rapidly. To the British, on the other hand, German economic recovery, as desirable as that may have been, had always to be balanced by measures of security against a revival of German aggression. The US tendency during the Level Industry talks to err substantially on the side of German recovery was therefore an alarming taste of things to come.[62]

The other notable feature of the Level of Industry talks was the opposition of the French government to loosening controls. To the French, US attempts to promote the West German economy were seen as tantamount to giving priority to Germany over France's legitimate desires for a modernised economy.[63] This stance by the French was both a threat and an opportunity for the British. On the one hand, Britain had to assist the United States in manoeuvring France towards a more positive attitude to West German economic (and political) reconstruction. On the other hand, Britain could use French support in order to counterbalance the preponderant US influence in West Germany.

By the time the West German currency reform was implemented in June 1948, British influence on economic policy within West Germany had already been eclipsed. What remained was a protracted and largely fruitless rearguard action. Of course, tripartite discussions on the future of German industry continued in 1948. Behind the scenes a rift had developed since the Level of Industry talks between the CCG officials in Germany, who found themselves in sympathy with the US aim of relaxing maximum limits on production, and the Foreign Office, which had resuscitated the element of permanent restriction in the plan.[64] Whether this was purely motivated by security considerations or whether the Foreign Office—with an eye on Britain's share of Marshall Aid—believed a higher level was incompatible with the UK's own steel plan[65] is not clear. At any rate, on prompting from the CCG, Bevin reviewed policy on the controls to be imposed on German industry in August 1948. Opinion in Whitehall had now shifted and limitations on capacity or production were viewed as impossible to enforce in the long term and hence of no value as security measures. Prohibitions of war- important industries on the other hand were still thought to be necessary.

62. PRO/FO371/65038/CE1772/CE1868.
63. FRUS, Vol. 2, 1947, pp. 997–9, Caffery to Marshall, 20 July 1947.
64. PRO/FO371/65038/CE1772/CE1868/71031/CJ389/CJ459/C1925.
65. A. S. Milward, *The Reconstruction of Western Europe 1945–51* (Methuen, London, 1984) p. 363.

The Cabinet was inclined to be more lenient in order to give any new West German government a fair wind, but Bevin, as always, had French interests also in mind.[66] The Foreign Office therefore supported the French position and the United States, for the time-being at least, had to agree in December 1948 to retain an upper limit on German steel.[67] The most divisive issue by far, however, was the knotty problem of dismantling. The root of the problem was the growing —and understandable—feeling in the US Congress, and among several members of the US Cabinet, that Allied policy on reparations and dismantling was incompatible with the promotion of West German and European recovery.[68] The US government exercised intense pressure on the British to relax their stance and for a time relations became strained.

Apart from the risk of losing political face, the overriding consideration here was security: 'neither the international situation nor the present political and economic position of Germany,' the Foreign Office wrote to the State Department in December 1948, 'dispel the possibility of a resurgence of German military power at a future date, whilst the danger of German war potential being put to effective use by an invading power has greatly increased'.[69] This was especially important as plants in the prohibited war industries had yet to be allocated and would thus survive if a moratorium on dismantling were imposed.[70] Such was Bevin's concern that the dismantling programme be carried out without delay, that when, in March 1949, the US Ambassador called on him to indicate that the fate of Marshall Aid depended upon British amenability over the reparations issue, Bevin 'wondered whether he should not even take [the] risk of a reduction in the amount of appropriation for European recovery.'[71] In fact, it never came to that: agreement was reached at the end of March on the retention of some additional industrial plant in Germany in return for a statement of policy on prohibited and restricted industries.[72] The terms of the agreement were soon overtaken by events, however. German resistance to dismantling, now joined by critical voices in Bevin's own party,

66. Cairncross, *Price of War*, pp. 182–4.
67. FRUS, Vol. 2, 1948, pp. 832–3, 836–41, 845–6; FRUS, Vol. 3, 1949, pp. 550–1; PRO/FO371/7104/CJ4816.
68. FRUS, Vol. 2, 1948, pp. 711–17, 719–21.
69. Ibid., pp. 838–47, memo from British Embassy to State Dept, 4 December 1948.
70. Cairncross, *Price of War*, p. 185.
71. FRUS, Vol. 3, 1949, pp. 559–60, Douglas to Acheson, 7 March 1949.
72. Cairncross, *Price of War*, p. 187.

convinced Bevin that it was time to negotiate a solution with the Germans before, as he put it, the policy 'fell down about our ears'.[73]

That solution was the Petersberg Agreement concluded between the Allies and the fledgeling Federal government in November 1949.[74] Under the terms of the agreement West Germany agreed to satisfy British and French security needs by cooperating with a Military Security Board and by participating in the International Authority for the Ruhr (IAR). In return, the Allies removed several industries from the prohibited list, and with one or two notable exceptions, such as the Krupp works in Essen and the Reichswerke in Salzgitter, agreed to an end to dismantling. A list of prohibited and restricted industries still remained and the ship-building industry, in particular, was still to be restricted. The upper limit on steel production of 11.2 million tons per annum was also retained, though in practice it was not enforced. Whilst these Allied concessions may not have seemed that generous to the Germans,[75] subsequent events were to bear out the soundness of Adenauer's approach. A year later with the Korean War upon him, Bevin was already proposing further relaxations.[76]

The Petersberg Agreement also signified the demise of the British strategy for influencing the face of German industry: the policy of playing off American and French interests in Germany was now no longer possible. Henceforth the premise upon which that policy was based—France's desire to restrict West German economic recovery—dissolved. The implications of this change are explained more fully in chapter 6, below. The IAR, upon which France had initially placed much of its hopes for controlling the German steel industry, turned out to be a paper tiger. The French response was to propose that the German coal and steel industry be subsumed within a European organisation which would satisfy French security and economic needs and provide West Germany with a way of attaining freedom from Allied controls. The Schuman Plan with its supranational authority was the sort of European initiative which

73. FRUS, Vol. 3, 1949, pp. 618–21, Bevin to Acheson, 28 October 1949.
74. For the Petersberg Agreement see K. Adenauer, *Erinnerungen 1945–1953* (Deutsche Verlags-Anstalt, Stuttgart, 1965), pp. 247–84; H. Lademacher, 'Das Petersberger Abkommen' in W. Först (ed.), *Zwischen Ruhrkontrolle und Mitbestimmung* (Kohlhammer/Grote, Cologne, 1982), pp. 67–87; H. Lademacher and W. Mühlhausen (eds.), *Sicherheit, Kontrolle, Souveränität* (Verlag Kasseler Forschungen zur Zeitgeschichte, Melsungen, 1985).
75. H.-P. Schwartz, *Adenauer. Der Aufstieg: 1876–1952* (Deutsche Verlags-Anstalt, Stuttgart, 1986), p. 687.
76. Cairncross, *Price of War*, p. 188.

the United States could heartily approve of. It was also, for that same reason, anathema to the British government whose rejection of membership effectively spelt the end of Britain's influence over the future of German—and European—industry.

British Policy—Exploitation and Suppression of Competition?

So far the British authorities have been depicted as juggling with the twin imperatives of economic reconstruction and security. By contrast, some but not all,[77] West German scholars have claimed that British policy was motivated in large part by a desire to exploit the resources of the British Zone for Britain's own ends and to suppress potential industrial competitors. Thus Plumpe[78] and Pingel[79] assert that the reduction of German competition was a component of British plans for Germany. Drexler, in his study of the textile industry, concedes that CCG officers were not agents for British industry. But he goes on to say that policy was influenced in some unspecified and undocumented way by the competitive interests of the British textile industry.[80] Werner Bührer in his study of the Ruhr steel industry quotes several contemporary German sources whose judgement of British policy was favourable but cites one source as claiming that some officials were hard-bitten representatives of the British Iron and Steel Federation.[81] On trade policy, several German historians have charged Britain with seeking to restrict a revival of German export trade.[82] The charge that most

77. See, for example, J. Foschepoth, 'Konflikte in der Reparationspolitik der Alliierten' in J. Foschepoth (ed.), *Kalter Krieg und Deutsche Frage* (Vandenhoeck and Ruprecht, Göttingen and Zurich, 1985), p. 195 and V. Berghahn, *The Americanisation of West German Industry 1945–1973* (Berg, Leamington Spa, 1986), p. 77.
78. W. Plumpe, 'Wirtschaftsverwaltung und Kapitalinteresse im britischen Besatzungsgebiet 1945–46', in Petzina and Euchner, *Wirtschaftspolitik*, p. 125.
79. F. Pingel, 'Der aufhaltsame Aufschwung. Die Wirtschaftsplanung für die britische Zone in Rahmen der aussenpolitischen Interessen der Besatzungsmacht' in Petzina and Euchner, *Wirtschaftspolitik*, p. 43.
80. Drexler, *Planwirtschaft*, pp. 52–3, 75.
81. W. Bührer, *Ruhrstahl und Europa. Die Wirtschaftsvereinigung Eisen- und Stahlindustrie und die Anfänge der europäischen Integration 1945–52* (Oldenbourg Verlag, Munich, 1986), p. 28.
82. Abelshauser, *Wirtschaft in Westdeutschland*, pp. 95–8; F. Jerchow, *Deutschland in der Weltwirtschaft 1944–1947. Alliierte Deutschland- und Reparationspolitik und die Anfänge der westdeutschen Aussenwirtschaft* (Droste, Düsseldorf, 1978) and M. Knapp, 'Die Anfänge westdeutscher Aussenwirtschafts- und Aussenpolitik im bizonalen Vereinigten Wirtschaftgebiet (1947–1949)' in M. Knapp (ed.), *Von der Bizonengründung zur*

frequently crops up, however, is that Britain's attachment to controls on German industry and her tenacious pursuit of dismantling reflected commercial rather than security motives.[83]

For the most part the evidence upon which these charges are based is slender. Often they rest on little more than the suspicions held by German protagonists at the time. It should, of course, come as no surprise to us that Adenauer believed that UK policy was intended to gain competitive advantage for British industry,[84] nor that his views should be widely shared by trade unionists, industrialists and German officials.[85] The belief, one suspects, rests on a shrewd if rather cynical assessment of what the Germans would have done under similar circumstances. It is clear, too, that many in the US administration harboured the same sort of suspicions.[86] But suspicions, however plausible or widely held, are not in themselves ground for conviction. The most compelling case for the prosecution so far is contained in Lademacher's study of the genesis of the Petersberg Agreement.[87] Lademacher's main evidence is that when the Foreign Office submitted a policy paper on the future of German and European industry in September 1949 its restrictive elements were perceived by General Robertson *durchaus zu Recht*[88] as designed to favour heavy industry in Britain.

To be clear, in refuting this interpretation I do not wish to encourage a counter-myth of dismantling. It was without doubt a mistaken and wrongheaded policy but, as is underlined in chapter 5, its economic effects were modest and, with the exception of the few plants Britain received as reparations, its main aim was security. British policy-makers in 1949, it must be remembered, had no way of knowing that the Federal Republic would develop into a stable democratic state and a pillar of the western alliance. If anything, the

ökonomisch–politischen Westintegration (Haag & Herchen Verlag, Frankfurt on Main, 1984), pp. 13–94.
83. For example, G. W. Harmssen, *Am Abend der Demontage—6 Jahre Reparationspolitik* (Friedrich Trüjen Verlag, Bremen, 1951); W. Treue, *Die Demontagepolitik der Westmächte nach dem Zweiten Weltkrieg. Unter besonderer Berücksichtigung ihrer Wirkung auf die Wirtschaft in Niedersachsen* (Niedersächsische Landeszentrale für politische Bildung, Hanover, 1967); A. D. Ahrens, *Demontage. Nachkriegspolitik der Alliierten* (Universitas, Munich, 1982); and Bührer, *Ruhrstahl*, p. 112.
84. Schwarz, *Adenauer*, pp. 681–2.
85. Lademacher and Mühlhausen, *Sicherheit*, pp. 38, 44; Bührer, *Ruhrstahl*, p. 112.
86. Lademacher and Mühlhausen, *Sicherheit*, p. 40.
87. Ibid.
88. Ibid., pp. 32–3.

indications were to the contrary. Moreover, memories of two world wars and of Germany's behaviour between them bred a justifiable concern for security in government circles.[89] The most telling criticism of dismantling, then, must surely be that given this aim of maintaining security against Germany the British pursued it in a manner which was singularly and conspicuously inept. The speed with which Germany rearmed in the 1930s and the ease with which dismantled plant was replaced in the 1950s testify to the ineffectiveness of dismantling as a long-term measure of security. Furthermore, in the face of US and German opposition, the policy was doomed to an ignominious failure which was to undermine much of what the British had been trying to achieve in Germany. In this respect the solution to the problem of security advanced by France and later embodied in the Schuman Plan was surely a more imaginative and constructive approach.[90]

That having been said, Lademacher's interpretation of the evidence on the motives behind dismantling ignores, I believe, the realities of the CCG's position and the distribution of power within Whitehall's German policy-making community. The CCG regarded it as almost a sacred duty to defend the interests of German industry and to protect it from the depredations of the 'reparations lobby'. There were good reasons, apart from residual colonial paternalism, why the CCG should pursue this policy. To administer a modern and populous country like Germany necessitated the cooperation of the occupied. Implementing policy was difficult enough at the best of times but if it had been known that the occupying authorities were acting out of self-interest then it would have seriously damaged their credibility. In its defence of German interests, moreover, the CCG could generally rely on the support of the major departments of state: the Foreign Office, for reasons already discussed, and the Treasury, because such a policy promised the lowest net costs to the Exchequer. It was also, of course, more in line with US policy.

Recent research lends support to this thesis. Tom Bower's latest book deals with British attempts to exploit German technology.[91] It

---

89. See the reports of Cabinet discussions on Germany in G. Warner, 'Britain and Europe in 1948: the View from the Cabinet' in J. Becker and F. Knipping (eds.), *Power in Europe? Great Britain, France, Italy and Germany in a Post-War World, 1945–1950* (de Gruyter, Berlin and New York, 1986), pp. 40–2.
90. See Milward, *Reconstruction*, pp. 362–420.
91. See T. Bower, *The Paperclip Conspiracy* (Michael Joseph, London, 1987), pp. 173–202.

makes a sorry chapter. British industrialists by and large were complacent, arrogant and indolent, missing many prime opportunities to gain worthwhile technology and plant. Where companies did make representations they were often met with a wall of bureaucracy. Most were excluded from consultations with the relevant ministries. Visits to Germany were permitted only through trade associations ('fair shares') and were frequently delayed. Only the Board of Trade seems to have been alive to the possible benefits and officials there were helpless in the face of CCG hostility. In the few cases where German experts were transported to Britain, moreover, they were rarely employed in worthwhile work: official caution and popular chauvinism defeating the best efforts of the Board's officials.

Similar problems beset the British Purchasing Agency (BPA), set up on the initiative of the Board to try to channel German exports directly to the needs of British reconstruction.[92] Economic conditions in Germany and lack of enthusiasm by the CCG meant the programme never really got off the ground and subsequent attempts failed due to the declining power of the British authorities in Germany. Other plans to expedite the removal of German machinery for use in British industry were no more successful. The multilateral deliveries scheme, aimed at making available certain key machines in advance of the final decision on dismantling, failed to live up to expectations: the CCG's Reparations, Deliveries and Restitution Division was too short-staffed to process all the applications and the Industry Division was reluctant to give up machinery needed by Germany. By the end of February 1947 only 19% of machines applied for had been released.[93] So frustrated did home departments in Britain become at the failure of these advanced reparations that in February 1947 a decision was taken to revoke the Potsdam reparations agreement so that the UK could receive by purchase 'certain urgently required plants', surplus to requirements, against credits paid to the German authorities for food and raw material imports. This scheme, the so-called 'Weir Plan', was quickly withdrawn, however, once the full implications of aban-

92. I. D. Turner, 'Being Beastly to the Germans? British Policy on Direct Imports of German Goods from the British Zone of Occupation to the UK, 1946–1948', *Journal of European Economic History*, forthcoming.
93. PRO/AVIA 49/119, minute by K. C. H. Greene (Ministry of Supply), 26 February 1947. All in all, the UK obtained only 299 machine tools with a total residual value of RM 5.5 million or $460,000 (Ibid., R. B. Tibbs, (UK Reparations Mission, Germany) to E. R. Wood (M of S), 28 October 1950).

doning Potsdam had been realised.[94]

At the micro level a similar pattern emerges. Alan Kramer has shown how local British officers made common cause with German officials to forestall the worst effects of dismantling in Hamburg.[95] My own investigations of the Volkswagen case reveal how pressure was brought to bear from the British motor industry at several stages during the occupation: in the first instance with the aim of breaking the works up and dispersing the machinery, then in 1946–47 with the purpose of suppressing Volkswagen exports, and finally in 1949–49 with the object of preventing so-called 'unfair competition' with British industry. None of these attempts were successful because they threatened the aims of the occupation: economic stability and reduction of British expenditure in Germany.[96] It must be added however that these cases do not prove that reparations were intrinsically valueless. Courtaulds success with West German rayon technology[97] and Soviet achievements in transferring German technology and plants to the Soviet Union testify to their economic potential.[98] It is merely that *British* reparations policy was an abject failure.[99]

The area where German resources were of most importance to Britain was probably the exploitation of raw materials. There were two senses in which this was detrimental to German interests: first, goods were diverted to overseas destinations, when, from the purely German point of view, they could have been better employed in the home market, and, secondly, such exports were often priced below current world prices. The practical considerations behind these issues are discussed in chapter 4, below. German historians have been understandably critical of the coal export policy on both of the above grounds.[100] It is worth bearing in mind, however, that the British received no direct benefit from this policy, which repre-

94. PRO/BT211/523, BOT/REP No. 91, 13 March 1947. Ibid., FOGS to Brussels, 15 March 1947.
95. A. Kramer, 'Demontagepolitik in Hamburg' in Foschepoth and Steininger, *Britische Deutschland- und Besatzungspolitik*, pp. 265–80.
96. Turner, 'British Occupation'.
97. Bower, *Paperclip Conspiracy*, p. 196.
98. A. C. Sutton, *Western Technology and Soviet Economic Development*, Vol. 3, 1945–1965 (Stanford University Press, Stanford, Cal., 1973), pp. 15–32 and *passim*.
99. This was also the view of General Robertson. See Lord Robertson, 'A Miracle? Potsdam 1945—Western Germany 1965', *International Affairs*, Vol. 41, No. 3, July 1965, pp. 401–10.
100. Jerchow, *Deutschland in der Weltwirtschaft*, pp. 262–6 and Abelshauser, *Wirtschaft in Westdeutschland*, p. 143; Pingel, 'Der aufhaltsame Aufschwung', p. 48.

sented an attempt on their part to reconcile the aims of their occupation with the interests of other European countries, whose industries had suffered under German rule.

Of greater value to the British economy was timber imported from Germany. Britain required large quantities of building timber to repair bomb-damaged buildings and assist in the ambitious programme of house-building after the war. The British Treasury under Chancellor of the Exchequer Hugh Dalton looked to the British Zone of Germany to provide much of the wood not obtainable in sufficient quantities in the UK.[101] The North German Timber Control was not averse to such aims—most of its officials, indeed, were on secondment from the Ministry of Supply—but transport and, above all, labour shortages restricted output and exports. Britain hoped to obtain between 1.25 and 1.5 million tons of timber per annum from Germany. Yet, by the end of August 1947, only some 1.1 million tons had actually been sent, much of it of doubtful quality, with a value of about £5.5 million.[102] The claim that the British decimated German forests to satisfy their own needs is insupportable.[103] Up to mid-1947 only around 5% of timber output was exported and timber felling was in any case light by comparison with wartime Britain, where two-thirds of all conifers in England and Wales had been cut down.[104]

Another valuable commodity from the British point of view was scrap iron removed from Germany. Balabkins has estimated that 3 million tons of scrap was taken in the form of war booty or reparations, whilst additional quantities were bought up at favourable rates by British agencies and commercial organisations.[105] According to Ministry of Supply records, however, the bulk of 305,000 tons of scrap metal purchased through the Scrap Export Agency, although of vital importance to the UK both 'materially and intrinsically' was not removed until 1950,[106] when Germany

101. PRO/CAB129/10, CP(46)218, 'The Cost of the British Zone in Germany', Memo by the Chancellor of the Exchequer, 4 June 1946.
102. House of Commons, *8th Report*, pp. 166–74, Evidence submitted by G. H. A. Golding, Controller General, North German Timber Control, 26 September 1947.
103. See F. Utley, *The High Cost of Vengeance* (Regnery, Chicago, Ill., 1949), pp. 278–80 and W. Treue, *Zehn Jahre Land Niedersachsen*, (Niedersächsische Landeszentrale für Heimatdienst, Hanover, 1956), p. 119.
104. See above, footnote 102.
105. Balabkins, *Germany under Direct Controls*, pp. 130–1.
106. PRO/AVIA49/119, R. B. Tibbs, (UK Reparations Mission Germany) to E. R. Wood (M of S), 28 October 1950. See also D. Burn, *The Steel Industry 1939–1959* (Cambridge University Press, Cambridge, 1961), p. 136.

was already well on the road to economic recovery.

Overall, it is impossible to escape the conclusion that British attempts to exploit the German economy were neither particularly concerted, nor especially successful. Taken altogether, the proceeds of the various schemes described above do not even begin to approach the amount of money the British were paying out for German food imports. The Germans, both at the time and since, have pointed to the scale of the costs of the occupation which the Länder authorities had to bear as evidence of Allied exploitation.[107] Yet, whilst there is some truth in this, in so far as such costs covered requisitioning of goods and services inappropriate to the conditions prevailing in the British Zone, it must be remembered that the occupying authorities were acting in place of a central government and were providing many of its functions —not the least of which was defence.

Conclusion

In sum, therefore the argument is not that the British were unsullied by thoughts of commercial gain but rather that such considerations were marginalised in practice and subordinated to the twin goals of economic recovery and security against a revival of German military might. The British treatment of German industry was, in short, *besser als ihr Ruf.*

---

107. See *Besatzungskosten—ein Verteidigungsbeitrag?* (Institut für Besatzungsfragen, Tübingen, 1950) and E. Wolf, 'Aufwendungen für die Besatzungsmächte, öffentliche Haushalte und Sozialprodukt in den einzelnen Zonen' in DIW, *Wirtschaftsprobleme der Besatzungszonen*, pp. 116–42. As a percentage of domestic product, occupation costs for the financial year 1946–47 were as follows: SZ–26.1%, USZ–15.1%, BZ–12.7%, FZ–28.0% (Ibid., p. 135). They increased after the currency reform, however.

4

The Uncontrolled Economy:
Ruhr Coal Production, 1945–8[1]

Mark Roseman

Introduction

For much of the period since the beginning of the 1950s, the idea
that there were any economic successes at all before 1948 would
have been met with polite scepticism.[1] The immediate post-war
years were viewed as a phase of economic chaos in which the main
achievements were negative in character—the extraction of reparations, for example, or the dismantling of German factories. The
traditional view was that recovery began only in summer 1948 with
the reinstatement of a largely liberalised market economy, the
creation of a new currency and the adoption of a bundle of tax
measures designed to encourage entrepreneurial initiative. Recently,
however, the tide has turned. A number of authors, notably Werner
Abelshauser, have suggested that the seeds of economic recovery
were sown long before the currency reform and indeed that the first
fruits of growth were reaped as early as autumn 1947.[2] The conventional contrast between ineffective controlled economy and successful market economy has been challenged. In a recent essay on
the economy of the British Zone, Falk Pingel argues that in sectors
in which the British, for their own reasons, had a strong interest,
respectable results were achieved from an early stage. The case of
mining shows, he believes, that where the British were *willing* to

1. The material for this piece was gained during research work for my PhD thesis
'New Miners in the Ruhr 1945–1958', Warwick University, 1988. I am indebted to the German Academic Exchange Service, the Leverhulme Trust and the
German Historical Institute, London for enabling me to carry out the field
work in Germany.
2. W. Abelshauser, *Wirtschaft in Westdeutschland, 1945–1948. Rekonstruktion
und Wachstumsbedingungen in der amerikanischen und britischen Zonen*,
(Deutsche Verlags-Anstalt, Stuttgart, 1975), passim.

promote rapid recovery, they were capable of it.[3]

The aim of the present contribution is to swing the pendulum back a little and to restore the status of chaos in the historiography of post-war Germany. Above all, the aim here is to demonstrate how ineffective was a lot of the economic policy-making in the pre-currency-reform period. Mining is a crucial test case because of its economic importance but even more because of the clear priority it was given. Whereas in April 1945 virtually nothing about the long-term economic future of Germany had been decided upon and the economic plans of the British and Americans were either punitive or nebulous or contradictory, there *was* agreement that Ruhr coal production should be maximised, at least in the short term.[4] The Potter–Hyndley report, the outcome of an Anglo-American mission to countries in north-western Europe, argued in June that economic collapse and serious disorder would result throughout the area unless it received immediate and sizeable injections of German coal.[5] And in July, American and British commanders in Germany received directives to the effect that Germany should export 10 million tons of coal up to December 1945 and a further 15 million tons in the first four months of 1946.[6] Yet despite all this commitment, what this contribution tries to show is just how unsuccessful British coal policy was initially and later, when coal production did begin to respond, how wasteful and shakey were the successes achieved.

Manpower Policy, 1945–6

The British organisation created to run the Ruhr mines, the North German Coal Control (NGCC), could not help but recognise that

---

3. F. Pingel, 'Der aufhaltsame Aufschwung. Die Wirtschaftsplanung für die britische Zone im Rahmen der aussenpolitischen Interessen der Besatzungsmacht', in D. Petzina und W. Euchner (eds.), *Wirtschaftspolitik im britischen Besatzungsgebiet 1945–1949* (Schwann, Düsseldorf, 1984), p. 46.
4. For full references to this and other points, see Roseman, 'New Miners'; see also Public Records Office (PRO)/FO942/178, Economic and Industrial Planning Staff (EIPS), 'The German coal industry. Report of the working party', September 1944; W. Milert, 'Die verschenkte Kontrolle. Bestimmungsgründe und Grundzüge der britischen Kohlenpolitik im Ruhrbergbau 1945–1948', in Petzina und Euchner (eds.), *Wirtschaftspolitik*, p. 105.
5. PRO/FO942/179, Combined Production and Resources Board: London Coal Committee, 'The Coal Situation in North West Europe. Report by the Potter/Hyndley Mission to North West Europe', June 1945.
6. Westfälisches Wirtschaftsarchiv (WWA) S22 (OMGUS) AG 45–46/103/1, Joint Chief of Staff to US Forces Berlin, 26 July 1945; Robertson to Clay, 21 September 1945.

Table 4.1 Workforce and production, 1945–6

Month	Workforce underground (at month's end)	as percentage of 1938[a]	Coal produced (tonnes)	as percentage of 1938[a]
1938				
average	228,813		10,607,000[b]	
1945				
October	157,415	68.7	3,607,000	34.0
November	166,958	73.0	3,844,000	36.2
December	174,740	76.4	3,909,000	36.9
1946				
January	177,756	77.6	4,394,000	41.4
February	179,295	78.4	4,088,000	38.5
March	180,790	79.0	3,875,000	36.5
April	181,148	79.2	3,629,000	34.2
May	180,728	79.0	3,927,000	37.0
June	180,410	78.8	3,794,000	35.8
July	181,573	79.4	4,493,000	42.4
August	182,986	80.0	4,485,000	42.2
September	184,250	80.6	4,197,000	39.6
October	186,421	81.5	4,618,000	43.6

[a] Workforce and production percentages are author's calculation.
[b] Production figure in 1938 is average monthly production.
Source: ZdKw (1946), 1, p. 3 and p. 20.

the key to increasing coal production lay in improving the manpower situation.[7] In mining, as in many other industries, the death
and disablement of miners called up for military service had left
large gaps in the workforce. In April 1945, the underground workforce had fallen as low as 127,525 men, little more than half the 1938
workforce (see table 4.1).[8] Because of the industry's long-standing
failure to recruit young labour, many of the workers remaining
were of retirement age. Accordingly, measures were begun immediately to replenish the depleted workforce. The NGCC's manpower
target was 320,000 miners,[9] roughly equivalent to the pre-war
figure, and designed to attain the 1938 production level of around
400,000 tonnes a day.[10]

Initially the NGCC devoted its energies to returning former

7. For more detailed coverage of the early period, see M. Roseman, 'Delayed
   Recovery. British Manpower Policy in the Ruhr Mines 1945–1947', in R. Lee
   (ed.), *Industrialisation and Industrial Development in Germany* (Routledge,
   London, 1989).
8. *Zahlen der Kohlenwirtschaft*, (ZdKw), No. 1 (1946), p. 20.
9. Above and below ground.
10. PRO/FO1005/345, NGCC Monthly Report No. 2.

miners to the industry and here it was quite successful.[11] Between April and October 1945, underground employment increased from 127,525 to 157, 415, while monthly coal production jumped from 268,000 tonnes to 3,607,000 tonnes. (By way of comparison, the equivalent figure in 1938 was over 10.5 million tonnes.) However, towards the end of August 1945, when the flow of former Ruhr miners began appreciably to slow down, the British authorities were under pressure to find a new source of manpower.[12]

This would not be a simple task. The supply of experienced men was drying up, so that recourse would have to be had to inexperienced men, or 'green labour' in official parlance. A significant proportion of the population was, by virtue of age, exhaustion or injury, unfit for heavy labour.[13] Then there was the problem that, despite the depressed economy, few workers were coming on to the labour market because the Reichsmark's loss of value encouraged a lot of economically meaningless employment. Big companies 'hoarded' their workforces in the hope of better times. In mid-1947, when a similar situation still prevailed, unemployment lay at 274,000 for the British Zone, or just 3% of the employed workforce. The authorities were to find themselves forced to engage in the complex and time-consuming task of screening and transferring workers in other employment.[14] A further difficulty for the authorities was that a combination of wartime evacuations, the official direction of expellees to rural areas with intact housing and the voluntary migration of many city dwellers had resulted in the bulk of usable and inessentially employed labour being not in the locality but in rural areas. Obtaining this labour would raise transportation and housing problems. Even for the existing Ruhr population, the authorities were engaged in a 'race against time' to provide accommodation before winter set in.[15]

The most serious hurdle, however, was that mining work, un-

11. PRO/FO 1005/345, NGCC Monthly Report Nos. 2–4; Manpower Division, CCG(BE), 'Report on Labour, Housing and Working Conditions in the Ruhr', (Lübbecke, 25 September 1945); PRO/FO942/183, (EIPS/97/146B), Economic Sub-Commission (ECOSC), CCG(BE), 'Brief for the Chancellor of the Duchy of Lancaster. Part 1: Hard Coal Production in the British Occupied Zone of Germany', 8 April 1946; *ZdKw*, No. 1 (1946), pp. 3, 20.
12. PRO/FO1005/1819, Manpower Division, 'Report . . .'.
13. Ibid.; PRO/FO1005/1947, 'Minutes of the committee to investigate coal production 1946 . . .'; Bundesarchiv, Koblenz (BA) Z40, 308, Zentralamt für Arbeit (ZfA), 'Das Arbeitspotential in der britischen Zone' October 1947).
14. PRO/FO1005/1819, Manpower Division, 'Report . . .'.
15. PRO/FO1005/1947, 'Minutes of the committee to investigate coal production 1946 . . .'.

attractive at the best of times, offered very little at the end of 1945. During the Third Reich miners' wages had dropped badly relative to other important industrial groups, a decline not made good after the end of the war.[16] In addition, miners now suffered from the food shortages that affected most urban areas. Many miners or their families saw themselves compelled to go on foraging trips into the country to obtain food.

These were difficult problems, yet they were surely not insuperable. There was no true scarcity of labour but rather a maldistribution of human and other resources. To right this maldistribution, the British had two options at their disposal. They could channel towards the mining community the resources—foodstuffs, consumer goods and building materials—that would ensure a plentiful supply of volunteers to the mines; or they could compel men to enter the pits. The British chose the second solution and in the autumn of 1945, the CCG's Manpower Division, on whom the job of finding new labour devolved, set the administrative wheels in motion to detect usable labour and to 'direct' (in other words, coerce) it to the mines. The actual detection and direction was largely carried out by the German labour exchanges; according to a reliable estimate, at the beginning of 1946 up to 50% of the total activity of German labour exchanges was devoted to finding new miners.[17]

Given this concentration of effort, it was not surprising that a steady stream of men began to arrive at the mines.[18] Yet the number 'recruited' stood in no relation to the time and energy expended.[19] An even bigger problem was that the directed labour did not stay in the mines, often fled in the first week of employment and frequently absconded with the work-clothing that was so hard to replace. Of 60,000 workers sent to the mines by labour exchanges up to March

16. K. Wisotzky, *Der Ruhrbergbau im Dritten Reich*, (Schwann, Düsseldorf 1983), pp. 146, 244ff.; Milert, 'Die verschenkte Kontrolle', p. 112.
17. 'Sechs Jahre Aussenstelle Bergbau des Landesarbeitsamtes Nordrhein-Westfalen', unpublished ms. 1952. I would like to thank Herr Nasskrendt of the Landesarbeitsamt Nordrhein-Westfalen (LAA NRW) for the loan of the manuscript.
18. PRO/FO942/183, (EIPS/97/146B), ECOSC, 'Brief for the Chancellor of the Duchy of Lancaster . . .'; August Niehues, 'Ruhrbergbau und Arbeitsvermittlung', *Arbeitsblatt für die britische Zone*, Vol. 1, No. 3, 1947, pp. 88–90; PRO/FO1005/1947, 'Minutes of the committee to investigate coal production 1946 . . .'.
19. 'Sechs Jahre Aussenstelle Bergbau', p. 3; WWA F35, 3495, German Mines Supplies Office (GMSO)Circular 161, 7 December 1945; PRO/FO1005/1822, Manpower Division Fortnightly Technical Reports for fortnight ending 29 December 1945 and 12 January 1946.

1946, only 18,000 were still there by the end of March. Between January and the end of September 1946 almost 50,000 men were dragged to the pits, yet over the same period the number of workers underground increased by less than 10,000 men.[20]

The newcomers' lack of skill coupled with their lack of motivation had a disastrous effect on productivity. In November 1945 the trend towards more normal coal production began to slow down and by the end of the year daily output per man/shift had fallen very considerably. Production ceased to climb in February, dropped sharply in March and regained its February level only in October 1946.[21] In other words, throughout most of 1946 coal production did not rise at all and stagnated at less than 40% of pre-war output. Between January and October the workforce barely grew. Against the backcloth of urgent European demand for coal, these results were striking indeed.

In June 1946, the labour exchange in Arnsberg gave an account of a recent recruitment action. A total of 68 men had been given a preliminary medical examination and issued with directions to work in the mines. For one reason or another 3 directions were withdrawn, leaving 65 men to be given a more thorough medical examination. Before this could be carried out 31 of the draftees had disappeared. Those remaining were duly examined and 13 found to be unfit for mining work. The lorry to take the fit men to the mines was late and by the time it had arrived 7 more of the 'recruits' had slipped away. Only 14 men were actually driven over to the mines and only 11 actually reported for work there. On the following day, just 2 were still present. Later, some of those who had left the mine made representations to the labour exchange in Arnsberg, complaining that their accommodation had been infested.[22]

Every works council and labour exchange could tell a similar story. They reveal that the directions were not properly policed. There were no guards at the hostel, no police at the labour exchange. When men were forcibly drafted from Holstein, for example, no guards accompanied them on the train. The directions were

20. PRO/FO1005/1947, 'Minutes of the committee to investigate coal production 1946...'; Archive of the Landes-Oberbergamt Dortmund (OBADA) I8010/723/47, unpublished statistics of the DKBL.
21. PRO/FO1005/1947, 'Minutes of the committee to investigate coal production 1946...'; PRO/FO942/183 (EIPS.97/146B), ECOSC, 'Brief for the Chancellor of the Duchy of Lancaster...'.
22. Staatsarchiv Münster (StaM), Arbeitsamt Dortmund, 47, Arbeitsamt Arnsberg to Präsident des LAA, Westfalen-Lippe, 28 June 1946, and subsequent correspondence.

not supported or accepted either by the draftees themselves or by those who should have been enforcing them. Works council and management made no effort to restrain the newcomers. Sometimes the works councillors, aggrieved by newcomers absconding with good work-clothing when the established workforce received nothing, actually invited unwilling recruits to return home before they were kitted out.[23] Even those who made the directions, the labour exchanges, seem to have given them so little support that the draftees were prepared to surface again at the exchange and make complaints.

Even when the newcomers stayed in the mines, it proved impossible to get much work out of them. The Mines' Inspectorate noted frequent complaints that the newcomers were not only refusing to do their share but were also intimidating the established workforce and preventing it from working properly. Although the NGCC repeatedly demanded tougher measures, management seemed unable to assert its authority.[24]

In other words, the administrative system as a whole was simply not geared up to coerce labour on a large scale. During the war, directions had been carried out within the framework of a police state. A centralised, efficient and ruthless network of security forces had backed up the system of labour controls and had intimidated the labour force into compliance. By contrast, the authorities in the post-war period were from the start hampered by lack of police. The British did not create a security administration to match the Nazis' police apparatus. This was undoubtedly a good thing, but it meant that their coercion policy was out of line with the general approach to occupation.

Even given the limitations to the security system, the directions' ineffectiveness was striking. It was clear that many German officials gave only half-hearted support. German officials in the labour administration found it very uncomfortable to issue labour directions in the name of the enemy, a feeling reinforced by the (widely known) fact that most of the coal produced was going for export and at prices well below the market rate.[25] (In fact, in order to avoid

23. For example, see Archive of the Gneisenau Mine, Dortmund (AZG) (now in possession of the WWA), File I/126, 'Declaration of miners' representatives . . .', 3 May 1946.
24. For example, OBADA I 3800/2263/46, Bericht des Fahrsteigers Göbbelsmann, 30 September 1946.
25. PRO/FO1005/1947, 'Minutes of the committee to investigate coal production 1946 . . .'.

greater unrest, the British were covertly feeding more coal into the zonal consumption than their international commitments allowed them, but this was kept secret to avoid a diplomatic row.)[26] It was generally felt that the British had no overall commitment to reconstruction as a whole, except where it suited their interests. Everyone knew of the Morgenthau Plan and the level of coal exports seem to prove that German recovery was a low priority. Therefore, few German saw the coal recruitment programme as a contribution to German recovery.

For their part, colliery managers were concerned also by the fact that conscription contributed little to the recovery of the industry. The mines were running on a loss-and-subsidy basis which covered operational costs but not depreciation, let alone allowing a profit. Every ton of coal mined was using up the reserves of the industry without putting anything back.[27] The influx of unskilled labour of all ages, often in poor condition, would in the long term only intensify the industry's labour problems and costs. The natural interest of the managers, therefore, was to pursue a more selective, gradual recruitment policy in the interest of long-term profitability and at the cost of maximising production in the short term.[28]

The most serious factor preventing management from asserting its will on the workforce was uncertainty about its own future. Managers in mining and in other industries were in a very peculiar, uncertain position. In some cases the top directors were in prison, in others the parent company was no longer able to control colliery policy. The chain of command had been broken and colliery managers often had to decide whose interests they should be serving. At the end of 1945, the British expropriated the mine owners and it seemed as if the pits might be socialised or nationalised on the British model. The trade unions were in the ascendant. Another more direct and personal threat was that of denazification. Managers feared being denounced to a denazification panel about their behaviour in the Nazi era. At the end of 1945, the Bergamt Dinslaken reported that discipline generally was very lax and an improvement could not be expected, 'bis die Aufsichtsbeamten 100%ig sicher

26. WWA S22 (OMGUS) AG 45–46/103/2, Echols to Clay, April 1946 (exact date illegible), ref: W–85224.
27. WWA S22 (OMGUS), BICO BISEC 11/104–1/39, Special intelligence report, 19 June 1948.
28. See chapter entitled 'Neubergleute', in P. Breder, *Geschichten vor Ort. Erinnerungen eines Bergmanns* (Glückauf Verlag, Essen, 1979); PRO/FO1005/1947, 'Minutes of the committee to investigate coal production 1946 . . .'.

sind, dass ihnen keine Unannehmichlichkeiten durch Ansch-
wärzereien und Anzeigen entstehen'.[29]

As a result of their insecurity *vis à vis* the workforce, the employers were unable to apply much pressure to the new recruits. In place
of forcing the recruits to work, managers favoured dismissing those
who would not do so. Yet, dismissals were clearly a measure of
desperation in a situation where the men *wanted* to leave the
industry. The frequency of Military Government instructions to the
mines not to dismiss the draftees suggests that the instructions had
little effect.[30]

The half-heartedness and hesitancy on the German side might
have been overcome or outweighed if the British had exerted greater
pressure and had intervened more directly. The crucial factor in
determining the negative outcome of the directions was the limited
willingness of the British themselves to sustain the logic of coercion.
In the first place, they felt constrained in the amount of pressure
they could put on the German administration because they saw
themselves as being dependent on its cooperation. The size of
Manpower Division and even more so of the NGCC bore no
relation to the tasks involved unless they were to delegate large areas
of their responsibility to German officials. This was true also of the
number of British troops and police available to enforce the conscription programme. The question as to why they were not larger
takes us beyond the limits of this study since it applied to all
sections of Military Government. In part the British probably felt
that they had no choice, since money was short and a British
administration would have been expensive. On the other hand at
least some of the costs might have been borne by the Germans so
that financial pressures can not be the sole explanation. The British
seem to have believed that a system of indirect rule, in which
German administrations carried out the bulk of the work, would be
less likely to arouse resistance and so, ultimately, would be more
efficient. There was much to support this view, but it meant that
policies could be implemented only with the cooperation or at least
on the sufferance of the German authorities.[31]

29. OBADA I 8018/1415/45, Bergamt Dinslaken to Oberbergamt Dortmund
    (ObaD), Lagebericht für November 1945, December 1945 and see Chapter 9.
30. OBADA I 8010/1824/46, Bergamt Krefeld, Lagebericht für Juli 1946;
    PRO/FO942/183, 'Brief for Chancellor of the Duchy of Lancaster . . .';
    WWA F26, 379, 1. RCD to Concordia, 17 January 1946 and subsequent
    memoranda in above and Files 380, 782 and 783.
31. PRO/FO1005/1947, 'Minutes of the committee to investigate coal pro-
    duction 1946 . . .'.

It could be argued that the British might still have supplemented the Germans' efforts by posting troops to the mines, guarding the new recruits' barracks and so on. Could they not have mustered the resources and the resolve to control a few thousand new miners? This is what the French, concerned at the failure of the Ruhr's export programme and themselves inclined to a tougher approach, continually demanded. Yet the British were loathe to arouse the opposition of the established workforce and risk depressing production. The British had not forgotten the lesson of 1923 when the French occupation had resulted in a policy of passive resistance, the miners reporting for work and then idly sitting in the pits.[32] It was not that the established workforce was particularly ill-disposed to the British. Indeed, labour was the only group initially to have high expectations of the occupying powers. But they could not be expected to endorse a coercive policy which appeared to maintain the methods of the Nazis and was directed at their own countrymen.[33] So, the British ended up trying to conduct a coercive policy in a non-coercive manner, hoping that new labour would knuckle down to mining the coal and undertaking very little when it turned out that they would not do so.

If rigorous controls and more draconian measures were out of the question, why was so little attempt made to enhance the attractiveness of mining work, above all by offering a meaningful remuneration in the form of considerably more foodstuffs, consumer goods and so forth?[34] Had this been done, it would have enabled the British to dispense with the whole sorry apparatus of coercion. Yet these resources were not forthcoming—a fact which becomes doubly perplexing when we find that the lack of incentives was also progressively sapping the *established* workforce's willingness to produce. The miners' standard of living actually deteriorated. In March 1946 they were hit hard, both physically and psychologically, by a cut in their rations.[35] The British had, in effect, not only

32. Ibid.; PRO/FO943/185, Doc. 103, 'Brief on special points arising from coal experts' report for use in Foreign Secretary's discussion with the French', October 1946; PRO/FO943/186, 'Informal meeting with Mr. H. E. Collins . . . at Norfolk House', 6 May 1947.
33. PRO/FO1005/1947, 'Minutes of the committee to investigate coal production 1946 . . .'.
34. For more detail, see Roseman, 'Delayed Recovery', passim.
35. BA Z40, 308, ZfA, 'Das Arbeitspotential in der britischen Zone'; OBADA I 3879/281/48, Bergbau AG Lothringen, 'Gutachten über die Kranken- und Unfallziffern', 31 May 1948; PRO/FO1005/1947, 'Minutes of the committee to investigate coal production 1946 . . .'.

not regenerated the workforce but actually reduced its productive capacity. To the miners, the food-cuts symbolised the unwillingness of the British to put something into the industry in return for what they were demanding from it.

There were, understandably enough, limits to what the British could be expected to offer from their own resources. The British budget was overburdened and the British population were in any case making some sacrifices to sustain occupied Germany. A more realistic option was to use German resources. The Germans made much play of the fact that coal was being exported at $10.5 a ton while the market price lay between $25 and $30 a tonne.[36] Had Germany actually received the full price, it was argued, there would have been no difficulty in boosting calories and hence the level of coal production. This was an oversimplification but Germany could certainly have earned more for its coal than it did. Even more productive than raising the price of exported coal would have been a decision to reduce the level of exports. The extra coal available for internal consumption could have been channelled back to the miners via the production of consumer goods and mining supplies. Alternatively it could have been used to produce finished goods for export, the proceeds of which could have been employed for food imports and so on[37]. Yet Britain neither altered the share of imports nor increased the price of exports.

Why? After all, these coal 'reparations' did not benefit Britain's economy; the coal exports went largely to other countries.[38] British policy can almost be explained in one word: France. In 1945 and early 1946 the British were far from seeing the Americans as their principal allies; cheap exports from Germany were the means to cement a European Alliance and France was undoubtedly the most important destination for these exports.[39] In addition, the French were growing ever more critical of British policy in the Ruhr and challenging their ability to control the area. Very worrying for the British was the fact that the French tried to enlist the support of the other Allied powers.[40] The British feared losing control over the

36. W. Abelshauser, *Wirtschaftsgeschichte der Bundesrepublik 1945–1980*, (Suhr-kamp, Frankfurt, 1983), p. 31.
37. Nordrhein-Wesfälisches Hauptstaatsarchiv (HStADüsseldorf) NW 53, 272, 'Notizen von der Konferenz im britischen HQ in Lübbecke am 9.5. 1945', Düsseldorf 13 May 1948.
38. Pingel, 'Der aufhaltsame Aufschwung', p. 48.
39. See, for instance, HStADüsseldorf NW 53, 272, 'Notizen von der Konfe-renz. . . .', Düsseldorf, 13 May 1948.
40. WWA S22 (OMGUS), AG 45–46/103/2 AGWar to OMGUS, 24 March 1946;

Ruhr to a quadripartite body and were keen to keep France sweet.[41]

There was still one option open to the British. They could still have used German stocks of food and consumer goods, or the existing scanty allocation of coal to German domestic use, to give the miners favoured treatment. The French continually demanded this, but it was just the type of ruthless measure the British were not prepared to undertake. From the start of the occupation there was a great sensitivity to the dangers of mass unrest that might result if too few resources were allowed for general consumption.[42] As the food situation in the British Zone worsened the British saw their freedom of manoeuvre grow ever smaller. Until it improved, the British refused to countenance giving extra rations to the miners even when these were offered by other countries and would not have been at the expense of the normal consumer.[43] It is this anxiety that explains why the miners suffered a ration cut in March 1946 like everyone else.

Had their production drive been more clearly orientated towards German recovery it is probable that the British would have been less nervous of giving the miners special status. True, no matter what policy was being adopted towards exports, the severe food shortage in spring 1946 would have disposed the general population against special rations for miners. But really the problem was one of legitimacy, not absolute shortages. There was no constituency in Germany or in Europe which was prepared to make a sacrifice for the miners, to prime the pump, as it were and begin a virtuous cycle in which coal production fuelled other industries and economies that in turn contributed to further growth in mining.

A Change of Approach, 1946–7

The failure of the regeneration strategy retarded recovery in Germany and the liberated countries alike. Coal was 'the life blood of

---

PRO/FO942/183, Duff Cooper to Bevin, 8 April 1946; PRO/FO942/183, EIPS/97/144, 'Ruhr Coal'.

41. PRO/FO942/182, Economics and Reparations Working Party Agenda for meeting 19 November 1945; PRO/FO942/183, EIPS/97/150, letter to Duff Cooper, April 1946; PRO/FO942/500, EIPS File 1330, 'Coal: technical advisers', passim.

42. WWA S22 (OMGUS), AG 45–46/103/1, Clay to WARCAD for Joint Chiefs of Staffs, 20 August 1945.

43. WWA S22 (OMGUS), AG 45–46/103/2, J. K. Galbraith and W. W. Rostow to General Clay, 31 May 1946; PRO/FO943/183, record of a conversation between Mr Blaisdell, Mr Galbraith and Mr Mark Turner, 11 June 1946.

German economy' and almost as important for western Europe.[44] It is barely an exaggeration to say that the fate of European reconstruction depended on whether the British would be able to regenerate the labour force in the Ruhr mines.

So it was inevitable that British policy towards the Ruhr mines would change. Neither politically, economically nor financially could the British afford to continue failing to get the coal. In addition, the maintenance of a policy that was not only contradictory and ineffectual but also blatantly undemocratic, cost them a lot of prestige within Germany. The only question was how quickly the pressure would reach a point where the British were forced to burst through the constraints preventing them from adopting a more consistent and successful approach.

What made it possible for the British eventually to adopt a different approach to the Ruhr mines were the progressive and interrelated changes in US policy and Britain's overall international orientation which took place during the spring and summer of 1946. As is well known, the British moved towards a more open recognition of their financial and economic dependence on the US.[45] Freed from some of their dependence on France, the British were able to give Germany's own need for coal a higher priority in their general economic strategy.[46] The Americans' new commitment to rapid recovery, as proclaimed in the Byrnes speech of September 1946, brought with it the offer of more help for the British Zone which would make an incentive strategy less of a burden on the population. In addition, Byrnes' public statement made it easier for the Germans to see the coal drive as part of a general recovery programme and thus gave Military Government the legitimacy to favour the miners with incentives.

In this changing climate, the British moved tentatively towards a new coal policy.[47] In September 1946, they made their first bold move, announcing an increase in miners' rations to 3,800 calories. Further rises and a 20% wage increase were soon to follow.[48] Finally, in January 1947, the points system was announced, making

44. HStaDüsseldorf NW, 53, 272, 'Conference held at Main HQ CCG(BE) on 10th May . . . '; WWA S22 (OMGUS), AG 45–46/103/2, J. K. Galbraith and W. W. Rostow to Clay, 31 May 1946.
45. Pingel, 'Der aufhaltsame Aufschwung', p. 48.
46. See Roseman, 'New miners', chapter 3.
47. For much more detail on the negotiations and progress throughout 1946, see Roseman, 'New Miners', chapter 3.
48. PRO/FO943/186, Doc. 147A, 'The coal industry in the British Zone'.

headlines in almost every country in the western world.[49] The basic
outline of the scheme was very simple: it consisted of special
coupons and points, graded according to earnings and job category,
with which the miners were able to buy goods otherwise virtually
unobtainable in Germany, except on the black market.[50] But it
represented a dramatic intensification of the policy of favouring the
miners with extra resources and attracted much attention abroad
because it was the first time that a major reward for success had
been offered the Germans. It was the most overt indication hitherto
of Allied commitment to rapid German recovery.

Together, these measures turned the tide in the coal supply. New
labour came flooding to the mines. During 1947, the workforce
grew faster that at any time in the Ruhr's history and it was this
dramatic increase that produced the vital coal (see table 4.2).[51] By
the autumn of 1947, the experts were agreed that output was
beginning to ease coal's stranglehold on the economy.[52] The easing
of the bottlenecks in coal and transportation prepared the way for
swift economic recovery and, as we know from Werner Abelshauser, it was at this point, in the closing months of 1947, that the
economic 'miracle' actually began.

Yet the story of coal from the autumn of 1946 onwards is not the
success story it seems. Though the stranglehold was somewhat
loosened, coal did not cease to be a bottleneck; in spring 1948, the
coal shortage became, briefly, as pressing as it had ever been.[53] The
results achieved in the industry were continually in jeopardy; there
were constant reversals and crises. Some of the resources necessary
to increase coal production were never supplied; with respect to
iron and steel and pit timber, the industry lived off its reserves, and
on the eve of the currency reform, the shortages were more acute
than ever. In other areas, massive resources were committed to the
industry—consumer goods for the miners, materials for miners'
housing and of course the human resource of new labour—but so

49. OBADA I8000/294/47, 'Bericht der Arbeitsgruppe Kohle über die Tätigkeit
    seit Anfang Dezember 1946', Düsseldorf 14 January 1947.
50. PRO/FO943/185, Doc. 127A, NGCC Production Branch, Memorandum,
    subject: Points system; Astrid Föllmer-Edling, 'Die Politik des IVB im
    Ruhrgebiet 1945–1948 (Die Anstrengung um die Erhöhung der Kohlen-
    förderung im Ruhrbergbau)', Unpublished dissertation, University of Bo-
    chum, 1977, p. 33ff.
51. See Roseman, 'New Miners', chapter 5.
52. BA Z40, 2, Deutsches Kohlenstatistisches Amt, 'Die Kohlenwirtschaft zu
    Beginn des Winters 1947–1948', Essen, November 1947.
53. WWA S22 (OMGUS), BICO BISEC 11/104–1/38, meeting of General Clay
    with BICO Staff, 14 May, 1948.

The Uncontrolled Economy

Table 4.2 Workforce, production and productivity, 1946–7

Month	Workforce size underground (at month's end)	Average daily production (tonnes)	Output per man-shift (underground) (tonnes)	Ration period beginning[a]	Calories received[b]
1938					
average	228,813	416,300	1.970		
1946					
October	186,412		1.227	14 Oct.	3,672
November	189,812		1.221	10 Nov.	3,373
December	193,069		1.231	9 Dec.	3,834
1947					
January	198,877	198,000	1.234	6 Jan.	3,586
February	203,288	212,800	1.253	3 Feb.	3,823
March	205,394	218,500	1.258	3 Mar.	3,645
April	207,391	204,300	1.199	31 Mar.	3,628
May	209,461	201,100	1.176	28 Apr.	3,643
June	212,599	203,400	1.181	26 May	3,570
July	217,940	208,900	1.192	23 Jun.	3,767
August	223,700	220,800	1.214	21 Jul.	3,795
September	227,577	224,800	1.229	18 Aug.	3,837
				15 Sept.	3,929
October	232,627	229,400	1.198	13 Oct.	3,855
November	238,267	260,700	1.212	10 Nov.	3,833
December	240,101	244,600	1.230	8 Dec.	3,780
1948					
January	240,755	237,100	1.196	5 Jan.	3,637
March	242,916	269,600	1.307		
June	244,916	265,800	1.307		

[a] Ration periods were exactly 28 days. They are aligned in the table with the month in which most of the ration period fell.
[b] Rations for underground workers.

Source: ZdKw (1946)1, p. 20 and p. 28; ZdKw (1946), 4, p. 2; ZdKw (1946), 7, pp. 32, 44; WWA S22(OMGUS) CO HIST BR 3/404–1/8, telegram from Wright to Adcock, 26 February 1948.

inefficiently and unevenly as to constitute a major drain on the economy.

Supplying Resources, 1947–8

As an example of supply problems, consider miners' housing. No one entering the Ruhr could fail to be struck, moved even, by the sheer scale of housing destruction. Of the 1,217,000 pre-war dwellings in the greater Ruhr area (i.e. the administrative area of the Siedlungsverband Ruhrkohlenbezirk (SVR)), only 196,000 remained undamaged. Of miners' homes, four-fifths were damaged or

107

destroyed.[54] A swift programme of repairs was doubly necessary: first, to house the new labour entering the Ruhr, and secondly to improve morale and productivity in the workforce generally.

By December 1945, a fair number of lightly damaged dwellings had been at least provisionally repaired (see table 4.3), a fact which owed as much to the private initiative of the miners and the willingness of the collieries to see part of their pit supplies illegally hived off to housing repairs as it did to the efforts of the authorities. Over the following months, however, progress dropped substantially. The failure to achieve much workforce growth was tacitly being used as an excuse to avoid giving the building programme priority. (The only important progress was that a number of the British and German agencies were created that were to play a key role in the more extensive housing measures of the following years.)[55] Thus, towards the end of 1946, when the workforce began growing more swiftly, the housing situation was completely unprepared and on 31 January 1947 the North Rhine-Westphalia (NRW) Manpower Department learned that there was no free barrack or hostel accommodation left in the Ruhr.[56] This was a major blow to the whole recruitment programme.[57]

The authorities had three options to deal with the crisis. In the short term, the only measure swift enough was more rigorous requisitioning of existing private accommodation. This was implemented very successfully although ruthlessly; the municipalities were, for instance, compelled to make *all* rooms discovered by housing inspections available to the mining programme. Over the year as a whole, some 23,000 billets for miners were found in private lodgings.[58]

This could not alone house all the labour required. A second option was to recruit exclusively local labour which would not

54. HStADüsseldorf NW9, 54, Wohnungsbezirkstelle Ruhr to Wiederaufbauminister (WAM) , 3 November 1947, appendix; private papers of Mr H. E. Collins, Anglo-American conversations regarding coal production, August–September 1947, A2, paper 1; Report on Miners' Housing.
55. For more detail on this period see Roseman, 'New Miners', chapter 2 and 4.
56. BA Z40, 451, Fielder to Director General, Housing Branch, 14 May 1946; HStADüsseldorf NW9, 112, Verbandsdirektor Siedlungsverband Ruhrkohlenbezirk (SVR) to WAM, 18 November 1949, appendix; NW53, 391, Lehr to Colonel Dalby, 25 February 1946, appendix; PRO/FO1005/1947, 'Minutes of the committee to investigate coal production 1946 . . . '.
57. HStADüsseldorf NW9, 55 Land Manpower Department to WAM 3 February 1947; Wohnungsbezirkstelle Ruhr to WAM, 3 February 1947.
58. Ibid., HStADüsseldorf NW9, 55, WAM, Referat Bergarbeiterunterkunft, Essen to Dept IVC, 1 July 1948; NW9, 112, WAM Dept IVC, memoranda 10 January 1948 & 12 January 1948.

Table 4.3 Ruhr miners' housing repairs

Quarterly period	Quarterly results	
1945		
III and IV	18,511	(av./quarter)
1946		
I	36,571	
II and III	15,570	(av./quarter)
IV	6,889	
1947		
I	5,158	
II	7,682	
III	5,611	
IV	5,597	
1948		
I	7,201	
II	6,225	

Source: HStad, NW9, 112, SVR monthly/quarterly reports.

make additional demands on housing. And indeed in the first part of 1947 around 70% of recruits came from within the Ruhr.[59] However, local supply was not inexhaustible and, as early as March, other key industries in the area were complaining about labour shortages. The chiefs of the British and US Manpower Divisions warned that economic recovery was threatened because other vital industries were being denuded of labour.[60] The only viable solution, therefore, was to increase the pace of building work. In May 1947, the Military Government endorsed an ambitious two-year plan that would meet all housing requirements both of the present workforce and of projected new recruits. The plan represented a dramatic intensification of the pace of building in the Ruhr and, once fully implemented, would absorb half of all building materials in the British Zone.[61].

Yet if we look at the housing results (see table 4.3) nothing of the

59. PRO/FO1005/1827, Manpower Report MP/LS/44026/32; WWA KI, 803/02, LAA NRW Monthly Report, February 1948.
60. PRO/FO943/185, Simpson to H. E. Collins 4 March 1985; PRO/FO1005/380, COPROD P(47)34.
61. HStADüsseldorf NW73, 282, Director SVR, Programme for erection of miners dwellings 'Ruhr 47/48', 28 March 1947; WWA S22 (OMGUS) 7/43–1/47, OMGUS PR Office release 3 April 1947; PRO/FO1005/380 COPROD P(47) 21; WWA S22(OMGUS), BICO BIECO 17/8203/12, BIECO/M(47) 12; building materials proportion is my calculation based on figures in Collins Papers, Loose Paper, Report on miners' housing, enclosure 'B': appendix B.

kind took place. Though, in the second quarter of 1947, the Verwaltung für Wirtschaft (VfW) (responsible since January 1947 for Bizonal resource allocations) increased the coal contingent almost thirteen times, the repairs completion rate rose only slightly. In August, normally the peak building month of the year, also the month when for the first time the full coal allocation envisaged by the plan was supplied, the completion rate was virtually as low as it had been at any time since the capitulation.[62] These results constituted a major embarrassment for all responsible. For several months during 1947, recruitment from many areas outside the Ruhr had to be curtailed. More serious was the waste and inefficiency of the whole operation. At a time when according to British sources 60% of the building materials in the British Zone were earmarked for miners' housing, the stream of repairs diminished to a trickle. In addition, it seemed necessary to send five memos for every brick laid in the Ruhr; for every house built there was a committee.

If one looks at the plan's provisions more closely it is apparent that in both quantitative and qualitative terms, too little account had been taken of Germany's general economic and housing situation. The plan had not attempted to make the difficult choice between improving housing quality or increasing quantity: it had done both. No provisional solutions had been accepted. Neither Nissen huts or temporary accommodation were envisaged and, an even more radical departure from existing standards of provision, all married men amongst the newcomers were to receive their own family accommodation within two years. Such goals, though desirable in themselves, could hardly be justified when fulfilment would mean many other priority consumers of coal, wood and other materials being neglected. Even those VfW officials who were advocates of special measures for the mines argued that it was impossible to provide for the building programme.[63]

Why then had the plan been authorised? One reason must be that the Allied authorities were continually under pressure to increase coal exports, so that there was a tendency to over-emphasise the needs of coal to the detriment of the rest of the economy. Yet it is doubtful whether the bipartite bodies had fully considered the implications of the allocations they demanded, for the plan had come into being more by brinkmanship than as a result of con-

62. HStADüsseldorf NW 9, 112, WAM Memo 01/314, 21 January 1948.
63. HStADüsseldorf NW73, 458, VfW, Arbeitsgruppe Kohle to WAM, 26 April 1947.

sidered planning. The original draft had been merely a theoretical exercise, designed to outline the theoretical requirements of a comprehensive housing programme.[64] At that time the Bipartite Economic Panel was actively considering *reducing* the coal allocation (in order to boost exports) for production of building materials, so the plan seemed destined to end up on that great unused pile of Worthy Memos on the Ruhr Housing Question.[65] However, the OMGUS Manpower Division, which in January 1947 had agreed to provide the Ruhr with 55,000 workers from the US Zone, was growing increasingly restive at the housing situation which was preventing more than a trickle of US Zone labour from getting to the mines. Finally, in exasperation, the chief of the Labour Allocation Branch, George Wheeler, authorised a press release stating that recruitment 'has had to be curtailed despite the continued coal shortage, because of shortage of housing materials'. The release had an immediate effect. General Clay, at that point in Moscow, sent an angry telegram pointing out that Wheeler's communiqué was 'absolutely inconsistent with our drive; it is a unilateral action completely at variance with our Bizonal Economic Agreement'.[66] An Anglo-American meeting to discuss the housing question was hurriedly organised; suddenly the SVR programme, from being a theoretical exercise, became the object of serious discussion. Results were demanded and the pressure was on to endorse the one detailed plan available. None of the Allied groups commissioned to look at the plan gave it more than a few days consideration. Perhaps Philip Rappaport, director of the SVR and the programme's author, was never quite explicit enough on the degree to which the plan was divorced from reality. More important was the fact that the division between British and German authorities had created a major communication gap.

This still does not explain the miserable results actually obtained, especially when the very considerable resources that *were* committed to the plan are taken into account. One key reason was that the very exaggerated nature of the programme increased opposition to it. The German body that would actually have to implement the allocations, the Verwaltung für Wirtschaft, was under no illusions as to its impossibility and undesirability. It proposed a more re-

64. HStADüsseldorf NW53, 465, Memorandum from Bate to WAM, 24 February 1947; BA Z40, 751, 'Discussion regarding the Housing Programme "Ruhr 1947/48" on 24 March 1947'.
65. WWA S22(OMGUS), Manpower 7/43–1/47, Communiqué 31 March 1947.
66. Ibid. and V. C. Stevens, Memorandum for Mr Werts, 1 April 1947.

111

alistic monthly coal allocation of something like half the plan figure.[67] In the summer however the bipartite authorities made the full coal allocation. But the VfW was never forced to make mandatory allocations of timber and other materials because the Bipartite Economic Panel was reluctant to constrict the VfW's freedom of action with a mountain of mandatory allocations. So, bolstered by the US Zone Länder's resistance to heavy consignments to the Ruhr, the VfW conducted a rearguard action in these materials, providing less than a fraction of the timber required by the plan. The result was that many projects for which the bricks and stone were available were held up by the absence of ancillary materials. For the first year of the plan only about one-sixth of wood ordered actually arrived.[68]

Apart from the feeling that the plan figures were inappropriate for the national economy, what strengthened the VfW's resolve was the enormous wastage and inefficiency that had characterised the programme from its inception. The fact that there were fewer repairs in August 1947 than there had been in February though the coal allocation had in the meantime increased by a factor of more than ten, was evidence that a huge amount of coal earmarked for miners' housing was seeping into other building projects and indeed other economic sectors in NRW. The British officer responsible for the administrative district of Arnsberg, into which fell a substantial portion of the eastern Ruhr area as well as some more rural parts of NRW, reported in May 1947 that, 'everywhere I go in this Regierungsbezirk I see building going on except in the Ruhr areas . . . Unless something is done to stop this tremendous leakage of building materials to the Black Market, I do not think we shall ever get enough houses built for the miners.'[69] By August 1947, the same observer reported that '*All* mining *Kreise* say that repairs for miners' housing are practically at a standstill owing to lack of building material and labour', a fact which he attributed to an 'incompetent and corrupt German administration' and to low fines for illegal building.[70]

The real problem, as Werner Plumpe has shown recently, was the

67. HStADüsseldorf NW53, 465, German memorandum on 3rd meeting of BECG working party on miners' housing.
68. HStADüsseldorf NW73, 481, Rappaport to WAM, 22 September 1947; NW73, 47, minutes of a meeting in Frankfurt on 22 January 1948, 26 January 1948.
69. PRO/FO1005/1603, HQ Military Government RB Arnsberg, Monthly Report, May 1947.
70. Ibid., Monthly Report, August 1947.

weakness of the regional administration.[71] The building inspector-ates were hampered by shortages of personnel, transport and paper.[72] The British were well aware of this but had proved unable, against industrial and other resistance, to create a tighter and more efficient bureaucracy.[73] Without a very major reform of the entire administrative system (and possibly not even then) no great im-provement could be achieved. The inefficiency was intensified by the fact that the municipalities, as the administrative level most exposed to popular pressure, were loathe to give the miners the degree of favouritism advocated on high and frequently allotted to non-miners houses constructed in the Ruhr 1947–8 programme.[74]

As if this were not enough to undermine the building programme and bolster opposition to it further south, there was another prob-lem: finance. At first sight it is strange that finance should have been a problem. In a planned economy, money could be expected to have little significance. Yet in respect to finance, the economy in the occupation period revealed itself not to be a planned economy at all. Finance had not been centralised in the same way as was the allocation of material resources and money led an independent existence.[75] In the case of miners' housing, for example, there was no procedure for Bizonal financing.

Even so, since generally there was more money in the economy than things to pay for, one might have expected the available supplies to have been exhausted long before the cash reserves ran out. The problem, however, was that to make even a small contri-bution might appear to be an admission of financial responsibility for miners' housing—an admission that no one wanted to make. One reason for this reluctance was the scale of the programme should it ever be fully implemented. The cost of new construction alone was getting on for ten times the entire NRW budget for new housing. The other reason was a general feeling that financial arrangements, unlike material contingents (which were seen by all

71. W. Plumpe, 'Auf dem Weg in die Marktwirtschaft: Organisierte Industri-einteressen, Wirtschaftsverwaltung und Besatzungsmacht in Nordrhein-Westfalen 1945–1947' in G. Brunn (ed.), *Neuland, Nordrhein-Westfalen und seine Anfänge nach 1945/46* (Hobbing, Essen, 1986), pp. 67–84.
72. HStADüsseldorf NW9, 55, WAM to HQ Military Government NRW, 13 March 1947.
73. Plumpe, 'Auf dem Weg in die Markwirtschaft', p. 73ff.
74. HStADüsseldorf NW9, 67, WAM, Dept IIIB3, 'Prüfungsbericht . . .', 14 May 1948.
75. See T. Horstmann 'Die Angst vor dem finanziellen Kollaps. Banken und Kreditpolitik in der britischen Zone zwischen 1945 und 1948', in Petzina und Euchner (eds.), *Wirtschaftspolitik*, p. 220 and chapter 2 in this book.

parties as temporary expedients prior to a currency reform) would have long-term implications. Thus, while NRW (the Land containing the Ruhr) argued that miners' housing was a national problem and that it could not shoulder the burden alone, the other Länder stuck to the view that housing was a matter for the individual Länder.[76]

Consequently, important building projects for which materials were available were held up by lack of money. Thousands of wooden prefabricated homes lay waiting in their yards for the finance to be settled. Unwillingly, the NRW Reconstruction Ministry agreed in September 1947 to consider financing individual projects on their own merits and it was on this basis that the tiny amount of new construction proceeded. Nevertheless financial complications still existed, the applications procedure slowed down the pace of building and by March 1948 less than half the (small amount of) money set aside by the NRW Reconstruction Minister for miners' housing had been spent.[77]

Deploying Resources: Incentives and Output, 1947

By 1949, the British intended there to be 300,000 men working underground, and throughout 1946 and 1947 this ambitious workforce target looked well within reach.[78] In December 1947 there were already 240,000 men underground, almost 50,000 more than a year before; it was the biggest single year's increase in the history of Ruhr mining and a sign just how irresistible were the twin sirens of extra rations and points system goods.

Yet production and productivity showed a much less favoured trend (see table 4.2). Though aware that the massive influx of new labour would slow down the rate at which individual output improved, the British had nevertheless anticipated a steady increase in productivity to around 1.4 tons and 1.5 tons per underground worker by the end of 1947. In fact average output per man/shift in 1947 showed virtually no improvement over the previous year's

76. HStADüsseldorf NW10, 91, WAM, Besprechungsnotiz, 19 September 1947; Reconstruction Ministry to Chef der Pressestelle, 14 June 1948.
77. HStADüsseldorf NW9, 56, Land Manpower Dept HQ NRW to Ministerial Director Rühl, WAM, 29 January 1948; NW10, 91, WAM, Besprechungsnotiz, 19 September 1947; NW53, 643, WAM to Personal Assistant of Minister Präsident, 4 March 1948.
78. PRO/FO943/185, ECOSC/P(46)45.

average and indeed was somewhat *below* that achieved at the end of 1946. Over the year, average production rose by only half the projected figure.[79] By the currency reform, the gap between target and reality had widened. Daily production had not gone much beyond 265,000 tons when it should have been well on its way to 400,000 tons.[80]

Was this simply a question of the newcomers' inexperience? It has been argued that the productivity of the experienced men (*Hauer*) rose substantially, while the newcomers' stagnated.[81] On closer examination, it transpires that this is a case of misleading terminology in the Anglo-American statistics: the term *Hauer* as it was used in the statistics denoted all faceworkers, irrespective of experience. In fact, from other statistics we know that new miners were more highly concentrated at the face than elsewhere in the mine.[82] In other words the concentration of newcomers were highest at the very point which was achieving the best results—suggesting that the inexperience of the newcomers was not the only, indeed not the major factor depressing productivity.

The question therefore remains why it was that the incentives offered were unable to achieve better productivity results. In spring 1947, 20% of all textiles available to Germans in the British Zone went to the miners, in other words one-sixtieth of the population received one-fifth of the goods. On average the miners were eight to ten times better supplied with household goods and clothing than the rest of the population.[83] As a senior US official put it: 'Large proportions of raw materials had been diverted from the German economy to an exclusive set of workers, who [have] not in return delivered the coal.'[84]

One problem was that, despite the incentives' programme, food was periodically in very short supply. In 1947, there were two real food crises in the Ruhr—in April and December. Miners themselves were not badly affected but their families—like other Ruhr

79. October 1947–March 1948 average daily production was 250,000 tons. The target had been 300,000 tons per day. My calculation is from *ZdKw*, Vol. 4, p. 3.
80. Ibid. and PRO/FO943/185, ECOSC/P(46)45.
81. Abelshauser, *Wirtschaft in Westdeutschland*, pp. 140–1.
82. For example, Bergbau-Archiv, Bochum (BBA) 30,34, annual report of Gutehaffnungshütte 1948–1949 and BBA 32/1509, Bergmännische Zahlenberichte 1948–1949, table 'Umschülerbewegung'.
83. PRO/FO943/185, extract from BIB/M(47)3; Parlamentsarchiv, Bonn, File 2,558, VfW Memorandum 23 February 1948.
84. WWA S22(OMGUS), BICO BISEC 11/103–2/16, minutes of the working party on the miners' points scheme, 21 August, 1947.

civilians—experienced an absolutely catastrophic fall. In May, citizens in Bochum were treated to just 629 calories a day, little over one-third of the survival minimum. By July, the Ruhr average was still only 1,260 calories.[85] It was a striking indication of the scale of German food shortages that rations in the Ruhr, the crucible of German recovery, should fall to such devastatingly low levels. The Military Governors felt, probably correctly, that it would be neither politically or economically advisable to give the Ruhr population as a whole any special consumer status.[86]

These crises were accompanied by major reversals in the upward trend of production. Until March 1947, productivity had risen rapidly but in April and May 1947 the trend was reversed abruptly and output per man fell well below the levels it had attained *before* the introduction of the points system (see table 4.2). Production was hit not just by a general fall in productivity and attendance but also by sporadic strikes, sometimes led by miners' wives, culminating in a 24-hour protest strike on 4 April in which 300,000 miners took part.[87] It was not until August that daily production attained the March performance. Another drop occurred in the December–January period.[88]

Many observers in the Ruhr believed the fall in the civilian ration to be the primary cause of the drop in production. They could point to the fact that married men, who felt forced to give an ever-increasing portion of their extra rations to their undernourished families, were directly physically hit by the ration cuts.[89] Yet

85. WWA S22 (OMGUS), CO Hist. Br. 3/406–1/22, NGCC, notes on NGCC; W. Abelshauser, *Der Ruhrkohlenbergbau seit 1945. Weideraufbau, Krise, Anpassung* (C.H. Beck, Munich, 1984), p. 40.
86. WWA S22 (OMGUS), AG 1947/178/1–2, telegram from Clay to Draper, 10 August 1947; WWA S22 (OMGUS) BICO BIECO 17/8203/12, BIECO/M(47)13: 15th meeting of BIECO, 19 May 1947.
87. OBADA I 8010/723/47, Berichte über die Lage im Ruhrkohlenbergbau, Februar-April 1947; Michael Clarke, 'Die Gewerkschaftspolitik der KPD 1945–1951, dargestellt am Beispiel des "Industrieverbandes Bergbau/Industriegewerkschaft Bergbau", im Ruhrgebeit', unpublished dissertation, University of Bochum, 1984), p. 35.
88. The December figures in the table may appear to be contradictory in that productivity rose, the workforce grew and yet daily production fell. The missing variable is absenteeism. Productivity is calculated on the basis of shifts worked and not on the basis of the number of workers on the company's books. If absenteeism rises sharply, it is perfectly possible for production to fall even though the number of workers on the books grows and shift productivity improves.
89. Even when the full civilian ration was being met, two out of five miners were in the habit of taking food home from the pits. Public Opinion Research Office, Political Division, Report No. 6, Part 1: 'The Ruhr miner and his family 1947' (Bielefeld, March 1948), p. 1.

though the food shortages were undoubtedly the *trigger* for the deterioration in productivity, the causes were more complex. As in the earlier period, the 'psychological' impact of the cuts was probably more decisive than their direct physical implications and productivity was harder and longer hit than the mere calorie loss would warrant.[90]

Part of the background to the disappointing performance was that in the 1945–46 period the British had aroused considerable hostility amongst the miners. Military Government had been slow to allow the unions to rebuild.[91] The expropriation of the former colliery owners at the end of 1945 had not been followed by attempts to democratise control.[92] Another irritant to the miners was the high level of coal exports at reparations prices.[93] And the biggest blow to morale had been the ration cut in March 1946. The negative impact of all these issues was skilfully articulated and mobilised by the communist element in the miners' union, I.V. Bergbau. For all these reasons, the British had a backlog of suspicion to overcome, a fact that became clearly evident in September 1946 when the grass-roots membership overturned union agreement to Sunday working.[94]

The British were therefore very concerned to build up confidence and, in the shape of the points system, introduced an incentives scheme which enabled the miners to obtain incentives *before* any great production increase had been achieved. The miners' union was able to gain a number of important concessions designed to limit the pressure on the contract-wage workers and to benefit those employees on fixed-time rates.[95] There were minimum and maximum limits to the points that could be earned, for example, and relatively generous terms for sickness and injury.[96] Thus, from the start, there was no very rigorous tie between incentives and output.

What then happened was that even before the spring food crisis,

---

90. This was certainly the view of the NGCC. See PRO/FO1005/380, COPROD P(47)22, NGCC Progress Report for 3 May 1947; VfW's comments in Abelshauser, *Der Ruhrkohlenbergbau seit 1945*, p. 41.
91. See chapter 10.
92. Milert, 'Die verschenkte Kontrolle', passim.
93. U. Borsdorf, 'Speck oder Sozialisierung. Produktionssteigerungs-Kampagnen im Ruhrbergbau 1945–1947' in H. Mommsen and U. Borsdorf (eds.), *Glückauf Kameraden! Die Bergarbeiter und ihre Organisationen in Deutschland* (Bund Verlag, Cologne, 1979), pp. 354ff.
94. Ibid.
95. The contract wage is the mining equivalent of the piece-rate. At that time all the most productive jobs were done on a contract-wage basis.
96. See Roseman, 'New Miners', chapter 3.

Mark Roseman

the goodwill and commitment that the scheme might have earned under more favourable circumstances was jeopardised by problems in supplying the goods for purchase. In February 1947, the DGB warned that the scheme was in danger of collapse.[97] Some goods failed to materialise altogether; others did not meet the quality expectations of the miners.[98] Then came the food shortages and it is easy to imagine the general mood in spring 1947. Hunger protests fused with political demands, an amalgam skilfully mobilised by the Communist Party. The socialisation movement reached its apogee.[99]

Even then, the points system would probably have been sufficient to restore productivity swiftly had it not been for the weakness of colliery managements. (In mining, unlike other industries, wage rates were established not at some regional bargaining level but by monthly, sometimes more frequent, contract negotiations for each face. More than in any other industry, wage levels were the result of a continuous battle between management and men. Under the points system, the number of points received—because they were tied to earnings—was ultimately governed by the outcome of wage negotiations at the face.) Miners found themselves in a good position to protect their cash and point earnings against falls in production because management continued to feel insecure. Despite repeated attempts to halt it, denazification dragged on.[100] The uncertain ownership situation and the threat of socialisation still troubled management. Even after a five-year moratorium on the socialisation question was introduced at American insistence in summer 1947, the managers' position remained uncertain.[101] The result was that the pit deputies—and behind them senior management—put up only limited resistance to miners' demands for more lenient contract rates, demands given extra legitimacy by the argument that food shortages and ill-health prevented any greater output.[102] Not food shortages alone, therefore, but a crisis of legitimacy and authority, exposed and exacerbated by food

97. DGB Archive, Düsseldorf, File 'Gewerkschaftliches Zonensekretariat, Britische Zone, 1947, 1', VfW to Economics Ministry, NRW and others, 25 March 1947, appendix 11.
98. Borsdorf, 'Speck oder Sozialisierung', pp. 354ff.
99. Clarke, 'Die Gewerkschaftspolitik der KPD', pp. 24 and 35ff.
100. PRO/FO1005/379, COPROD/P(46)12; WWA S22 (OMGUS), BICO BISEC 11/104-1/39, OMGUS ODI, special intelligence report, 'Some German Views of the Political, economic and sociological aspects of Ruhr Coal Production', 19 June 1948.
101. Interview with Bergassessor Wimmelmann in Ibid.
102. OBADA 18010, situation reports for January and March 1947.

118

shortages, was the real cause of low productivity.

In the summer of 1947, the Americans made considerable efforts to improve the link between incentive and output.[103] The points system was tightened up in a number of ways and the conditions for accidents and sickness made less generous. A supplementary three-phase programme of incentives was introduced. In Phase 1, mines were given a four-week production target which, if met, entitled the miners to so-called '10-in-1' or 'CARE' packets of luxury goods, foodstuffs, textiles, children's toys and other articles.[104] There were three such CARE Packet actions. The new output-oriented philosophy was apparent in the condition that a specific production target be met and that only underground workers receive the packet.[105] Phase 3 which began in January, was also linked to output and provided the miners with a variety of imported food and consumer goods on the basis of individual performance and that of the mine.[106] The intervening Phase 2, on the other hand, had no such productivity link and was simply designed to protect the miner from fluctuations in the food supply in the period between the first and second CARE packets.

These additions made some contribution to productivity but the weakness of the CARE Packet actions was that they produced a great deal of effort in the target month itself and a relapse as soon as the action ended. None of these measures filled the authority vacuum. The revised points system regulations contained the clause that contracts should periodically be reviewed to ensure 'dass sie einer normalen Leistung entsprechen'.[107] Yet this instruction, introduced in September 1947, could have little impact until the mining officials believed their situation to be more secure.

The Impact of German Management, November 1947–June 1948

It was partly to give management such security that the Allies decided to give the Germans more control over the industry. In

103. Föllmer-Edling, 'Die Politik des IVB', pp. 59ff; Roseman, 'New Miners', chapter 5.
104. WWA S22(OMGUS), CO Hist. Br. 3/404–1/8, BISEC memo(47) 25, 27 August 1947.
105. Föllmer-Edling, 'Die Politik des IVB', p. 74.
106. WWA S22(OMGUS), CO Hist. Br. 3/404–1/8, BISEC memo(47) 25, 27 August 1947.
107. Abelshauser, *Der Ruhrkohlenbergbau seit 1945*, p. 41.

November 1947, a German coal board came into being, the Deutsche Kohlenbergbau-Leitung (DKBL), consisting largely of industrial representatives but with some trade union representation. The NGCC was wound up and replaced by a smaller bipartite organisation, the UK/US Coal Control Group (UK/USCCG).[108] Military Government's influence continued to make itself felt in the mining industry for several years but the DKBL undoubtedly represented a considerable transfer of authority back to German management and reduced the scope for outside control.[109]

Productivity certainly responded though a renewed mini food crisis in spring 1948, the continuing uncertainty over the industry's future, the inherent limitations of the points system and unremitting supply problems all set limits to what management could or dared to achieve in terms of individual output (see table 4.2). In addition, there was one constraint on mining output whose impact was actually strengthened by the formation of the DKBL, namely, that existing coal prices offered management no incentive to maximise production.[110] In confidential discussions with the Americans, a senior management representative admitted that management was not trying to secure maximum output, nor could it be expected to, 'when we are only allowed to include 1.50 RM for the depreciation of our equipment per ton of coal mined for subsidy purposes, while our capital goods depreciate at the rate of from 2.00 RM to 2.20 RM or more per ton of coal extracted'.[111] The Americans concluded that 'it would seem that under existing price and subsidy policies the board of managers should keep production at the lowest possible level consistent with its members continuing in office'.[112]

In other words, there was an inherent contradiction between giving management greater freedom and authority, on the one hand, and failing to create proper incentives, on the other. It would be inappropriate here to dwell on all the circumstance governing the Allies' policy towards the domestic (i.e. non-export) coal price. Until summer 1947, Britain's attempts to increase it had been overridden by the other occupying powers in Berlin. Then, the

108. See Roseman, 'New Miners', chapter 5.
109. See, for instance, BBA 10, 594, Niederschrift über die Sitzung der Bergwerksleiter im Bezirk Bochum der DKBL am 25 Mai 1948 in which it was decided to dismiss all men guilty of three or more unexcused absences.
110. WWA S22 (OMGUS), BICO BISEC 11/104–2/3, UK/USCCG report, 'Review of hard coal production in the Ruhr', 10 June 1948.
111. WWA S22 (OMGUS), BICO BISEC 11/104–1/39, OMGUS ODI, special intelligence report, 19 June 1948.
112. Ibid.

Americans had come round and a modest price rise was implemented. Thereafter the biggest resistance came from the German authorities, worried that dearer coal would undermine German price stability.[113] Over the following years, the resistance to granting coal an economic price and the failure to supply an alternative incentive was to be perhaps the biggest weakness in the Germans' reconstruction strategy.

Once management gained control over the industry, the impact of this pricing policy swiftly made itself apparent. In January 1948, the DKBL's Director-General, Heinrich Kost, proposed to the UK/USCCG that recruitment in future be restricted to covering wastage and that increases in production be obtained only by improving productivity.[114] Though the Coal Control Group rejected these proposals, which clearly put more emphasis on improving productivity than maximising production, underground recruitment between January and June 1948, did in fact do little more than cover wastage.[115] In reports to the Control Group, the DKBL argued that shortages of mining supplies had severely limited the collieries' ability to absorb new labour.[116] The main reason, as meetings between senior colliery representatives and the DKBL's manpower experts made apparent, was that both mines and DKBL were ill-disposed to any great increases in workforce size and labour costs.[117]

Similarly, management devoted an increasing proportion of the labour force to development and preparatory work and away from current production, thus strengthening a trend already apparent in 1947. Between 1946 and 1948, the number of contract workers grew faster than the face workforce, a sign that an increasing number were being put to development work.[118] Though the Coal Control Group was well aware of this problem it was able to do little about it.[119] There is little doubt, therefore, that the available capacity was

113. Roseman, 'New Miners,' chapter 5.
114. PRO/FO1005/1624, minutes of 5th meeting of UK/USCCG, 16 January 1948.
115. Ibid. and *ZdKw*, Vol. 7, p. 32.
116. WWA S22 (OMGUS), BICO BISEC 11/104–1/39, 'Extract from the March 1948 report by German coal mine management'.
117. BBA 32,741, Direktorenbesprechung 30 January 1948; PRO/FO1005/1624, UK/USCCG, minutes of 8th Meeting, 27 February 1948; minutes of 10th Meeting, 2 April 1948.
118. My calculation from H. H. Bischoff, 'Arbeiterzahl und Förderanstieg', *Glückauf*, Vol. 87, No. 23/24, 1951, pp. 565–7, table 7 and OMGUS figures.
119. WWA S22 (OMGUS), BICO BISEC 11/104–2/6, verbatim minutes of the meeting with Military Governors and Bizonal officials, 14 June 1948.

not being fully utilised and that coal production was not being maximised.

Summer 1948—A Turning Point

April 1948 saw an important change in the method of mine financing in preparation for the currency reform. Hitherto, the mines had received from the British Zonal budget frequent injections of cash which varied in size according to their operating losses. From April onwards, these payments ceased and were replaced by a new per-ton subsidy from the Bizonal budget. Because payment was on a fixed per-ton basis, and was not as generously calculated as the earlier *ad hoc* subsidies, the mines had to watch their spending much more closely.[120] Before, they had at least been protected from operating losses (though not covered for depreciation), but now, careful management was needed to avoid bankruptcy.

The impact of this change was to reduce Allied control. In the first place, the new financing procedure was in German hands and the level of subsidy paid to the mines was now a subject for German decision. Secondly, UK/USCCG had to acknowledge that the mines had no option but to concentrate on productivity. It did not cease to press for increases in production, but it was obvious that the mines had to put themselves on a firmer financial footing.

In two senses summer 1948 marked the end of an era. On the one hand, it saw the end of direct Allied control over production policy and, on the other hand, an end to the controlled economy. It also saw the disappearance of many of the problems outlined above. Management's new confidence, in conjunction with the restored value of the currency, reinstated the link between payment and output. In the course of 1948 there was a major shift of power away from labour. The currency reform ended the black market and supply shortages rapidly became a thing of the past. In other words the massive wastage and inefficiency in resource allocation, procurement and deployment that had characterised the earlier period were in most respects eliminated. Indeed, it is hard to believe that high growth rates could have been maintained by an economy operating as the pre-1948 economy had done.

120. WWA S22(OMGUS) BICO BISEC 11/104-2/3, UK/USCCG, review of hard coal production, 10 June 1948.

On the other hand, the currency reform did not mark the end of the industry's problems. Indeed in some areas, notably housing, progress was actually retarded by the financial and economic changes of summer 1948, as the coal price was not freed and the market was thus prevented from channelling resources to the industry in line with coal's value to the economy. Whatever advantages this may have had for national growth and price stability, it prevented the mines from making essential investments. It was not until 1951 that the West German government could be prevailed upon to make the necessary capital transfers.[121]

Nevertheless, the difference between the problems of the 1946–8 period and those after the currency reform, was that the former seem symptomatic of a fundamental lack of legitimacy and authority in the pre-currency reform economic system, whereas, after 1948, coal's problems, at least in this intensity, were virtually unique. 'Coal', not 'the economy', had become the problem.

121. See Chapter 2.

5

British Dismantling Politics, 1945–9: A Reassessment

Alan Kramer

Introduction

It is now time for a reconsideration of the historical problem of dismantling after the Second World War. The dismantling of industrial plant was the only aspect of two interrelated policies of the western Allies, reparations and industrial disarmament, which entered into the popular memory of Germans in the post-war era. In spite of this, no monographs have appeared on dismantling in the British Zone of Germany, the most heavily industrialised zone and consequently the zone with the highest concentration of dismantled plants. This stands in contrast to the long and rich tradition of historical research on reparations and disarmament after the First World War. Lorna Jaffe, who deals with British policy on German disarmament in the period from 1914 to 1919 in her book *The Decision to Disarm Germany*, lists in her bibliography no less than eighteen articles and books just on British war-aims policy and the disarmament of Germany;[1] works on the reparations question *after* the Treaty of Versailles are legion. The paucity of scholarship on dismantling after 1945 may have something to do with the fact that contemporary German accounts were prepared with an openly political intention: to persuade the dismantlers to desist and the Germans to resist.[2] The few subsequent German publications have not been entirely free from a certain anachronistic, even nationalistic flavour.[3]

1. L. S. Jaffe, *The Decision to Disarm Germany. British Policy towards Postwar German Disarmament 1914–1919* (Allen & Unwin, London/Boston, 1985).
2. G. W. Harmssen, *Reparationen, Sozialprodukt, Lebensstandard. Versuch einer Wirtschaftsbilanz* (Trüjen Verlag, Bremen, 1948).
3. This is above all true of H. D. Ahrens, *Demontage, Nachkriegspolitik der*

125

Alan Kramer

Thus Wilhelm Treue, whose booklet on dismantling in Lower Saxony appeared in 1967, had the express intention of showing that 'dismantling was not of the slightest economic use' (i.e. for the countries receiving reparations), and that Britain's main motivation was the weakening of German commercial competition.[4] An article in 1979 by Walter Först examined dismantling only from the point of view of the attempts made by the German side to prevent it.[5] Neither Treue nor Först used British sources; Treue stated that this was not necessary, since the attitude and behaviour of the British occupation forces in the dismantling question emerged clearly enough from German archival sources. It was not his task, argued Treue, to track down sources which would show in detail the links between the commercial interests of firms and private individuals in Britain and the execution of dismantling policy: that, he wrote, was the duty not of German, but of British historiography.[6] Such self-restraint did not, however, prevent him from leaving the accusations stand.

The purpose of this article is first to take a fresh look at the development of British policy on reparations and industrial disarmament from wartime planning through to post-war implementation. It is worth emphasising that along with the well-known disagreements between the British and US governments over the extent of the dismantling programme, there were also conflicts within the British administration which have not previously figured in writing on the subject. The chief protagonists were the Foreign Office and the Treasury on the one side, who were interested essentially in politically realisable reparation and disarmament aims within the overall framework of minimising the strain on British resources by allowing the reconstruction of the German economy. On the other side were the supply departments, such as the Board of Trade and the Ministry of Supply, and the Admiralty, which

Alliierten, Universitas, Munich, 1982). But see also W. Treue, *Die Demontage-politik der Westmächte nach dem Zweiten Weltkrieg. Unter besonderer Berücksichtigung ihrer Wirkung auf die Wirtschaft in Niedersachsen* (Niedersächsische Landeszentrale für polistische Bildung, Hanover, 1967); D. Scriverius, 'Die britische Demontagepolitik im Spiegel der Überlieferung des Haupstaatsarchivs Düsseldorf', in C. Scharf and H.-J. Schröder (eds.), *Die Deutschlandpolitik Grossbritanniens und die britische Zone 1945–1949* (Steiner, Wiesbaden, 1979), pp. 93–101; W. Först, 'Die Politik de Demontage', in W. Först (ed.), *Entscheidungen im Westen* (Grote, Cologne, and Berlin, 1979), pp. 111–43.
4. Treue, *Demontagepolitik*, pp. 41–5, 89.
5. Först, 'Politik der Demontage'.
6. Treue, *Demontagepolitik*, pp. 7–8.

pursued the policy of attempting to restrict German economic competition and to exploit German technical capital and know-how for the benefit of the British economy. The eventual politics of dismantling were to emerge from this complex web of relationships between Whitehall and the occupation authorities in Germany. We are fortunate that the development of British policy on reparations from 1941 to 1949 has now been the subject of a lucid treatment by Alec Cairncross.[7] Sir Alec was in Berlin in the winter of 1945–6 as the Treasury representative in the British team for the negotiations with the United States, the Soviet Union and France over the reparations plan. His book is partly based on his personal memoirs of the negotiations, but it is also particularly good on the early stages of British reparations policy from 1941 to 1945. For the period during which the bulk of the dismantling was carried out, from 1946 to 1950, Cairncross provides only a brief overview of the development of British policy, and does not deal with dismantling in the British Zone.

The second intention of this study is to explain the different categories of dismantling, to discuss the progress of the British dismantling programme together with the political reactions it produced, and finally to assess the overall economic effects of dismantling in West Germany, in particular in the British Zone.[8]

Wartime Policy Development

British government planning for the fate of post-war Germany did not begin in earnest until 1943, when the Foreign Office produced its first memorandum on the subject. Although this paper dealt with the Germany's future borders, the problems of a future armistice and the prevention of German rearmament, it left aside the question of the future of the German economy.[9] As early as 1941, however, reparations had begun to interest officials in several government

---

7. A. Cairncross, *The Price of War. British Policy on German Reparations 1941 to 1949* (Blackwell, Oxford, 1986). See my review in the *Bulletin of the German Historical Institute London*, Vol. 9, No. 3, November 1987, pp. 23–5.
8. This article is based on my doctoral thesis, 'Die britische Demontagepolitik am Beispiel Hamburgs 1945–1950', Hamburg University, 1987, due to be published by Christians Verlag, Hamburg, 1989. The author would like to thank the German Historical Institute London for a scholarship which enabled him to carry out a part of the research in the Federal Republic of Germany.
9. L. Woodward, *British Foreign Policy in the Second World War*, Vol. 5 (HMSO, London, 1976), pp. 25–31.

departments, and in December of that year the Treasury produced a memorandum which outlined the thinking of an interdepartmental committee on 'Compensation to be Required from the Enemy'.[10] Under the guidance of the celebrated economist John Maynard Keynes, as economic adviser in the Treasury, the committee came to the conclusion that the payment of reparations in cash would be unwise, and that deliveries in kind should be limited to a time-span of, say, five years. Indeed it was 'not in Britain's interests' to make high reparations demands.[11]

The Treasury memorandum provoked a response in the form of a paper by Hugh Dalton, President of the Board of Trade, which outlined a drastic reparations policy. This was based on the idea that Britain should adopt the policy of doing what Nazi Germany would do to a defeated Britain, and it concluded that British export opportunities would be better in a Europe 'in which Germany was largely disindustrialised, while other States . . . were industrialised'.[12] In November 1942, another Labour member of the War Cabinet, the Minister of Aircraft Production, Sir Stafford Cripps, argued that the security of Europe depended on reducing German economic power and raising that of its neighbours.[13] On a recommendation of the Dalton memorandum, a committee of expert representatives from interested ministries to examine the reparations question was set up under chairmanship of the legal adviser in the Foreign Office, Sir William Malkin.

Drawing explicitly on historical experience, the Malkin Committee linked, for the first time, the aim of reparations with that of 'economic security'. The latter was a key concept for the British attitude to the German economy and the dismantling question throughout the period from 1943 to 1950, albeit with changing implications as circumstances changed. For the Malkin Committee it meant the complete disarmament of Germany and the destruction or removal of all armaments industries including the aircraft industry, together with the prevention of any German attempts to reintroduce a policy of autarky.[14] These measures were based on the

10. Cairncross, *Price of War*, p. 18.
11. Ibid.
12. Quoted in T. D. Burridge, *British Labour and Hitler's War* (Deutsch, London, 1976), p. 66.
13. Woodward, *British Foreign Policy*, vol. 5, pp. 11–12.
14. From the summary of the report for a speech by Keynes in the State Department, Washington, on 28 September 1943, in J. M. Keynes, *Collected Writings*, Vol. 26, *Activities 1941–46: Shaping the Post-War World: Bretton*

key premises that the victorious Allies would always be in the position, if necessary, to wage war against Germany and that the economic measures would not only be effective for a long time but also be capable of being implemented in the long term. There can be no doubt that the memory of the failure of the Versailles disarmament policies in the 1920s and 1930s was never far from the minds of the members of the Malkin Committee, and in particular from that of the member who dominated the proceedings, Keynes.

This applies all the more to the reparations question. Keynes, who had first acquired his international reputation for his critique of the Versailles reparations policy,[15] called the Dalton memorandum a plan for 'organised enslavement'.[16] However, Keynes had never condemned reparations as such, only the amount of reparations demanded and the manner of payment as monetary transfers. The Malkin Committee hoped to avoid the kind of problems reparations had caused after the First World War by stressing that reparations policy should be moderate in order to take into account both war damage in Germany and the necessity of maintaining an adequate standard of living. The report of the Malkin Committee, which was completed in August 1943, refused to commit itself to naming a fixed overall sum for the reparations to be demanded; moreover reparations deliveries were to be completed within five years, unlike the 1921 reparations agreement under which reparations payments were to be made until 1966 or the Young Plan of 1929 under which payments would have continued until 1988.

Nevertheless, Germany could make a substantial contribution to the reconstruction of Europe, and the Malkin Committee recommended taking reparations in the following ways:

(i)   Once-for-all deliveries from capital assets, for example, machine tools, ships, rolling stock, agricultural equipment.

(ii) Once-for-all deliveries of raw or semi-manufactured materials from stock, surplus to peacetime requirements, for example, steel and cattle.

(iii) Deliveries in kind from current production of semi-manufactured and manufactured goods for use in the construction industry and for the repair of transport systems, for example,

Woods and Reparations, edited by D. Moggridge (Macmillan and Cambridge University Press, Cambridge, 1980), pp. 370–3.
15. See Keynes, Collected Writings, Vol. 2, The Economic Consequences of the Peace (Macmillan and Cambridge University Press, Cambridge, 1977).
16. Keynes, Collected Writings, vol. 26, p. 337.

Alan Kramer

cement and steel.
(iv) Deliveries in kind from current production of ships and rolling
stock, agricultural equipment and fertiliser.
(v) The provision of German labour, especially for reconstruction
tasks.[17]

The policy of dismantling German industry arose out of two of the
aims defined in the Malkin Report: economic security through
measures of industrial disarmament, and reparations deliveries of
capital assets. From 1944, although the Malkin Report was no
longer used as a starting point for further policy recommendations,
the idea of a reduction in Germany's overall industrial capacity was
studied in detail by the official committee dealing with the economic
aspects of post-war Germany and Europe, the Economic and Industrial Planning Staff (EIPS). At its first meeting, in March 1944,
the EIPS decided to carry out studies on various branches of
German industry in the post-war period. In August 1944, it presented its 'Report on Issues Affecting the Economic Obligations to
be Imposed on Germany', which attempted to maintain a balance
between restrictive economic measures for the purpose of ensuring
military security and measures intended to rehabilitate the German
economy.[18] Overall, the EIPS recommendations were relatively
moderate, especially when compared with the US Treasury Secretary, Henry J. Morgenthau's proposal to destroy Germany's entire
industrial base. Drastic measures, that is prohibition and elimination, were only to be taken in a few strategically important industries. The central recommendation of the report to allow the German
steel industry an annual production of 10 to 12 million tons became
the basis of all future British planning for the German economy,
and the reason given for this proposed level is characteristic of
British policy towards the German economy: it was seen as an
appropriate amount to safeguard Germany's economic base, but
without Britain having to fear the loss of its own export markets.[19]
Although no decision had been made on whether reparations from

17. From the summary of the Malkin Report, in Keynes, *Collected Writings*, vol.
26, pp. 363–4.
18. Public Record Office (PRO)/FO1005/959, EIPS Report, pp. 358–9. See also
chapter 3 in this volume.
19. EIPS, Report of the Working Party on Steel, 31 May 1944, cited in G. Müller,
'Sicherheit durch wirtschaftliche Stabilität? Die Rolle der Briten bei der
Auseinandersetzung der Alliierten um die Stahlquote des 1 Industrieniveauplans vom 26 März 1946', in D. Petzina and W. Euchner (eds.) *Wirtschaftspolitik im britischen Besatzungsgebiet 1945–1949* (Schwann, Düsseldorf, 1984),
p. 68. For the intention of the EIPS to eliminate Germany's export industry,
see also PRO/FO942/52, minutes of the EIPS meeting on 6 May 1944.

130

the current production of industry would be taken, the EIPS calculations for the level of the steel industry left no surplus for such deliveries. The EIPS report was approved by a committee of ministers in August 1944, and a slightly modified version formed the basis of the British negotiating position in the four-power talks on the future level of German industry in winter 1945–6 in Berlin.

Britain and the Level of Industry Negotiations in Berlin, 1945–6

The British role at the Berlin four-power negotiations on the level of industry for Germany has been dealt with by Gloria Müller, in relation to the most important sector, the steel industry; it has also been covered exhaustively by Alec Cairncross.[20] To spare the reader the details of these negotiations, it is best to summarise the main developments as a rearguard struggle by the British delegates who were attempting to preserve enough industrial plant to enable the German population to maintain a standard of living equivalent to the European average while not burdening the occupying powers with the cost of financing necessary German imports. The Soviets, the French and even the Americans wanted to reduce German economic activity to a considerably lower level than that proposed by the British. This can be seen most clearly in the disagreements over the future of the steel industry, which occupied a central position in the economy because of its key role in most manufacturing industries. Britain argued for the reduction of Germany's steel production to 10.5 million tons annually, or about half the 1936 production of 19.5 million tons.

The Americans initially proposed a maximum production of 7.8 million tons, the French 7 million and the Soviets 4.6 million tons. In protracted and increasingly bad-tempered negotiations the Brit-

---

20. Müller, 'Sicherheit durch wirtschaftliche Stabilität?' pp. 65–86; Cairncross, *Price of War*, chs. 5–7; A. Cairncross, *A Country to Play With. Level of Industry Negotiations in Berlin 1945–46* (Colin Smythe, Gerrards Cross, 1987). In this memoir, originally written in 1952, Cairncross presents the perspective of an economic expert in charge of the Economic Advisory Panel, preparing the British position for negotiations with his counterparts in the Technical Committee, and he records little of the higher-level negotiations in the Economics Directorate and the Coordinating Committee. Fascinating though this memoir is, it does not aim to provide a systematic treatment of the negotiations, for which the reader is best served by Müller, read in conjunction with B. U. Ratchford and W. D. Ross, *Berlin Reparations Assignment. Round One of the German Peace Settlement* (University of North Carolina Press, Chapel Hill, NC, 1947).

ish delegation came down to 9 million tons when they realised the gulf that separated them from their partners. Then General Clay, the American member of the Coordinating Committee, the second-highest body, and in effect the only decision-making body, of the four-power the Allied Control Authority (ACA), persuaded his Soviet counterpart to accept a total steel-making capacity of 7.2 million tons, with a maximum production level of 5.8 million tons. However, the British delegate, General Robertson, refused to accept anything below 7.5 million tons of steel-making capacity.[21] Finally Sokolovsky, the Soviet member of the Coordinating Committee, made the decisive concession, and agreed on 10 January 1946 to a production limit of 5.8 million tons with a maximum steel-making capacity of 7.5 million tons. This would have been the end of the story, but two days later Robertson announced that he was not prepared to accept 5.8 million tons of steel production as the basis of planning for the rest of the economy. After consulting London, Robertson declared that the British government could not agree to a policy that would condemn the German people to eternal poverty, hunger and slavery: no civilised nation had the right to impose such a peace on a defeated enemy. Robertson maintained that Britain had only agreed to a level of 7.5 million tons provided the overall plan for the German economy were based upon this figure. A plan on the basis of 5.8 million tons could not be realised without turning Germany into a wilderness. To the surprise of the other delegates, Robertson went on to say that retaining a capacity of 7.5 million tons also meant, according to the British interpretation, that this quantity would actually be produced. Sokolovsky's accusation is undoubtedly correct that Robertson was trying to give a fresh interpretation to an agreement already reached.[22] Work on the rest of the Level of Industry Plan could only be completed when the deadlock was resolved (a) by the Soviet agreement to dismantle for reparations only those steel plants which were no longer necessary for a capacity of 7.5 million tons, and (b) by the British agreement to cooperate in drawing up the rest of the plan on the basis of 5.8

21. Murphy to Byrnes 22 and 31 December 1945, in United States, Department of State (ed.), *Foreign Relations of the United States* (cited as FRUS), Vol. 3, 1945, pp. 1484–6 and 1499–1501. See also Ratchford and Ross, *Berlin Reparations Assignment*, p. 123.

22. Ratchford and Ross, *Berlin Reparations Assignment*, pp. 127–30; Murphy to Byrnes 8, 11 and 13 January 1946, FRUS, Vol. 5, 1946, pp. 481–8. The discussion of the steel negotiations in Cairncross, *Price of War*, pp. 107–8, is too brief; for a better account, see Müller, 'Sicherheit durch wirtschaftliche Stabilität?'

million tons of actual annual steel production.[23] The British struggle for a higher level of industry thus foundered on the determination of the US to negotiate a compromise with the Soviet Union. By March, consensus had been reached with regard to all the individual levels of economic output and the balance of trade. The figures were arrived at not on the basis of the economic and technological needs of an advanced country, but as the result of what two senior American economic advisers called a 'political poker game',[24] in which, after haggling over numbers, General Clay overcame the differences between the proposed levels by applying the 'rule of four', that is, by averaging out the four figures.[25]

Although the proposals were criticised in London by Cabinet ministers, especially because of the expected balance of payments deficit in the British Zone, Foreign Minister Bevin argued in favour of accepting because he felt there was no point in fighting on alone against the USSR, France and the US for a higher level of industry.[26]

The German Section in the Foreign Office and the British Military Government in Berlin had also advised acceptance of the plan, above all because they anticipated that the obvious disparities and inconsistencies in it (e.g. between the low level of steel production and the higher production levels in the steel-using industries) would soon make necessary an upward revision of the plan.[27] Finally, the British delegation in Berlin managed at the last hour to secure the reluctant agreement of the Soviet Union and France to review the plan if there were a change in its basic assumptions. These were (i) that Germany was to be treated as an economic unit, (ii) that the population would not exceed 66.5 million, and (iii) that German exports would be sufficient to pay for necessary imports, so that the occupying powers would not have to bear the burden of supporting Germany.[28] Just how much this agreement meant in practical terms must have been clear to all participants at the time: in effect a review required the unanimous decision of all four powers. It was already apparent that the Soviet Union and France were running their own

---

23. Clay to War Department, cited Murphy to Byrnes 31 January 1946, FRUS, Vol. 5, 1946, p. 496.
24. Ratchford and Ross, *Berlin Reparations Assignment*, pp. 172–3.
25. Cairncross, *Price of War*, p. 124.
26. A. Bullock, *Ernest Bevin: Foreign Secretary 1945–1951* (Heinemann, London, 1983), p. 266.
27. Müller, 'Sicherheit durch wirtschaftliche Stabilität?', pp. 78–80.
28. Murphy to Byrnes 27 March 1946, FRUS, Vol. 5, 1946, p. 553. This agreed formula for a possible revision did not form part of the plan, but was taken as an additional decision of the Coordinating Committee.

zones as independent entities, and no progress had been made towards setting up central administrative agencies as an essential prelude to treating Germany as one economic unit.

The 'Plan for Reparations and the Level of the Post-War German Economy' was published on 26 March 1946, seven weeks later than the original deadline. Under its terms German economic capacity and production were to be reduced to 50–5% of the 1938 level, or roughly 75% of the 1936 level, corresponding in fact to the level of production in the year 1932, when unemployment stood at 6 million. The steel industry was to be reduced to 30% of its pre-war level, the chemical industry to 40%, heavy engineering to 31%, and machine-tool manufacturing to 11.4%.[29] In order to eliminate Germany's capacity for waging war, certain industries, for example, arms, ammunition, aircraft, ship-building, synthetic fuels, light metals, radioactive substances, were to be completely forbidden and the equipment for their manufacture destroyed or dismantled for reparations. The plan was considerably more drastic and covered a wider range of industries than British experts had originally wanted. Nevertheless, it would be wrong to ascribe the plan, as was frequently done in contemporary German campaigns against dismantling and as is still sometimes done in recent history books,[30] to the influence of Roosevelt's Treasury Secretary, Henry J. Morgenthau, who in 1944 had put forward a plan to deindustrialise Germany and turn it into an agricultural land. The Level of Industry Plan reflected rather the desire for security on the part of the Soviet Union and France coupled with their need for massive reparations. It also represented the last attempt by Britain and the US to reach a consensus with the Soviet Union over the future of the German economy.

The Turn in British Policy on Four-Power Rule in Germany

The Berlin negotiations had shown the British that they were in danger of isolating themselves diplomatically if they insisted on pursuing policies designed to preserve in Germany an adequate

29. F. Jerchow, *Deutschland in der Weltwirtschaft 1944–1947. Alliierte Deutschland- und Reparationspolitik und die Anfänge der westdeutschen Aussenwirtschaft* (Droste, Düsseldorf, 1978), pp. 203–4.
30. For example, C. Klessmann, *Die doppelte Staatsgründung. Deutsche Geschichte 1945–1955* (Vandenhoeck & Ruprecht, Göttingen, 1982), p. 105.

industrial base, and that without American support they could not achieve their objectives at four-power level. Dismantling in the western zones never took place to the extent laid down by the Level of Industry Plan. In fact the plan reinforced the will of the British government to continue its relatively moderate policy with respect to reparations and the treatment of the German economy in its zone, and it also lent added impulse to the idea already mooted in the Control Commission for Germany (CCG) in 1945 of treating the western zones as a separate economic unit, for which 'alternative estimates' for the level of industry would be prepared.[31] By early 1946, even before the Level of Industry Plan had been completed there were discussions at the highest level between the Foreign Office and Field Marshal Montgomery, the Military Governor of the British Zone on the possibility of breaking with the Potsdam Agreement and setting up a West German government in order to prevent the spread of communist influence in Germany.[32] These deliberations were, according to the German historians Pingel, Steininger[33] and Foschepoth,[34] the beginning of a reorientation in British policy towards Germany, which can be dated to a conference in the Foreign Office on 3 April. At this meeting, John Hynd (the junior minister with responsibility for the administration of the British Zone in Germany) proposed that the British government should cooperate more closely with the Germans, strengthen the western zones and set up a German administration in the British Zone with economic powers. Bevin took these ideas even further and asked his officials to prepare a study on the possibility of a joint administration of all three western zones.[35] Bevin presented these

---

31. The Economic Planning Committee (British Zone) of the CCG had held a conference on 11 September 1945 in Bad Oeynhausen at which it was agreed that without the cooperation of the Soviets and without information on the extent of removals of industrial equipment from that zone it would be impossible to produce plans on the basis of economic unity. The only alternative was to treat the western zones as a economic unit and to prepare 'alternative estimates' for this eventuality. See PRO/FO1014/358, Economic Planning Committee Paper no. 20, 29 September 1945.
32. F. Pingel, "Die Russen am Rhein?" Zur Wende der britischen Besatzungspolitik im Frühjahr 1946', *Vierteljahrshefte für Zeitgeschichte*, Vol. 30, No. 1 1982, pp. 105–6.
33. R. Steininger, 'Die Rhein–Ruhr-Frage im Kontext britischer Deutschlandpolitik 1945–46', in H. A. Winkler (ed.), *Politische Weichenstellungen im Nachkriegsdeutschland 1945–1953*, (Vandenhoeck & Ruprecht, Göttingen, 1979), p. 118. See also chapter 1 in this volume.
34. J. Foschepoth, 'British interest in the Division of Germany after the Second World War', *Journal of Contemporary History*, Vol. 21, No. 3 1986, pp. 391–411.
35. Pingel, '"Russen am Rhein?"', pp. 106–7.

ideas to the Cabinet on 7 May 1946 in the form of a memorandum in which emphasis was laid on the necessity of maintaining a reasonably high standard of living in order to prevent the communists from exploiting the economic distress. To this end it would be necessary to 'organise our own zone as an independent unit according to our own ideas, bringing in the other western zones as we can'. It would also be necessary to revoke the Level of Industry Plan and 'reduce reparations to a sensible level', which would give the Germans hope for their future.[36]

However, the negotiations in Berlin had shown the British that support from the Americans was not likely to be forthcoming for so radical a change in policy, with its implication of breaking the Potsdam Agreement and of thus wrecking collaboration with the Soviet Union in the Allied control of Germany. In this situation, the 'reparations stop' announced by General Clay on 3 May must have come at a very opportune moment for Bevin and the Foreign Office, since it directed the attention of the world towards the lack of economic unity in Germany and the assumed guilty party, the Soviet Union. It prepared the ground for Bevin's long statement on Germany at the Paris Council of Foreign Ministers (CFM) on 10 July, in which he stated that if there were to be no progress on economic unity (in the sense of interzonal trade and common export–import policy), then the British government would have to organise its zone in such a way that it would no longer be a burden to the British taxpayer.[37] It was immediately following this threat that the US Secretary of State, Byrnes, made his offer to merge the US Zone with any other occupation zone—an offer which was taken up, just as was intended, only by the British government.[38]

Even before the turn in British policy towards Germany in spring/summer 1946 there was consensus among policy-makers on the necessity of an upward revision of the Level of Industry Plan—irrespective of whether Germany was to be treated as an economic unit or a West German state was to be created.[39] Because it was impolitic to be seen as the cause of the division of Germany,

36. R. Steininger, *Deutsche Geschichte 1945–1961. Darstellung und Dokumente in zwei Bänden* (Fischer, Frankfurt on M., 1983), Vol. 1, pp. 188–93.
37. United States Record, Council of Foreign Ministers, Second Session, 339th meeting, . . . 10 July 1946, FRUS, Vol. 2, 1946, pp. 864–8.
38. Steininger, 'Rhein–Ruhr-Frage', p. 130. See also chapter 1 in this volume.
39. PRO/FO371/55601/C4086, C. Steel (head of the CCG Political Division) to Sir William Strang (FO), 10 April 1946; PRO/CAB134/597, Overseas Reconstruction Committee (ORC), 3 February 1947.

the Foreign Office always used a dual approach: the Soviet Union's 25% share of the reparations from the western zones was not placed in question, in order to maintain the fair distribution, if not the original extent, of reparations. However, when EIPS presented a draft revised plan in October 1946, this was based on the concept of the western zones as a separate economic entity.[40]

Dismantling in the British Zone, 1945–7

Only a few weeks after the end of the Berlin negotiations the change in British policy had consequences in the dismantling of industry. Dismantling, in the sense of the removal of machines, had begun in armaments factories in October 1945, and measures of industrial disarmament, for example, the destruction of equipment used in the production of war material, had started by July 1945. At the end of May 1946 the gantries (large steel structures under which ships were formerly built) of Blohm & Voss, Hamburg's biggest shipyard, were demolished in a spectacular series of explosions, as part of the programme of eliminating Germany's industrial war potential. When preparations were made to demolish the gantries of the next shipyard, the Howaldtswerke, the trade unions and politicians of all parties joined forces to protest. The gantries were saved when the Hamburg Military Government, which was in any case opposed to the destruction, managed to have the measure temporarily suspended. The delay coincided with the turn in British policy towards Germany, and at a meeting of ministers it was decided to slow down the programme of industrial disarmament in the ship-building industry and postpone the destruction, because it was recognised that Britain 'might be obliged to abandon the attempt to administer Germany as a unit', in which case 'industrial disarmament . . . would require complete reconsideration'.[41]

As the entire question of the level of industry and reparations was once again in abeyance, progress on dismantling in the British Zone from May 1946 to March 1947 was very slow. In August 1946, for

40. PRO/FO1005/961, 'EIPS Report on the Proposed Revision of the "Plan for Reparations . . ."' (22 October 1946), EIPS/P(46), pp. 1–6.
41. PRO/FO371/55383/C6597, telegram COGA (John Hynd) to CCG Berlin 21 June 1946; see, PRO/FO371/55384/C7173, minutes of the meeting of ORC (46) 9th meeting, 21 June 1946. For further details on the demolitions carried out at the Blohm & Voss yard and the planned demolition at the Howalts-werke, see Kramer, 'Die britische Demontagepolitik', chapter 4.3.2.

example, dismantling was being carried out in only four plants, in September, in five, and by the end of the year no more than 73,500 tons of equipment had been dismantled.[42] There were procedural and technical reasons for the slow pace of dismantling, and also low efficiency of labour. For example, before dismantling could start, factories had to be selected, their equipment inventoried, each item had to be valued, and the valuation had to be approved by a quadripartite directorate. Valuations were slowed down because the German valuers employed suffered from poor concentration as a result of the general lack of food.[43] By the end of 1946, however, the valuations of 185 factories in the British Zone had been approved, but dismantling was only being carried out at fourteen plants, and the first five factories were not completely dismantled and packed until April 1947.[44] The lack of progress clearly was not caused by technical problems, but was the result of decisions on political priorities, and in this period the promotion of economic recovery took precedence. The low priority accorded to dismantling was reflected in the unpopularity of the work among the staff of the Military Government who, as a report of the Board of Trade noted, regarded reparations as an 'indefinite obligation and a nuisance'.[45] The pace of dismantling was not increased until the time of the Moscow CFM, March–April 1947, when, as Bevin expected, the Inter-Allied Reparation Agency (IARA) and the Soviet Union made renewed complaints about the slow pace of reparations deliveries and industrial disarmament.[46]

The Revision of Dismantling Policy

The slow progress of dismantling up to March 1947 stands in sharp contrast to the anxiety of the British government to reach an early agreement with the US over the revision of the Level of Industry Plan. In September 1946, Generals Clay and Robertson agreed to

42. *Monthly Reports of the CCG (BE)*, August, September and December 1946.
43. PRO/FO1014/152, 'Notes of a Conversation between Mr Whitham (Reparations Division) and Brigadier Armytage (Hamburg Military Governor) at a Meeting held . . . 9 July 1946'.
44. *Monthly Reports of the CCG (BE)*, December 1946 and April 1947.
45. PRO/FO943/7, report on reparations by Dakin, Board of Trade, November 1946.
46. For the record of the Moscow Council, see FRUS, Vol. 2, 1947; see also memorandum from the Inter-Allied Reparation Agency to the Council of Foreign Ministers, n.d., probably early January 1947, ibid., pp. 392–3.

begin a joint study for the revision of the plan.[47] Against the background of reports that the Soviet Union was suffering 'indigestion' from a surfeit of dismantled equipment from Germany, Clay received a proposal from the Soviet Military Governor Sokolovsky to suspend dismantling for ten years and instead deliver goods from current production.[48] While the idea of current reparations was seriously considered by the US Military Government, among other reasons in order to open the Soviet Zone and the rest of eastern Europe to US influence,[49] Bevin and the Foreign Office decisively rejected the idea. In the event of such a proposal being raised at the Moscow Council, Bevin drew up a list of preconditions which, as he stated, the Soviet Union would never accept. This would keep the way open for the reconstruction of the economy in the British–US Bizone.[50]

The British–US joint study did not get under way until May 1947, eight months after the original decision. Why should there have been such a long delay, when Britain was urging an upward revision on the Americans, the recipient nations were becoming impatient over the lack of deliveries and the Germans were beginning to acquire more political autonomy? The reasons tell us much about the different approaches to German policy adopted by Britain and the US. In December 1946, when the two foreign ministers met with the two Military Governors to discuss the Bizonal fusion, Bevin remarked that the figure of 11 million tons of steel capacity originally proposed by the British had turned out to be justified. General Clay objected that 11 million tons of steel represented a 'dangerous war potential', and refused to countenance a Bizonal

---

47. PRO/FO943/36, Robertson (Berlin) to COGA, 17 September 1946.
48. Caffery to Byrnes 24 August 1946, FRUS, Vol. 5, 1946, pp. 593–4; Durbrow (US *chargé d'affaires* in Moscow) to Byrnes 4 September 1946, *ibid.*, p. 601.
49. For example, Murphy to Byrnes 25 October 1946, FRUS, Vol. 5, 1946, pp. 632–3. See also a personal memorandum from Clay to Byrnes of November 1946: 'The acceptance of this principle [i.e. reparations from current production] would require as a condition the full political unification of Germany, thus extending Western liberalism to the borders of the countries now under Communist influence.' J. E. Smith (ed.), *The Papers of General Lucius D. Clay. Germany 1945–1949* (Indiana University Press, Bloomington, Ind., 1974), Vol. 1, p. 282.
50. Cabinet paper by Bevin, 17 October 1946, PRO/CAB129/12, quoted in Steininger, *Deutsche Geschichte*, Vol. 1, pp. 216–18. The idea expressed by Cairncross (*Price of War*, p. 166) that Bevin did not abandon hope of 'some accommodation with the USSR' until the end of 1947 does not seem plausible in the light of this Cabinet paper. See also the subsequent Cabinet discussion in January and further memorandum to the Cabinet in February 1947, in *Price of War*, pp. 168–70.

revision of the level of industry.[51] As far as we can tell, at this stage US planning did not envisage either a Bizonal revision or an overall increase. US policy was thus rather schizophrenic: on the one hand, Clay wanted to begin talks on the political fusion of the Bizone, an unmentionable subject in view of the delicate state of east–west relations, but, on the other, found a Bizonal revision of the Level of Industry Plan impracticable.

At the Moscow CFM Bevin again urged the Americans to begin talks on the revision of the Level of Industry Plan on the basis of 10 million tons of steel production and suggested issuing an immediate public declaration to this effect. The Americans refused, and Marshall recommended a six-week postponement. There are four reasons which explain why the British government was in a hurry to revise the plan. First, while Britain and the US were both put under pressure from the IARA to speed up reparation deliveries, Britain could not afford to ignore the interests of the smaller west European nations in case they turned out to be necessary as a counterweight to US predominance in Europe. Secondly, the supply ministries in London were pressing the Foreign Office to expedite reparation deliveries urgently wanted in British industry. As Britain could not be certain of being allocated those plants it regarded as essential, for example, the Hermann–Goering steel works in Salzgitter, the EIPS recommended increasing reparation deliveries to all nations, including the Soviet Union.[52] Thirdly, although Bevin was disillusioned with the results of dismantling thus far, quoting a Board of Trade study to the US Secretary of State, Marshall, which showed a loss of value through dismantling and transfer of 70–80% of the original value, he saw no practical alternative.[53] It was important, Bevin stated, to give the Germans a clear picture of the future of their industry, for they could hardly be expected to cooperate in rebuilding a democratic state until they knew how much and in what form they had to pay reparations.[54]

The fourth reason for British impatience was closely connected with the fear that the US and the Soviet Union might yet come to an

51. PRO/FO943/30, 'Anglo-American Discussions on Germany. Interview between the British and American Secretaries of State and the British and American Deputy Military Governors, 3 December 1946. Note prepared by Mr Playfair.'
52. PRO/CAB134/597, ORC, 3 February 1947.
53. Bevin–Marshall talks 5 April 1947, FRUS, Vol. 2, 1947, p. 309.
54. Statement by Bevin at the Moscow Conference on 31 March 1947, FRUS, Vol. 2, 1947, pp. 300–1.

understanding, which would have diminished Britain's status as the third world power. The British government certainly wanted to tie the US to its obligations in the Bizone and to its presence in Europe, but it also wanted to carry out its own political programme in Germany as fast as possible, partly to counter the threat of the 'Americanisation' of Germany.[55] When the Anglo-American working party began its deliberations in May 1947, it soon became apparent that American views on the future of the German economy had changed radically. The American group now proposed a steel-making capacity of 14 million tons and raising most of the other production limits.[56] The negotiators agreed in the end on 10.7 million tons maximum production and capacity, a figure very close to the British position.[57]. The two sides could not however reach agreement on the list of prohibited industries: the Americans wished to retain the prohibition on aluminium, magnesium, beryllium and vanadium which the British proposed to lift; and the British wanted to maintain the ban or production restriction on a number of industries including heavy engineering, machine tools and ship-building. The question of prohibited industries was therefore left out of the Revised Plan and was due to be resolved later. These disputes are now well known and need no further elucidation here.[58]

'Multilateral Deliveries'—Myth and Reality

Before dealing with dismantling in accordance with the list published in October 1947, it is intended to discuss the removals of industrial equipment from factories which were not on the list. These removals, because they were shrouded in mystery, were frequently the object of criticism by Germans and were condemned as particularly obnoxious actions. Prime among such removals were the 'multilateral deliveries'. In contemporary German accounts the

55. J. Foschepoth, 'Konflikte in der Reparationspolitik der Alliierten', in J. Foschepoth (ed.), *Kalter Krieg und Deutsche Frage. Deutschland im Widerstreit der Mächte 1945-1952* (Vandenhoeck & Ruprecht, Göttingen and Zurich, 1985), p. 187. See also A. S. Milward, 'Grossbritannien, Deutschland und der Wiederaufbau Westeuropas', in Petzina and Euchner (eds.), *Wirtschaftspolitik im britischen Besatzungsgebiet*, especially pp. 31 and 33.
56. PRO/FO1036/9, minutes of FO meeting, 7 May 1947.
57. Revised Level of Industry Plan, reprinted in Harmssen, *Reparationen*, Part 1, pp. 91–8.
58. Cairncross, *Price of War*, pp. 175–8, 182–7.

quantity of multilateral deliveries and their negative effects on the economy were often exaggerated. The origins of the multilateral deliveries lay in the slow progress of dismantling in 1945 and 1946. The term was created by analogy with the 'unilateral deliveries' which were reparations deliveries of individual items, chosen by the CCG without reference to four-power bodies, and sent only to Britain and not to the other countries entitled to reparations.[59] The unilateral deliveries, known also as the 'Mills Scheme' after its progenitor Sir Percy Mills, chief of the CCG Economic Division, consisted of machines urgently needed in Britain which could otherwise only be obtained after a long delay. The programme of unilateral deliveries had to be abandoned in early 1947 because it came under attack from the other members of IARA, the international body which distributed reparations, for giving the occupying power unfair advantage.

Multilateral deliveries were designed to overcome both problems: that of maintaining the supply to Britain of urgently needed machines, and that of ensuring the appearance of fair distribution of reparations to all recipient nations. This was achieved by sending secret lists of urgently needed machines from the supply ministries, based on information on availability given by the CCG, to the British delegation at the Assembly of IARA. The British delegation submitted 'padded' lists of requirements to the Assembly and in negotiations was able to fall back on its real demands.[60] Suspicions that Britain was circumventing the correct procedure were voiced at the IARA Assembly, and Yugoslavia threatened to move a motion accusing the UK of being a 'swindler', but the British delegation managed to ride out the storm.[61]

When the multilateral deliveries scheme was presented to the ACA it was opposed by the Americans, who said that the British should follow their example and speed up the dismantling of armaments plants to provide reparations. The scheme, as the American member of the Economic Directorate, General Draper, pointed out, represented a reversal of the normal four-power procedure of declaring plants available and allocating them between east and

59. See Kramer, 'Die britische Demontagepolitik', chapter 3.4 for further details on unilateral deliveries and booty.
60. PRO/FO943/16, J. Selwyn, Board of Trade, to Sir Desmond Morton, IARA, 4 December 1946; PRO/FO371/53101/UE 5724, telegram from Morton to FO (and Board of Trade), 30 November 1946.
61. PRO/FO943/17, telegram from Morton to FO, 27 February 1947; PRO/FO943/17, Morton to FO, 8 March 1947.

west.[62] Despite the opposition of the US, and even though the two divisions of the CCG most concerned with operating the programme, the Reparations, Deliveries and Restitution Division and the Trade and Industries Division, demanded the withdrawal of the programme on the grounds of its impracticability,[63] the British government decided to go ahead with multilateral deliveries.

After its announcement to IARA in November 1946 the programme came into effect in February 1947 when it was presented by the Reparations Division to regional officials of the CCG.[64] Apart from the proponent of the programme, Sir Percy Mills, and his successor as President of the Economic Sub-Commission, Sir Cecil Weir, most of the CCG staff concerned appear to have been reluctant to carry out the multilateral deliveries. It is hardly surprising that the Military Government were poor at public relations in this respect and made no official announcement about the programme to the German people. The first meeting on the subject between British and German zonal officials did not take place until July 1947.[65] Soon the German zonal authorities were engaged in creating legends—about the destination of the machines and about the extent of the removals — which have survived in some historical writing on dismantling.[66] One of the officials in the department of the zonal economic administration which dealt with the dismantling question, Dr Kutscher, claimed that the great majority of multilateral deliveries went to Britain.[67] In fact, France, Yugoslavia and Greece each received more multilateral deliveries than Britain. However, the accusations did contain a grain of truth. Britain took for herself the most valuable machines. The average value of each item delivered to countries other than the UK was RM 4,565 while the average value of the items delivered to the UK was RM 17,707.[68] Another accusation had less basis in fact: in December 1947

---

62. PRO/FO943/16, William Draper to Sir Cecil Weir, 30 November 1946.
63. PRO/FO943/16, Dakin, Board of Trade, to Knight, UK Reparations Mission. c/o RDR Division, Detmold, early December 1946.
64. PRO/FO/1014/5, minutes of Deputy Regional Commissioner's Conference with heads of branches, 24 February 1947.
65. Bundesarchiv–Zwischenarchiv Hangelar bei Bonn (BA–ZwA), B102/3755, Aufzeichnung Dr Kutscher, 18 July 1947.
66. See Treue, *Demontagepolitik*, pp. 53–4.
67. BA–ZwA B102/3800, Entwurf einer Aufzeichnung von Dr Kutscher für Dr Semler (Director of the Verwaltung für Wirtschaft, the German Economic Administration), 5 December 1947.
68. Calculated from BA–ZwA B103, Box 214, Item 2193. 'Summary B' of the 'British Emergency Delivery Scheme' (the official name for multilateral deliveries), Records and Statistics Section, RDR Division, 18 August 1949. For further details, see table 3.5 in Kramer, 'Die britische Demontagepolitik'.

Kutscher wrote that he had been unofficially informed that the British had planned to remove 40,000 machine tools.[69] One year later he raised this to 70,000.[70] Military Government had, in reality, only declared an interest in 6,379 machines, of which 2,731 were not approved for removal by the Industry Division or rejected by the recipient country. In the end, only 3,648 items were delivered under the programme, and at most 4,324 machines were actually removed from factories. Their reparations value (after depreciation) was a little over RM 20 million, a disappointing result for a scheme expected to yield RM 75 million worth of reparations.[71]

These facts were in the main available to the German authorities (e.g. in the Monthly Reports of the CCG), and it is therefore pertinent to ask why such exaggerated and false claims were made. The reason was probably in order to bring pressure to bear on the British to curtail the multilateral deliveries by encouraging opposition. Certainly, if it were the intention of the German authorities to create disquiet, they succeeded, helped by the lack of information given by Military Government on the entire question of dismantling up to October 1947. Representatives of the Chambers of Industry and Commerce in the British Zone, meeting in Remscheid in June 1947 to discuss reparations and dismantling, voiced the fear of 20,000–30,000 machines being confiscated for multilateral deliveries.[72]

The Control Commission was well aware of the widespread anxiety among German industrialists caused by the multilateral deliveries. The CCG insisted on the cessation of the programme to coincide with the publication of the dismantling list in October 1947, and successfully warded off an attempt by the London supply departments to have another 1,700 machines seized for last-minute delivery in September 1947.[73]

---

69. BA–ZwA B102/3800, 'Entwurf einer Aufzeichung von Dr Kutscher ... 5 Dezember 1947.'
70. BA–ZwA B102/3800, Dr Kutscher to Dr Rud. Wedemeyer, 6 December 1947.
71. BA–ZwA B103, Box 214, Item 2193, 'General Summary' of the 'British Emergency Delivery Scheme', Records and Statistics Section, RDR Division, 18 August 1948. See also the section on the British Purchasing Agency, the 'Weir Plan', and technical reparations in chapter 3.
72. Archiv der Handelskammer Hamburg C1211/10, Vol. 1: 'Vermerk Dr Zinkeisen. Betr.: Sitzung am 16. Juni 1947 in Remscheid.'
73. PRO/FO 371/65209/CJ1645, telegram from Lübbecke to Foreign Office, 23 September 1947, originator not named, but probably General Robertson.

The Confrontation with Reality: Dismantling Politics, 1947–9

Less well known and less understood than the development of dismantling policy is the actual implementation of the programme and the interaction between the different levels of British policy-making and the German authorities. Before turning to a discussion of dismantling in the British Zone, we should examine the question of the extent of the influence of the commercial interests of British industry. There is in fact very little evidence of direct influence on government policy on the selection of branches of industry, or on the selection of individual factories for dismantling. There was almost no chance before mid-1946 for British firms to make their wishes felt, although in 1945 the Economic Sub-Commission of the CCG developed a questionnaire to be sent out to industry associations in Britain in order to name and locate German firms whose technological know-how could be exploited or which were trade rivals. In one case, a questionnaire answer—given by a private firm in Glasgow instead of by the industry association—contributed to the decision to dismantle a named rival firm three years later in Hamburg, but such cases of direct influence were exceptions.[74] Indeed, at a meeting with the Board of Trade on 16 May 1946, the Federation of British Industry complained that it had not been consulted over the Level of Industry Plan and expressed its disappointment that its members had so far received no reparations.[75] There was, on the other hand, 'considerable indirect consultation' between British industry and the Trade and Industry Division of the Control Commission, as the CCG representative at this meeting pointed out in defence. But as Sir John Woods, the highest-ranking Board of Trade official, said, the primary aim in drawing up the Level of Industry Plan had been 'security', to be gained through the destruction of German war potential. Woods added that British export industries would enjoy a substantial advantage while Germany was still in chaos.[76]

After publication of the dismantling list in October 1947 the Foreign Office prepared a report requested by Bevin on allegations that dismantling policy had been influenced by the personal inter-

74. For further details, see Kramer, 'Die britische Demontagepolitik', chapter 3.3.2.
75. PRO/BT11/2697, 'Brief for Meeting with the German Committee of FBI', and minutes of the meeting on 16 May 1946.
76. Ibid.

ests of British manufacturers. The report admitted that the first Level of Industry Plan 'contained an element of UK commercial interest', but the subsequent revision of the plan in the light of Germany's balance-of-payments position 'had forced [the Control Commission] to eliminate this'.[77] It is true, as the report stated, that it was highly unlikely that a British manufacturer would be able to obtain equipment specifically requested from a particular German plant through corrupt influence, because the Germans were able to propose substitution of plants and because allocation of reparations passed through three phases outside the control of the CCG or of an interested party: (1) four-power allocation between the Soviet Union and IARA, (2) allocation by IARA among member nations, and (3) public tender to the trade in the UK.[78] However, the report was somewhat disingenuous in claiming that commercial interest was completely absent from British policy on the level of industry, for while the restrictions on steel output and ship-building were primarily justifiable as security measures, the breathing-space they provided for British exports was a valuable by-product.[79]

On 16 October, seven weeks after the proclamation of the Revised Plan, the Revised Dismantling List for the Bizone was published. The list, containing the names of 496 plants in the British Zone (and a further 185 in the US Zone), was the result of a complex selection procedure by Control Commission staff which also involved confidential talks with German economic and industrial experts. Although there was no consultation with German zonal authorities or with German politicians, at regional level there was close cooperation between the Military Government and the Land economics departments with the aim of selecting plants for dismantling so as to cause the minimum of dislocation for the economy.[80]

The CCG drew up comprehensive plans before the publication of the dismantling list to deal with possible resistance. Since Mili-

77. PRO/FO 371/65213/CJ2682, Haviland to private secretary to Bevin, 20 November 1947.
78. Ibid.
79. That the lack of competition from the German economy did indeed provide a breathing-space for British industry until 1950 or 1952 is confirmed by A. Cairncross, *Years of Recovery. British Economic Policy 1945-51* (Methuen, London, 1985), p. 132.
80. Interview between the author and W. Kägeler (formerly official in the Department of Economics, Hamburg), 25 April 1983. See also 'Bericht über die am 7.5.1948 stattgefundene Mitgliederversammlung des Wirtschaftsverbandes Maschinenbau, Teil A, Ausführungen von Dipl.-Ing. Kägeler, Amt für Wirtschaft . . .', Staatsarchiv Hamburg, Vorstandsakten Blohm & Voss, K793 U20 I, and PRO/FO1014/811, discussions with Senator Borgner.

tary Government was dependent on the cooperation of the Germans for carrying out dismantling, a number of strategies were laid down in advance, ranging from peaceful persuasion of workers by the unions and the German authorities, via the direction of labour, to the combatting of mass disturbances.[81] At the end of September 1947 Robertson informed the Foreign Office that he was sceptical about the chances of carrying out dismantling successfully. The mood in Germany was, he said, extremely bad. Under these circumstances the programme of dismantling could not be implemented. It would not be possible to persuade German politicians to accept the list.[82] But Robertson's pessimism turned out to be misplaced.

The announcement of the dismantling list was accompanied with a considerable public relations effort. Robertson's speech to the press and his radio broadcast (in German) were discussed beforehand in the Foreign Office and carefully edited.[83] The British authorities closely monitored the German reaction to the publication of the list. The overall impression, the CCG noted with relief, was that the list was not as bad as expected. The SPD was not opposed to the dismantling of war plants, but expressed its concern over the economic effects of the dismantling of other factories. The CDU recognised Germany's moral obligation to pay some form of reparation, but doubted whether the remaining industrial capacity would be sufficient to maintain a modest standard of living.[84] The leading German politicians in fact did 'accept' the dismantling programme. Although the Zonal Advisory Council (the German representative body in the British Zone broke off its session as a protest, there was no response to a call for an extraordinary meeting to discuss the issue.[85] The Länder acquiesced in the matter and soon began formalised cooperation with the CCG in the form of 'Anglo-German Mixed Commissions' which were set up in each of the four regions of the Zone. These commissions embraced the CCG departments concerned with dismantling, German politicians, officials, and representatives of the unions and of the chambers of industry

81. PRO/FO371/65209/CJ1498, Robertson to the Regional Commissioners, 14 August 1947.
82. PRO/FO371/65209/CJ1645, telegram from Robertson (Lübbecke) to FO, 23 September 1947.
83. PRO/FO371/65210/CJ1760.
84. PRO/FO371/65211/CJ2007, Military Governor Berlin to FO, 17 October 1947.
85. *Akten zur Vorgeschichte der Bundesrepublik Deutschland*, ed. Bundesarchiv and the Institut für Zeitgeschichte (Oldenbourg, Munich and Vienna, 1982), Vol. 3, p. 674.

and commerce. They had limited powers to exchange plants on the list for others of equal reparations value, but had no powers to intervene in the dismantling of armaments plants. Their main task was to schedule dismantling in order to minimise the disruption to industry and labour.

Dismantling of factories deemed surplus to the economy as laid down in the Revised Plan began in most cases in early 1948; dismantling of war plants (198 in the British Zone) had in the main begun in 1947 and was nearing completion. Regional differences in the structure of industry meant that dismantling had varying economic, social and political consequences: workers made redundant by dismantling in the city-states Hamburg and Bremen were normally able (before the currency reform in June 1948) to find alternative work, whereas employment in small industrial towns in Lower Saxony and North Rhine-Westphalia often depended on a single factory due for dismantling. According to a survey by the Deutscher Städtetag in November 1947, 49,857 jobs were expected to be lost through dismantling, but only 10,883 workers were expected to remain without employment.[86] It is therefore not surprising that dismantling in Hamburg proceeded smoothly, and that Hamburg remained peaceful even when the shipyard Blohm & Voss was entirely dismantled in 1948 and 1949. By contrast, dismantling in the Ruhr area and in Lower Saxony led to open confrontation and violent clashes between protesting workers and dismantling teams in which police and troops had to intervene.

But apart from differing re-employment prospects, there are three other reasons why dismantling in Hamburg produced less conflict than in Lower Saxony and the Ruhr area. First, dismantling in Hamburg was carried out by the firms' own employees, which meant that there were no opportunities for tension between dismantlers and the former workforce. Secondly, cooperation between the British and the German authorities was particularly effective. This was based on mutual trust originating in the many attempts made by the Hamburg Military Government to defend the interests of the region's economy. Thirdly, differences in economic structure meant that dismantling in Hamburg and Schleswig-Holstein was completed more rapidly than in the rest of the British Zone. Dismantling in Hamburg was largely completed by the end of 1948.

86. Staatsarchiv Hamburg, Senatskanzlei II 039.26–2, Vol. 3, No. 2, 'Finanzielle Auswirkungen der Demontage. Ergebnisse einer Rundfrage vom 10 November 1947 vom Deutschen Städtetag'.

The dismantling of the large steel works in North Rhine-Westphalia and Lower Saxony only began in 1948, and thus coincided with the politicisation of dismantling.

Until the summer of 1948, dismantling ran smoothly throughout the zone, mainly because the German people were preoccupied with other issues: the lack of food, the black market, and mounting east–west tensions. For Walter Schmid, the official responsible for the dismantling question in the Bizonal Verwaltung für Wirtschaft (VfW), this was an unsatisfactory situation, but although he criticised his superiors for their lack of action, there was no intervention in dismantling politics. For example, Hermann Pünder, the director of the VfW, refused a request from Schmid to raise the question of dismantling politics in his talks with the Military Governors on 14 April 1948.[87] Schmid even threatened to resign over the neglect of his subject, but to no avail.[88] Only after the currency reform did German politicians take up the issue. On 25 June 1948, Ludwig Erhard raised the question in a discussion with Roger Stevens, the Assistant Under-Secretary of State in the Foreign Office, proposing the replacement of dismantling with reparations from current production.[89] A few days later Pünder submitted a memorandum to Clay and Robertson whose title, 'Demontagen und ERP', signified the direction the anti-dismantling campaign now took. Politicians, officials, and industrial consultants turned to contacts in the Congress, the Marshall Plan administration and in US business circles to try and have the programme of dismantling reduced.[90]

It was fortunate for the German campaign to influence Anglo-American dismantling politics that it coincided with the growing tendency of the economic and political imperatives of the Marshall Plan and of the Cold War to become the determining factors of US foreign policy. The campaign also coincided with the general politicisation of West Germany as the antagonisms between the parties became ever clearer after the currency reform. As the first Federal

87. Bundesarchiv, Koblenz (BA) Z35/289 No. 132, Note on discussions between Schmid and Kutscher, Verwaltung für Wirtschaft, Höchst, 26 February 1948; see also BA, B102/3883.
88. Ibid.
89. BA B102/3883, note (28 June 1948) on discussion with Stevens on 25 June 1948. Stevens replied that there would be no change in the Level of Industry Plan and that the Allies had merely committed the error of not having implemented the plan in good time.
90. V. Berghahn, *Unternehmer und Politik in der Bundesrepublik* (Suhrkamp, Frankfurt on Main, 1985), pp. 80–2. The description of the contacts cultivated by Ruhr industrialists in the USA is one of the few merits of Ahrens, *Demontage*.

elections approached, politicians of all parties sought to make capital out of their opposition to dismantling, which by 1949 had come to be seen as a purely British activity. The increasing pressure exerted in winter 1947–48 by the Marshall Plan administration and some US congressmen, then by the US Military Government in Germany and finally in 1949 by the US Department of State on the British government to stop dismantling did not go unnoticed by the German campaigners. However, the flood of protest notes, memoranda and resolutions had if anything negative consequences on British dismantling politics. Within the Foreign Office it was often stressed that yielding to German pressure would mean a loss of prestige, thus endangering occupation policy as a whole.[91]

This was the policy adhered to until September 1949, when Bevin became convinced that dismantling could no longer be carried out against the mounting tide of German opposition.[92] The French government was reluctant to abandon the dismantling programme, but showed willingness to compromise when Bevin and Acheson joined forces to persuade Schuman.[93] With the signing of the Petersberg Agreement in November 1949 by the three western powers and the new Federal German government, the dismantling programme was curtailed and during the course of 1950 it was ended.[94]

Conclusions

The economic losses sustained through dismantling can be assessed in several different ways. IARA distributed reparations from the western zones to the value of $524,745,599 in 1938 prices, of which $143,514,107 were accounted for by deliveries of industrial capital equipment.[95] Because of inflation, the 1938 dollar prices would have

91. Cf. e.g. PRO/FO/371/70933/CJ4645, D. Johnston (FO) to C. Mayhew MP, brief for a debate in the House of Commons on 22 September 1948. For the increasingly acrimonious dispute between the governments of Britain and the USA over reducing the extent of dismantling, see Cairncross, *Price of War*, pp. 180–9, and Bullock, *Ernest Bevin*, pp. 600, 620–1, 638–9, and 662–3.
92. Memorandum of conversation by Acheson, Washington, 15 September 1946, FRUS, Vol. 3, 1949, pp. 599–600.
93. Acheson to Schuman, 30 October 1949, FRUS, Vol. 3, 1949, pp. 622–5; Acheson to McCloy, 30 October 1949, ibid., pp. 625–6.
94. For the Petersberg Agreement see H. Lademacher and W. Mühlhausen (eds.), *Sicherheit, Kontrolle, Souveränität, Das Petersberger Abkommen vom 22, November 1949. Eine Dokumentation* (Verlag Kasseler Forschungen zur Zeitgeschichte, Melsungen, 1985).
95. Inter-Allied Reparation Agency, *Report of the Secretary-General for the Year 1951*, (Brussels, 1952), Statement I and Statement II.

to be more than doubled to reflect the 1951 price levels.[96] The 1951 reparation value of dismantled industrial equipment was thus approximately $287 million, or DM1.2 billion. However, IARA did not have the intention of identifying the losses to the German economy, but of providing guidelines for the distribution of reparations among the nineteen recipient nations; the reports of the Agency contain only the reparations values after depreciation according to a fixed formula. Both the market value and the replacement cost would have been somewhat higher. The reparations figures given by the Agency also did not include deliveries from the western zones to the Soviet Union and Poland.

In the 1950s the West German government computed the losses to the economy through reparations and came to the conclusion that the value of dismantled equipment (after depreciation, price basis 1938), amounted to RM 2 billion, or RM 2.96 billion at replacement cost.[97] The figure of RM2 billion, which is probably the most realistic estimate of losses through dismantling, represented a reduction of the gross fixed capital of West Germany in 1948 of 3.51%.[98] However, this figure has to be relativised: it should be seen in the light of new industrial investment from mid-1948 to 1950 of DM10.2 billion.[99]

Although dismantling itself thus represented a relatively minor loss to industry, the exact macro-economic loss is not easy to determine, since there were unquantifiable losses caused, first, by the production limits or prohibitions in certain industries. While the steel-production limits were already exceeded in 1950 and 1951, the restrictions on ship-building and shipping were strictly enforced by the Allied High Commission and remained an impediment for several more years.[100] Secondly, the rate of investment was undoubtedly affected adversely by dismantling: until the publication of the dismantling list in October 1947 industrialists were reluctant to invest in new plant if they did not know the fate of their factory.

96. Ibid., p. 18.
97. BA–ZwA B102/171465, Mindesttabellierung der Demontagekartei, Teilkartei A, Bundesamt für gewerbliche Wirtschaft 1.4.1958. Figures altered to exclude losses of ocean-going ships.
98. Gross fixed capital (Brutto–Anlage–Vermögen) in mid-1948 was approximately DM56 billion—calculated from the tables in K. Pritzkoleit, *Gott erhält die Mächtigen. Rück- und Rundblick auf den deutschen Wohlstand* (Karl Rauch, Düsseldorf, 1963), pp. 283 and 286–7.
99. Ibid., p. 283.
100. See R. Stödter, *Schicksalsjahre deutscher Seeschiffahrt 1945–1955* (Mittler, Herford, 1982).

However, the main reason for negative net investment in this period was not the fear of dismantling, but the lack of a firm currency. Counterbalancing these unquantifiable losses to the economy was the impulse dismantling gave to the modernisation of some factories through reinvestment in up-to-date machinery. However, such 'hidden benefits' of Allied dismantling policy are equally difficult to quantify; this area would require further research on a micro-economic basis.

By 1948, dismantling had become an anachronism. Although its economic parameters did not change fundamentally, British dismantling policy, which in 1945 and 1946 had been particularly 'liberal' in comparison with that of the Allies, was seen in 1949 as particularly restrictive. In the context of the Marshall Plan it made little economic sense, and in view of US hegemony in West Germany it was not capable of completion. The demand for 'economic security' from Germany, incongruous though it now seems in the context of the Marshall Plan and the Cold War, still had some meaning for the British government. After the end of the war, the British government had been the first to view the Soviet Union as the main potential aggressor in any future conflict in Europe. But the British did not go as far as the Americans in the conclusions to be drawn from this perception. In London, unlike in Washington, Germany in 1949 was still regarded as a potential menace to world peace.[101] The British government therefore sought to maintain medium-term measures of economic security and in March 1949 Bevin proposed that the industry restrictions and prohibitions remain in force for a further five years.[102] The chance of retaining a further breathing-space for British exports was implicit in this policy, even though this intention was never expressly stated by the decision-makers in the Foreign Office. In fact in March 1949 the Cabinet laid down that 'no aspect of reparations policy was to be influenced by considerations of protecting British industry against fair competition by the Germans'.[103] Although the industry restrictions were to remain in force for some time, the overriding consideration of British policy towards Germany was no longer security through negative economic measures, but through the economic,

101. See Bullock, *Ernest Bevin*, p. 663.
102. Douglas to Acheson 16 March 1949, FRUS, Vol. 3, 1949, p. 569.
103. Cabinet meeting 8 February 1949, CM 10 (49), cited in Bullock, *Ernest Bevin*, p. 663.

political, and military integration of West Germany into the west.[104]

104. PRO/CAB134/600, ORC (48)9, FO memorandum for the ORC 1 April 1948; PRO/CAB128/13, CM56 (48), Cabinet minutes, 16 August 1948; PRO/FO371/70603/C10710, memorandum Kirkpatrick, 25 November 1948, cited in Steininger, *Deutsche Geschichte*, Vol. 2, p. 298.

6

Allied–German Negotiations on the Deconcentration of the West German Steel Industry
Isabel Warner

The early phase of the Allied occupation of Germany from 1945 to 1949 has been the subject of a vast amount of valuable historical research.[1] The *limbo* period, that is, the transition from full occupation to full sovereignty, of the early 1950s, remains, however, to a large extent under-researched, a state of affairs that is rapidly being remedied due to the increasing availability of archival material for this period.[2] In this context an analysis of the negotiations that took place between the Allied High Commission (AHC) and the Federal government from January 1950 to March 1951 leading to a deconcentration settlement for the West German steel industry can help shed light both on Allied differences over occupation policy and the Federal Republic's *Staatswerdung*. With the formation of the Federal government in September 1949, West Germany emerged as a formal, but by no means sovereign state, since it was still subject to Allied control. Yet in terms of a European economic reconstruction and in view of the political and military realities of the Cold War it became ever more obvious to the western Allies that the Federal Republic would have to be incorporated into the western bloc. This realisation accorded the Germans a certain room for manoeuvre and the Federal Republic became more of a political actor in its own—

1. See Chapter 12.
2. See W. Benz, *Die Gründung der Bundesrepublik. Von der Bizone zum souveränen Staat* (Deutscher Taschenbuch Verlag, Munich, 1984); M. Knapp (ed.), *Von der Bizonengründung zur ökonomisch-politischen Westintegration* (Haag & Herchen Verlag, Frankfurt on Main, 1984); H. Guldin, 'Aussenwirtschafts-politische und aussenpolitische Einflussfaktoren im Prozess der Staatswerdung der Bundesrepublik Deutschland 1947–52', *Aus Politik und Zeitgeschichte*, B32/87, 1987, pp. 3–20; L. Herbst (ed.), *Westdeutschland 1945–55. Unterwerfung, Kontrolle Integration* (Oldenbourg, Munich, 1986).

albeit still limited—right. As the deconcentration of the steel industry was one of the last outstanding issues of the Allied occupation
and given that a German government would have a great interest in
the fate of its country's basic industry, an Allied–German dialogue
was largely inevitable.

For the sake of clarity, the argument in this chapter can be
summarised as follows:

(i) From January to September 1950 the dialogue was rather
one-sided since the Federal government was not able to produce common, concrete deconcentration proposals. The Allies
in turn, had difficulties deciding on the modalities of a deconcentration law.

(ii) By linking two separate issues, that is to say the deconcentration of the steel industry (which dated from the *restrictive* phase
of the occupation) and the Schuman Plan (which was a feature
of the post-1949 phase centering around the necessity for
European integration) the Federal government was able to
forge diverse German interests into a united front and hence
exert pressure on the Allies to revise their deconcentration
plans. In this way the best deconcentration settlement possible
under the circumstances was achieved. This in turn acted as a
precondition for domestic approval of the Schuman Plan which
marked an important step forward on the path to German
sovereignty.

Naturally this whole process was not without its difficulties, nor
was it without repercussions on the Allied side:

(i) The French, who had initiated the Schuman Plan, were able to
gain greater influence over the deconcentration.

(ii) The Americans were able to out-manoeuvre the British whose
concept of deconcentration they did not share, at the same time
achieving their aim of binding the Federal Republic to western
Europe.

(iii) Finally the British, whose influence had declined steadily,
found themselves compelled to endorse a deconcentration
agreement they had had no part in negotiating, for fear of being
made responsible for the failure of the Schuman Plan.

Before turning to the negotiations *per se*, it is necessary to take a
brief look at initial Allied deconcentration policy in order to determine the scenario that presented itself to the nascent German
government in late 1949.

Initial Allied Deconcentration Measures 1945–9

There was general agreement among the Allies in the immediate post-war period that Germany should never again be in a position to endanger world peace. To this end Article 12 of the Potsdam Agreement of August 1945 stipulated that 'the German economy shall be decentralised for the purpose of eliminating the present excessive concentrations of economic power as exemplified in particular by cartels, syndicates, trusts and other monopolistic arrangements'. In view of the importance of the steel industry within a war economy and considering that 78% of German crude steel production was controlled by six steel concerns located in the Ruhr—*die Waffenschmiede des Reiches*—the deconcentration of the steel industry was bound to rank high on the list of Allied priorities.[3] It was, however, to take a full year before first steps in this direction were taken. This was largely due to Allied inability to agree on a four-power law prohibiting excessive concentrations of economic power. Discussions on the law, which was to cover all areas of the economy where concentrations were manifest, that is, the chemical industry,[4] the banking sector,[5] as well as the coal and steel industries, had started in October 1945. Deadlock was soon reached over the question of what constituted an excessive concentration and whether the law should be mandatory or not.[6] This prompted the British, in whose zone the bulk of the steel industry was located, to take unilateral action.

On the 20 August 1946 the British Military Governor informed his colleagues on the Allied Control Council (ACC) that he had taken control of the steel industry in his zone. The North German Iron and Steel Control (NGISC) was established as the controlling body for the steel industry. It was to be advised in its task of

3. The six concerns in question were the Vereinigte Stahlwerke AG, Fried. Krupp, Hoesch-Werke AG, Klöckner-Werke AG, Gutehoffnungshütte AG and the Mannesmann AG.
4. For Allied deconcentration policy in the chemical industry see R. Stokes, 'Recovery and Resurgence in the West German Chemical Industry: Allied Policy and the IG Farben Successor Companies 1945–51', PhD thesis, Ohio State University, 1986.
5. For Allied deconcentration policy in the banking sector see T. Horstmann, 'Alliierte Bankenpolitik nach dem Zweiten Weltkrieg in Westdeutschland. Neuordnung und Rekonzentration der deutschen Grossbanken 1945–56', PhD thesis, Ruhr-Universität Bochum, 1986.
6. When Law No. 78 was finally promulgated in the British Zone in February 1947 it had already been overtaken by developments in the deconcentration of the steel industry, which was thus exempted from its purview.

planning and executing the deconcentration by a German body, the Treuhandverwaltung (TV). Deconcentration guidelines were set out in a plan by the Metallurgy Branch of the British Element of the Control Commission of July 1946.[7] Hereby the vertical complexes in the steel industry were to be split up through the complete segregation from the former steel combines of those plants that were to remain in production. Despite war damage and dismantling of plants scheduled for reparations, steel capacity was still in excess of the 5.8 million tons per annum permitted by the Level of Industry Plan of March 1946. The old concerns were to be liquidated and no return to vertical integration under single management was to be permitted. Under no circumstances was the property to be returned to the former owners. The finances of these plants—henceforth called steel unit companies—were to be organised in such a way as to facilitate transfer to public ownership in whatever manifestation was ultimately chosen. There was, however, no doubt in the British mind that socialisation was the most desirable option.[8]

By late November the NGISC had produced a plan and 'Operation Severance', as it came to be known, was launched in January 1947. The first four unit companies went into operation on the 1 March. In line with the British aim of socialising the basic industries of the Ruhr, the supervisory boards of the new companies comprised five representatives from management and the labour force respectively. An eleventh man, a member of the TV, made up the picture. Thus, in effect, the British had instituted codetermination in the German steel industry. By 1948 twenty-four unit companies had been segregated out of the eight major steel combines in the British Zone, representing four-fifths of the iron and steel plant in West Germany. The right to use the assets of the former combines was witnessed by a *Betriebsbenutzungsvertrag*, a leasing agreement. Each segregated company was capitalised at RM 100,000 and working capital was to be obtained from private and public funds.

Meanwhile the British socialisation programme for the basic industries of the Ruhr was encountering numerous setbacks.[9] After

7. Public Record Office (PRO) /F0371/71143A/CK503, memorandum on the control of the german iron and steel industries, 6 July 1946.
8. R. Steininger, 'Die Rhein-Ruhr-Frage im Kontext britischer Deutschlandpolitik 1945–46' in H. A. Winkler (ed.), *Politische Weichenstellungen in Nachkriegsdeutschland 1945–53* (Vandenhoeck & Ruprecht, Göttingen, 1979), pp. 41–166.
9. R. Steininger, 'Reform und Realität. Ruhrfrage und Sozialisierung in der anglo-amerikanischen Deutschlandpolitik 1947–48', *Vierteljahreshefte für Zeitgeschichte*, (VfZ), Vol. 27, No. 2, 1979, pp. 172ff. See also H. Lademacher, 'Die

settling internal differences over the modalities of the programme, the government proceeded in February 1947 to initiate its first phase, that is, the appointment of trustees. This drew instant protests from the French and the Benelux governments, who felt that this posed a risk to their security. There was also concern over its effect on foreign-owned property in the Ruhr. Thus the British were forced to defer the appointment of trustees by the end of the month.[10] In view of the creation of the Bizone, in which Britain became the junior partner due to its increasing financial difficulties, the Americans were able to gain greater influence over the fate of the Ruhr industries. As they maintained that a deconcentration of the steel industry could only take place while maintaining a framework of private enterprise within the Ruhr,[11] the outlook for the British policy of socialisation was bleak.

While there was agreement within the US administration that cartels should be destroyed, differences existed over the extent of deconcentration that should take place. These differences bear investigation since they did on occasion carry over into Germany and influence events there. This was essentially a dispute between two factions. The first group, known as the trust-busters, was centred in the US Treasury and Justice Departments. It advocated that the Ruhr steel concerns be broken down into small units that would pose no risk to Allied security, nor present a future competition for Allied industry. Against this was set a second group representing business interests with good contacts within the US Military Government in Germany. It was intent on merely curtailing the quasi-monopolistic position of certain steel concerns, permitting relatively large units which would serve the envisaged economic recovery of Europe.[12]

The fact that most of General Clay's advisers in the Economic Division of the US Military Government were from this second group was reflected in the American criticism of Operation Severance. The Americans felt that it had led to the creation of companies that were economically unsound and not capable of competing in a world market for steel products. Moreover, they maintained that

britische Sozialisierungspolitik im Rhein-Ruhr-Raum 1945 bis 1948' in C. Scharf and H.-J. Schröder (eds.), *Die Deutschlandpolitik Grossbritanniens und die britische Zone 1945–49* (Franz Steiner Verlag, Wiesbaden, 1979), pp. 51–92.

10. Steininger, 'Reform und Realität', p. 186.
11. V. Berghahn, *Unternehmer und Politik in der Bundesrepublik* (Suhrkamp Verlag, Frankfurt on Main, 1985), p. 96.
12. Ibid., pp. 88ff.

the nature of the German steel industry was such as to necessitate a degree of vertical integration in order to defray the high costs of extracting steel from the Ruhr ores. Finally, they objected to the fact that the issue of the title to the steel concerns remained clouded as the ensuing uncertainty was having a negative effect on labour productivity and the procurement of loans for capital investments.[13] Consequently, the British and Americans attempted to iron out their differences in the formulation of a bipartite law on the re-organisation of Germany's coal, iron and steel industries.

The British accepted the American contention that only a re-presentative, freely-elected German government should decide whether the ultimate ownership of the steel industry should be private or public. This point was firmly anchored in the Preamble to Law No. 75. Thus British socialisation policy was effectively deferred—though not precluded—as the British were not prepared to sanction any act, such as the sale of new stock, that would settle the ownership issue in favour of private ownership. In addition, the British added the proviso that persons having furthered the ag-gressive designs of the Nazi Party were not to be permitted to return to positions of control within the industry. The Americans in turn did not approve the British concept of total reorganisation, which they felt would disturb property rights to a greater extent than was necessary for the purposes of deconcentration.[14] These underlying differences were not solved by the promulgation of Law No. 75 on the 10 November 1948.

On the reorganisation of the steel industry, the law foresaw that the assets seized by Military Government, listed in a number of schedules accompanying the law, should be handed over to a Steel Trustee Association (STA), a German body appointed by the Allies. It was eventually appointed in August 1949, but did not proceed beyond the exploratory stage in its task of devising deconcentration plans for quite some time. When the French joined the Bizone the new bipartite Steel Group was renamed the Combined Steel Group (CSG). The inclusion of the French made it necessary to *harmonise* Law No. 75, making its implementation a function of the AHC, which had succeeded Military Government in June 1949. To the

13. OMGUS Special Report to the Military Governor, 'The Ownership and Control of the Ruhr Industries', November 1948, pp. 1–4.
14. H. G. Schmidt, 'The Reorganisation of the West German Coal and Iron and Steel Industries under the Allied High Commission for Germany 1945–52', Office of the US High Commissioner, Historical Division, September 1952, pp. 18–20.

existing differences between the British and American conceptions, the French added their traditional fear of a powerful steel industry concentrated in the hands of a hostile German government, which found expression in their vehement objection to the ownership clause in the Preamble to Law No. 75. The only tangible results of five years of occupation as regards the deconcentration of the steel industry were thus twenty-four unit companies whose viability was in dispute, and an inability on the part of the Allies to agree on a framework for the industry's reorganisation.

German Attempts to Initiate a Deconcentration Dialogue

The initial problem facing the Federal government was that of gaining access to the deconcentration process. This was after all an area of policy for which Article 2b of the Occupation Statute of April 1949 reserved the Allies special powers, even if Article 4 did state that the Federal government could, after prior notification of the Allies, take measures and pass legislation in this field, as long as this did not conflict with Allied measures. In view of mounting rumours that the Allies were thinking of revising Law No. 75, Ludwig Erhard, Minister of Economics, raised the issue with Chancellor Adenauer in late 1949. He argued that while the Federal government was responsible for the eventual decision on the owner-ship of the steel industry, it was impossible to deal with this question in isolation from that of the reorganisation. Thus responsi-bility for the deconcentration should be transferred to the govern-ment, whereby the AHC would retain its powers of control in accordance with Article 2b. The CSG and the Combined Coal Control Group were, however, to be stripped of their executive powers of control. The STA and the Deutsche Kohlenbergbau-Leitung (DKBL) were to be put at the government's disposal in an advisory capacity. Erhard proposed to start immediately with the elaboration of a legal solution for the ownership issue and simul-taneously initiate deconcentration plans.[15] In a note of 22 January 1950 Adenauer suggested action along these lines to the AHC.

Not surprisingly the CSG's reaction was that the note was 'a clever move in a campaign to destroy Law No. 75'. It recommended a rejection of Adenauer's offer, feeling that 'any reorganisation by

15. Bundesarchiv (BA)/B102/17184, Erhard an Adenauer, 22 December 1949.

the German Government would be subject to political pressure embarrassing both to itself and the AHC'.[16] There was concern that the former owners would try to circumvent deconcentration through the government. Rising concern within industrial circles on the uncertainty over the reorganisation had indeed produced a number of proposals.[17] Yet Erhard conceded that most of them were rather one-sided, concentrating on the ownership question, whereas a viable economic settlement hinged on a solution that was technically operational.[18] The government's claim that the STA's expert advice be put at its disposal should be viewed in this context. Heeding the CSG's advice, the AHC informed Adenauer that it was preparing its own plans for the revision of Law No. 75. The government had to content itself with the prospect of an advisory role in the implementation of the law. Finally, the AHC showed itself willing to accept any proposals the government might wish to make, but did point out that it also intended to consult other German interests.[19] There could be no better indication that the Allies were not prepared to relinquish the opportunity of reorganising the German steel industry in accordance with their own views. Nor were they prepared to let the Germans decide the divisive issue of ownership before actual deconcentration plans had been drafted and approved, thus ensuring the continuity of Allied policy.[20] Yet, the Federal government for its part was going to have difficulties elaborating concrete deconcentration proposals for quite some time.

The second problem facing the Federal government in this initial period was the need for a common German approach. As the AHC had indicated, it was also consulting other German organisations, most notably the Deutsche Gewerkschaftsbund (DGB). This is not surprising in view of the unions' traditional links with the British

16. Schmidt, 'Reorganisation', p. 48.
17. BA B102/17184, Lehr an Erhard, 7 November 1949. The proposal by Robert Lehr, a member of the Executive Board of the Vereinigte Stahlwerke, was representative of industrial thinking of the time. He claimed that the immunity of private property would have to be guaranteed under deconcentration and advocated solving the ownership question by exchanging shares in the old companies for shares in the new steel unit companies.
18. BA B102/133877, Erhard an Adenauer, 23 February 1950.
19. PRO/F0371/85691/CE987, McCloy to Adenauer, 23 February 1950.
20. PRO/F3071/85690/CE581, General Macready (Office of the British Economic Adviser) to R. B. Stevens, 6 February 1950. 'To my mind it is of vital importance that we should not allow the Germans to legislate on the deconcentration of German industry as appears to be suggested by the Chancellor, and above all we should not allow them to settle the question of ultimate ownershp until a plan of deconcentration has actually been drawn up and approved.'

dating from the early occupation period. The DGB, which favored a reorganisation in terms of public ownership with strong trade union participation,[21] must also have appeared a more amenable partner for discussion, having stated in November 1949 that despite reservations it saw in Law No. 75 the possibility for constructive new beginnings. However, this ran counter to Adenauer's efforts to concentrate all contacts with the AHC in the government,[22] and could only serve to erode the government's status as the legitimate German representative. Further, this practice would detract from the weight of any future proposals the government was to submit, as Erhard pointed out to the Chancellor in March 1950.[23] The government was dismayed to learn how well informed the DGB was on Allied plans for the revision of Law No. 75—the same plans that it had so far been denied an insight to.[24] Thus the DGB's claim that the French High Commissioner intended to delete that part of the Preamble referring to German responsibility for the ownership decision,[25] prompted severe protests to the AHC. Adenauer was finally granted a meeting with the High Commissioners on the 5 April 1950 to discuss the redrafting of Law No. 75. German fears that the only tangible concession acquired on deconcentration was about to be lost, were allayed. However, Adenauer was informed that there were doubts within the AHC as to whether the ownership provision should remain completely unqualified, the fear having been expressed that it might be operated in such a way as to constitute a menace to security.[26]

Allied Differences on Law No. 27

Matters had rapidly come to a head within the AHC on the

21. BA B102/85690, Stellungnahme der Gewerkschaften zur Neuordnung der Grundstoffindustrien, 28 März 1950.
22. H. P. Schwarz, *Adenauer. Der Aufstieg: 1876–1952* (Deutsche Verlagsanstalt, Stuttgart, 1986), pp. 672–3.
23. BA B102/133877, Erhard an Adenauer, 18 März 1950.
24. BA B102/17184, Vermerk über eine Besprechung mit dem Vertreter und dem General Counsel des Amerikanischen Hohen Kommissars am 21 Januar 1950, 24 Januar 1950. 'Mr McClain erwiderte, dass dem deutschen Wunsche auf Einsichtnahme in die alliierten Gesetzentwürfe nicht entsprochen werden könne. Die Hohen Kommissare seien jedoch bereit, der Bundesregierung die beabsichtigten Pläne bekanntzugeben, sobald die deutsche Bundesregierung den Hohen Kommissaren Vorschläge für eine deutsche Mitwirkung unterbreitet hätte.'
25. BA B102/17184, Aktenvermerk von Herrn Bomke, 27 Februar 1950.
26. PRO/FO371/85694/CE1603, telegram from Wahnerheide to Foreign Office, 6

ownership clause. While giving ground gradually on other points involved in the revision of the law, the British had held their position on the Preamble. The French, on the other hand, were just as obdurate in their insistence that the provision should be deleted. In late March the French Ambassador had called on the Foreign Office to propose a compromise, whereby the clause was to be removed from the Preamble and instead each High Commissioner was to make a declaration of intent. M. Massigli was informed in no uncertain terms that there was no prospect of the British agreeing to 'any such rather shabby solution'.[27] While sympathetic to French security fears, the Americans felt bound by their earlier acceptance of Law No. 75. When the issue came up at the AHC Council meeting of 14 April 1950, the French High Commissioner made good on his earlier threats and appealed to his government on the majority decision. Since the British government did not feel the need to raise the issue at the forthcoming Council of Foreign Ministers in London, a veto in Germany was the only recourse left to the French. Under the Agreement on Tripartite Controls action was automatically suspended for thirty days. At the end of that period the law would be operative unless stopped by action at government level. As it transpired the French government made no formal protest. Instead the French High Commissioner was instructed not to sign the law, but to arrange that it should be promulgated by the Chairman of the AHC. As a result the law, henceforth known as Law No. 27, became effective as of 16 May 1950.

This incident is of particular interest in view of the fact that a week earlier the French Foreign Minister, Robert Schuman, had made his proposal for the creation of a European Coal and Steel Community (ECSC).[28] It seems paradoxical that the French should invite the German government to pool its coal and steel industries with those of France, while at the same time attempting to deny it the right to decide the eventual ownership of these industries. There is doubtless a lot of truth in the Foreign Office speculation that the proposal was motivated by the French realisation that it was impossible to perpetuate the existing restrictions on the German steel level.[29] Furthermore, fundamental elements of French policy towards Germany were in danger of being overtaken by current

April 1950.
27. PRO/F0371/85693/CE1488, Kirkpatrick to Lord Henderson, 28 March 1950.
28. For the text of the Schuman Proposal of 9 May 1950 see *Foreign Relations of the United States* (FRUS), Vol. 3, 1950, pp. 692–4.
29. R. Bullen (ed.), *Documents on British Policy Overseas: The Schuman Plan, the*

developments with no hope of compensation. German steel production was higher than that of France[30] and this was silently accepted by the Americans despite the projected steel surplus for 1953. Washington and London were favourably disposed towards German rearmament, at least in principle.[31] Finally, the Americans, who had come to the conclusion that the problem of Germany's economic potential concentrated in the Ruhr could only be solved in a European framework, had been urging France to take steps in this direction for quite some time.[32] The proposal was thus more than a selfless visionary gesture on the part of France. Indeed, the head of the French Planning Commissariat, Jean Monnet, had pointed to the central question of the control of Germany's economic potential and competitive capacity in an internal memorandum of 3 May, which had served as a basis for the proposal.[33] As concerns the timing of the proposal, Schuman admitted to the Foreign Office that it was intended to deflect the otherwise embarrassing wrath of the French parliament over the anticipated defeat on the Preamble to Law No. 27. He ended on a jocular note, expressing the hope that at some time in the near future the French and the British might be aligned in a majority against the Americans.[34] However, events were to show that the exact opposite was to take place. While the British had decided early on not to join this new European venture, the Americans viewed it favourably. Dean Acheson soon overcame his initial suspicion that it was intended as a supercartel in line with the European tradition for cartel agreements, which were an anathema to the Americans.[35] The fact remains that the commencement of the Schuman Plan negotiations on the 20 June 1950 marked a new phase for the deconcentration of the steel industry, as the French had created a new frame-

---

Council of Europe and Western European Integration, May 1950–December 1952 (HMSO, London, 1986), Series II, Vol. 1, p. 56, Foreign Office minute from Rickham to Lincoln, 15 May 1950. The permitted level of German steel production had been increased from 10.7 million tons per annum in August 1947 to 11.1 million tons per annum in April 1949.

30. Bericht der Stahltreuhändervereinigung, *Die Neuordnung der Eisen- und Stahlindustrie im Gebiet der Bundesrepublik Deutschland* (C. H. Beck, Berlin and Munich, 1954), p. 3. West Germany (not including the Saar) had a crude steel production of 38.2% in 1950 as compared with 27.3% for France.
31. Schwarz, *Adenauer*, p. 732.
32. FRUS, Vol. 3, 1949 pp. 622–5, letter from Acheson to Schuman, 30 October 1949.
33. G. Ziebura, *Die deutsch–französischen Beziehungen seit 1945. Mythen und Realitäten* (Neske, Pfullingen, 1970), pp. 195–200.
34. PRO/F0371/85696/CE2288, memorandum by Kirkpatrick, 18 May 1950.
35. J. Monnet, *Mémoirs* (Fayard, Paris, 1976), pp. 356–7.

work within which to deal with the German problem. A problem whose solution was made all the more pressing for the Americans by the onset of the Korean War five days later. This framework was, however, to become increasingly linked with the deconcentration of the steel industry under Law No. 27.

A German Proposal Emerges

The promulgation on the 14 September 1950 of Regulation No. 1 to Law No. 27, which decreed the liquidation of the six major steel combines in the Ruhr, placed Adenauer in an extremely delicate, position. It only served to emphasize that the advisory role promised the Federal government had not materialised. On the other hand, it was becoming increasingly difficult to explain to the German public and parliament that while the German delegation in Paris was supposedly taking part in the ECSC negotiations as an equal,[36] the Allies could reorganise those industries whose future integration was being decided without consulting the Federal government. These considerations prompted the Office of the Chancellor to reconsider the German approach.[37] It was recognised that as the AHC could not be expected to abandon deconcentration, it was necessary to influence the form it would take. Yet if the steel industry was to remain competitive within the framework of the ECSC, it would have to retain a measure of *Verbundwirtschaft*— vertical integration with coal. Therefore it was necessary to overcome persistant opposition to integration in order to arrive at a common German position on the number of steel companies to be created and the extent of their vertical integration, before starting negotiations with the Allies. The immediate result of the linkage between the Schuman Plan and deconcentration was the unremitting pressure exerted on the Ministry of Economics in the following months to produce the relevant proposals. To this end the Cabinet issued a deadline for a preliminary framework of proposals by mid-October.

When these proposals arrived they were very limited indeed. They did not satisfy Adenauer, who felt that the Ministry of

---

36. For an account of the Schuman Plan negotiations see W. Diebold, *The Schuman Plan. A Study in Economic Cooperation 1950–59* (Frederick A. Praeger, New York, 1959), pp. 60ff.
37. BA B136/2456, Vermerk von Dr Rust, 25 September 1950.

Economics could have played a more active role in deconcentration,[38] and called for new proposals by the end of the month. By deciding early on that it was preferable to aim for a cooperation with the STA, rather than to risk lagging even further behind the Allies in the formulation of deconcentration plans by wasting time finding its own experts,[39] the Ministry of Economics had placed itself in an intractable situation. As the STA felt compelled to adhere to the CSG's order not to permit the government an insight into its reorganisation plans, the Ministry of Economics had to rely on information from the black market regarding these plans.[40] However, Erhard's pressure on the AHC to relax this stricture finally paid off and a meeting with the STA took place on the 26 October. Thus the Ministry of Economics was able to coordinate its proposals for steel unit companies with those of the STA.[41]

Now all that stood in the way of a German proposal was the unresolved question of *Verbundwirtschaft*. This problem was tackled the following day in the course of discussions, chaired by the Ministry of Economics, between representatives from the STA, the DKBL, the former steel concerns and the mining unions. Whereas in the past the majority of Germany's coal mines had been controlled by the steel industry, Heinrich Kost, the head of the DKBL, who came from the independent mining industry, intended to use the reorganisation to free the coal industry from this historical domination. In this he was supported by the miners' union, the IG Bergbau. Differences emerged rapidly, with the DKBL maintaining that even if coal mines were to be linked with steelworks, they would have to remain independent in the sense that the steel industry did not try to influence their economic policy. Further the captive mines were also to be subject to the DKBL's reorganisation plan for the coal industry. The representatives of the former steel concerns were willing to forego that part of their mining property not essential to the domestic supply of their steelworks within the framework of reorganisation. If principles governing vertical integration were to be established, however, they should only apply to

38. U. Enders and K. Reiser (eds.) *Die Kabinettsprotokolle der Bundesregierung*, Vol. 2 (Harald Boldt Verlag, Boppard, 1982), pp. 423–4.
39. BA B102/17184, Vermerk von Dr Risse, 17 April 1950.
40. BA B102/60661, Vermerk über die Tätigkeit des Bundeswirtschaftsministeriums auf dem Gebiet der Entflechtung, 21 Oktober 1950.
41. BA B102/60661, Vermerk über die Besprechung am 26 Oktober im Bundeswirtschaftsministerium mit den Herren der Stahltreuhändervereinigung, 30 Oktober 1950.

the latter mines. In the midst of all this the Ministry of Economics repeatedly tried to fashion some form of consensus. Agreement was finally reached on the fact that although in the past more than 50% of coal output had been controlled by the steel industry, the figure in terms of actual requirements was nearer 25%. Yet the DKBL felt unable to endorse the principle that where coal was needed by steelworks an ownership-type relationship—*eigentumsmässiger Verbund*—should also exist in those cases where steelworks were located at some distance from coalfields. When pushed on this point, it agreed reluctantly provided no more coal than was actually required was tied. The only source of general agreement was the dilemma posed by Germany's need for some form of vertical integration if it was to remain competitive within the framework of the ECSC.

The compromise reached after three hours of spirited discussion reflected the underlying disagreements. It was agreed that where steelworks were located near coalfields—*unmittelbarer technischer Verbund*—as was the case in the Hamborn, Oberhausen, Dortmund, Gelsenkirchen and Bochum areas, an ownership-type relationship should exist. On the other hand, the question of the economic necessity of such a relationship in cases not subject to these conditions was still under review. Finally, the coalmining companies were in all cases to be created as legally independent companies.[42] This last point went a long way towards fulfilling the DKBL's demands. The Ministry of Economics greeted this rather vague compromise enthusiastically, as it was finally able to send Adenauer German deconcentration proposals. The proposal on vertical integration was based on the agreement reached at the meeting of 27 October, although no individual coal mines were singled out for integration at this stage. Further, the creation of seventeen steel unit companies was recommended. This was followed by a list of five cases still under consideration. Although the plan was far from complete, the Cabinet decided to send it to the AHC post-haste to pre-empt the CSG's plan which was rumoured to be in the making. The High Commissioners passed the German plan of 3 November 1950 to the CSG for comment, which decided to incorporate the government's proposals into the plan it was elaborating in conjunction with the STA.

The CSG's plan was based on an outline presented by the

---

42. BA B102/60666, Stenographischer Bericht über die Sitzung im Bundesministerium für Wirtschaft, 27 Oktober 1950.

American Chairman to his French and British colleagues on the 18 October. It was motivated by his desire to achieve deconcentration in the shortest possible time in view of rumours concerning an imminent German proposal, and by the wish to remove the problem from German influence. Whereas the British were gratified that the plan was largely based on old British proposals for Operation Severance, they felt it was dangerous to exclude the Federal government from expressing its views at the proper time or from participating in the actual implementation of the reorganisation.[43] These views did not pass unnoticed among Britain's allies. The CSG's plan of 30 November 1950 called for the creation of twenty-nine steel unit companies and pointed out that as the Federal government's suggestions for the steel industry were based on the same work as those presented by the STA, it was not necessary to answer them in detail. The CSG approved sixteen of the seventeen companies proposed by the government and agreed to accord two further cases special treatment. Its plan then went on to examine the five remaining cases. Whereas the STA advocated creating six companies out of these assets, the CSG wanted to create eleven, maintaining that they would still be large enough to operate efficiently and competitively. On the 12 December 1950 the plan was approved by the Council of the AHC and sent to Adenauer. It was significant that it did not include proposals for the vertical integration of coal mines with steelworks, the Allies preferring to defer the issue until after the creation of the steel unit companies. The five cases subject to disagreement (see table 6.1) were to form the basis of discussions during the course of the following month. It was evident that the Federal government meant business, its delegation at the ECSC talks in Paris having requested an adjournment of the Conference in December so that a settlement on deconcentration could be reached with the Allies in Germany. By making progress on the Schuman Plan, and more specifically German acceptance of Articles 60 and 61 on cartels and concentrations,[44] dependent on an acceptable deconcentration settlement, the Germans were now in a position to bargain with the Allies.

43. PRO/F0371/85700/CE5842, monthly progress report no. 5 on the reorganisation of the coal and iron and steel industries, Office of the Economic Adviser, 20 November 1950; PRO/F0371/85701/CE6337, monthly progress report no. 6 on the reorganisation of the coal and iron and steel industries, Office of the Economic Adviser, 16 December 1950.
44. For the Schuman Plan negotiations on cartels and concentrations see Berghahn, *Unternehmer*, pp. 138–43.

Isabel Warner

Table 6.1 Differences between the CSG and STA proposals for steel unit companies as listed in the CSG plan of 30 November 1950

STA		CSG
1	Hüttenwerk Huckingen Wdt. Mannesmannröhrenwerke]	1
	Hüttenwerk Niederrhein Westfälische Union]	2
2	[Bochumer Verien [Wurag	3
3	⌐ Henrichshütte Huckingen]	
	Gussstahlwerk Witten	4
	Stahlwerke Bochum	5
4	Hüttenwerk Ruhrort-Meiderich	6
	Rheinische Röhrenwerke	7
5	Georgsmarienhütte Stahlwerke Osnabrück]	8
	Hüttenwerk Haspe	9
6	Dortmund Union	10
	Hüttenwerk Hörde	11

Source: Stahltreuhändervereinigung (1954), pp. 422–3.

Forging a Franco-American Alliance

With the adjournment of the ECSC Conference it became imperative for the French to act. Their main concern was to eliminate vertical integration in the German steel industry, which they felt provided for discriminatory practices. Under such a system steel producers were able to obtain coal from their subsidiaries at concealed prices and in times of coal shortages could receive preferential treatment to the detriment of other importers such as France. French dependence on German coal and coke supplies dated from the development, after 1890, of a large basic steel industry using minette ores. Minette ore was successfully smelted only with a large input of metallurgical coke. This came either in the form of German coke made from Ruhr coal or of suitable grades of Ruhr coking coals for transformation into coke in France.[45] As the International

45. A. S. Milward, *The Reconstruction of Western Europe 1945–51* (Methuen, London, 1984), p. 130. Milward does, however, point out that the precise extent of French import-needs from Germany never seems to have been

Authority for the Ruhr (IAR), which was set up in 1948 to determine the distribution of German coal and coke between domestic consumption and export, had not lived up to French expectations, they were looking for other possibilities to assure their needs.

When the French had raised the issue of *Verbundwirtschaft* back in September 1950 in the course of a meeting of the AHC's Economics Committee, in an attempt to sound out their allies, it had been agreed that vertical integration of coal and steel could only be authorised if specific technical reasons justified this. However, the US contention that the latitude left by this agreement subjected it to more or less liberal interpretation pending the position taken on the Ruhr coal-sales organisation, the Deutsche Kohlenverkauf (DKV),[46] was not reassuring. As the DKV's monopoly would put the steelworks on the defensive in terms of their coal supply, the Americans felt it might be necessary for them to own mines. The British, who had always opposed vertical integration, albeit for the very different reason that it impeded socialisation, were viewed unfavourably as too accommodating to the German desire to participate in deconcentration.[47] Thus French representatives in Germany concluded that they would have to abandon their more lenient approach to the DKV—based on the desire to facilitate control of the coal industry by the IAR—and join the Americans in their quest to dissolve it, in order to obtain US support on *Verbundwirtschaft*.[48] Furthermore, as the British upheld the German claim for retention of the DKV, the US would also be in need of an ally.[49]

This alliance was formalised during a meeting in Monnet's office on the 19 December 1950. It was agreed that the deconcentration programme under Law No. 27 was a necessary precondition for the achievement of the aims of the Schuman Plan and that the operation of the Schuman Plan would safeguard the objectives of deconcentration under Law No. 27.[50] This alliance is not altogether surprising. In early 1950 there was a fresh influx of personnel at the

accurately determined, as the whole issue seemed to have become entangled in the intricacies of international power politics.

46. The DKV was set up on the 4 February 1948 as a successor to the North German Coal Distribution Office. It regulated the sale of coal along the lines of the former syndicates.
47. Archives Nationales (AN) 81 AJ 138 télégramme de Francois-Poncet, 25 septembre 1950.
48. AN 81 AJ 137, note de Valery, 24 octobre 1950.
49. PRO/T230/182, minutes of a meeting in the Foreign Office re: Schuman Plan/Law No. 27, 29 January 1951.
50. AN 81 AJ 137, compte rendu d'une réunion le 19 déc. 1950 entre experts Américains et Français, 21 decembre 1950.

US High Commission. This was heralded suspiciously by the British as the 'arrival of trust-busting lawyers, angling to take over the work of deconcentration purely as a decartelisation measure'.[51] This appears to have been an after-effect of yet another clash between the two factions within the US administration, which erupted just before General Clay's departure from Germany in May 1949, in the course of which trust-busters in Germany had alerted Congress to the slow progress on deconcentration and decartelisation.[52] It is difficult to determine how this round was decided as Clay's successor, John McCloy, had connections in both camps and appears to have adopted a middle course. He was, however, flanked by trust-busting watchdogs. In addition, McCloy's long-standing friendship with Monnet probably also had a hand in facilitating this coalition.[53]

The details of the Franco-American alliance were worked out in a meeting between experts two days later. In return for supporting the Americans on the DKV, the French managed to secure their agreement that coal assets should be organised as separate legal entities which would sell to affiliated steel plants at market prices on invoice including taxes attributable to the transaction. Having accepted that a degree of vertical integration would be permitted, the French managed to eliminate the nuances in the American opinion as to how much coal would come under the control of the steel industry. The former American view that an amount *not to provide for the entire requirements* of the affiliated steelworks be permitted, was revised to read an amount *providing for substantially less than the entire needs*. Under these circumstances the French agreed to eight cases for which the Americans approved an integration. The Americans in turn accepted that coal output of mines owned by steelworks or subject to delivery contracts, would come under the emergency allocation powers of the High Authority to be created under the Schuman Plan. As regards the grouping of steel unit companies, it was decided that some concessions could be made to the Germans to secure their acceptance of deconcentration.[54] Thus the stage was set for in-depth negotiations with the Federal government.

51. PRO/F0371/85691/CE1016, Harris-Burland to Stevens, 27 February 1950.
52. Berghahn, *Unternehmer*, pp. 98–9.
53. J. Gillingham, 'Die französische Ruhrpolitik und die Ursprünge des Schuman Plans', *VfZ*, Vol. 35, No. 1, 1987, p. 21.
54. AN 81 AJ 137, note par le Président Français du Groupe Controle d'Acier, 22 decembre 1950.

Discussions on Steel Unit Companies

The first problem dealt with was that concerning the grouping of steel assets. On the 21 December 1950 a meeting was convened in the Ministry of Economics to prepare a German position on the five cases subject to disagreement with the CSG.[55] It was attended by representatives from the STA, the steel concerns and the DGB. The representative from the Ministry of Economics proceeded to outline the Federal government's position. A combination of the first set of plants into one company was advocated in order to provide the Westdeutsche Mannesmannröhrenwerke, which had lost certain assets through dismantling, with a broader economic base. The technical justification offered was that this combination would permit an exchange of its excess Martin steel with the excess Thomas steel of the Hüttenwerk Huckingen. For the second group of steelworks, which the STA wanted to separate into two companies, the Ministry of Economics recommended the creation of one company. This was the only case in which disagreement with the STA existed, based on the Ministry's contention that the Bochumer Verein would not be viable on its own. The combination of the Hüttenwerk Ruhrort-Meiderich with the Rheinische Röhrenwerke was deemed necessary as the latter produced only 20% of its own steel requirements, while Ruhrort-Meiderich was mainly a producer of semi-finished steels and had always acted as its supplier. Thus the one would get an assured market for its products in times of overproduction and the other an assured supply of raw materials in times of shortage. In addition, the government recommended joining the August Thyssen-Hütte, which was not considered viable in terms of current production, to this combination. Due to the poor geographical location and near complete dependence of both the Georgsmarienhütte and the Stahlwerke Osnabrück on orders from the Federal Railways, their combination with the Hüttenwerk Haspe was considered beneficial. This was with particular regard to their complementary production programmes. The combination of the final set of assets was upheld on the grounds of their shared installations and complementary rolling programmes. It was recognised that this would constitute the most powerful combination in Germany, but it was argued that there would be no domination in any rolled product. However, the DGB did feel that the govern-

55. BA B102/60666, Aktenvermerk von Dr Thiesing, 21 Dezember 1950.

ment had been unduly influenced by the industrialists in proposing this combination of former Vereinigte Stahlwerke assets. The meeting ended on a note of general unanimity, although the DGB made its support contingent on a satisfactory settlement of the codetermination issue.[56] The DGB was demanding that codetermination measures initiated by the British under Operation Severance for the steel industry, be incorporated into a codetermination law or *Mitbestimmungsgesetz*. Adenauer consequently intervened in the discussions between industrialists and the DGB on this law in order to secure trade union support for the German deconcentration proposals.[57]

These proposals formed the basis of the Federal government's memorandum to the AHC of the 27 December 1950 on the reorganisation of the steel industry. This was followed by a series of meetings with the Americans at the beginning of January 1951 to discuss the German counterproposals. The German proposals for the first three sets of steel assets were rejected, as the Americans could see no technical justification for their combination. However, as concerned the last two cases, the Ministry of Economics was able to report that the Americans had showed a more accommodating attitude. While it was agreed that compromises were usually unsatisfactory, they were still deemed preferable to a solution dictated by the Allies. After all it would be a substantial success if the Americans were to accept the combination of Dortmund Union with the Hüttenwerk Hörde which would lead to the creation of a unit company with an annual capacity in excess of 2 million tons of crude steel.[58]

The results of these meetings were reflected in the government's second memorandum to the AHC of the 14 January 1951. It stressed that in the interests of reaching an agreement the government was willing to accept the CSG's proposal for the first group of steel assets. As for the second grouping, the government was willing to go beyond the STA's proposal for the creation of two companies, proposing instead the creation of three separate companies. One consisting of the combination Bochumer Verein/Wurag, the other of the Henrichshütte Hattingen/Gussstahlwerk Witten, while the Stahlwerke Bochum were to remain independent. However, the

---

56. BA B102/60686, Schreiben des DGB Bundesvorstandes an Staatsekretär Schalfejew, 22 Dezember 1950.
57. H. Thum, *Mitbestimmung in der Montanindustrie. Der Mythos vom Sieg der Gewerkschaften* (Deutsche Verlagsanstalt, Stuttgart, 1982), pp. 79–86.
58. BA B102/60666, Aktenvermerk von Dr Thiesing, 13 Januar 1951.

government retained its position on the three remaining cases, as well as advocating that the August Thyssen-Hütte's creation as a unit company be deferred. The memorandum was accompanied by a note on the principles of *Verbundwirtschaft*, promising more detailed proposals shortly. However, it was conceded that the German steel industry's present ownership of 56% of Ruhr coal output could be reduced to 25%.[59] This figure still contrasted considerably with the 10% envisaged by the Americans for the eight cases of integration agreed on with the French in December. This made for protracted negotiations, now that the Germans had finally managed to get the Allies to confront the issue of *Verbundwirtschaft*. The Americans would also be faced with a strengthened Federal government. For, as British representatives in Germany had remarked in December, 'the DKBL, possibly under the influence or pressure from the Federal Government are now adopting an attitude on this question which is totally opposed to the British and French opinion, and is largely at variance with American ideas upon a reasonable measure of integration of ownership between coal and steel'.[60] In addition, the DGB had agreed to tolerate the *Verbundwirtschaft* compromise reached in the Ministry of Economics on the 27 October 1950. As a trade-off for the IG Bergbau, the DGB was advocating an inclusion of the coal industry in the codetermination law.[61]

Meanwhile in Paris the Schuman Plan Conference, which had resumed session on the 15 January 1951, was not making much progress. The German delegation remained adamant in its resistance to Articles 60 and 61 of the ECSC treaty. In reports back to Bonn, Walter Hallstein, the leader of the German delegation, emphasised the need to reach a settlement rapidly. Soon all other outstanding issues in Paris would be ready for initialling, and higher political considerations would make it difficult for the Germans to hold up the signing of the treaty for much longer.[62] Simultaneously, Hallstein was exerting pressure on Monnet in Paris. His claim that the Federal government was willing to sign the treaty, but would be forced to point out at the time of ratification that the deconcentra-

59. Bericht der Stahltreuhändervereinigung, *Neuordnung der Eisen- und Stahlindustrie*, pp. 447–54.
60. PRO/F0371/85701/CE6337, monthly progress report no. 6 on the reorganisation of the coal and iron and steel industries, Office of the Economic Adviser, 16 December 1950.
61. Thum, *Mitbestimmung in der Montanindustrie*, p. 66.
62. BA B102/4378, Vermerk von Dr Schäfer für Erhard, 14 Januar 1951.

tion measures as they now stood had been imposed on Germany, prompted Monnet to urge the Americans to make some concessions in Germany that would make the Schuman Plan acceptable there.[63]

Discussions on Verbundwirtschaft

The main differences between the Allies and the Germans on the issue of vertical integration can be summarised as follows. While the Allies felt that the German steel industry's coal and coke require- ments could be adequately secured by long-term contracts, the Germans maintained that this would not be sufficient if they were to preserve similar advantages enjoyed by the steel industries of countries which had adequate supplies of indigenous high-grade ores. The poor and varying quality of German ores made it necessary for blast-furnace managers to be able to change the quality of coke charged into the furnace at short notice. Further, the Germans maintained that with only about 25% of coal output annexed by steelworks, this would not interfere with the interests of other consumers. The argument that *Verbundwirtschaft* would involve the supply of coal and coke at preferential rates was countered by the allegation that supplies by jointly owned collieries at standard market rates were envisaged.

However, it was impossible to start negotiations on the details of vertical integration in the absence of concrete German proposals. The Americans feared that these proposals would be sent directly to the CSG, thus involving the British before an American/French/ German settlement had been reached.[64] This is not surprising, for while the Americans had come to accept that steelworks were to be permitted links with coal mines providing for up to 75% of their coking coal requirements, the British had always maintained that combined ownership proposals should be examined on a case-by- case basis on the grounds of economic necessity. Further, they were only to be approved if actual physical links existed between the steelworks and the mine. They were not prepared to support *a priori* some arbitrarily fixed percentage of coal assets to be annexed by steel companies.[65] The British, on the other hand, had very

63. AN 81 AJ 137, extraits d'une conversation téléphonique entre M. Monnet et M. Bowie, 15 janvier 1951.
64. AN 81 AJ 137, Report from Cleveland to Tomlinson, 16 January 1951.
65. PRO/T230/182, minutes of a meeting in the Foreign Office re: Schuman Plan/Law No. 27, 29 January 1951.

different worries of their own. While realising that the issue of *Verbundwirtschaft* was rapidly gaining importance in Germany, the Foreign Office complained of not having been informed on the current discussions between the Americans and the Germans on this issue. Furthermore, as it appeared to be the last obstacle to the conclusion of the ECSC treaty, it was necessary to know the relevant details of the latter, so as not to make decisions in Germany on Law No. 27 which might obstruct the Schuman Plan.[66] However, as the British were reluctant to go beyond the lines of the Paris liaison agreement, established for countries not participating in the plan, this served only to increase their isolation.

When the joint STA/DKBL proposals were finally sent to Erhard on the 17 January 1951, they constituted twelve cases in which either ownership links or participations were envisaged, with the coal mines remaining legally independent (see table 6.2). They were to serve as a basis for negotiations with the Americans which continued throughout the month of February. The fact that they soon reached deadlock was not so much due to French inflexibility as to problems of a more technical nature. Reports that the Federal government had decided in an extraordinary Cabinet meeting that Hallstein should not be authorised to initial the ECSC treaty until Erhard had reached a satisfactory agreement on outstanding deconcentration issues, prompted Monnet to issue new instructions to French representatives in Germany. Under these terms, the cases for which a coal–steel liaison was acceptable could, if justifiable, be increased beyond the original eight agreed on with the Americans.[67] However, as the Americans contended that in no case should more than 75% of the coking coal requirement of a steelworks be covered by an affiliated mine, the problem hinged on how this requirement should be calculated. Whereas the Americans calculated maximum figures for steel production on the basis of output during the years 1939 to 1943, coal production was based on the target figures for 1953. The Germans maintained that steel production should also be calculated on the basis of 1953 target figures. There were also differences on the probable amount of coking coal that would be produced by the affiliated mines in the course of the year 1953. In addition, different methods were used to calculate the capacity of German blast furnaces and thus their coke requirements. These

66. Ibid.
67. AN 81 AJ 138, télégramme de M. Bérard, 30 janvier 1951; AN 81 AJ 137, projet d'instructions de M. Monnet, 30 janvier 1951.

Isabel Warner

Table 6.2 Proposals for integration of steelworks, with coalmines

German proposals based on the STA/DKBL Plan of 17 January 1951	Federal Government's proposals of 14 March 1951
1 August Thyssen-Hütte	
– Beeckerwerth	– Beeckerwerth
– Lohberg	
2 Hüttenwerk Ruhrort-Meiderich	
– Friedrich Thyssen 4/8	– Friedrich Thyssen 4/8
– Friedrich Thyssen 2/5	– Friedrich Thyssen 2/5
– Westende	– Westende
3 Hüttenwerk Oberhausen	
– Osterfeld	– Osterfeld
– Jacobi	
4 Eisenwerke and Gussstahlwerk Gelsenkirchen/Mühlheim-Meiderich	
– Alma	– Alma
– Pluto	– Pluto
– Holland	– Holland
– Bonifatius	
5 Bochumer Verein	
– Carolinenglück	
– Graf Moltke	Still subject to examination
– Engelsburg	
6 Dortmund Union/Hüttenwerk Hörde	
– Hansa	– Hansa
– Westhausen	– Westhausen
– Hansemann	– Hansemann
7 Westfalenhütte	
– Kaiserstuhl I & II	– Kaiserstuhl I & II
– Dorstfeld	– Fürst Leopold
– Oespel	– Baldur
8 Hüttenwerk Huckingen	
– Consolidation	Still subject to examination, but
– Königin Elisabeth	the mine consolidation will not be
– Wilhelmine Victoria	proposed
9 Hüttenwerk Haspe/Georgsmarienhütte/Stahlwerk Osnabrück	
– Viktor-Ickern	– Viktor-Ickern
– Königsborn	
– Werne	
– Alter Hellweg	
10 Hüttenwerk Ilsede-Peine	
– Friederich der Grosse	– Friederich der Grosse

178

11 Maximillianshütte	
– Hugo	Still subject to examination, but
– Essen Sputh	the mine Hugo will not be
	proposed
12 Hüttenwerk Rheinhausen	
– Rossenray coalfields	– Rossenray coalfields

Source: BA B109/1125; AN 81 AJ 137; Stahltreuhändervereinigung (1954), pp. 455–7.

differences led to varying evaluations of entire plants and made for extremely difficult negotiations.

Meanwhile British isolation was increasing. It was becoming ever more obvious to the British that some sort of agreement would be reached in Germany on vertical integration. The British High Commissioner reported back to London that traditional British allies in the coal industry and among the trade unions would probably accept the agreement. Should it be also be supported by the French, the British would be placed in a very delicate position.[68] Ernest Bevin summarised the British dilemma accurately. On the one hand, the British government did not wish to be jockeyed into accepting agreements on important aspects of Law No. 27 arrived at as the result of discussions in which it had taken no part, and that were contrary to British policy. On the other hand, it did not wish to lay itself open to the charge of sabotaging the Schuman Plan.[69]

Moving Towards a Compromise

In a note to Adenauer of 12 February 1951, McCloy attempted to clarify the situation as it stood.[70] In view of the Schuman Plan, which the Americans welcomed as a step towards a strong European community, a greater degree of flexibility on deconcentration was possible. However, he pointed out that the Americans were not authorised to act in the name of the AHC. They could merely recommend the eventual settlement resulting from the German––American talks to their Allied colleagues. The assumptions underlying these talks were that the ECSC would be established and that the settlement arrived at would be presented to the AHC by the

68. Bullen, *Documents on British Policy Overseas*, pp. 388–90, telegram from Kirkpatrick to Bevin, 9 February 1951.
69. Ibid., pp. 392–3, telegram from Bevin to Kirkpatrick, 13 February 1951.
70. BA B136/2458, McCloy an Adenauer, 12 February 1951.

Federal government as a common solution. These provisions constituted an American attempt to bind the Germans firmly to the Schuman Plan, removing the possibility for a reopening of the ECSC negotiations due to German claims of a dictated deconcentration settlement. The note went on to state that while the Americans were willing to concede the amalgamation of the Georgsmarienhütte with the Stahlwerke Osnabrück and the Hüttenwerk Haspe, as well as the combination of the Dortmund Union with the Hüttenwerk Hörde, the concessions made on vertical integration were considered the absolute limit. It was agreed that certain steelworks would be permitted integration with coal mines to an extent of 75% of their coking coal requirements. However, this was subject to objective calculations—a requirement some of the German calculations did not satisfy. McCloy ended with the admonition that should the urge to achieve additional concessions result in the rejection of the Schuman Plan, all concessions made to date would automatically be suspended. This did not leave Adenauer much room for manoeuvre and his reply was to take some time in coming.

Simultaneously the Americans were attempting to secure British support for the eventual settlement. Acheson dispatched his principal adviser on German affairs to London with warnings that the consequences of a failure of the ECSC would be dangerous for Allied policy in Germany.[71] Fears that the French might refuse to proceed with German rearmament and the relaxation of controls, should the German problem not be solved, were very real in terms of the forthcoming Four-Power Conference at which the Americans did not want to arrive with a negative balance sheet.

A series of meetings were held in the Office of the Chancellor late February in an attempt to break the deadlock on *Verbundwirtschaft*. The individual cases were for the first time calculated on the basis of the US figures and it emerged that with the exception of the Ilsede–Peine case, the STA/DKBL proposals would have no hope of being approved, as all mines would exceed the 75% formula. As no solution was forthcoming, the idea that the link between the Schuman Plan and a deconcentration settlement should be renounced in order to prevent a rash decision on *Verbundwirtschaft* found increasing support.[72] Yet McCloy had been very clear on the con-

71. Bullen, *Documents on British Policy Overseas*, pp. 404–5, telegram from Bevin to Sir O. Franks, 17 February 1951.
72. BA B109/129, Tätigkeitsbericht der STV Abt. Technik für Februar 1951, 15

sequences of such a move. The dilemma facing Adenauer was that while he recognised the necessity of Germany's association with the Schuman Plan he was unwilling to risk its failure before parliament due to low domestic, and especially industrial, support for the deconcentration settlement on which it hinged—largely due to his own efforts. The steel industry, which was still smarting from the fact that it had not been represented in the German delegation to the ECSC negotiations,[73] saw the issue of *Verbundwirtschaft* as its last chance to influence developments. This holds especially true in view of the fact that as of August 1950 Monnet had effectively limited the influence of the expert committees, in which it was represented, on the Schuman Plan talks.[74]

Adenauer reaffirmed his acceptance of the 75% formula in the course of a meeting with McCloy on the 2 March 1951. He maintained, however, that it would have to be based on future production figures. This met with American resistance, and so Adenauer asked McCloy to negotiate directly with the steel industrialists. Adenauer was in fact passing the buck. As he had not been able to break the stalemate created by industrial intransigence, it was now up to the Americans to remove this last obstacle to a settlement. Whatever settlement transpired Adenauer would be able to point to higher political considerations necessitating its acceptance. While the underlying implication would be that the industrialists had not been able to modify the compromise, he was thus forced to submit. This is in character with Adenauer's belief that economic considerations would have to take a back-seat to the more important political implications of the Schuman Plan.[75] McCloy duly met with the industrialists on the 5 March. He informed them that recent talks with the French had established that German acceptance of the 75% formula based on current production capacity, calculated on the basis of the US figures, was indispensible to an agreement.[76] Despite the promise that the interpretation of the formula would

---

März 1951. On the basis of the American calculations the STA/DKBL plan would have led to an average commodity coverage of 107.5%, whereas the German calculations produced a figure of 58%.

73. W. Bührer, *Ruhrstahl und Europa. Die Wirtschaftsvereinigung Eisen- und Stahlindustrie und die Anfänge der europäischen Integration 1945–52* (Oldenbourg Verlag, Munich, 1986), pp. 180–3. Bührer does show, however, that the steel industry was by no means underrepresented in the expert committees.
74. Berghahn, *Unternehmer*, pp. 130–6.
75. E. Wandel, 'Adenauer und der Schuman Plan. Protokoll eines Gesprächs zwischen Konrad Adenauer und Hans Schäffer vom 3 Juni 1950', *VfZ*, Vol. 20, No. 2, 1972, p. 196.
76. BA B109/129, Auszug aus einem Vermerk von Dr Sohl, 7 März 1951.

not be unduly rigid, the industrialists were faced with a *fait accompli*. They had no choice but to resign themselves to this turn of events, realising that this was the only way to rid the steel industry of the remaining Allied controls. These talks led to acceptance by the US of four of the German proposals for the integration of steelworks with coal mines. Five further cases were accepted partially and three remained subject to examination. As a result 16% of the Ruhr's future coal output would remain tied to the steel industry.

The results of this meeting were communicated to Adenauer and directly influenced his compromise proposals of 14 March 1951.[77] In making his proposals, Adenauer adhered to the framework established by McCloy in February. Yet he added the proviso that should one of the proposed solutions not stand the test of economic viability, measures taken under Law No. 27 should not preclude amendment through the High Authority subject to the provisions of the Schuman Plan. The Chancellor went on to recommend the creation of twenty-four steel unit companies (see table 6.3). These included the two combinations already conceded by the Federal government in January. Furthermore, Germany bowed to the Franco-American view that the Gussstahlwerk Witten, a prosperous plant, should not be used to rehabilitate the Henrichshütte Hattingen. Thus it went beyond its former proposal, now recommending the creation of four separate companies out of these assets. Hereby the Bochumer Verein was to be combined with the Wurag, while the other three companies were to remain independent. The Federal government was also forced to renounce its position on the Hüttenwerk Ruhrort-Meiderich/Rheinische Röhrenwerke amalgamation, agreeing instead to their creation as two separate companies. However, its views had prevailed on the last two cases subject to dispute. The August Thyssen-Hütte was also included in the list of companies to be created, albeit with the proviso that its creation be deferred subject to the outcome of further talks. That covered twenty-five of the CSG's original twenty-nine companies. Adenauer advocated that the remaining four companies be treated as Schedule C companies. As companies listed in Schedule C to Law No. 27 had recourse to a provision whereby they were only included in the reorganisation at the express request of their owners,

---

77. Bericht der Stahltreuhändervereinigung, *Neuordnung der Eisen- und Stahlindustrie*, pp. 455–7.

Table 6.3 Federal Government's proposals of 14 March 1951 for the creation of steel companies

No.	No. on the CSG's list of 30 November 1950	Description of plants
1	1	Deutsche Edelstahlwerke
2	3	Eisenwerke & Gussstahlwerk Gelsenkirchen/Mülheim-Meiderich
3	4	Gussstahlwerk Oberkassel
4	5	Hüttenwerk Ruhrort-Meiderich
5	6	Hüttenwerk Niederrhein/Westfälische Union
6	7	Rheinische Röhrenwerke
7	8	Hüttenwerk Oberhausen-Gutehoffnungshütte-Geselkirchen
8	9	Stahlwerke Bochum
9	10/11	Hüttenwerk Haspe/Georgsmarienhütte/Stahlwerk Osnabrück
10	12	Westfalenhütte Dortmund/Hoesch Hohenlimburg
11	15	Hüttenwerk Huckingen/Wdt Mannesmannröhrenwerke
12	16	Stahl- und Walzwerke Grossenbaum/Kamerichwerke
13	17	Hüttenwerk Rheinhausen/Westfälische Drahtindustrie
14	18	Hüttenwerk Geisweid/Stahlwerk Hagen
15	19/20	Hüttenwerk Hörde/Dortmund Union
16	21	Bochumer Verein
17	21	Henrichshütte Hattingen
18	2	Gussstahlwerk Witten
19	23	Maximillianshütte
20	24	Siegerland-Charlottenhütte-Friedrichshütte
21	27	Hochofenwerk Lübeck
22	28	Rasselstein-Andernach
23	29	Luitpoldhütte
24	22	August Thyssen-Hütte (its creation was to be deferred)

It was recommended that the following plants be treated as Schedule C companies:

	13	Stahl- und Röhrenwerke Reizholz
	14	Ilseder Hütte
	25	Reichswerke
	26	Buderus'sche Eisenwerke/Stahlwerk Röchling-Buderus

Source: Stahltreuhändervereinigung (1954), pp. 455–6.

the government evidently hoped that they would be decontrolled.

On the issue of vertical integration, Adenauer's note foresaw affiliations based on the condition that the coal-mining assets were to be created as legally independent companies. They were to supply the steelworks to which they were linked in accordance with customary trade practices, their output being subject to the same rules governing distribution within the ECSC as companies that were not integrated. The individual proposals concerning the allocation of mines to steelworks were reflective of the 5 March meeting (see table 6.2). Finally, Adenauer also accepted the dissolution of the DKV within three months of the completion of the reorganisation. Thus the last obstacle to the Schuman Plan negotiations had been removed and the ECSC treaty was duly initialled on 19 March 1951. Now all that remained was official acceptance of Adenauer's compromise proposals by the AHC.

To this end, the German proposals were discussed in the Economics Committee on 21 March. Whereas the American and French representatives recommended Council approval of the compromise, the British member reserved his position, thus giving the British Cabinet the opportunity to discuss the proposals the following day. While the Cabinet recommended that the High Commissioner accept the settlement, British approval was not unqualified.[78] In the course of the Council's meeting of 29 March 1951, the British High Commissioner outlined his government's objections. When considering the proposals in the framework of Law No. 27, the general British impression was unfavourable. Vertical integration was deemed incompatible with the aims of the law as it provided a possibility for the re-emergence of trusts. Nor did the technical reasons presented in favour of such a system appear valid. Finally, the individual cases had not been examined on a Tripartite basis. Acceptance of the steel proposals would lead to the conservation of the Klöckner concern and provide the Vereinigte Stahlwerke with a base for the re-establishment of its former empire. Finally, the dissolution of the DKV was not judged essential to the enforcement of the law. It was acknowledged, however, that the problem could not be resolved without considering its repercussions on the Schuman Plan, the Germans having made their participation contingent on concessions in the deconcentration. Thus the British were will-

---

78. PRO/CAB128/19/CM(51)22, conclusions of a meeting of the Cabinet, 22 March 1951.

ing to accept the compromise, subject to the provisos that (i) the combined ownership of coal and steel companies should take the form of holding companies with separate subsidiaries, rather than that of completely integrated companies; (ii) failure to ratify the ECSC treaty would have to result in the whole question being reviewed.[79] Hence the AHC was able to inform the Federal government on 30 March 1951 that it accepted the German compromise and would promulgate the necessary regulations for its implementation.

In sum it is possible to say that the Schuman Plan served both to modify the deconcentration of the West German steel industry under Law No. 27 and to remove it from British influence. Indeed, the Federal government had managed to secure a better deconcentration settlement than it could have hoped for in January 1950. The CSG's original proposal for twenty-nine steel unit companies was reduced to twenty-four and one of these would be exceptionally powerful in terms of annual crude steel capacity. Furthermore, concessions had also been obtained on *Verbundwirtschaft*. Whereas the Americans and the French had envisaged in December 1950 that the German steel industry should dispose of no more than 10–12 million tons of coal production, this figure had been doubled to 21 million tons.[80] The British, on the other hand, had not been able to exploit the unique opportunity of putting their deconcentration concept into practice in the Ruhr. The decline of Britain's influence in its zone of occupation in Germany was symptomatic of its transformation from a major to a secondary power in the post-war world. Although the deconcentration of the West German steel industry was by no means complete in March 1951 as important details still remained to be worked out, the settlement reached with the Allies provided a framework within which to do this. In addition, the uncertainty that had prevailed in the Ruhr due to the pending deconcentration had now been removed, as the future structure of the successor companies had been clarified, thus enabling the Federal Republic to participate in the European common market for coal and steel on equal terms with the other member countries, and bringing it a step closer to real sovereignty.

79. AN 81 AJ 137, procès-verbal de la 59e séance du conseil de la Haute Commission Alliée, HICOM/M(51)9, 29 Mars 1951.
80. AN 81 AJ 137, compte rendu de la visite faite à M. Willner, 3 février 1951.

PART III

Democratic Rebirth Under British Control

7

British Democratisation Policy in Germany
Barbara Marshall

Introduction

The 'democratisation' of Germany was one of the key phrases of
Allied occupation policies in Germany. It implied not only a
thorough denazification and re-education of the German people but
also an occupation of at least twenty years because the objectives
were essentially long-term. There were basic flaws inherent in the
concept: liberal 'democracy' as understood by the western powers
had to be built on the cooperation of the Germans. This, in turn,
prevented radical structural changes which would have to have been
introduced against the will of the Germans—unless the British were
willing to cooperate with those Germans who themselves wished
radical changes. This the British were unwilling to do. Moreover,
very soon after the war the international scene changed, leading to a
rapid rehabilitation of Germany, the former enemy, and the fore-
seeable end of the occupation. Any more direct attempt by the
Allies to intervene in West Germany's internal political development would be deflected by delaying tactics until the Germans had
regained their sovereignty.

Wartime Planning for a Future German Democracy

In the course of Britain's wartime planning for post-war Germany
little official thought had been given to her political future after
military defeat was secured. Churchill's predeliction for military
matters is well documented and little discussion about Germany's
future internal political development had taken place at Cabinet
level. Although it was generally assumed that a 'democratic' Germany would provide the best guarantee against a resurgence of

189

German aggression, no concrete plan for Germany was ever formulated. There were several reasons for this. First, there was the general uncertainty as to the international situation at the end of the war. In Europe this might bring about the predominance of the Soviet Union which Britain would have to face alone if the United States were to turn their wartime utterances into practical politics and withdraw from Europe. British plans for Germany were therefore predicated on the continuation of the Allied wartime coalition. This precluded the development of precise and independent British plans for the treatment of Germany. Secondly, there was the fear that 'Germany', even after her eventual defeat, would still be a potential threat to British security. Lord Vansittart's central tenet, that Germans were bellicose by nature, had left its mark on the British establishment. This distrust extended to all Germans. As a result there was no group inside Germany on whom the British felt able to rely for these plans. As Attlee put it: 'It was an illusion to imagine that there was a normal Germany to which one could revert. There had been no normal Germany for fifty years or more, except one governed by a centralised and militaristic machine.'[1]

Even cooperation with pre-Hitler German democrats was no option. The British held these German democratic politicians in extraordinarily low esteem. This was even the case when the German politicians' anti-fascist stance was well known and where they had actually fled to Britain or spent years in concentration camps for their beliefs. The British considered them as having been too feeble to prevent Hitler's rise to power, and now they were seen as a 'spent force' and basically untrustworthy.[2] In the eyes of the British these old-style democrats remained incorrigible nationalists at heart. The British dilemma was clear: they had to build up democracy in Germany with undemocratic people. 'In the absence of potential democratic leaders, after ten years Nazi repression any . . . [German] government could probably only be representative of the old Germany and might well ensure the survival of those very elements of militarism which it is our fundamental aim to destroy.'[3]

One way forward out of the contradiction seemed to be to build up democracy 'from the bottom upwards' with the help of new

1. Quoted in L. Kettenacker, 'Grossbritannien und die zukünftige Kontrolle Deutschlands' in J. Foschepoth and R. Steininger (eds.), *Britische Deutschland- und Besatzungspolitik 1945–49* (Schöningh, Paderborn, 1985), p. 37.
2. A. Glees, *Exile Politics during the Second World War* (Oxford University Press, Oxford, 1982).
3. Kettenacker, 'Grossbritannien', p. 39.

190

democratic forces which were to emerge in Germany as a result of re-education.[4] It was recognised, however, that beneath the nationalist and aggressive policies perpetrated by German central governments there had existed a healthy democratic tradition at local level going back to the reforms of Freiherr von Stein in the early nineteenth century. Democracy in Germany had mainly failed at the top.[5] A future democracy in Germany therefore had to make use of these democratic traditions: together with a weakening of central power through a federal structure should come the rebirth of German democracy from the lowest level.

These ideas formed the basis of a number of wartime directives and Military Government handbooks which in 1944 and 1945 were issued to troop commanders for the treatment of the German people after their military defeat.[6] Political activities, public meetings, etc. should be allowed and freedom of speech and of the press guaranteed. Military commanders should be neutral towards the different emerging political groups.[7] There was also to be a democratic trade union movement, provided for in the Anglo-American SHAEF directive of 9 November 1944. Wartime plans for the *military* occupation were therefore characterised by a pragmatic approach: Germany was to be thoroughly disarmed, National Socialism and militarism were to be eradicated once and for all, but the long-term aim was 'to lay the foundations for the rule of law in Germany, and for the eventual cooperation in international life by Germany, to encourage individual and collective responsibility in Germans'.[8]

However, these British ideas did not become occupation policies after the war because the Americans adopted Joint Chiefs of Staff (JCS) Directive 1067 in April 1945 which was based on the harsher, more punitive principles put forward by the US Treasury Secretary Morgenthau in 1944. The British never accepted the political aspects of this directive, and this disagreement was one of the reasons for the absence of jointly agreed Anglo-American policies in Germany at the end of the Second World War.

4. See chapter 8 of this volume and B. Marshall, 'German Attitudes to British Military Government 1945–47', *Journal of Contemporary History*, Vol. 15, No. 4, 1980, pp. 655–84.
5. R. Ebsworth, *Restoring Democracy in Germany. The British Contribution* (Stevens and Son, London, 1960), p. xiii.
6. U. Schneider, 'Britische Besatzungspolitik 1945', PhD thesis, University of Hanover, 1980.
7. F. S. V. Donnison, *Civil Affairs and Military Government. North West Europe, 1944–46* (HMSO, London, 1961).
8. Ibid., p. 195.

Barbara Marshall

From War to Cold War

After unconditional surrender, German political activists spontaneously formed themselves into 'Antifascist Committees' (Antifas) in which the left predominated, although initially bourgeois members often also took part.[9] These committees had a variety of objectives which differed in their degree of radicalism according to the political composition of the local parties. However, they all wanted to see a thorough purge of all traces of National Socialism from public life and give practical help to all in need—such as returning concentration camp inmates or the homeless. They also worked to prepare the way for the emergence of democratic parties and trade unions which in due course would assume power in Germany. Only a few Antifas considered themselves as an alternative, embryonic power structure for a future Germany.

These first political stirrings by the Germans were not popular with the Allies and on 2 June 1945 a general ban was declared throughout the western zones. For the time being the priority of the British was to restore basic services and to 'run' their zone as efficiently as possible. For this they established 'indirect rule' in towns and villages by appointing politically trustworthy German administrators some of whom had already been selected during the war.[10] These administrators wielded almost unlimited power in local affairs being the link between the population at large and British Military Government. Soon an 'unholy alliance' emerged between these powerful German local authorities and Military Government: both viewed German political initiatives with suspicion. The priorities of British Military Government and German administrators alike were to bring some sort of order to the chaos of the post-war situation. Any spontaneous German *political* grouping, particularly if they challenged the existing status quo, would complicate this task. German committees such as Antifas therefore found themselves sandwiched between British and German authorities, and for this reason alone had no chance of exercising any lasting influence on German political developments. But even later when, after the Potsdam Conference, political parties were allowed to come into the open, they were considered 'unhelpful' for the orderly running of the cities' affairs. In Hanover the Oberbürger-

9. Stadtarchiv Hanover, 'Material Nagel'. See also L. Niethammer *et al.* (eds.), *Arbeiterinitiative 1945* (Hammer, Wuppertal, 1976).
10. Schneider, 'Britische Besatzungspolitik', p. 42.

meister, himself an old Social Democrat, warned SPD leader Schumacher that 'there must be no doubt that politics must not interfere
with the German administration'.[11]

This view was shared by the British, albeit for different reasons.
In fact, the principles behind British plans for democratisation had
been reassessed. Whereas the wartime directives had assumed that
German democracy at the local level prior to 1933 had been healthy,
this interpretation had been changed by W. A. Robson, a Professor
of Public Administration at the London School of Economics.
Robson was in close touch with the Administration and Local
Government Section of the British Element of the Control Commission for Germany (CCG) at the time of the German surrender
when the CCG were waiting in London for their imminent departure to Germany.

According to Robson a fundamental reorientation of the German
people was required on four main points:

(i) That bureaucracy, however efficient, was no substitute for
self-government.
(ii) That 'local self-government' does not, as many learned German apologists had claimed, mean administration by local
officials, but involves effective control by popularly elected
representatives.
(iii) That the pre-Nazi government was not democratic.
(iv) That the expert and the professional administrator should only
be the adviser and the instrument of executive action, and not
the maker of administrative policy.

What was needed in Germany was a lesson in basic democracy as
practiced in Britain: 'In the British Zone we envisaged authorities
like the more rural county councils in our own country, to which
until recently only independents were elected and where politics
were taboo'.[12]

The rules of the political game called 'democracy' were to be
learned in an almost unpolitical, formal way. Political parties and
trade unions would emerge only later, after a 'period of reflection'
which was expected to produce new political forces and personalities. The democratisation of German public life was thus to take
place mainly in three areas: the reform of local government as
advocated by Robson, with a gradual emergence of constitutions at

11. Stadtarchiv Hanover, Oberbürgermeister Brakte Papers, File 22, OB, Brakte
to Kurt Schumacher, 30 August 1945.
12. Ebsworth, *Restoring Democracy*, p. 22.

Barbara Marshall

the higher level such as the Länder on a similar pattern, the reform of the civil service and the delayed and measured licensing of (new) political parties capable of exercising executive power. For the time being no organisation was to refer to 'Germany' in their statutes, the future of the German nation-state being still uncertain.[13]

However, British expectations were not fulfilled. The 'period of reflection' was shortened by the licensing of parties in the Soviet Zone on 11 June and by the relentless pressure of German politicians whose main priority was to regain their freedom of action. From early summer of 1946, moreover, a change of British policy in Germany could be detected.[14] The commitment to four-power control in Germany was weakened and the fusion of the British and US Zones heralded the beginning of a process which was to lead ultimately to the division of Germany. The onset of the Cold War made the development of political structures urgent. The first democratic local government elections were held in the British Zone in the autum of 1946. Elections at Land level followed in April 1947. Moreover, in Zonal Directive 57 of 1 December 1946 the British handed the right of self-government back to the Germans at Land level. The democratic constitutions which were being worked out in the Länder were no longer perceived as a continuation of the leisurely build-up 'from the bottom upwards' but they served the purpose of securing the long-term interests of Britain in Germany, as did the Basic Law for the Federal Republic later.[15]

Local Government Reform

The way in which local affairs were run in the immediate post-war period could only be a temporary device. As we have seen, instead of introducing democracy at the local level the British had made the German administrators even more authoritarian and powerful. The Oberbürgermeister and Bürgermeister of the cities and towns were

13. H. Pietsch, *Militärregierung, Bürokratie und Sozialisierung. Entwicklung des politischen Systems in den Städten des Ruhrgebiets, 1945–48* (Walter Braun, Duisburg, 1978), p. 31.
14. See chapter 1 of this volume and J. Foschepoth, 'Grossbritannien und die Deutschlandfrage auf den Aussenministerkonferenzen 1946–47' in Foschepoth and Steininger (eds.), *Britische Deutschland- und Besatzungspolitik*, p. 65.
15. F. R. Pfetsch, 'Die Verfassungspolitik der westlichen Besatzungsmächte in den Ländern nach 1945', *Aus Politik und Zeitgeschichte*, B22/86, 31 May 1986, pp. 3–17.

the main point of contact between the British and the German population at large and much of the communication between them went through these official German channels. The (Ober)Bürgermeister were also responsible for the police and for denazification,[16] not only of their own administration but also for that of the economy. On their suggestion, the British dismissed or reprieved politically suspect personnel. Expediency and efficiency were, of course, the priorities of the 'first hour'. However, as some kind of normality was re-established, the German officials themselves felt the need to involve more of the public in the running of local affairs, if only to provide the population with more information about the reasons for their misery.[17] The British, on the other hand, tackled local government reform rather suddenly after the election victory of the Labour Party in July 1945. No other British policy in Germany can be so directly attributed to the change of government in Britain. Although the final declaration of the Potsdam Conference in August spoke of a 'restoration' of democratic local government, in Germany the British introduced their own independent programme.

The aims of the reform were (i) to decentralise the German administrative structure as a whole (as much of the British Zone was in the former State of Prussia this meant effecting radical change in the traditional Prussian system of government) and (ii) to introduce at local level the 'dual system' as it existed in Britain. As we have seen, the British had assumed that excessive power in the hands of the Prussian government had been responsible for much of German aggression in the past. Decentralisation was therefore seen as the necessary framework within which democratic self-government at the local level would operate. However, when the Allies first moved into Germany some kind of German administrative structure was necessary for first practical measures. For this reason the old Prussian state offices of Regierungspräsident (regions) and Oberpräsident (county) were temporarily revived. By the time local government reform was tackled in earnest in late 1945 these offices had again taken root in the German administrative machine and only a massive British interference would have been able to dislodge them. Moreover, a centralised system was also reintroduced by the

16. See chapter 9 in this volume.
17. B. Marshall, *Origins of West German Politics* (Croom Helm, London, 1988), p. 100. Stadtarchiv Hanover, Niederschriften über Besprechungen mit den Dezernenten und dem Stadtbeirat, 16 October 1945.

creation of Sonderverwaltungen, set up either to carry out tasks formerly performed by the Prussian ministries like the Ministry of Finance or to cater for the new needs of the post-war situation such as the distribution of building materials. There were also some central offices which survived the war such as the Reich Food Estate (see below). The centralising nature of these zonal institutions was at odds with the British-style decentralised local government.

The British model provided for democratically elected local councils each of which chose a mayor as a representative figurehead. The council would form a number of smaller subcommittees where members could develop expertise in a given field and thus provide effective control of the administration. These subcommittees, as in Britain, were to be run by non-political civil servants, headed by the town clerk who was accountable to the council. In dividing the functions of the old-style (Ober)Bürgermeister in this way the British hoped to eradicate the Führerprinzip in local affairs—that excessive power concentrated in the hands of leading local officials which had been disguised under 'efficiency' and had generated fundamentally undemocratic attitudes. These new institutions were, however, only gradually introduced between the autumn of 1945 and 1946.

The Germans were ambivalent towards these British proposals. On the one hand, German local administrators had welcomed the British objective to decentralise the administration as a whole. Already before and during the Weimar Republic they had campaigned for more autonomy for the cities, the office of Regierungspräsident being the particular target for their wrath, having had the responsibility for overseeing the cities' activities. In this respect the interests of German local politicians and British Military Government overlapped, and the failure of the British to bring about changes when the traditional administrative structures in Germany at the end of the war were at their most vulnerable came as a great disappointment.

On the other hand, the changes proposed in local government were not popular. There seemed to have been considerable (real or pretended) confusion among the Germans as to how the new system was supposed to work with information particularly in the smaller cities coming slowly and mainly by word of mouth. It was, for example, not known how much the new-style (Ober)Bürgermeister would be paid, an important consideration for the weighting of the new office within the overall structure. The new system was alien to the Germans who considered this kind of change in the post-war chaos a waste of time and, in any case, unnecessary in view of old democratic German local government traditions. However, both arguments were firmly rejected by the British: 'Whatever democratic traditions you may have had in Germany it was not strong enough to withstand the attacks of Nazism, and it is therefore necessary to amend it . . . We regard [the changes] as the cornerstone of our scheme for the political re-education of Germany, pending the introduction of the elective system . . .'[18]

Nor was there any support from those Germans who might benefit from the reforms: the political parties. For these the possible gains of the reforms were heavily outweighed by the losses they entailed. An important part of the reforms were changes in the traditional German civil service to introduce the non-political British-style 'public servant' (see below). This exclusion of civil servants from political activity would mean heavy losses particularly for the SPD who could ill-afford the disappearance from the political scene of their most experienced (civil-servant) members.

In accordance with the British concept that local government should operate 'unpolitically' the members of the first small local advisory councils were appointed (often on the advice of the (Ober)-Bürgermeister) on the basis of their status in society, not according to the parties the candidates had belonged to in the past. This meant effectively that candidates with the 'wrong' political background, such as communists, could be excluded. Not surprisingly, the British found the Germans rather unresponsive to their changes:

> The organisation and selection of councillors . . . are now in full swing . . . The German mind, never a highly flexible mechanism, is very slow to grasp the principles involved. This means additional explanation and supervision by Military Government whose job in this respect would be much simpler if a press campaign could be started to initiate a still bemused public in the mysteries involved in governing themselves . . .[19]

This 'unpolitical' approach to the selection of local politicians was continued even during the selection of the members of the next,

18. PRO/FO371/55610/C1322, Brigadier Bridges, Director of the Administration and Local Government Branch, Internal Affairs and Communications Division, CCG, to Regierungspräsidenten of the British Zone, 4 February 1946.
19. PRO/WO171/7990, monthly report of Detachment 504/720, Military Government, October 1945 Appendix C (Civil Administration).

larger councils, the Nominated Representative Councils (NRCs) which were to work out the cities' constitutions or statutes (and later those of the Länder partionments). Indeed if it was discovered that council members or (Ober)Bürgermeister were members of political parties these would be dismissed or retained only temporarily to prevent further disruption of the emerging system.[20] It was a rather absurd situation because the attempts of the local government reformers took place in late 1945–early 1946, at a time when the political parties had already been given a licence to operate at Kreis or district level. It was abandoned only reluctantly in the face of outspoken German opposition. British observers agreed that their first intentions in Germany had been mistaken:

> we soon found that it was unrealistic to plan on the assumption that the new politicians would be prepared to behave like independents. Whether we like it or not, the Germans who were prepared to accept political responsibility wanted their parties back ... To be non-political meant either that one had been a Nazi or that one did not have the moral courage to show one's colours and was therefore a potential Nazi.[21]

Besides the setting up of the NRCs the initial task facing the British was to strip the (Ober)Bürgermeister of their power. They were given the choice of either carrying on as (Ober)Bürgermeister in name as head of council with essentially a representative function, or of becoming Oberstadtdirektor (town clerk), and thus continuing their administrative work, albeit under political control by the council. Most officials in the British Zone shrewdly chose the latter.

From the beginning the British insisted that, with the exception of specific subject areas which remained the prerogative of Military Government, the NRCs *were* the city governments. Their first task was to work out local constitutions which tended to be based on those previously in operation either pre-1933 or in many cases even during the Third Reich, with modifications to redefine the role of the (Ober)Bürgermeister and assure democratic accountability. Discussions centred around the openess of council debates—their easy accessability had been badly exploited by the Nazis—and the professional qualifications of the leading administrative experts such as the town clerk. As long as a qualification in law was the prerequi-

20. Hauptstaatsarchiv Hanover, Z50/Acc32/63 No. 92a II, Brigadier Lingham to Ministerpräsident Kopf, 13 February 1946.
20. Ebsworth, *Restoring Democracy*, p. 23.

site, the office would remain in the hands of a privileged few, the 'Juristenmonopol'. The Germans also clashed with the British over the provisions in the local constitution relating to former members of the NSDAP. Here the Germans wanted a clause permitting the involvement of ex-Nazis in local affairs at a later date but the British insisted on their exclusion. Although the British won in 1946, the Germans left no doubt that these clauses of the constitution would be changed as soon as an opportunity arose.[22]

While these debates on the local constitution were going on the council had regrouped into the necessary committees which took on much of the decision-making powers for local government. A detailed study of one city in the British Zone, Hanover, has shown that the system worked well, with the council becoming *the* mouth-piece for German public opinion towards the occupying authorities, and the addressee of numerous petitions and requests for help from the population.[23] This part of local government reform can be considered as having been successful; indeed it represents the policy with the longest lasting effect. Although it was vigorously debated by the Germans at the end of the occupation when they had the possibility to make changes, the advantages of keeping British institutions outweighed the upheaval involved in the return to German traditions.[24] For this reason it is still in operation in many German cities today.

Länder Constitutions and the Basic Law

The British were slower than the other Allies in tackling the question of the Länder constitutions. There were two main reasons for this. First of all there was the general uncertainty of Germany's future: the setting up of self-governing German states at a time when the problem of the German nation-state was not yet solved seemed premature. Secondly, the British Zone covered much of the territory of the former state of Prussia which, as the Allies had already decided during the war, was to be dissolved into smaller units. It was, however, not until 1 November 1946 that this process

22. Marshall, *Origins*, p. 103. W. Rudzio, *Die Neordnung des Kommunalwesens in der Britischen Zone, Zur Demokratisierung und Dezentralisierung der politischen Struktur: eine britische Reform und ihr Ausgang* (Deutsche Verlags-Anstalt, Stuttgart, 1968).
23. Marshall, *Origins*, p. 108–11.
24. Rudzio, *Neuordnung*, p. 234.

of reorganisation was completed with the setting up of the Land Niedersachsen (Lower Saxony). From then on the British Zone consisted of four Länder: North-Rhine-Westphalia (which had been set up largely to accommodate the industrial complex of the Ruhr), Schleswig-Holstein, Hamburg, and Lower Saxony (Bremen was still at that time a US enclave).

At this stage these Länder formed the highest German units of government. However, the Länder governments were subordinate in practice to the zonal administrations such as the Central Offices for Food and Agriculture in Hamburg and for Economics in Minden. These offices were geographically dispersed over the whole zone so as to avoid the impression that a 'zonal government' was in the making. They nevertheless acquired a measure of authority in relation to the Länder who, notwithstanding the declared intentions of the British to decentralise, found their rights more limited than had been anticipated. It has been claimed that by the end of 1946 'the general distribution of powers left the *Länder* in about the same position as did the Weimar Constitution. While their legislative jurisdiction was somewhat smaller, their administrative competence had been increased.'[25] Mention should also be made of another zonal office, the Zonal Advisory Council. This was composed of leading German politicians of the British Zone. However, as the name suggests, this body had a strictly advisory function and any attempt by the Germans to extend its powers was promptly blocked by the British.[26]

In the course of 1945 and 1946 the governments and parliaments of the Länder were nominated by the British. But only with Ordinance No. 57 of 1 December 1946 was a legal framework created within which the state governments and legislatures could act more independently. Democratic elections to the Länder parliaments were held in April 1947; the first task of these newly created assemblies was to work out constitutions for their areas. Ordinance 57 was intended to be a pragmatic set of guidelines rather than a detailed constitutional framework, but it satisfied the requirements of Britain's policy towards Germany at this point: it would prevent an easy change in the status quo of the territorial arrangements in Germany and secure Britain's control over her zone of occupation

25. P. H. Merkl, *The Origins of the West German Republic* (Oxford University Press, Oxford, 1963), p. 12.
26. A. Dohrendorf, *Der Zonenbeirat der britisch-besetzten Zone. Eine Rückblick auf seine Tätigkeit* (Schwartz, Göttingen, 1953).

at a time when future Allied cooperation over Germany had become less likely and the division of Germany emerged as a realistic alternative.[27]

In this first phase of constitutional development certain aspects of the reforms of local government were repeated at state level, such as the introduction of a modified British-style voting system, the separation of political and administrative offices and the ban on political activity by civil and public servants. Any reference in the constitutions to a German nation-state was prohibited so as not to prejudice future international arrangements; each Land government was to be collectively responsible to its parliament; parliamentary committees were to take on most of the assembly's legislative work and each member of parliament had the right to initiate legislation.

When, later in 1947, four-power cooperation in Germany came effectively to an end British thinking on the constitutional arrangements in the Länder of their zone changed: the constitutions now were to express the fact that they were no longer considered provisional arrangements. Certain British principles such as the division of powers between the executive, legislature and judiciary were to be incorporated, as well as the independence of judges and the exclusion from political activity of civil servants. The constitutions were to be put to a plebiscite in order to involve the whole population in the fundamental decision of their political future. The way in which the British approach to the German problem had changed was also indicated by the fact that the Länder were now allowed to include in their constitutions passages indicating that they considered themselves part (*Gliedstaaten*) of a future German nation-state—something the British had previously prevented. Increasingly, Germans were encouraged to develop their own initiatives, although all draft constitutions still had to be submitted to the British for approval. Moreover, with Bizonia in operation the British also became more amenable to American constitutional proposals. This applied particularly to the inclusion of articles referring to the protection of human rights. The difference in approach between the British and Americans was clear: 'the main differences between the British drafts and the US constitutions are that the former, in effect, deal only with the structure of the State—and that very briefly and not always adequately—while the latter deal with this subject in considerable detail and also cover . . .

27. See n. 14, above.

additional subjects-[Basic Human Rights and Duties; Man and Society].'[28]

The British priority was the smooth functioning of the governmental machine, provided that certain basic constitutional principles were maintained, such as the control of the executive by the electorate and the legislature and the legislative prerogative of the assemblies which the latter could not delegate. All wider issues such as the social or economic order were to be left to legislation by a future German government.

Given this general, pragmatic British approach it was not surprising that the Germans themselves determined increasingly the contents of their respective constitutions. Specific German traditions and experiences ultimately proved more important than the influence of the British. Under the impact of the Cold War and the general shift in Allied policies towards Germany in favour of rehabilitation even such fundamental features of British policy as the voting system and the ban on political activity by civil servants could be ignored. At Land level, more than in the communities, the contradictions between different aspects of British policy in Germany became apparent. The practical necessities of the times seemed to demand the introduction of central agencies, even if this reduced the role of the lower levels of the federal structure, the devolution of power to whom had been regarded as so vital for Germany's democratisation. The Americans, on the other hand, had always favoured a more decentralised, federal system, the practical problems of the post-war period notwithstanding. With their influence in Germany growing, their approach to the emerging political structures ultimately prevailed. The US preponderance manifested itself as early as the autumn of 1946 when the first offices of the planned combined Anglo-American Zones (Bizonia) were set up.

By the time the Germans debated the Basic Law for the emerging Federal Republic the objectives of the Allies in Germany had become even more modest. All crusading ideas about the implanting of 'democracy' in Germany had been replaced by considerations of safety from a possible alliance of the new West German state with the east, by keeping control of the Federal Republic's foreign and military affairs in the form of an Occupation Statute. As a guarantee against the resurgence of a German threat to her neighbours as decentralised a system in Germany as was reconcilable with admin-

28. Pfetsch, 'Verfassungspolitik', p. 8.

istrative efficiency should be introduced. Federalism seemed to be the most useful form of political organisation not only from the western Allies' point of view but also because it obscured the fact that with the setting up of the Federal Republic the separation of Germany into two states had become a reality. On the other hand, the federal system also seemed to offer sufficient flexibility for a future reunification and thus seemed to keep all options open. The six western powers (including the Benelux countries) which met in London from February to June 1948 to come to an agreement on the form of a future West German state emphasised that:

> the Constitution should be such as to enable the Germans to play their part in bringing to an end the present division of Germany not by the reconstitution of a centralised *Reich* but by means of a federal form of government which adequately protects the rights of the respective states and which at the same time provides for adequate central authority and which guarantees the rights and freedoms of the individual.[29]

For these reasons a federal system was the most acceptable form of organisation also for those Germans who had to take on the task of working out a constitution and might be blamed for the division of their country. When the minister presidents of the western zones were called to Frankfurt on 1 July and given instructions by the Allies to convene a Constituent Assembly to work out a constitution there was still considerable reluctance among the Germans to proceed. Only under the impact of the Berlin blockade was the Allied proposal finally accepted.

Germans and Allies agreed that the Constituent Assembly or 'Parliamentary Council' should be composed of members of the Länder parliaments and that the latter should ultimately vote the new constitution into existence. On 10 August, a small constituent council of legal experts (one from each Land) was selected by the minister presidents and met on the Chiemsee island Herrenchiemsee for two weeks to prepare discussion papers for the wider Parliamentary Council. This group of constitutional specialists with their 'position papers' in effect pre-empted important decisions. For example, 'democracy' was understood as a perfectly organised machinery, the contents of which were not even discussed. Otto Suhr (Berlin) thought that a majority of those present was too

29. Merkl, *Origins of the West German Republic*, p. 19.

'wedded to tradition' (*traditionsgebunden*). In Berlin they had argued about the problem of professional civil servants in a democracy and about socialism. On Herrenchiemsee it was tacitly assumed that there *was* a professional civil service.[30] The full Parliamentary Council met for the first time on 1 September in Bonn. There was instant agreement with the Allies' wish to see a federal system in Germany. Indeed, even 'without any specifications by the Allies, there can hardly be any doubt that the German authorities would have drawn up a democratic constitution for a federal system'.[31] This meant that previous German plans based on all-German neutralist concepts had been abandoned in favour of one government and one parliament for the western zones.[32] On the other hand, the Germans were at pains to play down the impression that a separate state was created by insisting that they were not working out a constitution but an administrative and organisational statute. The Herrenchiemsee draft papers gave direction to the Council's debate: legal not socio-political considerations predominated. The latter were left to future legislation.

The Parliamentary Council was less free in its deliberations than the Länder parliaments. It had to deal with more than one occupation power and its proposals would fundamentally affect the economic and political order in Europe. The Allies therefore watched the proceedings closely. Because of their interference the deliberations went through two crises: the first in November 1948 during the debate on the functions and powers of the upper house, the Bundesrat, and the second in March 1949 in connection with the clauses concerning the fiscal administration of Germany. In both cases the crises occurred because the occupation powers appeared to be siding with one or other of the German parties and were resolved by inter-German compromises which the Allies finally accepted. In the first place the Bundesrat emerged as a second chamber with a suspensive veto. The second crisis was longer and more serious: the Allies made their approval of the Basic Law dependent on a (to them) satisfactory division of powers of the financial administration between the two levels of government.

All in all, the Basic Law was far more influenced by past German experiences than by Allied interference. Where the latter was exer-

30. F. Wiesemann 'Die Gründung des deutschen Weststaats' in Institut für Zeitgeschichte (ed.), *Westdeutschlands Weg zur Bundesrepublik 1945–49* (Beck, Munich, 1976), p. 127.
31. Merkl, *Origins of the West German Republic*, p. 117.
32. Wiesemann, 'Grundung', p. 128.

cised, it was resented by the Germans and therefore almost counter-productive. This applied, for example, to the 'military-style' Frankfurt recommendations to the minister presidents in July 1948 which the Germans were very reluctant to accept. There was generally more Allied interference in the deliberations of the Basic Law than there had been in that of the state constitutions of the US Zone. It seems likely therefore that a large part of the Allied intervention was inspired by the British authorities. Although dif-ficult to qualify, it seems that complaints by German politicians like Schumacher that the Allies had meddled with the most basic right of a people—the right to write its own constitution without inter-ference[33]—reflected a more general German unease: the Basic Law had been forced upon them in too great haste, too soon after military defeat and with the political future of the whole of their country too uncertain to be openly welcome.

Civil Service Reform

Of the three areas in which the British attempted to reform the administrative structures in Germany, that of the civil service was the most controversial. Changes in the German civil service had been included in Britain's earliest reform programmes, and the final imposition of a civil service law by the Allies on the emerging Federal Republic came as late as 18 February 1949 (Law No. 15). The prolonged duration of Allied efforts in this area alone indicates the great importance attached to it both by the Anglo-American occupying authorities and the Germans. Yet despite Allied efforts the traditional structure of the German civil service re-emerged with the founding of the Federal Republic. Not only were the rights of the Beamte anchored in the Basic Law (Article 131) but a special civil service law of 17 May 1950 went much further: it compensated all those civil servants who had lost their jobs 'as a consequence of the war' either in the form of lost employment in their former home areas in the east or as a result of Allied denazification policies.

This failure of the Allies was all the more remarkable in that at the end of the war both the German public and the Allies were ready for a 'change of elites in public administration' and the disappear-

33. Merkl, *Origins of the West German Republic*, p. 116. See also E. Kogan, 'Der entscheidénde Schritt', *Frankfurter Hefte*, vol. 3, 1948, pp. 586–91.

ance of the top administrative 'layer' seemed to make such a change possible.[34] But here even more than in other areas the slowness of the Allies' response to the German situation mitigated against a successful occupation policy. There were other inhibiting factors as well. Even in the course of wartime planning in Britain there were tendencies to rebuild the traditional pre-Hitler German civil service. Clearly such continuity excluded a radical restructuring of the civil service after the war. Similarly, because of the failure of the occupying powers to take immediate action, the (temporary) legal basis for the employment of civil servants in 1945 remained the German civil service law of 1937, albeit stripped of its Nazi provisions. This provided a continuity of status, rights and conditions for the civil service which it was difficult to dislodge later. All these obstacles to change were compounded by a shortage of skilled personnel at all levels of British Military Government which could have taken this controversial matter firmly in hand.[35]

The programme for the reform of the civil service was included in the British 'Directive on Administration, Local and Regional Government, and the Public Services' of September 1945. In fact the entire Part II of the directive was devoted to it. There were three fundamental changes which the British thought essential. First, the large, monolithic state-controlled civil service should be separated into a number of smaller services according to the level of government at which the individual was employed. As in Britain only officials employed directly by central government should be classed as 'civil servants'. Secondly, there was to be a ban on any political activity by the civil servants. Thirdly, the traditional privileged status of the Beamter who had acted as a representative of 'state authority' was to be replaced by the new concept of the politically neutral public servant. These criticisms of the German system were partly based on an idealised view of the system in Britain. Moreover, it demonstrated, 'a selective view which saw class privilege [*Kastendünkel*] in Germany but which ignored the social exclusivity of the [British] Civil Service where the Administrative Class was the almost exclusive reserve of 'Oxbridge' graduates'.[36] The directive contained a great number of detailed proposals for change but it did

34. W. Benz, 'Versuche zur Reform des öffentlichen Dienstes in Deutschland 1945–52', *Vierteljahreshefte für Zeitgeschichte*, Vol. 29, No. 2, 1981, pp. 216–45.
35. U. Reusch, 'Versuche zur Neuordnung des Berufsbeamtentums' in Foschepoth/ Steininger (ed.), *Britische Deutschland und Besatzungspolitiks*, p. 176.
36. Reusch, 'Versuche', p. 177.

not have the force of law and remained a declaration of intent. From the beginning there was vociferous German opposition, often led, as we have seen, by the Social Democrats. Moreover by mid-1946 a sea change of British policy had begun, culminating in Directive 57 of December 1946 in which the Germans were given back much of the control over their own affairs.

A more promising field for reform seemed to open up for the Allies with the creation of a new set of institutions in 'Bizonia' with their own public servants. It was here that British and Americans acting jointly tried to ensure that German legislation was enacted according to Allied guidelines in respect of two specific proposals: first that there should be a *Personalamt*, comparable to the British Civil Service Commission, and secondly, a new civil service law setting out conditions of service according to Allied thinking should be created. The Bipartite Control Office (BICO) reissued previous guidelines and repeatedly exhorted the Germans to produce the required legislation. Eventually, on 22 April 1948, a transitional law for the 'Legal Position of Public Employees of the United Economic Area' was enacted.[37] German acceptance of the law, however, was only ever tactical. The 'principle of incompatibility' embodied in the law which excluded civil servants from political activity was unacceptable to the Germans. Finally, on 15 February 1949, the Bizonal occupation authorities promulgated their law for 'Administrative Employees of the United Economic Area' which incorporated all their previous demands, at a time when the Parliamentary Council, 65% of whose members were Beamte, was exercising the German democratic right of self-determination. It was an ill-considered move by the Allied authorities, destined to be superseded. In the event, Article 131 of the Basic Law satisfied all the demands of the Beamte, reflecting the power of the best-organised pressure group in the Parliamentary Council.

An examination of the various attempts to reform administrative structures reflects the steadily narrowing options which the British had in Germany. Whereas they could simply dictate the institutional framework of local government in Germany, by the time the constitutions of the Länder and later of the Federal Republic were elaborated the scope for British influence had markedly diminished. The views of the other western Allies had to be taken into account and, what was perhaps more important, the wishes of the

---

37. Benz, 'Versuche zur Reform', p. 227.

Germans themselves. The latter were able to push their views through much more strongly than they had been able to in the first period of the occupation when the British reformed local government. Thus the British did not succeed in getting their way on important issues such as the voting system or the political activity of civil servants. In the last analysis, the contradiction of Allied policy in Germany, the attempt to 'democratise by democratic means', worked in favour of German traditionalism.

The Political Parties

Whether the British liked it or not they had not been able to prevent the emergence of political parties. The Social Democrats and the communist KPD had the organisational advantage over the 'bourgeois' camp because their members had maintained contact throughout the Third Reich and were now ready for political action. Their first aim was to be allowed to operate freely. Military Government, on the other hand, saw in the ban of all political activities a period of 'reflection' for the Germans at the end of which a stronger and more deeply rooted democracy would emerge, based on new political forces. However, the decision of the Soviets on 11 June to license political parties and trade unions in their zone led to an acceleration of developments in the British Zone as well. By July the British Foreign Office thought the lifting of the ban on parties in the British and US Zones was 'desirable'.[38] British observers in Germany agreed on the possible consequences of further delays: 'the longer we refuse the Germans the right of political activity the greater the danger will be of Nazis and rabid nationalists covering their tracks and taking refuge in other groups . . . and of the politically uneducated Germans becoming even more misguided . . .'[39] But it was not until after the Potsdam Conference that the British Military Governor, Field Marshal Montgomery, announced the imminent licensing of political parties. This was formalised in the Zone Directives Nos. 10 and 12 of 15 September 1945.

However, as we have seen, British Military Government would have preferred further delays. One additional reason for this was the

38. PRO/FO371/46868/CO238, Foreign Office memorandum 'German Political Questions', 9 July 1945, p. 21.
39. PRO/FO371/46934/CA772, 21st Army Group, Political Intelligence Summary No. 6 for period ending 17 August 1945.

general uncertainty of members of Military Government as to the precise nature of occupation policy, as well as a chronic shortage of manpower. As late as January 1946 the average commander was reported as '[thirsting] for political guidance, but a chronic lack of experienced personnel made it impossible to satisfy it. It has not hitherto been possible to maintain a special staff at Lubbecke to deal with problems arising from German political activity . . .'[40] When a 'German Political Branch' was set up at Zonal Headquarters in the autumn of 1945 it consisted of only three men. They were not only to maintain an overview of political developments throughout the zone but also to advise Military Government personnel and Germans alike—clearly an impossible task. This explains to some extent the insistence on a slow and controlled licensing process of the parties which started with the September directives. Local activists were warned immediately that 'the decision on these applications [for a licence] will take a long time, as all applications have to go to headquarters at Bad Oeynhausen'.[41] In the event the parties could function above district level only from December 1945 after undergoing prolonged and detailed scrutiny of their organisations, leaders, members and constitutions. Their applications, to be submitted in six copies (five in English, one in German), were returned for the slightest irregularity.

A further reason for British caution when approaching political activities in Germany was their suspicion that under the guise of 'democratic' groupings some potent German force might re-emerge which could threaten British security. This distrust was directed in the first instance particularly against the German left where parties and trade unions together might form a potentially dangerous combination. Again it was the rather vague notion that the Germans were 'political' where in British eyes they should approach matters from a non-political stance which gave the British cause for concern. Thus Hanover Military Government reported in November 1945:

> The German still persists in regarding trade unions primarily as a political . . . force. Although this outlook is based on experiences in Imperial Germany and under Weimar it receives strong reinforcement at

40. PRO/FO371/55610/C11763, Office of Political Adviser to Commander-in-Chief, Advance HQ, Berlin to Bevin (FO), 12 January 1946.
41. Stadtarchiv Hanover, II–L–40a, 'Ergebnis der 97 Besprechung zwischen dem Stadtkommandanten und Oberbürgermeister Bratke, 27 September 1945'.

this time when political parties are limited to *Kreis* level whilst the trade unions have no similar limitations. The danger of the parties going 'underground' by amalgamation with Trade Unions is causing K[reis] Detachments considerable concern and will need constant watching.[42]

It seems however, that it was not only a lack of overall policy and suspicion of *all* Germans regardless of their political allegiances which determined the British approach to political activities in Germany. There was also a specific notion of how 'democracy' had to work in the defeated enemy country. As we have seen, it was to work 'from the bottom upwards' at the local level. But applied to the political parties it also implied that the British would abstain from giving preference to any particular group and, if necessary, disadvantage some to help the full range of political options to emerge. As Schumacher complained in the summer of 1945, 'suddenly there is only to be democracy . . .'[43] In other words the blanket imposition of 'democracy' made no distinction between the parties of the left with their proven anti-fascist track record and the rest of the parties whose position had been in some cases ambiguous. The British felt that allowing the SPD to make use of its organisational advantage would be against the interest of democracy in Germany for several reasons: the SPD might become too closely associated with British Military Government and be later disowned by the Germans as the 'party of the Allies'. On the other hand, the SPD might come to dominate the German political scene too much and thus prevent other and—it was hoped new—parties from exercising their political rights. The fact that many members of Military Government were not in sympathy with the political objectives of the SPD nor with Schumacher as a person may also have played a role. Above all, the British view of 'democracy' as almost a game with fair rules but vague content underpinned their attitude. Indeed, the British saw in this approach the embodiment of liberal principles in their policies in Germany: they were to create a general framework which the Germans themselves should fill.[44]

The question arises as to the impact of this British approach on the political parties in Germany. This was profound in a direct, but

42. PRO/WO171/7990, monthly report of Detachment 504/720, Military Government, November 1945, Appendix A.
43. Stadtarchiv Hanover, K. Schumacher, 'For a New and Better Germany', 2nd half of August 1945.
44. Interview with Noel Annan, 25 April 1985. Lord Annan was a member of the CCG's Political Division.

also an indirect way. Contrary to popular belief the SPD was *dis*advantaged. The loss of its organisational advantage over the other parties in the summer of 1945 has to be seen in context with other Military Government measures which worked against that party, such as the ban of the party's own youth or sport sections—a traditional way for the left to recruit members. The SPD was also not able to run its own party newspaper; only party 'information sheets' were initially allowed, and that only after a long and exhausting struggle between party activists and Military Government. Moreover, the party never received official support from the Labour Party (now in office) as might have been expected. On the other hand, the SPD fared better in local government in the British Zone than the other parties.[45] It provided the greatest numbers of officials and, in a period when the Allies were in control and the parties were unable to exercise power directly, the placing of party members in crucial administrative positions was the main method by which the parties hoped to exercise some influence. However, even this minor advantage seemed in jeopardy when the British, in the course of the proposed local government reform, thought of introducing a clause which banned civil servants from political activity. After numerous complaints by the SPD, involving even Labour Party members and the press in Britain, the clause was dropped.

The main beneficiary of Military Government policy was in fact the CDU. This was particularly the case in the Rhineland where the Catholic Church was powerful and the Catholic Centre Party had had its traditional power base. Without the Military Government ban on political activity in the immediate post-war period the pressure on the constituent parts of the emerging new party to re-establish themselves as separate entities would have been greater than the collective will to form a new political group.[46] Certainly in areas without a strong Centre Party presence, such as in the east and north of the British Zone, prolonged and difficult negotiations took place before the new party finally emerged. Even then the fact that the party did not have to exercise real power allowed it to obscure some of its inherent contradictions. Later these lost some of their importance when the general political climate moved more to the right under the impact of the Cold War.

In many other respects the British achieved unintended results. Whereas they had wanted a 'period of reflection' for the Germans

45. Pietsch, *Militärreigierung*, p. 190.
46. Ibid., p. 170.

after the end of the war which would lead to a new and vigorous democracy more deeply rooted in society, they encouraged by their ban on all political activity the very continuity which they wanted to prevent. Thus *all* major parties when they eventually emerged rebuilt their old organisations and with functionaries who had already been in their posts before 1933. Even the 'new' CDU could use the organisations of the pre-1933 Centre Party and sometimes those of the nationalist DNVP. There was also no deeper understanding for democracy and the reasons for its collapse. This is well illustrated by the way the issue of National Socialism was approached by the parties. In Hanover, for example, the largest bourgeois party was the Niedersächsische Landespartei (NLP), a regional party of Lower Saxony. In May 1945, its leader, who had already been party leader before 1933, appealed to party members to 'eradicate thoroughly [*mit Stumpf und Stil*] the weed of National Socialism . . . which [was] entirely un-German'.[47] By March 1946, a marked change in the party's attitude had taken place. Instructions to party speakers refer to the 'determination not to look backwards . . . We should not talk about collective guilt. Under no circumstances should we admit that the German people are guilty of the war.'[48] In the same city, the liberal FDP in the summer of 1945 was unequivocal in its condemnation of National Socialism: '[The party] is determined, in clear recognition of the crimes committed by Hitler and the obligations which arise from them for the German people, to work for an honest reconciliation and compensation [*Wiedergutmachung*].' However, by January 1946, the party was following a more aggressive line, announcing its determination to fight socialism in all its guises, 'be it as National or Inter-National Socialism'.[49] A similar point can be made about the CDU. Whereas the early party, in its Cologne Guidelines of October 1945, vehemently rejected National Socialism as having 'covered the name of Germany throughout the world with shame and dishonour', the party in Hanover, in January 1946, made no reference at all to the past. On the contrary, the leader of the new local party asserted: 'we demand that christians recognise the fact that they made one of the greatest sacrifices in Hitler's Germany and that they contributed decisively to the defeat of National Socialism'.[50]

47. Stadtarchiv Hanover, Akte 'Die Zulassung der politischen Parteien'.
48. Marshall, *Origins*, p. 188; Hauptstaatsarchiv Hanover, VVP5/11, 'An den Parteivorstand der NLP', 28 February 1946.
49. Marshall, *Origins*, p. 184; *Neuer Hannoverscher Kurier*, 25 January 1946.
50. Ibid.

On the left, by the autumn of 1945, first spontaneous attempts at creating a united working-class party had failed. Without any outside encouragement the small groups left at the end of the Third Reich were unable to sustain a separate identity and had to drift into the SPD which thus acted as the *Magnet* as Schumacher hoped it would. Left-wing activists like those in Hanover blamed the Allies for this state of affairs:

> The remaining illegal small groups which were essentially SAP [Sozialistische Arbeiterpartei] friends, Socialist Front and ISK [Internationalen Sozialistischer Kampfbund] had offered their practical cooperation as soon as the Americans occupied the town. Political discussions about longterm objectives were pushed into the background. *Realpolitik* was the word. This found its manifestation in the so called Reconstruction Committees. No one talked about the so-called 'historical' parties. No one believed they would reappear in their full 'glory'. The concept of the workers movement was the unity of the working class as the lesson of the past. A new socialist movement ought to have been the consequence. That it came differently, we owe to the restoration efforts of the allies who knew no other aim but the reformation of the state of pre-1933. The Russians . . . led the way. While we were still arguing about what kind of political movement could emerge from the committees, they created *faits accomplis* in their zone.[51]

It seems that as far as political parties were concerned the British were partially successful within their own terms of reference in that a general framework was created in Germany in which a variety of parties could operate. However, by banning smaller parties on both right and left in the early phase of the occupation the British seemed to repeat what they had also practised in their reform of local government: the export of British institutions abroad. Unlike the experience of the Weimar Republic, a British-style two-party system with one smaller third party emerged in Germany. Later election results, moreover, seemed to indicate that the German people preferred the CDU to the SPD and that the British therefore may have worked in the direction in which the Germans wanted to go anyway. On the other hand, the British did not succeed in their desire to see 'new' political forces emerge in Germany. The ban on

51. O. Brenner, Hanover, to J. Lang, New York, 12 February 1947 in H. Grebing and B. Klemm, (eds.) *Lehrstücke in Solidarität. Briefe und Biographien deutscher Sozialisten, 1945–49* (Deutsche Verlags-Anstalt, Stuttgart, 1983), pp. 145–9.

all political activity in the first crucial months prevented this, as did British nervousness which saw in parties or trade unions potential opposition groups which would endanger their security.

Conclusions

The analysis of the British policy of 'democratisation' of public administration in Germany showed that this was only a limited success. The contradiction between the liberal content of the programme which depended for its long-term functioning on the cooperation of the Germans and its imposition by force if it was to bring about results with which the Germans did not agree was already obvious to some British at the time. But force was acceptable to the Germans in the early phase of the occupation; indeed, it had been expected. It was however, not used because it went against basic British principles and also because it would have involved a vast amount of expenditure which Britain could not afford. Moreover, all plans for reform were based on a long occupation and the emerging Cold War with the growing US involvement and the break-up of four-power cooperation in Germany led to a distortion of initial British intentions. In the short run, all Allied policy was able to provide was an institutional framework. By being in control in Germany they shielded German officials and politicians from blame for the appalling circumstances of the time. Unlike the Weimar Republic, Bonn did not have to shoulder the responsibility for the past. For the German population, however, it took time to overcome the credibility gap which the existence of political structures without real power represented. With economic prosperity and political stability this has eventually been achieved.

8

Priming the Pump of German Democracy. British 'Re-Education' Policy in Germany after the Second World War

David Welch

Introduction

The policy of 're-education' adopted by the Allies in different forms after the war represents a political experiment unique in modern history.[1] The rationale behind Britain's policy of re-education in the period 1945–55 was to change the political behaviour and social outlook of the German people by means of a fundamental restructuring of all the means of opinion and communication. In practice this control was to extend beyond the press, radio and cinema, to include the entire education system.

As I shall show, the all-embracing nature of a term like 're-education' facilitated policy shifts which allowed the British to move (according to the rapidly changing nature and eventual collapse of the 'Grand Alliance') from 'guilt mobilisation' to the 'projection of Britain', and eventually to embrace seriously German public opinion and the possibility of German sovereignty. It has been argued that Britain did have a properly conceived plan for re-educating Germany that consisted of responsible government, the federation of Germany and European partnership. The notion of responsible government and the idea of a federal Germany becoming a partner within a reconstructed Europe was based on the British conception of a new German society. Such a society it was argued could only emerge through a process of 're-education'.[2] The

1. The research on which this chapter is based was made possible by the generous financial support from the Nuffield Foundation.
2. See K. Jürgensen, 'British Occupation Policy after 1945 and the Problem of Re-educating Germany', *History*, Vol. 68, No. 223, June, 1983, pp. 225–44.

wartime planning of re-education and its post-war implementation reveals that there really was no formulated and agreed policy between the various ministries concerned. Rather, compromises emerged from the intense rivalries that existed within the British administration; between those 'liberals' who felt that not all Germans were bad and who wished to go so far as to encourage even strong cultural links, and others, particularly in the Foreign Office, who took a much tougher line believing that the entire German nation should be brought to account through a process of 'guilt mobilisation'. British occupation policy was therefore a gradual process that emerged, on the one hand, from certain premises that had been formulated during the inter-war period based around an historicist interpretation of German national character traits and, on the other hand, as a result of pragmatic short-term improvisations in response to changing political circumstances.

Wartime Planning

The debate polarised around Robert Vansittart of the Foreign Office and his younger acolytes. Writing in 1941, Lord Vansittart, in attempting to explain Germany's past and present, held that all Germans were responsible for the Nazi tyranny.[3] 'Vansittartism' as it became known, was a political creed that embraced all shades of the political spectrum in Britain and retained some influence within the Foreign Office, and later with junior officers of the post-war Control Commission for Germany (CCG). However, in May 1942, Vansittart was roundly defeated when he attempted to carry a motion in the House of Lords on post-war policy towards Germany. Rather than accept the Vansittart view of the 'vicious and guilty German race' their Lordships preferred, instead, to stress the need for a just peace and 're-education'.[4] The issue was not seriously raised again in the Lords until a year later when, in March 1943, a new, significant element was introduced into the discussion. Viscount Cecil of Chelwood posed the rhetorical question of what should be done after Nazism was destroyed and Germany disarmed. He replied that Germany should be given the opportunity of

3. R. Vansittart, *Black Record: Germans Past and Present* (Hamish Hamilton, London, 1941). This was based on Vansittart's broadcasts.
4. House of Lords, Parliamentary Debates, May 1942. The debate took place on 19 and 21 May.

're-educating herself'.[5] The idea of self-help under British guidance is a recurring theme in the numerous discussion papers and official briefings that began to appear in 1943 and 1944. 'Re-education' as opposed to punishment and suppression was now being adopted in some quarters as part of British post-war planning.

The potential role that the mass media would play in this 're-education' process was first seriously discussed in the summer of 1943. On 11 August 1943, the Political Warfare Executive (PWE) set up a German subcommittee under the chairmanship of Con O'Neill, the former head of the News Department of the Foreign Office, who had, until Munich, worked in the Diplomatic Service in Berlin. During the previous month O'Neill had prepared a secret paper on 'Lines for Emergency Plan; Propaganda to Germany after her Defeat', which began with the words: 'Our long term aim is presumably to integrate Germany into a peaceful and prosperous European order.'[6] O'Neill argued that the tone which had been adopted in BBC broadcasts should be maintained—that of the strong but just enemy. The paper concluded with the somewhat ironic sentiment in the light of the eventual policy of projecting British values that 'no attempt should be made in the German way to ram the conquerer's culture down the conquered's throat'.

In October 1943, O'Neill became Secretary of the subcommittee of the Post-Hostilities Planning Committee, the chairman of which was John M. Troutbeck of the Foreign Office, who had just been appointed adviser to the Cabinet on Germany and given the task of coordinating British policy. In December Troutbeck set out a memorandum on the 'Regeneration of Germany' in which he argued that in order to destroy the political outlook and traditions upon which Germany society had been based it would be necessary 'to stamp out the whole tradition on which the German nation has been built'.[7] A month later the War Cabinet received a secret report from O'Neill on the 'Re-education of Germany' which suggested certain principles that should govern the British approach. Again the paper repeated the notion that 'Germans alone can re-educate their fellow countrymen'.[8] These two important papers highlight a number of different attitudes that were contained within British

5. House of Lords, Parliamentary Debates, 10 March 1943.
6. Public Record Office (PRO)/Foreign Office(FO) 898/370, 6 July 1943.
7. PRO/FO371/39093; Troutbeck entered the FO in 1920 and was transferred to the Ministry of Economic Warfare in 1940.
8. PRO/FO371/39093, the memorandum is dated 27 January 1944.

wartime planning during this period. Troutbeck's interpretation was clearly based on a number of prevailing assumptions that were critical of Germany's past, while O'Neill was more concerned to accept that Germany could change and would be willing to participate in peaceful cooperation. In July 1944, the Cabinet's Armistice and Post-War Committee (chaired by the Deputy Prime Minister, Clement Atlee) received an authoritative directive which outlined short- and long-term objectives on the re-education of Germany.[9] This directive was particularly concerned to detail the role of education in occupied Germany. For the period immediately after the close of hostilities the first aim was to eradicate Nazi and militarist values while the long-term objectives were to re-establish standards of 'respect for objective facts . . . and to foster interest in the ideas of popular democracy, such as freedom of opinion, speech, the press and religion'. Interestingly enough, re-education was to be put into practice first of all with German prisoners of war who were to be segregated according to their political affiliations into categories of 'black' (Nazis), 'grey' (followers) and 'white' (anti-Nazis).[10]

The notion of 'two Germanies' (or in this case, 'three'), was also taken up by Professor E. R. Dodds of the Foreign Office Research Department in a detailed paper on the failure of democracy in Germany since 1918. Although pointing out the weak liberal traditions in Germany, Dodds concluded that the failure of the Weimar system 'does not compel us to believe that Germans are permanently incapable of self-government'.[11] Drafted by Dodds in late 1944, this was a period of heated reaction against punitive suggestions emerging from the United States. In a minute appended to Dodd's report Troutbeck referred to it as 'a most impressive paper' but nevertheless felt compelled to add that Germans were unlikely to become democrats, 'at any rate in this century'.[12] The more enlightened policy-makers were keenly aware in drawing up plans for re-education that they should not make the same mistakes as the peace-makers of 1919. However, 're-education' was such a vague

9. PRO/FO371/39095, 3 July 1944. The draft directive came from the Armistice and Civil Administration Organisation which initially consisted of ten members from different departments and organisations.
10. See H. Faulk, *Die deutschen Kriegsgefangenen in Grossbritannien: Re-education* (Gieseking, Munich and Bielefeld, 1970).
11. PRO/FO370/46880. See also A. M. Birke, 'Geschichtsauffassung und Deutsch-
landbild im Foreign Office Research Department', *Historisches Jahrbuch* (Görres Gesellschaft, Freiburg and Munich, 1984), Vol. 104, pp. 372–91.
12. PRO/FO370/46880. The FO received Dodd's report on 13 February. Troutbeck's minute although undated was probably written in early March.

umbrella term, that it could be used to justify a wide range of policy initiatives.[13] For some it was seen as a means of reinstating Germany into the mainstream of European economic and political life while at the same time persuading Germans of their responsibility for Nazism and its atrocities. For others re-education was the vehicle for German atonement and 'guilt mobilisation'. In fact both policies were argued by individuals in the different policy-making departments. The two policies were not mutually exclusive nor were they necessarily contradictory. They were made in the context of the various tripartite agreements and in the light of revelations of the horrors of Nazi concentration camps and the concomitant need to respond to public opinion in Britain.

As early as December 1944, even before the images of the death camps had appeared, Richard Crossman, who by this time was deputy head of the Anglo-American Psychological Warfare Division (PWD),[14] pointed to a discernible shift towards guilt mobilisation when he complained bitterly that 'the sudden and violent change of policy directives necessitates a complete transformation of our task in Germany'. His own views of this new 'hard' line were clear enough: 'We should seek to destroy National Socialism, but we would assume that the mass of the people would be glad to be rid of it . . . Now all Germans are to be regarded as potentially dangerous, as sharing in guilt, as a people apart.'[15]

The Start of the Occupation

In April 1945, the PWD, with Crossman clearly the moving spirit, attempted to soften official policies by searching for signs of anti-Nazi activity and suggesting that such 'noble and inspiring' Germans who had resisted the Nazis be entrusted with positions of responsibility.[16] Not only did such notions question the morality of guilt mobilisation but they also implied a short occupation without the need for long-term 're-education'. Crossman's attempts to find

13. This was confirmed in an interview given to the author by Michael Balfour, 13 March 1987.
14. Crossman was formerly with the British Political Warfare Executive. PWD was a division of Eisenhower's Supreme Headquarters, SHAEF, with a combined Anglo-American staff. It was dissolved with the rest of SHAEF in July 1945.
15. PRO/FO371/46729, 20 December 1944.
16. PRO/FO371/46894, unsigned PWD Guidance Notes, dated 21 April 1945.

'good' Germans and publicise them drew an instant response from C. E. Steel who was temporarily with Supreme Headquarters Allied Expeditionary Force (SHAEF) and soon to become head of Political Division. Writing to Troutbeck, Steel doubted the wisdom of prematurely boosting 'these dubiously repentant Huns', claiming: 'I cannot believe that the British Government are prepared at this moment to admit the existence of a democratic Germany, or even the germ of one.' Instead, Steel suggested a stiff rebuke to Crossman ('who is engaged in pushing his personal views on the German problem') and PWD to 'lay off re-education and German resistance'.[17] Nevertheless, there were those in the Control Commission, like Michael Balfour of Public Relations and Information Services Control (PR/ISC), who attempted to make a distinction between 'collective guilt' and 'collective responsibility'. In a draft paper entitled 'German Guilt—to plug or not to plug', Balfour argued that the question of guilt was fundamental to Britain's relationship with the German people. With one eye clearly on the experiences of Versailles he suggested that, 'Unless . . . justice . . . can be established, it will remain (in German eyes) merely the kind of settlement which the victorious side imposes by force of arms at the end of the war . . .'[18]

Indeed, one of the dominant themes in ISC's first policy directive for the week beginning 13 May 1945 was 'the common responsibility of all Germans for Nazi crimes'. Refering to a propaganda campaign that was to be launched to show the German people the horrors of Belsen and Dachau, the directive went on to state that 'the moral responsibility for these crimes must be laid wholly and solely on the German nation'.[19] According to ISC, which was responsible for media policy, radio and press would be specifically designed to inculcate a sense of individual responsibility among its German audience.[20] However, once British troops began the occupation of Germany, the desirability (or otherwise) of distinguishing between collective responsibility and collective guilt became obscured by the more pragmatic considerations of bringing order to a vanquished nation. Memos pontificating on the moral dimension of

17. PRO/FO371/46894, Steel to Troutbeck, 3 May 1945.
18. PRO/FO1056/22. Balfour became Director of Information Services Control in April 1946. See a similar discussion paper intended to brief Control Commission Officers on 'War Guilt: German Arguments—British Answers.' It contained eight stock answers to anticipated questions.
19. PRO/FO1005/739, 12 May 1945.
20. PRO/FO1005/739, Information Control Directive No 5, 20 June 1945.

the occupier's role tended to disappear in a bureaucratic maze. Moreover it was such a fine distinction that in September 1945 in a note minuted by the head of PR/ISC, Major General Alec Bishop, it was decided that ISC would continue to emphasise German war guilt, as long as it was 'considered to be psychologically desirable'.[21] Collective responsibility or collective guilt were thus interchangeable according to the needs of the moment. What did remain constant was that Britain anticipated a long occupation during which time Germans would undergo 're-education' and political sovereignty would only be handed over step-by-step.[22]

Notions like 're-education' assumed as axiomatic that there would be a long period of colonial-style occupation. Collective complicity and the shift to guilt mobilisation also allowed the British to reflect once again on German national character traits and to ruminate on whether re-education was possible at all for such a people. For example, in March 1947, writing in the *British Zone Review* (the official journal of the Control Commission), one staff-writer actually recommended inter-marriage to dilute wicked Teutonic blood![23] Such views were not uncommon, for guilt mobilisation was not simply a response to the barbarism unleashed by Nazism; its roots and antecedents can be traced to the prevailing ignorance about Germany that resulted in historical stereotypes being adopted in all walks of life in Britain from the Labour Cabinet down to middle-ranking officers in the Control Commission. Witness the absurd official pamphlets that were intended to brief new Control Commission Officers coming into Germany about what they could expect from the former enemy and the attitude they should therefore adopt ('don't know how to make tea', 'they exalt death', 'fond of music'). In this immediate post-war period, according to Lord Annan of the Political Division (whose officers were supervising the political side of the Control Commission): 'Military

21. PRO/FO1056/25, 22 September 1945. PR/ISC was initially headed by Alec Bishop and together with Education Branch was responsible for the implementation of re-education. See Bishop's draft outline 'Can We Re-educate Germany?' (PRO/FO1056/21, November 1945) which was eventually printed in the *British Zone Review*, 8 December 1945.
22. See Duff Cooper's memo to Foreign Secretary Ernest Bevin contemplating a Germany of *1966*, PRO/CAB21/1872, CP(46)223, ORC(46)52, 16 July 1946. Cooper was in Paris at the time and the memo was in support of French dismemberment plans.
23. 'Educating Germany: An Englishman's View', *British Zone Review*, 15 March 1947. This journal provides a revealing insight into the attitudes of middle-ranking officers charged with carrying out occupation policies such as re-education.

Government officials resembled civilised and agreeable officers in a rather forward-looking Bedouin country—tending to treat Germans in the beginning very much as intelligent natives.'[24]

British Policy on Education

The Allied Control Council (ACC) was set up by tripartite proclamation in Berlin on 5 June 1945. The Potsdam Agreement had laid down certain principles for the occupying powers known as the 'Four D's: de-militarisation, de-nazification, democratisation and deindustrialisation. Educational policy had also been governed since July 1945 in accordance with the principles laid down at Potsdam, by which the signatories undertook that 'German education should be so controlled as completely to eliminate National Socialist and militarist doctrines and to make possible the successful development of democratic ideas.'[25] To this end, Education Branch, under the direction of Donald Riddy, moved to Germany as a division of CCG to implement 're-education' policy, receiving instructions from both the Military Governor in Berlin and from the Control Office in London. However, Education Branch's direct responsibility for education stopped at the end of 1946 when in accordance with the British policy of decentralising Germany, responsibility for education was handed over to the new Länder governments. Ordinance No. 57 on the 'Powers of *Länder* in the British Zone' meant that Britain no longer had governmental power in the field of education; instead their authority was confined to supervision and the power of veto.[26] Nevertheless, working from Control Council Directive No. 54 (Basic Principles for the Democratisation of Education in Germany), Education Branch in its new advisory capacity continued to persuade the German academic profession to introduce new educational legislation in order to provide the framework in which democratic ideas could successfully flourish.[27]

24. Annan originally made this remark in an interview for a BBC television programme on the occupation of Germany. He subsequently confirmed it in correspondence with author, 20 February 1987. Annan recalls that in the early days they were determined that there should be no repetition of the 'stab-in-the-back' excuse prevalent after 1918.
25. This came from part III, paragraph 7.
26. See PRO/FO371/55898, statement of 19 November 1946 anticipating Ordinance 57, and PRO/FO371/64387, policy instructions in the light of ordinance 57.
26. PRO/FO371/64387, 'Basic Principles for the Democratisation of Education in

However, in April 1947, Robert Birley (former headmaster of Charterhouse) became Educational Adviser to the Military Governor, Sir Brian Robertson, with responsibility for reconstructing the German education system. Riddy was considered not tenacious enough in the face of his superiors in the struggle for resources. Ordinance 57 demoted an already humble branch with a modest head, and so the appointment of Birley, a grand figure with grand powers, was meant to compensate. Like Heinz Koeppler who was in charge of the prisoner-of-war programme at Wilton Park,[28] Birley viewed the task facing Britain as pre-eminently a spiritual one and he therefore proposed to re-educate only those Germans 'deeply tainted with Nazi ideology'.[29] For idealists like Birley, then, 're-education' (a term he didn't like) was seen as a means of rebuilding the cultural links between Germany and the civilised world which the Nazis had been so concerned to destroy. Indeed, of all the divisions within the Control Commission, Education Branch continued to object to the term 're-education'. As late as June 1948, in response to a draft paper set out by the Military Governor and his Regional Commissioners which concluded that 'We are all agreed that 're-education' is one of the chief objects of our Occupation . . .',[30] Education Branch felt compelled to reply: 'We detest the word 're-education' as much as the Germans. This is an Education Branch, not a 'Re-education' Branch, and the word has never been used in our directives'.[31]

Birley and his staff believed that because their Educational Control Officers worked 'on the ground' (a favourite term) and there-

---

Germany' which outlined 10 basic points, 3 June 1947. Although the decision to decontrol education was widely supported within Education Branch, it was not without its critics. See, for example, T. J. Leonard's (Textbook Section) 'urgent SOS' to Arthur Deakin demanding an interview with Bevin, PRO/FO371/64386, Leonard to Deakin, 5 January 1947.

28. At the end of the war, Britain had 2.7 million prisoners outside Germany. Koeppler's Wilton Park opened in January 1946 as a residential college where prisoners could undertake a six-week course and discuss in a relaxed atmosphere burning issues of the day. From January 1947 civilians from Germany were brought over to participate in the courses.

29. PRO/FO371/70714, Birley memorandum on education in the British Zone, 20 December 1946. See also, A. Hearnden (ed.), *The British in Germany: Educational Reconstruction after 1945* (Hamish Hamilton, London, 1978), including Birley's contribution on 'British Policy in Perspective'. See also, A. Hearnden, *Red Robert: A Life of Robert Birley* (Hamish Hamilton, London, 1984).

30. PRO/FO371/70713, Military Governor's conference with Regional Commissioners, 24 June 1948.

31. PRO/FO371/70713, brief for Military Governor supplied by Education Branch, 29 June 1948.

fore came into much closer contact with 'ordinary' Germans than any other division within CCG, their role was to establish mutual trust and an exchange of ideas, not to force 're-education' down German throats. Ironically enough it was precisely the refusal of Education Branch Officers to give orders and to insist that their guidance be obeyed in the face of entrenched German academic opinion that resulted in the adoption of an education system that virtually went back to 1933. In recent years Britain's failure to introduce thorough-going reforms in the field of education has come under increasing criticism from Germans themselves who have claimed that Education Branch could have saved German education from the problems that were to beset it many years later had they adopted a coherent policy of educational reform and been prepared to carry it through.[32] Largely as a result of impeccable 'liberal' motives, the opportunity to break with the past had been lost.

Information Control: Projecting the British Way of Life

The other part of the Control Commission primarily concerned with re-education was the PR/ISC Group. On 18 August 1945, PR/ISC, originally part of Political Division of the CCG, became a separate group organised into two branches, Public Relations (PR) and Informations Services Control (ISC) under Major-General Bishop and later C. Sprigge. ISC was charged with the control of 'all media by which information is conveyed to the Germans'.[33] The failure of Education Branch to remould the German education system should not lead to broad generalisations about any British reluctance to meddle with German institutions. A case in point was PR/ISC's role in manipulating the British-sponsored media that were to play a primary part in re-educating the tastes of the German public. The methods of presentation that were to be employed in the media were seen not as a means of re-establishing German culture but as a means of projecting British values and the British

---

32. See M. Halbritter, *Schulreformpolitik in der britischen Zone 1945–9* (Beltz, Weinheim, 1979), and M. Heinemann (ed.), *Umerziehung und Wiederaufbau* (Klett-Cotta, Stuttgart, 1981). See also, S. B. Robinson and J. C. Kuhlmann, 'Two Decades of Non-Reform in West German Education', *Comparative Education Review*, Vol. 11, No. 3, 1967, pp. 311–30; and W. Burmeister, 'Were the British too Neutral?' *Adult Education*, July, 1978.
33. PRO/FO936/148.

way of life. With the onset of the Cold War, the media were to play an increasingly important role in this context. As early as May 1945, a Foreign Office paper had declared that the media were to re-educate the German public 'so that they may unconsciously become more accessible to the ideas and standards for which Britain stands'.[34] It was anticipated that the Head of PR/ISC would decide on the extent to which the media would be employed for re-education purposes. In practice, however, it was never as simple as this; PR/ISC did not operate in isolation and therefore would often be forced to respond to changing political events outside of its control. In each of the Corps Districts and in the British Sector of Berlin, there were Information Control Units organised into sections dealing with a separate information media—press, publications, films and entertainments, but not broadcasting. Whilst these units received direction on policy and technical matters from ISC, they retained a close contact with Military Government through Information Control Officers on the staff of HQ Military Government Regions. Initially news and other material for directly controlled and licensed newspapers, and for the German Broadcasting Service, was provided by the German News Service at Hamburg under the direct control of ISC.[35]

Press and Radio: The Quest for Objectivity and Pro-British Attitudes

Of all the media, the press and radio were probably the most important for carrying out the task of 're-education'. Most of the senior PR/ISC officers appeared to attach little importance to the value of film.[36] On 14 July 1945, a memorandum by the CCG had set out a five-stage plan for the German media. As far as the press was concerned the long-term goal was an 'objective' press which could separate fact from comment and at the same time interpret His Majesty's Government policy. In other words, it should be impartial and pro-British! The problem was to get the Germans to see things the impartial and British way: 'If we succeed in giving the German reader this impression (of impartiality) it will be all the

34. PRO/FO898/401, 29 May 1945.
35. By March 1947, ISC employed a staff of approximately 360 officers of all grades, PRO/FO371/64578.
36. This point was put to me by Michael Balfour, interview 13 March 1987.

David Welch

easier for us to introduce those items which are intended to influence him into identifying his interests with those of this country without his resenting them as propaganda.'[37] The press like other media was to be recast in the British mould.

According to one PR/ISC report, the fundamental problem was that the German press was at the time of surrender 'so rotten in its structure, so thoroughly impregnated with Nazism, and so completely subservient to the Propaganda Ministry, that it had to be rooted out, and re-created from the bottom up'.[38] The rooting-out process was carried out by SHAEF, the building-up was handed over to CCG and PR/ISC. During the SHAEF planning period it was considered essential that the new licensed German press should be independent of party or political interests. Accordingly, PR/ISC set about granting licenses on the assumption that this policy would be maintained. In order, then, that re-education could take effect, PR/ISC had originally intended to introduce a licensed German press over carefully phased stages with a zonal newspaper serving as a model of what was wanted. Instead, a ministerial decision in the summer of 1945 (no doubt influenced by the speed with which the Americans and Russians were granting licenses in their zones) completely reversed this policy and directed that a party-political press should be licensed. Under the direction of Major N. B. J. Huijsman, the newly appointed Controller of Press and Publication Branch in PR/ISC, the overt Military-Government-run German-language press was replaced by a licensed press. By the middle of 1947, there were approximately forty licensed newspapers representing the point of view of the main political parties in the British Zone. They consisted of four pages (later increased to eight) and appeared twice a week only.[39] The intention had been to keep these licensed papers under close control with ISC subjecting them to pre-publication censorship and post-publication scrutiny. In practice, however, both the censorship and the scrutiny proved too big a job for ISC's already overstretched officers and was eventually given up as a lost cause.[40]

In July 1947, in a detailed and highly critical report on the licensed German press in the British Zone, Major Huijsman stated

37. PRO/FO945/848, 14 July 1945.
38. PRO/FO1056/195.
39. The circulation of the individual newspapers and their party affiliations can be found in K. Koszyk, *The German Press under British Occupation* (Neue Gesellschaft, Siegen, 1983).
40. Interview with Michael Balfour, 13 March 1987.

226

that the fundamental problem that still had to be solved was the creation of a new, progressive and pro-British press which 'will help us now and will outlive the occupation—i.e., a press which can put across the British point of view without losing the German public's support'.[41] The practical effects, however, of the licensing policy had been to create political party newspapers that reflected the views of their parties which were by and large anti-CCG. Also the licensing of a political press had led, in the interest of fairness, to fixing circulations in proportion to voting strengths. This allowed a large portion of the available circulation to represent the views of outspokenly anti-British parties such as the German Communist Party (KPD). Huijsman estimated that out of a total circulation of five million copies in the British Zone, less than one million could be considered 'to have consistently given a fair picture of British policy'. PR/ISC's concern was not simply that there was a lack of pro-British publicity, but more damagingly, that the press might become a vehicle for *anti*-British publicity. The report concluded gloomily that 'the air is dark with wings of press chickens coming home to roost'.

The one exception was the zonal newspaper *Die Welt* which began its life on 2 April 1946 as both a German-language imitation of *The Times* and a covert mouthpiece for CCG policies run by the Press Production Unit. It was considered by PR/ISC to be the most authoritative and credited channel through which British policy reached the German public. However it was invariably judged by Germans to be the official voice of occupation policy.[42] The dualistic character of *Die Welt*—to serve as a paragon of independent German journalism and to be the 'camouflaged' spokesman for His Majesty's Government policy—was never fully resolved. In fact, in February 1947, Sprigge, head of PR/ISC, was formally asked by *Die Welt*'s German editors that it be officially recognised as a British paper. They argued that it was only fair to acknowledge this when asked by readers to explain why it was so superior in quality and was allowed such a large circulation.[43] A month later the British Press Adviser, Peter Mendlesohn, wrote: 'Much was achieved to make the paper a near mouthpiece of CCG. But the basic difficulty remained. We still have to use German editors to express our own

41. PRO/FO1056/195, 15 July 1947.
42. PRO/FO371/64516, monthly reaction reports no. 12, 28 June 1947.
43. PRO/FO1096/9, 11 February 1947.

views and of course they don't express them well or willingly.'[44]
Nevertheless, PR/ISC continued to press for making *Die Welt* into
a daily newspaper. One report stated: 'The advantages are obvious.
750,000 subscribers in the British Zone could receive a daily newspaper of four pages of carefully selected and well-edited news and
information which would give them a balanced and well-informed
picture of world and German events, and the British case.'[45] However the German reading public remained suspicious of the paper
and it was constantly attacked for its allegedly privileged position.[46]
PR/ISC also recognised that if *Die Welt* were to be published daily
in order to reinforce an already important 'British' instrument for
influencing public opinion, then this might result in a popular
outcry, 'and such a professional feeling against *Die Welt* as to make
it virtually impossible to retain any German staff'.[47] Although *Die
Welt*'s circulation reached one million at the beginning of 1949,
from then on it ran into difficulties and with its circulation falling
was eventually sold to Axel Springer in September 1953.

The German Broadcasting Service in the British Zone, known as
the Nordwestdeutscher Rundfunk (NWDR) was originally controlled by the Broadcasting Control Units at Hamburg and
Cologne, which eventually amalgamated into a single unit. These
units came directly under ISC Branch and had no representatives in
the Information Control Units. In the case of broadcasting the aim
was to avoid too many official items and to create a service where,
subject to necessary controls, 'Germans would speak to Germans
and take their full share in the re-education of their own people.'[48]
Under a policy agreement between the BBC and PR/ISC and signed
by Bishop (of PR/ISC) in December 1945, the respective functions
of the BBC German Service and NWDR were settled by means of a
division of labour. The NWDR was to provide for the British Zone
a 'Home Service' on the lines of the BBC Home Service. It was
agreed that in order to retain its audience and to build effectively a
new tradition in German broadcasting, NWDR should not be too
obviously concerned with 're-education' or even with any manifest

44. PRO/FO1096/9, 4 March 1947.
45. PRO/FO1056/193, 24 September 1947.
46. PRO/FO371/64516, monthly reaction report no. 11, 29 December 1946. See
    also, H. D. Fischer, *Re-educations- und Pressepolitik unter britischem Besat-
    zungsstatus. Die Zonenzeitung 'Die Welt' 1946–50* (Droste, Düsseldorf, 1978).
47. PRO/FO1056/193, brief on BICO Frankfurt telegram, 24 September 1947.
48. Parlamentsarchiv, Bonn, 91/050401. This contains a wealth of information on
    German broadcasting during this early occupation period. See also,
    PRO/FO1056/193.

attempt to raise German cultural standards. It was also agreed that excessive attention to the political and historical re-education of the Germans would destroy its credibility and as a result entertainment was not to be transparently 'edifying' and information not too obviously 'instructional'.[49]

The German Service from London was part of the BBC European Service and spoke with a British voice. Its transmissions, introduced with the words 'Here is England', were addressed to an audience all over Germany.[50] Under the agreement mentioned above, the re-education of the German people was to 'be the direct, though by no means exclusive, concern of the BBC German Service'. The projection of Britain, in the widest sense of the term, was seen as one of its main tasks, 'and will contribute directly to the end of re-education'. In order to counter the more overt propaganda disseminated by the BBC and to allow it to function 'more efficiently as a long-term means of influencing the German mind', NWDR would 'not unduly increase the proportion of British official announcements and relays from outside Germany to programmes originated by Germans on the spot. Control Commission policy, for instance, should be explained *by Germans*; and regular relays, as opposed to occasional relays of special programmes, should generally be avoided.'[51] In the early period, NWDR broadcast general news bulletins seven times daily and presented special reports on agriculture, sport and religion, together with news commentaries. By the end of 1945, NWDR was capable of broadcasting for fouteen hours a day and was ready to stand on its own feet.

When Hugh Carleton Greene moved from the BBC German Service and took over control of NWDR in the autumn 1946, he sought to create a German version of the BBC—a fee-based monopoly independent of party and state: 'My task as I saw it was to

---

49. PRO/FO1056/26, 15 December 1945. This division of labour had been worked out by the BBC and PR/ISC in November and they agreed to meet regularly to sort out any conflicts of interest. In fact, tension between London and PR/ISC continued even after this agreement with PR/ISC continuing to believe that the BBC were using too many news items about Germany and not enough about Britain.
50. The original opening sentence had been 'This is the German Broadcasting Station'. However, when Hugh Greene took charge of the BBC German Service he changed it to a ringing 'Here is England, Here is England', arguing that this was *not* another Germany and therefore more challenging to the German audience. Interview with Hugh Greene, 11 January 1985.
51. PRO/FO1056/26, definition of functions of BBC German Service and NWDR, 15 December 1945. See also PRO/FO953/819, which contains reports on NWDR.

produce a constitution which would take account both of German and British experience and if possible produce a synthesis which would work and, given time, might be acceptable as a lasting solution.'[52] Like the press, the immediate problem confronting NWDR was to keep the political parties at arm's length. Greene, like so many 're-educationalists' was less concerned with the vices of Nazi radio than with the shortcomings of broadcasting during the Weimar period.[53] This was particularly important because, as the zonal radio station, NWDR was also responsible for broadcasts to schools. Although he disliked intensely the term 're-education', and saw it as 'a clumsy concept', as Controller of Broadcasting in the British Zone, Greene viewed 're-education' as conducting a debate with those Germans willing to listen (and learn).[54] In these early days, men like Peter von Zahn, Axel Eggebrecht, Hans Schmidt-Isserstedt and Ernst Schnabel were encouraged to broadcast in an atmosphere of comparative freedom which gave NWDR programmes their distinctive character. Thus under Greene's guidance NWDR was intended to become a German station which would inform and entertain and diffuse democratic values simply by exemplifying them.[55] It was also Greene's task to give NWDR a legal status and knit it into the social and political life of post-war Germany. After much debate within Germany, NWDR's charter was finally issued as an appendix to Military Government Ordinance No. 118. The character came into force on 1 January 1948 and NWDR thereby became the first German broadcasting organisation to acquire a legal status after the end of the war. It provided NWDR with a position of independence hitherto unknown in German broadcasting.[56]

52. Quoted in Sir Hugh Greene, *The Third Floor Front* (Bodley Head, London, 1969), p. 52.
53. In many ways it can be argued that the long-term intentions of many British 're-educationalists' were to reform the institutions of the Weimar Republic. See Professor Dodd's survey of Weimar institutions, above note 11.
54. Interview with Hugh Greene, 11 January 1985.
55. For a highly critical report on the state of radio by two Education Branch Officers in February 1946 in which they claim that the press was more objective and that radio was too moralistic and concerned with guilt mobilisation see, PRO/FO1049/525, 20 February 1946. Axel Eggebrecht, on the other hand, in his introduction to a collection of essays entitled, *Zornige alte Männer* (Rowohlt, Hamburg, 1979), claims that he has never experienced such complete liberalism in broadcasting as under British control.
56. For a mass of material relating to the history, organisation and finance of the station and including the charter of NWDR (translated into English on 4 October 1947), see Parlamentsarchiv, Bonn, 91/050402. Greene's own verdict on his time with NWDR was that he was 'only partially successful' in that he achieved a situation where broadcasting was not under the control of central

Physical and Psychological Problems of Re-Education

There can be little doubt that Political Division and PR/ISC saw the press and radio as important means of implementing CCG's declared policy of 're-education'. However they were hampered by a number of problems, both physical and technical, that should not be underestimated. The biggest limitations on the dissemination of 'information' was the lack of paper and the shortage of wireless sets. Taking *Die Welt* as an example, there was a little over 1 newspaper to every 4.5 persons in the British Zone by the end of 1947. Even those who were able to purchase a newspaper were severely restricted in the amount of information they could obtain; the shortage of paper dictating the meagre number of printed pages allowed. With only two paper mills in the British Zone working to capacity, a PR/ISC report of September 1947 concluded: 'Until paper supplies are adequate we shall be quite unable to keep the German public adequately informed on current events, let alone correct the impression of the past twelve years.'[57] *Die Welt* alone would have required an additional 300-plus tons of newsprint per month in order to have become a daily publication.[58]

A similar situation applied to broadcasting. In March 1946, a BBC monitoring unit divided obstacles to listening to the radio in Germany into physical and psychological categories. The physical obstacles included lack of food and shortage of radio sets and spare parts, whereas the most important psychological barrier was that the BBC was inextricably connected in German minds with British policy; any failure of that policy led to a decline in BBC prestige in German eyes.[59]

These psychological barriers were also identified by PR/ISC who likened information control to a 'trough' and the German public to

government but failed to detach it from party political interference. Interview with author, 11 January 1985. See also, M. Tracey, *Das unerreichbare Wunschbild. Ein Versuch über Hugh Greene und die Neugründung des Rundfunks in Nordwestdeutschland nach 1945* (Kolhammer-Grote, Cologne, 1983).

57. PRO/FO1056/93.
58. To have printed *Die Welt* daily would also have created enormous distribution problems. The report estimated that it would have required an increase in petrol consumption from 36,000 litres per month to 70,000 litres, which could only have come out of mandatory Military Government allocations.
59. BBC Archive, 'Evidence on the German Audience for British Broadcasts', 6 March 1946. See same report dated 14 January 1947 where it was estimated that in the whole of Germany there were some 7.5 million radio licenses and on average four listeners per set or 30 million radio listeners throughout Germany. ISC estimated that the BBC was retaining an audience in the British Zone of something over 2 million for its news service.

David Welch

a 'horse'. PR/ISC recognised that the reaction of the German public to information was conditioned by many factors outside of their control. Above all it was influenced by the fact of occupation:

> No nation with any self-respect will willingly accept the word of an Occupying Power, particularly when this Power is concerned not only with teaching a new way of life, but also with condemning much that forms part of the individual German's heritage. Under these conditions it is not unnatural that anti-occupation rumours and humour flourish. Another influence is the precarious economic state of the German people; hunger and an uncertain economic future are not conducive to reasonableness.[60]

The BBC in particular seems to have suffered in the immediate post-war period. From German correspondence with the BBC German Service it would appear that Germans did not compare the occupation with what Goebbels had threatened, but with the type of treatment that the BBC seemed to promise during the war.[61] The failure of the CCG to deliver the civilised treatment that people like Dick Crossman had been arguing for affected the BBC's credibility after the war. This was partly explained by the BBC's remarkable popularity with Germans during the war—something the BBC never fully appreciated. After the war the BBC German Service suffered in comparison with NWDR which was perceived by many Germans as the authentic voice of the vanquished under occupation.[62] The BBC, on the other hand, was more inclined to be associated with pedagogic re-education and 'guilt mobilisation'. One of the consequences of this was outlined in June 1946 when a BBC Research Listener Report established from over 2,000 letters received during May that a 'sharp rise in the curve of anti-British feeling' had led to 'a new German national sport of weighing up the rival merits and personal advantages of democracy and communism'.[63]

60. PRO/FO1056/93.
61. See BBC Archive, 'Evidence on the German Audience for British Broadcasts', report dated 6 January 1946 based on 4,115 letters received during December: 'The main psychological danger to holding our German audience appears to lie in the widespread disillusionment and disappointment among anti-Nazi elements and their feeling that there is a wide disparity between British policy as represented by the BBC during the war and British post-war practice by Military Government.'
62. For examples of this see Parlamentsarchiv, Bonn, 91/05402.
63. BBC Archive, 'Evidence on the German Audience for British Broadcasts—the Political Listener', 6 June 1946.

The Cold War and the Promotion of British Interests

Most of the reports of German public opinion suggest that the popularity of the British, which had declined since the occupation, improved during the bleak winter of 1946–47, although continued attempts at 're-education' remained unpopular. By the summer of 1948 the political situation had changed dramatically and 're-education' had almost disappeared from CCG policy directives. With the Russians blockading Berlin, the three western Military Governors had agreed upon the structure for a federal constitution for western Germany. Nevertheless, some British officials, including Sir Stuart Crawford, head of the Educational Department, were still insisting that re-education was 'the chief objective of our occupation'.[64] For some time, however, there had been growing concern felt, among others, by Raymond Gauntlett, the new Director of Information Services Division (formerly PR/ISC), that the ideas and objectives emanating from Education Branch and particularly Birley were 'resulting in a weakening of British projection'.[65] In a confidential note to Robertson, Gauntlett spelt out the danger of Birley's idealism: 'Birley wants an organisation which in a general, vague way will influence German Education and Culture and which will treat British projection as pure incidental. I believe that approach to be fundamentally wrong.'[66] According to Gauntlett 'an effective Information Service should be assisting and promoting British policy and projecting British civilisation . . . so that the maintenance of British influence throughout the information-cultural field will be assured with the new (Western) German Government'.[67] Birley clearly objected to this crude 'projection of Britain' theme, and argued that such a policy would force him to 'find false beards for my Education Control Officers'.[68] Nevertheless, in October 1948, Robertson set out the future objectives for Education Branch and Information Services Division. This draft paper, which became policy on 5 November with only minor revisions, represented a minor victory for Gauntlett. It can also be seen as a pragmatic response to the international climate of the Cold War and to the constraints of public opinion in Britain. The crucial

64. PRO/FO371/70713, quoted in Jürgensen, 'British Occupation Policy', p. 237.
65. PRO/FO1056/152, 16 October 1948. Gauntlett became Chief of Information Services Division in April 1948 as a result of changes in ISC.
66. Ibid.
67. Ibid.
68. PRO/FO1056/152.

David Welch

paragraph reads:

> A cardinal principle of the future organisation ... will be directed towards the projection of the British point of view. While the promotion of culture in Germany and the establishment of a live press in Germany may have intrinsic virtues, these are not objects to which the money of the British taxpayer can properly be devoted save insofar as they constitute a medium for the furtherance of British policy and British ideas.[69]

Thus by the end of 1948, Robertson was transforming Information Control into public relations on behalf of the British 'way-of-life' while pedagogic 're-education' withered into 'cultural relations' on the lines of the British Council. After all, a West Germany fit to bear arms as a bulwark against communism could hardly need 're-educating'.[70]

German Attitudes Towards the British

Now instead of the 're-education' of an 'incorrigible' German race there was an urgent need to discover exactly what were German attitudes to British military rule. Once the British rediscovered the 'other Germany' they became conscious of the need to gauge public opinion and regularly to receive detailed reports about the mood of the German people.[71] Most of the divisions within the Control Commission became involved in the collection of such data, although interdepartmental rivalries prevented the coordination of such material. As we have seen, the BBC's Listener Research Unit evaluated German listeners' letters and provided monthly reports for the German Service Director which were read by Political Division.[72]

69. PRO/FO1056/152, 'The Future Organisation of Education Branch and Information Services Division', 27 October 1948. For later policy instructions regarding the future organisation of these two branches, see PRO/FO371/76811, 10 February 1949.
70. On 11 April 1949, in a letter to Sir Ivone Kirkpatrick of the Foreign Office, Robertson argued for increased expenditure on British cultural activities in Germany by claiming that: 'we should look on our cultural programme as something which is important for political reasons as well as merely for the projection of British culture', PRO/FO317/76819.
71. Despite the importance of German public opinion, very little serious work has been undertaken in this field. See B. Marshall, 'German Attitudes to British Military Government 1945–47', Journal of Contemporary History, Vol. 15, No. 4, 1980, pp. 655–84.
72. BBC Archive, 'Evidence on the German Audience for British Broadcasts',

ISC initially produced specific reports on German reactions to the newly created mass media, but from March 1946 their 'German Reaction Reports' covered most of the burning issues of the day.[73] PR also edited and published the *British Zone Review*, the official organ of the CCG which was published fortnightly and had an average circulation of 15,000 copies. Although the paper was primarily produced to foster a unity of purpose among CCG personnel, it was widely distributed among newspaper proprietors and therefore dealt regularly with German attitudes. In November 1946, however, the Governmental Sub-Commission of the Control Commission, no doubt prompted by the more sophisticated sampling techniques employed in the US Zone, called for more 'quality, selectivity and objectivity' in analysing German public opinion.[74] As a result, Political Division set up its own Public Opinion Research Office (PORO) charged specifically with the combating of rumours and providing more precise information about German attitudes and developments in the British Zone. These surveys were conducted either by means of overt interviewing techniques on a particular subject or by a rigid questionnaire. The list of names was drawn from the food-office lists in 'order to eliminate choice and chance' and appended to every report was the extraordinary disclaimer issued by the General Secretariat of PORO which suggested that 'educated' Britons might find German views 'irritatingly naive and stupidly illogical'.[75]

These early reports, which were divided into general and specialised matters, tended to concentrate on topics dealing with Allied ordinances, currency reform, the black market, food and clothing. It is only towards the end of 1948 that they began to ask the Germans what they thought of the British and British values. PORO's analyses of these reports invariably pointed to the failure of 're-education' whether (in their own words) 'measured by a willingness to obey British instructions without grumbling or in terms of the progress of the mass of the people towards a virile

April 1946. Most of these reports appear to have been written by Christina Gibson.
73. For a detailed breakdown of these 'German Reaction Reports', see PRO/FO371/64516. For example, report no. 13, 10 March 1947 contains highly critical German comments about the nature of British occupation. One question even asks 'Is it wrong for Germans to bring children into the world?' For a detailed account of German views on the impartiality or otherwise of the mass media, see report no. 14, 20 April 1947.
74. Marshall, 'German Attitudes', p. 659.
75. See PRO/FO1056/130, PORO reports.

western democracy'.[76] For example, in a report carried out in September 1947 after two years of British occupation, over 6,000 Germans of both sexes (chosen at random) were asked (by German interviewers) whether National Socialism was (a) a bad idea or (b) a good idea badly carried out. The survey found that about 50% of both sexes thought Nazism was 'a good idea badly carried out'. One important conclusion appeared that those educated during the Nazi period (i.e. under 30 years old) were still not convinced of the 'basic wrongness of Nazism'. This bore out similar surveys carried out by PORO in July 1947 on a smaller sample and a major survey conducted by the Americans which differed by only 5%. Indeed, the American survey found that only 24% of those under 30 years were prepared to say that Nazism was 'bad'.[77]

Similarly, after two important public announcements by Lord Pakenham (Chancellor of the Duchy of Lancaster) and Robertson on the objectives of the British occupation, a major survey was carried out in December 1947 into 'German Ideas on the Objectives of the British Occupation'. It discovered that 50% of those questioned considered that the 'ruin of the German economy' was Britain's prime objective. The 'building of democracy' came a very poor second. PORO suggested that the worsening food situation was a factor in 'this disappointing result of British persuasion and information supply'. PORO concluded: 'It seems that the Germans will accept nothing until they judge themselves fully fed.'[78]

These surveys tell us something not only about German opinion and feelings, but they reveal also the attitudes of the British official to Germans, many of whom had served in the colonial service and who found it distasteful to 'sell' Britain or to assuage German public opinion. PORO was particularly concerned that Germans should not take advantage of these questionnaires to 'insult us' and consequently often felt compelled to add eccentric interpretations to the statistics. In December 1948, for example, Duncan Wilson of Political Division asked PORO to find out whether 'Germans like us or not'. Statistically, the survey carried out among 4,000 Germans,

76. PRO/FO1056/130, morale report no. 4, 1–15 October 1947, dated 21 October 1947.
77. PRO/FO1056/130, report no. 111A, Attitudes to National Socialism. Official British comments on this report can be found in PRO/FO371/70651, 23 February 1948. For details of the American survey see, OMGUS report no. 72 in A. J. Merritt and R. L. Merritt, *Public Opinion in Occupied Germany: the OMGUS Surveys 1945–49* (University of Illinois, Chicago, Ill., 1970), pp. 30–3, 171–2.
78. PRO/FO1049/1391, report no. 170, January 1948.

found that 68% of men and 69% of women attributed to the British 'good' characteristics (hard-working, intelligent, self-controlled, generous, brave, progressive and peace-loving), whereas 32% of men and 31% of women thought the British to be 'conceited, cruel, backward and domineering'. Nevertheless, the head of PORO, in a covering letter to Wilson, added: 'I believe that the German race, is unstable and that it tends to have a greater ambivalence in love and hate than almost any other nation except, perhaps, the Japanese. This theory is borne out by their violence in physical love making and known prediliction for extreme sentimentality mixed with great brutality.'[79]

What use, if any, these reports had and whether they made an impact on policy decisions it is difficult to say. They appeared to be eagerly received by the divisions, many of whom were starved of such information. And despite occasional challenges to their quality and worthiness, PORO remained responsible for their sampling techniques and successfully defended their right to circulate reports without alterations. Despite obvious limitations, they provide a revealing insight into German public opinion under occupation.

The Long-Term Impact of Re-Education

The precise impact and the long-term effects of notions such as 're-education' are difficult to assess. The roots and antecedents of the thinking behind 're-education' can be traced to the experiences of Versailles and the peace settlements following the First World War. In 1945, politicians of all shades of opinion were determined not to repeat the mistakes of 1919, and 're-education' seemed the most humane solution to the 'German problem'. It was also borne out of a contemporary belief in the 'power' of propaganda to persuade, and as such was very much a product of wartime psychological warfare extended into the occupation period. Because of its all-embracing nature, 're-education' lent itself to a combination of high idealism, arrogant colonialism, and pragmatic improvisation. It did *not* however lead to a coherent and carefully coordinated programme of implementation and fizzled out as it deserved to. Its long-term implications for the Federal Republic of Germany cannot

---

79. PRO/FO1049/1391, 'Popularity of the British in Germany'. The letter was signed by James R. White on 3 December 1948.

be separated from the occupation itself which allowed a period of transition without the self-destructive recriminations that followed the First World War. The enthusiasm with which Germans embraced liberal democracy and the speed of their economic recovery surprised and baffled those in the Control Commission and forced many to re-examine their assumptions about Germany. Even Sir Robert Vansittart was persuaded to write in *The Times* in 1954: 'My lifelong antipathy to Germany is well-known yet for once in all the blue moons of existence I acknowledge a German Government and a German tendency which might be turned to the account of Christian Civilisation . . .'[80] In the final analysis, the concept of 're-education' and the manner in which it was implemented, reveals as much about the nation that engaged in 're-education' as it does about the society that was to be 're-educated'.

80. *The Times*, 31 May 1954.

9

Denazification in the British Zone
Ian Turner

Introduction

This chapter looks at one of the most controversial and least understood aspects of the British occupation: the denazification programme. Denazification was the negative aspect of the measures undertaken by the Allies to reform German society. Like the democratisation of the political system and the re-education of the German people its aim was to ensure that Germany would never again pose a security threat to Britain and her allies. Like these other policies, too, denazification in the British Zone was based on the view that Nazism was not an historical accident but the latest manifestation of the bellicose German national character. As such the British authorities were generally sceptical of the value of replacing one set of elites with another which would share the same defects. Consequently, British denazification policy never attempted an 'artificial revolution' but tried instead to strike a balance between the needs of security and the demands of a shattered economy.

The British opposed the radical and comprehensive measures proposed by the Americans. But even the more moderate occupationally related measures carried out in the British Zone caused sufficient chaos and disruption to provoke serious concern. Administratively, the process engulfed British and German officials alike in a deluge of directives and policy documents. By late 1946 and especially from 1947 onwards, the British sought means to get themselves off the hook as quickly as possible. Devolution to the Germans was one method but this brought problems of control with it and was not universally popular within the CCG. The other device was the categorisation process which was seen as a means of rehabilitating many of the less-serious offenders. When categorisa-

239

Ian Turner

tion itself was devolved to the Länder the British were caught between their desire for a speedy conclusion and their policy of non-intervention. The conclusion was therefore protracted and unsatisfactory from both sides.

Denazification—Artificial Revolution or Rehabilitation?

The earliest academic studies seem to have been in general agreement with popular opinion at the time that denazification was not just a failure of conventional magnitude but went beyond that to attain the monumental proportions of a full-fledged fiasco.[1] Indeed, so bleak was the picture painted by early commentators of denazification that an academic reappraisal of the policy was inevitable sooner or later.

The revisionists in this case—John Gimbel[2] and, most notably, Lutz Niethammer[3]—point out that previous analyses of denazification, including the two most significant academic studies by Montgomery and Fürstenau,[4] are based on the assumption that the aim of denazification policy was to bring about in Germany an 'artificial revolution', that is to say, the removal of the old discredited ruling class and its replacement by a new elite.

Niethammer refutes this thesis. He claims that denazification had a dual character and that at least as important as the removal of elites was the rehabilitation of individual Nazis by the German denazification panels, the so-called *Mitläuferfabrik*, whose function it was to cleanse the German people of the brown stain on their past so that they could resume their place 'mit frischer weisser Weste in die Gesellschaft zurückgeschickt'.[5] According to Niethammer's re-

1. J. H. Herz, 'The Fiasco of Denazification in Germany', *Political Science Quarterly*, Vol. 63, No. 4, December 1948, pp. 569–94. See also W. E. Griffith, 'Denazification in the United States Zone of Germany', *Annals of the American Academy of Political and Social Science*, Vol. 267, No. 1, January 1950, pp. 68–76.
2. J. Gimbel, 'American Denazification and German Local Politics, 1945–1949. A Case Study in Marburg', *The American Political Science Review*, Vol. 54, March 1960, pp. 83–105; *idem.*, 'The Artificial Revolution in Germany. A Case Study', *Political Science Quarterly*, Vol. 76, No. 1, March 1961, pp. 88ff; *idem.*, *A German Community under American Occupation, Marburg 1945–1952* (Stanford University Press, Stanford, Cal., 1961).
3. L. Niethammer, *Entnazifizierung in Bayern* (S. Fischer, Frankfurt on Main, 1972).
4. J. D. Montgomery, *Forced to be Free. The Artificial Revolution in Germany and Japan* (Chicago University Press, Chicago, Ill., 1957); J. Fürstenau, *Entnazifizierung* (Lüchterhand, Neuwied and Berlin, 1969).
5. Niethammer, *Entnazifizierung*, p. 13.

240

searches, the importance of the rehabilitation aspect of denazification in the US Zone rose with the increasing tendency of US policy towards consolidation and economic reconstruction, so that although the denazification programme as a whole was extended and apparently intensified in a series of *ad hoc* policy decisions in response to public pressure in the United States, the severity of the purge was an illusion cultivated by General Clay to draw public attention away from his tacit promotion of German recovery.[6]

Niethammer's stress on the dual character of the denazification process and the importance of developments in the international political climate in determining the shape of policy has left its mark on the most recent scholarly works on the subject.[7] So much so, in fact, that Wolfgang Krüger, commenting on denazification in North Rhine-Westphalia, felt able to praise the rehabilitation of former Nazis as 'der grösste Erfolg der politischen Säuberung', adding: 'Man wüsste genau, welche Gefahren der jungen Demokratie drohten, wenn breite Bevölkerungskreise auf Dauer aus der politischen Gemeinschaft ausgeschlossen worden wären.'[8]

Despite these newer works, the perceived view of denazification remains coloured by the concentration of research on the American practice, whilst the motives and principles behind the policy of the French and the British,[9] to say nothing of the Soviet Union,[10] have yet to be fully explored. This chapter, therefore, represents an attempt to investigate the political conception underlying British denazification policy and to show how over time the priority shifted between denazification and the pragmatic demands of economic efficiency.

6. Ibid., p. 240.
7. K.-D. Henke, *Politische Säuberung unter französischer Besatzung* (Deutsche Verlags Anstalt, Stuttgart, 1981); D. Stiefel, *Entnazifizierung in Österreich* (Europaverlag, Vienna, 1981); W. Krüger, *Entnazifiziert!* (Hammer, Wuppertal, 1982).
8. Krüger, *Entnazifiziert!* pp. 158–9.
9. Henke's study deals principally with the alternative German procedure developed in Württemberg-Hohenzollern, whilst Krüger's thesis concentrates more on the practice of denazification than the underlying intentions of the policy.
10. See the excellent resumé in Henke, *Politische Säuberung*, pp. 14–6, and for the official line, W. Meinicke, 'Die Entnazifizierung in der sowjetischen Besatzungszone 1945 bis 1948', *Zeitschrift für Geschichtswissenschaft*, Vol. 32, No. 10, 1984, pp. 969–79.

Ian Turner

British Denazification Policy—Origins and Development

Denazification and the 'German National Character'

It has rightly been said that one of the main factors determining denazification policy as practised in the various zones of occupation, was the view held by Allied policy-makers of the nature of National Socialism and its causes.[11] The increasingly sceptical view which developed amongst many Foreign Office officials as the war drew on as to the inherent suitability of the German character for democracy, and the consequent rejection of the belief in 'das andere Deutschland' which this entailed is discussed elsewhere in this book.[12] Once the proposition was accepted that Nazism was neither the product of unique historical circumstances, nor the outward manifestation of a society dominated by a certain set of elites, but was rather endemic to the German national character, then the possibility of destroying National Socialism by replacing those in power with another set of Germans disappeared and the concept of an 'artificial revolution' was nullified. The Vansittartist view of the German problem was reflected in the attitude of British officialdom to German refugees. Emigré intellectuals like the neo-Marxist Franz Neumann had a considerable influence on the planning of US denazification policy.[13] The Foreign Office[14] and the Control Commission for Germany (CCG),[15] however, generally viewed German refugees with suspicion.

Of course, as with other aspects of British policy, there were differences in opinion and approach amongst the various divisions of the Control Commission. The Political Division seem, from the records available, to have been the most ardent proponents of an 'artificial revolution' and at every opportunity pressed for greater participation by and reliance on German anti-Nazis.[16] An excerpt from a press release, prepared by the division to accompany the

11. Henke, *Politische Säuberung*, p. 9.
12. See chapters 7 and 8 of this volume.
13. See Niethammer, *Entnazifizierung*, pp. 15, 47–50 and Griffith, 'Denazification', p. 68.
14. A. Glees, *Exile Politics during the Second World War* (Oxford University Press, Oxford, 1982); T. Bower, *Blind Eye to Murder* (Deutsch, London, 1981), pp. 169–70.
15. See R. Ebsworth, *Restoring Democracy in Germany* (Stevens and Sons, London, 1960), p. 10.
16. The influence of Political Division can be seen most clearly in those sections of ZPI3 devoted to the political composition of German Denazification Panels.

announcement of a new policy instruction in April 1946, although designed principally for public consumption nevertheless conveys something of Political Division's thinking on denazification:

> This is an opportunity for the anti-fascist forces in Germany to make themselves felt. Working class institutions, such as the Trade Unions, and the Workers' Representative Councils in factories, should produce some of the men best able to advise Military Government accurately and impartially on this quest of denazification. This is an opportunity for political parties to assert their influence and establish their leadership in the continuing struggle against the remnants of Fascism . . . The administration, the factories, the universities, the professions, can no longer be allowed to harbour men who are the enemies of democracy. It is the task of German democrats to expose them everywhere. The petty Nazi informer and the sinister Nazi propagandist, must give way to the forces of German democracy.[17]

The attitude of Political Division was not shared by the rest of the Control Commission, however. The CCG's Intelligence Division, for instance, seems to have nurtured a profound suspicion of all Germans. The division's outpost in Lower Saxony responded in mid-1946 to the findings of a survey of public opinion in Brunswick:

> We know that you appreciate that Nazism is not an isolated phenomenon, but must really be considered to be the logical culmination of the trends which have dominated German thought for at least the past 150 years. Our problem is therefore of far greater import than whether Nazis can become democrats. It is indeed whether Germans can become democrats, if we consider the word 'democrat' to be synonymous with what we understand as the British way of life, the fundamental ideal for which we have fought two world wars.
>
> As the disease is far more deep-seated then Nazism, it is dangerous to assume that we can always accept unconditionally the views of any German body, no matter how carefully we may have chosen the members, with regard to what we believe to be their understanding of the ideals we are seeking to inculcate.[18]

Similar sentiments were expressed in a confidential memorandum

---

17. PRO/FO1005/1387, SCDP(46)21, Press Releases on ZPI3, considered at the fourth Meeting of the Standing Committee on Denazification, 12 April 1946.
18. PRO/FO1010/27, 13 Regional Intelligence Staff to Detachment 120, Military Government, 22 June 1946.

on denazification by Lower Saxony's Regional Commissioner, General Macready, when he urged great caution in the appointment of 'so-called nominal Nazis' to high positions in the administration or industry:

> Nazism is more than a political creed—it is designed to appeal to all the inherent German characteristics of militarism and domination. The nominal Nazi . . . is still a German . . . A common association with the now vanished, though discredited regime, will tend to promote cliques of Germans of similar temperament and background. While paying lip service perhaps to the tenets of democracy, they may still be 'bad' Germans in the European sense and only waiting the opportunity to start some fresh Germanic venture. The next Hitler will not necessarily be a Nazi.[19]

The consequence of this widespread view of the 'German mentality' was to shift the focus of British denazification away from the main concerns of the Americans in Germany—to remove the National Socialist elites and punish those who were implicated in the regime—towards a narrower conception concerned primarily with ensuring the removal from positions of authority of individuals fundamentally opposed to the objects of the British occupation. To quote General Robertson, the British Military Governor, on the subject:

> Our interest in Denazification is quite different from that of the Germans. Apart from war crimes, we are chiefly concerned with security i.e. we wish the German administration and German industry to be staffed with people who are not dangerous to the aims of the occupation. For the Germans, however, the question is largely one of justice and retribution upon individuals who have oppressed and persecuted their fellow citizens and brought disaster upon their country. Criticism of our denazification measures is scarcely ever now based on security considerations but emanates from political opponents of the Nazis i.e. mainly Left-Wing Parties both in Germany and outside it.[20]

Denazification in the Early Phase

The first recorded expression of Anglo-American denazification

19. PRO/FO1010/27, 229/MG/41/SEC, 'Denazification', Macready, 16 June 1946.
20. PRO/FO371/64352/C3969, Robertson to Jenkins (COGA), 7 March 1947. See also Bower, *Blind Eye to Murder*, p. 197.

policy is contained in the Directive CCS 551 issued by the Combined Chiefs of Staff on 28 April 1944.[21] It specified as its main aims the destruction of 'Nazism–Fascism and the Nazi hierarchy' and the maintenance of law and order. The primacy of security and scope for interpretation which it embodied were fully in line with British thinking.

The SHAEF planners in the German Country Unit in London charged with translating the objectives of CCS 551 into practical policy came in the main from a police background. In order to carry out the necessary purge, the planners foresaw the creation of a Special Branch, analogous to the British police department which deals with political affairs, as part of the Public Safety Branch of Military Government, the organisation primarily concerned with the reorganisation and supervision of the German police. To enable its officers to conduct the operation 'einheitlich, routinemässig und ohne Vorkenntnisse',[22] the Public Safety (Special Branch), or PSSB, was provided with a concrete set of categories for dismissal and arrest and a list of criteria, in the main consisting of membership or offices held in certain Nazi and state organisations. To facilitate PSSB investigations, a questionnaire was devised, universally referred to as the *Fragebogen*, which as Colonel Halland, the British head of Public Safety Branch, explained to his Control Commission colleagues was 'an old police technique similar to that used in 1940 in this country'.[23] The categories, lists of criteria and the procedure for vetting were incorporated into both the 'Handbook of Military Government in Germany',[24] and the SHAEF Public Safety Manual,[25] issued in August and September 1944, respectively.

The willingness of the British to adhere to SHAEF policy on denazification declined virtually from the moment Allied troops set foot on German territory. The reason for this reluctance was the progressive extension and intensification of denazification ordered by the United States in response to US domestic criticism of

21. F. S. V. Donnison, *Civil Affairs and Military Government: North West Europe, 1944–46*, (HMSO, London, 1961), p. 359; Niethammer, *Entnazifizierung*, p. 57.
22. Niethammer, *Entnazifizierung*, pp. 58–9.
23. PRO/FO1005/343, CO/MISC/M(44)4, 'Machinery for Purging and Vetting of German Personnel', minutes of special meeting on 5 December 1944, 6 December 1944. Presumably, Halland was referring to the investigation of aliens in Britain.
24. For the SHAEF Handbook see P. V. Hammond, 'Directives for the Occupation of Germany', in H. Stein (ed.), *American Civil–Military Decisions* (University of Alabama Press, Birmingham, Ala., 1963), pp. 335ff.
25. Copy in PRO/WO220/231.

Military Government leniency towards former Nazis. The first stage in this process was the modification of SHAEF policy represented by the Directive FACS 93 issued on 6 October 1944 in direct response to Treasury Secretary Morgenthau's and President Roosevelt's condemnation of SHAEF policy.[26] The new pre-surrender directive laid down that:

> Under no circumstances shall active Nazis or ardent sympathisers be retained in office for purposes of administrative convenience or expediency. The Nazi Party and all subsidiary organisations shall be dissolved. The administrative machinery of certain dissolved Nazi organisations may be used when necessary to provide certain essential functions, such as relief, health and sanitation, with de-nazified personnel and facilities.[27]

This new SHAEF directive marked the almost complete nullification of the element of discretion in the removal of Nazis from office. Moreover this was not the end of the process, for following the allegedly scandalous practices of Military Government in Aachen,[28] a new directive on the 'Removal from Office of Nazis and German Militarists' was issued by SHAEF on 24 March 1945 which virtually doubled the list of criteria for removals and deprived local commanders of any residual powers of discretion that they had retained.[29]

The British responded critically to this creeping intensification of the denazification programme and refused to implement US directives fully in their zone.[30] This left something of a vacuum in British denazification policy, however, for although the SHAEF publications still covered the pre-surrender period of occupation, there was still no agreed post-surrender policy. Thus when the Director of Civil Affairs at Field Marshal Montgomery's Headquarters 21 Army Group requested a clear directive on the removal of Nazis from industry in July 1945, he was informed by the Control Commission in London that British policy was embodied in the first sentence of the UK redraft of the US overall directive (JCS 1067) of 26 July 1945 to the effect that: 'All members of the Nazi

---

26. PRO/FO371/46799/C1048, 'Treatment of Nazis', Draft for ATCA Committee by Troutbeck (FO), March 1945.
27. Donnison, *Civil Affairs . . . North West Europe*, p. 203.
28. C. Fitzgibbon, *Denazification* (Michael Joseph, London 1969), pp. 88–97; Griffith, 'Denazification', pp. 68–9 and I. Lange (ed.) *Die Entnazifizierung in Nordrheinwestfalen* (Republica Verlag, Siegburg, 1976), p. 13.
29. Henke, *Politische Säuberung* p. 22; PRO/FO371/46799/C1223.
30. Bower, *Blind Eye to Murder*, pp. 163–5; PRO/FO371/46799/C1397.

Party who have been more than nominal participants in its activities and all other persons hostile to Allied purposes should be removed from public and semi-public office and from positions of major responsibility in important private undertakings.'[31] Apart from a collection of specialist directives originally drafted for submission to the European Advisory Commission (the inter-Allied body which had tried during the war to hammer out an agreed policy for Germany), and since issued in booklet form to the Commander-in-Chief in Germany,[32] this less than totally watertight statement of policy was all the guidance that the authorities in London were prepared to offer. The absence of clear guidelines was due not least to a concern in Whitehall to await the outcome of the Potsdam Conference before issuing a general post-surrender directive on denazification.[33] In fact it was to be mid-September before a new directive specifically for the British Zone was issued on the 'Arrest, Removal and Exclusion of Nazis from Office' which, whilst adhering to the spirit of the SHAEF Handbook and the section of the Potsdam declaration on denazification,[34] nevertheless 'allowed sufficient latitude for the German administration and economy to be built up'.[35]

British Zone Denazification Policy—Characteristics and Defects

In view of the hostility with which the British regarded the US-imposed SHAEF directives, it is perhaps not surprising that, as has been generally remarked, British denazification policy in the phase of zonal autonomy was characterised by caution.[36] The British

31. PRO/FO371/46799/C4890, Office of Chief of Staff London to Director of Civil Affairs, HQ 21 Army Group, 31 July 1945. See also Donnison, *Civil Affairs . . . North West Europe*, p. 366.
32. See I. D. Turner, 'British Occupation Policy and its Effects on the Town of Wolfsburg and the Volkswagenwerk 1945–1949' PhD thesis, Manchester University, 1984, pp. 885–6. There was no specialist directive on the denazification of industry.
33. PRO/FO371/46799/C1397, Troutbeck to Green (WO), 26 July 1945.
34. For the provisions of the Potsdam Agreement on denazification, see W. G. Friedmann, *The Allied Military Government of Germany* (Stevens and Sons, London, 1947), pp. 262–3; Fürstenau, *Entnazifizierung*, p. 46; Stiefel, *Entnazifierung in Österreich*, pp. 21–2 and Krüger, *Entnazifiziert!*, pp. 27–8.
35. PRO/FO1005/1387, SCO/P(46)1, 'Denazification in the British Zone and the Treatment of Ex-Nazis and Militarists', Part 1, 'Review of Present Denazification Policy', 19 February 1946. Lange, *Entnazifizierung*, p. 14, gives 10 September as the date of issue but does not include the text of the directive which I have also been unable to locate.
36. Fürstenau, *Entnazifizierung*, pp. 30, 42–3; Krüger *Entnazifiziert!*, pp. 14, 42; Friedmann, *Allied Military Government*, p. 114.

exhibited none of the missionary zeal of the Americans who at that stage were still determined to pursue extensive denazification, decentralisation and decartellisation as a prelude to a rapid withdrawal from the Continent. As one Control Commission official was to comment in retrospect: 'I knew that the Germans had blotted their copybook, but we had to live with them for the next three hundred years.'[37]

In practice, the first wave of denazification carried out behind the advancing armies by the US Counter-Intelligence Corps and the British Field Security Service made use of the SHAEF categories. Town mayors were required to submit lists of officials with their former party affiliations indicated. Inclusion in one of the standard categories meant dismissal and in some cases internment as a dangerous Nazi.[38]

Following the German surrender and the stabilisation of occupation zones, British Military Government officers based their actions, for want of anything better, on an instruction which had originally been designed for purging financial institutions.[39] The instruction provided for two types of removal: dismissal and suspension pending further investigation. Criteria for the first category included membership of the NSDAP before April 1933, office in certain Nazi organisations and employment by the Gestapo. The second category was more elastic and encompassed 'active Nazis', 'convinced supporters of the regime' and former officials in German-occupied Europe. The decision in each case was to be made on the basis of *Fragebogen* distributed to the heads of administration. In fact, altogether the process of conducting the purge was left to the responsible Germans admittedly acting under British supervision. At this stage denazification was directed primarily at persons in positions of authority within local government and administrative organisations.

If for the most part the British harboured no illusions about their ability to transform German society by the removal of its elites and were certainly not tempted into a zonal registration of the entire adult population in order to mete out general retribution for the evils of National Socialism, then their denazification policy was nevertheless not without its defects. In the first place, the lack of a

---

37. Bower, *Blind Eye to Murder*, p. 30.
38. Information on denazification in practice from Turner, 'British Occupation', pp. 257ff.
39. 'Instructions to Financial Institutions and Government Financial Agencies (Personnel) No. 3', March 1945. See Lange, *Entnazifizierung*, pp. 69–79.

zonal register meant that denazification in the British Zone was largely an occupationally related process.[40] For people in responsible positions in industry or public administration, and for applicants to such positions, denazification was the supreme occupational hazard of the period. The rationale behind this feature of British denazification was sensible: not only was the British Zone thereby spared the prospect of an investigation into the lives of several million people, with the inevitability of a series of general amnesties and exemptions when the sheer bulk of administrative work threatened to overwhelm the authorities, but it could be cited as evidence of the British intention to remove the 'big Nazis' whilst leaving mere followers in peace.

The restriction of denazification to positions of responsibility, a logical consequence of British concern with security first and foremost, was not uncontested within the CCG. In a plea to military commanders to extend the application of denazification to workers who were ardent Nazis, Political Division (German Political Branch) wrote, 'The object of our Denazification Policy is to remove any Nazi, in any position, who by his previous conduct, rendered himself odious to his fellow men, and nothing in ZPI No. 3, nor in ACA Directive No. 24, should be taken to limit the scope of Denazification.'[41] Mostly, however, the concern within the CCG was with restricting the scope of denazification. Thus the Public Safety Branch at Hanover voiced their concern at reports of people in subservient positions being dismissed which if continued would, it was felt, result in unnecessary waste of manpower, a forcing of people to eke out a livelihood as common labourers 'or by less desirable activities and in a consequent danger of widespread dissatisfaction'. It was of the utmost importance that all unnecessary denazification should be avoided, the communication concluded.[42]

In fact, by November 1947, 2,144,022 *Fragebogen* had been evaluated in the British Zone out of a total population of some 22 million people,[43] approximately one-fifth of whom would have been members of the NSDAP or associated organisations.[44] In

40. Largely, but not exclusively: evidence of having undergone denazification was also required for political office holders, potential students and by those seeking a permit for interzonal travel. See Lange, *Entnazifizierung*, p. 36.
41. PRO/FO1005./1387, SCD/P(46)11, App.'A', 16 March 1946.
42. PRO/FO1010/27, 229/MG/1752/1/PS, 21 June 1946.
43. PRO/FO1033/42, 'Denazification Statistics for the British Zone', PSSB, Berlin, 23 December 1947.
44. See M. Balfour and J. Mair, *Four-Power Control in Germany and Austria 1945–1946* (Oxford University Press, London, 1956), p. 171.

reality, therefore, the occupational character of denazification meant that many of those whose past records would have placed them in a dismissal category were able to lie low by working in clerical or other non-responsible positions or by dealing in barter or black market transactions. These people were later able to re-emerge once the process of denazification had been terminated without having suffered any form of political disqualification. Moreover, this defect was exacerbated by the differences in denazification policy amongst the various zones.[45] Thus, any person who anticipated professional and other disqualifications in the US Zone was well advised to move to the British Zone where, provided he kept a low profile and did not apply for a senior position, his chances of evading denazification were good.[46]

Even within the British Zone, denazification was far from being uniform in its implementation. As we shall see, the number of directives and policy instructions issued by Headquarters rapidly burgeoned, threatening to submerge the Military Government officials on the ground, and the German bodies which subsequently assumed some of the responsibility, with a flood of paperwork. Directives were followed by instructions and instructions were supplemented by a succession of appendices until the whole lot was superseded by a revised instruction or a new directive. Add to this the fact that many regional and local Military Government detachments issued their own guidelines and interpretations of the policy directives and that many officials and German bodies received these statements of policy belatedly or not at all, then it is not difficult to realise why one commentator described the procedure in the British Zone as an *Entnazifizierungswirrwarr*.[47]

45. Fürstenau, *Entnazifizierung*, p. 148.
46. A case often cited as an example of the effects of lack of interzonal uniformity is that of Heinrich Nordhoff, the long-time Generaldirektor of the Volkswagenwerk. Nordhoff had been made a Wehrwirtschaftsführer for his wartime services as head of Opel's Brandenburg truck plant but had been refused employment in the US zone before eventually taking up his post in Wolfsburg in the British Zone.
47. Quoted by Fürstenau, *Entnazifizierung*, p. 192. See also: Lange, *Entnazifizierung*, pp. 5, 22–3. For an amusing insight into the realities of Military Government in the early days and the relation or lack of relation, between policy directives and what actually happened, see Donnison *Civil Affairs . . . North West Europe*, p. 30.

Quadripartite Denazification Policy

The Allied declaration of policy agreed at Potsdam on 2 August 1945 contained a paragraph on the removal of Nazis from office which was identical with the formula given to 21 Army Group quoted above. Although inclusion in the Potsdam agreement was not in itself a reason why policy should be determined at quadripartite level, denazification was evidently regarded as one of the prime aims of the occupation and a policy area where inter-zonal uniformity was highly desirable. For this reason, when the Allied Control Authority (ACA) was set up in August, a Nazi Arrest and Denazification Sub-Committee was formed, reporting to the Public Safety Committee of the Authority's Directorate of Internal Affairs and Communications. The subcommittee met for the first time on 31 August and it was agreed that the first priority should be the drafting of a common policy directive for arrest of Nazis and the removal of implicated persons from office.[48]

As a basis for the directive the subcommittee used an American draft which was 'a near replica of the July directive' issued in the US Zone.[49] Indeed it soon became clear that the Americans were making the running in the subcommittee, pushing for a wider measure of denazification than the British were prepared to contemplate. The British pinned their hopes on the inclusion of a clause, later paragraph 5 of the final directive, which permitted retention in office of individuals who came under the mandatory removal clauses of the directive where there was positive evidence that he was 'not more than a nominal Nazi and is not a militarist and is not hostile to the Allied cause . . .', and on what was to become paragraph 8b, which provided for temporary retention of an individual judged indispensable at the discretion of the zonal commander. To achieve this latter clause the British were prepared to mount determined opposition to a joint Soviet–American front.[50] Nevertheless, the directive, when finally approved by the Allied Control Council (ACC) on 12 January 1946, contained eight categories and

48. Minutes of the subcommittee at PRO/FO1005/635.
49. Griffith, *Denazification*, p. 70. Dir. 24 is in Friedmann, *Allied Military Government*, pp. 311–12 and B. Ruhm von Oppen, *Documents on Germany under Occupation, 1945–1954*, (Oxford University Press, London, 1955), pp. 102–7. See also Krüger, *Entnazifiziert!*, pp. 28–9.
50. PRO/FO1005/635, minutes of 11th, 12th, 13th meetings of the Nazi Arrest and Denazification Sub-Committee, 17 October 1945 to 24 October 1945. See also Niethammer, *Entnazifizierung*, p. 298.

ninety-eight individual groups of people subject to compulsory removal and exclusion and a further twenty-two groups comprising career officers in the German armed forces and 'persons who represent Prussian Junker tradition' who were earmarked for discretionary removal and exclusion.[51]

In London, the Foreign Office had been watching the development of quadripartite denazification policy with concern. Con O'Neill at the German Department described the policy as 'sheerest madness', remarking that, 'as an example of systematic and meticulous imbecility it would be hard to beat'.[52] When the directive was finally issued, the FO seized on the vague formulation and wide room for interpretation it offered, with O'Neill minuting: 'We have seen and deplored this paper before. It now remains for our people in Germany to ignore the letter of the law and act in the spirit of common sense.'[53]

Denazification in the British Zone after Control Council Directive 24

Even prior to the issue of ACC Directive 24, the British had started to give consideration to the possibility of transferring a portion of responsibility for the denazification programme to the Germans. The move had obvious advantages: the process would be speeded up, the specialised knowledge and experience of the Germans exploited, and British personnel could be relieved of some of the administrative burden of denazification. Moreover, by associating the Germans more closely with the programme, the British authorities could hope to deflect any criticism away from themselves. The establishment of German advisory committees on denazification had, in fact, been suggested in a paper by the CCG's Joint Intelligence Committee as early as September 1945,[54] and had subsequently been advocated by the Control Commission's Political Division.[55]

51. The list of removals also included mayors and police chiefs, categories which the British had hoped to exclude from denazification. See PRO/FO1005/635, minutes of the 13th meeting of the Nazi Arrest and Denazification Sub-Committee, 24 October 1945 and PRO/FO1005/623, minutes of the 9th Meeting of the Allied Public Safety Committee, 26 October 1945.
52. PRO/FO371/46800/C8985, minute by O'Neill, 1 December 1945. See also Bower, *Blind Eye to Murder*, p. 188.
53. PRO/FO371/55434/C790, minute by O'Neill, 28 January 1946.
54. PRO/FO1005/1388, JIC(CCG)45/6, 1st draft considered at 3rd meeting of CCG's Standing Committee on Denazification (SCD), 25 September 1945.
55. PRO/FO1005/1388, Political Division to Chief of Staff, 30 October 1945 discussed at 6th meeting of SCD, 13 November 1945.

There was still a residual reluctance within the Control Commission to delegate any responsibility for denazification to the Germans and it was only towards the end of the year when the Nominated Representative Councils were functioning at province and Regierungsbezirk level,[56] that an instruction was issued establishing German Advisory Committees at these levels of government to assist in the assessment of those in the discretionary removal classes.[57]

Following the announcement of Directive 24, this instruction was superseded by Zonal Policy Instruction (ZPI) 3 of January 1946 which established a whole system of German Denazification Panels, German Review Boards and British Review Boards down to Kreis level.[58] These German bodies had no formal executive powers, and in each case PSSB retained the ultimate authority. But there was no getting away from the fact that involving the Germans in the denazification process in this way inevitably meant giving them greater influence. In fact, the operation of these committees proved extremely controversial. They were composed of political nominees, predominately from left-wing parties, who on occasion used their positions to settle old scores with political opponents. The bourgeois parties and the churches in particular were vociferous in their criticism of what they felt were unfair decisions by the committees.[59] However, the rationale behind transferring executive responsibility to the Germans became increasingly compelling as time passed and the pressure to bring denazification to a quick conclusion mounted. In early March 1946 the CCG's Standing Committee on Denazification Policy established a working party under the former Deputy Chief of the Internal Affairs and Communications Division, Brigadier Heyman, to 'plan measures to bring . . . [denazification] to a final conclusion and to deal with the hard core which would remain'.[60]

56. See chapter 7 of this volume.
57. IA and C Division Instruction 28 of 3 December 1945 in Lange, *Entnazifizierung*, pp. 101–3 and PRO/FO1010/27, INTR/5161/HQ, 3 December 1945.
58. See Lange, *Entnazifizierung*, pp. 233–41. ZPI3 went through two further versions. Full details of the amendments and additions and the rules for the composition and duties of the committees can be found in Lange, *Entnazifizierung*, pp. 241–65, 297–329 and in the survey of British policy in Krüger, *Entnazifiziert!*, pp. 31–43, 50–1.
59. See Turner, 'British Occupation', pp. 274–8.
60. *Monthly Report of the CCG (BE)*, Vol. 1, No. 2, July 1946, p. 13. The SCD was established by a decision of the Chiefs of Staff's Conference of 8 August 1945 (CSBZ/M(45)11 Min. 10 quoted in Office of Chief of Staff to Divisions, 10 August 1945 in PRO/FO371/46799/C4897). Originally conceived as a

Parallel with the deliberations of the Heyman Working Party, discussions were proceeding in the Nazi Arrest and Denazification Sub-Committee of the ACA on a directive for 'The Arrest and Punishment of War Criminals, Nazis and Militarists and the Internment, Control and Surveillance of Potentially Dangerous Germans'.[61] The object of both sets of discussions was the formulation of a policy for the categorisation of those who were affected by the removal and exclusion clauses of Directive 24 so as to facilitate the restriction and control of the activities of individuals considered hostile to Allied purposes. Here, too, considerations of security were uppermost in British minds.

The Heyman Report, which in its first form was considered by the Standing Committee in late March,[62] made provision for the vast majority of cases to be categorised by German Denazification Panels. The Standing Committee, with General Robertson's support, pressed for maximum possible transfer of power to the Germans. In order to speed up the process it instructed Public Safety Branch to plan for handover to the German bodies by September 1946.[63] At this point, the Regional Commissioners, with Internal Affairs and Communications (IA and C) Division and Public Safety in support, mounted a concerted attack against any proposal to abandon denazification to the Germans. The German Denazification Panels, they claimed, not PSSB, were the real bottleneck in the system and any withdrawal of Public Safety control at this stage would be extremely unwise in view of what the Regional Commissioners held to be an inherent tendency of the German bodies towards partiality and corruption.[64] Moreover, as General Macready in Hanover observed, under present rules denazification in his province would be impossible to complete inside thirty-two

---

form of court of appeal it developed into a policy-making body. Its first meeting was on 1 September 1945 and in March 1946 it became the Standing Committee on Denazification *Policy* (SCDP). (PRO/FO1005/1388 and PRO/FO1005/1389.) The Committee was chaired by General Templer and was composed of representatives from the service divisions and the Chiefs of Intelligence, Political, Legal and Trade and Industry, Manpower and IA and C Divisions.

61. See PRO/FO1005/636, minutes of meetings of the Nazi Arrest and Denazification Sub-Committee and PRO/FO1005/624, minutes of meetings of the Allied Public Safety Committee.
62. PRO/FO1005/1386, minutes of the 2nd meeting of the SCDP, 20 March 1946.
63. PRO/FO1005/1386, minutes of the 9th meeting of the SCDP, 2 July 1946.
64. PRO/FO1005/1387, SCD/P(46)46, 'Speeding up of Denazification', IA and C Division, 28 June 1946; PRO/FO1005/1386, minutes of the 9th meeting of SCDP, 2 July 1946. See also Bower, *Blind Eye to Murder*, p. 199.

weeks and would very likely take another year at least.[65]
The Heyman Report in its final version was approved by the
Cabinet's Overseas Reconstruction Committee (ORC) in July 1946
and constituted both British zonal policy on categorisation and the
British negotiating basis for the discussions proceeding in the
ACA.[66] The quadripartite discussions proved slow and intractable,
however,[67] and the British were anxious to commence categorisation as soon as possible, not least because they needed to release by
October 1946 approximately 10,000 individuals who had been
detained in the first wave of arrests and for whom the British
authorities had neither the manpower resources to guard nor adequate winter accommodation to house. Only by implementing a
scheme for categorisation could these internees be downgraded and
released with any semblance of legitimacy.[68] As a result, a memorandum submitted by the Chancellor of the Duchy of Lancaster,
John Hynd, was passed by ORC and issued as ZPI38 of August
1946.[69]

ZPI38 soon ran into a storm of criticism from the Germans. In
Hamburg, the trade union and party members on the panels
threatened to resign unless the instruction was revoked. Aside from
the absence of sufficiently severe sanctions for the less dangerous
offenders in category III of the new scheme, there was a strong
widespread objection to the classification of militarists (i.e. former
regular officers in the Armed Forces) in the same categories as
former Nazis and war criminals.[70] The CCG back-tracked and
agreed to issue a separate directive on militarists. In the meantime,
ZPI38 was held in suspended animation and the process of categorisation had yet to begin when the ACC directive, confusingly
numbered 38 as well, was issued in October 1946.[71]

65. PRO/FO1005/1387, SCD/P(46)46, 28 June 1946, App. E, Macready to
Gaffrey (IA and C), 21 June 1946.
66. PRO/FO371/55438/C8251, telegram COGA to Berlin, 18 July 1946.
67. For good examples of the increasingly testy confrontations between the
Anglo-American and Soviet representatives see PRO/FO1005/636, minutes of
the 24th meeting of the Nazi Arrest and Denazification Sub-Committee, 10
May 1946.
68. PRO/FO1005/1387, SCD/P(46)41, 26 June 1946, App. A, Berlin to COGA,
nd; PRO/FO371/55438/C8374, brief for the Secretary of State on Hynd
memorandum of 13 July 1946.
69. PRO/FO371/55439/C12776, Wilson to Dean, 18 October 1946.
70. PRO/FO371/55439/C12776, CCG to COGA, October 1946.
71. Lange, *Entnazifizierung*, p. 25. ACC Directive 38 is in Friedmann, *Allied
Military Government* pp. 314–26, and Ruhm von Oppen, *Documents* pp.
168–79.

The provisions of ACC Directive 38 as regards the categorisation of war criminals and Nazis were implemented by Zonal Executive Instruction (ZEI)54 of 30 November 1946,[72] supplemented by British Zone Ordinance 79 of 24 February 1947 on the 'Categorisation of Less Dangerous Nazis',[73] and by the final verion of ZPI3 of 7 March 1947.[74] Readers might like to spare a thought for the German and British officials at whom this cascade of paper was directed.

The Dilemma of Denazification

The dilemma posed by denazification in the British Zone has been commented on by many observers.[75] Thus, in Donnison's judgement:

> It was clear to the British element of the Control Commission, then still in London, that this policy created a conflict between the need to purge German society of Nazism and the need, not merely to keep the revived German administration working, but to provide the inhabitants of the British Zone with food, water and some protection from disease. If famine, pestilence, and anarchy were to supervene, suffering would not be confined to the Germans ... Furthermore, it was precisely the development of such conditions that would favour the recrudescence of Nazism or the emergence of Communism. It was the pressure of these self-regarding considerations that ultimately decided how the conflict would be resolved within the British Zone.[76]

It is apparent from the available evidence that in the first few months following the capitulation, the British were, indeed, intent on minimising the effect a 'holocaust of sudden dismissals'[77] would have in Germany and concentrated their efforts primarily on win-

72. Lange, *Entnazifizierung*, pp. 269–96.
73. CCG (BE), *Military Government Gazette*, No. 4, pp. 418–19.
74. Lange, *Entnazifizierung*, pp. 297–329.
75. Fürstenau, *Entnazifizierung*, p. 44; Stiefel, *Entnazifizierung in Österreich*, p. 36; Krüger, *Entnazifiziert!*, p. 34; U. Schneider, 'Britische Besatzungspolitik 1945', PhD thesis, University of Hanover, 1980, p. 118; H. Balshaw, 'The British Occupation in Germany, 1945–1949, with Special Reference to Hamburg' DPhil. thesis, Oxford University, 1972, p. 125 and V. Dotterwich, 'Die Entnazifizierung', in J. Becker, T. Stammer and P. Waldmann (eds.), *Vorgeschichte der Bundesrepublik Deutschland. Zwichen Kapitulation und Grundgesetz* (Wilhelm Fink Verlag, Munich, 1979), p. 135.
76. Donnison, *Civil Affairs ... North West Europe*, pp. 365–6.
77. Colonel Hume, Military Government Commander for RB Hanover, on 16 July 1945. Quoted by Schneider, 'Britische Besatzungspolitik', pp. 118 and 252.

ning the 'Battle of the Winter'. Thus, instructions for the denazification of industry, when issued, were hedged with such qualifications as 'action taken against firms or individuals must NOT be such as might hold up the production or distribution of food or impair the housing or health situation during the winter'.[78] Partly for reasons of expediency, therefore, and partly out of a perception of where the greatest security threat was likely to come from,[79] the initial political purge affected most immediately the administration, the educational system, the police and public services.[80] By the end of 1945, the denazification of industry in the British Zone had barely begun, a fact registered with increasing concern within the Control Commission hierarchy.[81] From November 1945 until July 1946, the CCG leadership both at zonal and regional level made repeated attempts to encourage an intensification of denazification in industry, constantly reiterating that it was British policy to give priority to denazification before reconstruction.[82]

Nor was this merely rhetoric on the part of the CCG. For the first year of the occupation, it seems that the British were prepared to sacrifice some economic efficiency for the sake of denazification.[83] Certainly, this did not apply to all sectors of the economy—the agricultural administration is a notable exception[84]—but for many

78. PRO/FO1010/27, HQ 30 Corps, 'Denazification of Business Concerns', 29 September 1945.
79. As Stiefel points out in *Entnazifizierung in Österreich*, p. 125, denazification was the mirror-image of nazification so that as the public service was the most heavily indoctrinated section, it became the prime target for purging.
80. PRO/FO1005/1388, 'Progress of Denazification', paper by Public Safety Branch, discussed at the 8th meeting of SCD, 4 December 1945.
81. PRO/FO1005/1388, minutes of the 6th meeting of SCD, 13 November 1945.
82. PRO/FO1005/1388, minutes of the 7th meeting of SCD, 20 November 1945; PRO/FO1005/1387, SCD/P(46)1, App. F, Office of DMG and COS Lübbecke to all Divisions, 10 December 1945; PRO/FO1010/2, minutes of General Conference, 19 November 1945; PRO/FO1010/27, 229/MG/41/SEC, 'Denazification', Macready, 26 June 1946 and Deputy Regional Commissioner, Hanover, to REO, 23 July 1946. See also DGB, Akte 'Britische Zone Allgemeines 1945-9', Ausschuss für die politische Bereinigung, Sitzung 28 Januar 1946.
83. DGB, 'Britische Zone Allgemeines 1945-9', Ausschuss für die politische Bereinigung, 28 Januar 1946; PRO/FO1010/27, confidential memorandum on denazification, Macready (RC), 26 June 1946 and Deputy Regional Commissioner to Regional Economic Officer, 23 July 1946. See also, H. G. Marten, *Die unterwanderte FDP* (Musterschmidt, Göttingen, 1978), p. 173. Compare Schneider, 'Britische Besatzungspolitik', p. 142, although his remarks are primarily addressed to the early days of the occupation when retention of experts was more common.
84. Balfour and Mair, *Four-Power Rule*, p. 175; Friedmann, *Allied Military Government*, p. 142.

Ian Turner

large and important areas it holds good. The Ruhr coal industry, for example, a crucial sector in many respects, lost so many of its technical and managerial personnel that production was retarded and industrial safety impaired.[85] Such was the concern of the occupying authorities that by May 1946 they were considering suspending denazification in the coal industry indefinitely.[86] Forestry and timber production,[87] potash and salt mining are further examples of economic sectors severely hit by the policy.[88]

Perhaps the clearest evidence of British intentions was the denazification of the Volkswagenwerk in Wolfsburg. Here was a factory which was producing cars under CCG control primarily for use by the occupying authorities and which enjoyed a privileged status in the economy of the British Zone. Although initially spared the full force of denazification, the process was resumed in 1946 following a CCG investigation. Between 17 and 19 June, 179 works employees, almost all from managerial and supervisory positions and including several key executives, were dismissed. The disruption caused by denazification, the uncertainty which surrounded the process of appeal and reinstatement, and the fear and suspicion which the policy evoked, all hindered production at the works.[89]

The reaction to the official denazification drive in industry from the CCG's economic divisions was not long in coming. Bitter protests were received from Military Government officials, battling to get the German economy moving again, about the catastrophic effects of denazification in their sectors.[90] Even so, denazification did not always take priority over efforts to restore the economy. In some cases the importance of the economic sector to the British Zone was such as to ensure that relaxation of the conditions and even wholesale exemptions from denazification were permitted. Agriculture and eventually the coal industry are two such instances.

85. Donnison, *Civil Affairs ... North West Europe*, p. 410.
86. *Akten zur Vorgeschichte der Bundesrepublik*, Vol. 1, pp. 521–26; Parlamentsarchiv, Bonn, XII/ZB 192, memorandum from British Liaison Staff ZAC to German Secretariat ZAC, 2 May 1946; *Monthly Report of the CCG (BE)*, Vol. 1, No. 5, October 1946, p. 28; Fürstenau, *Entnazifizierung*, pp. 112–14; Lange, *Entnazifizierung*, p. 31.
87. PRO/FO1010/4, Petterson (Senior Economic Controller, Hanover Region), 'Denazification and Export Programmes', 10 May 1946.
88. PRO/FO1010/27, Trade and Industry Division (Military Government Hanover), 'Denazification of Potash and Salt Mines', 5 June 1946.
89. See Turner, 'British Occupation', pp. 211–12.
90. PRO/FO1005/1387, SCD/P(46)12, App. A, 'Denazification of German Industry', 15 March 1946 approved by ECOSC on 11 March 1946 and forwarded for discussion at the 2nd meeting of SCDP, 20 March 1946.

In other cases, hard-pressed functional officers strove to retain essential personnel by a variety of means, both fair and foul. As far as the former method was concerned, the Allied denazification legislation offered a number of openings. Temporary retention of individuals under paragraph 8 of Directive 24 was the most obvious. Figures for June 1946 show that outside of Hanover Region only 29 people were officially retained under this clause.[91] For Hanover, 168 were retained in the mandatory dismissal class above (see table 9.1).[92]

Another possibility was for Military Government functions to sponsor an appeal against a decision of the German Denazification Panels and PSSB. After March 1946, in fact, all those whose appeal was supported by Military Government were automatically retained in office pending the result of appeal to the German Review Boards, provided PSSB judged their *Fragebogen* to be 'sufficiently clean to warrant the reasonable assumption that . . . [their] appeal will ultimately be successful'.[93] Again there was a glaring disparity between Hanover, where, in May 1946, 966 cases of recommended dismissals were retained pending appeal, and the other regions where there were only 20 such cases altogether.[94]

Quite apart from these legitimate means of evading the full force of denazification, some functions resorted to the simple subterfuge of ignoring instructions altogether. Thus, when the British Zone's transport administration was investigated in late 1947, the authorities discovered 'what can only be interpreted as a deliberate attempt by both the German Executive Joint Committee and the Bipartitite Control Panel for Transport to sabotage the denazification of the Transport Administration'.[95] Nor was this instance an isolated case, as visitors to the British Zone including the World Federation of Trade Unions were to testify.[96]

Once the German appeal bodies were in place, the wave of dismissals was in any case reversed. In the Volkswagenwerk, for example, out of just under 200 employees dismissed by recommen-

91. PRO/FO1005/1386, Annex II to App. A to HQ/06101/10/Sec G, 25 June 1946.
92. This may, of course, be because the Hanover figures were a closer reflection of reality.
93. PRO/FO1010/27, Public Safety, Hanover Region, 27 March 1946. Procedure was relaxed still further by the final version of ZPI3 in March 1947.
94. PRO/FO1005/1386 Annex I to App. A to HQ/06101/10/Sec G, 25 June 1946.
95. PRO/FO371/64747/C15312, M. L. Priss (FO), 1 December 1947.
96. For the WFTU's critical remarks see PRO/FO371/55509. See also Fenner Brockway's comments in *German Diary* (Gollancz London, 1946), pp. 26–7 and Bower, *Blind Eye to Murder*, p. 172.

Table 9.1 Temporary retentions of individuals under paragraph 8 of ACC Dir. 24 (Hanover Region)

Mandatory removal category	1 mth	2 mth	3 mth	4 mth	5 mth	6 mth	7 mth	8 mth	Total
Administration	6	1	0	0	0	0	0	1	8
Communications	5	1	0	0	0	0	0	0	6
Industry	9	0	0	0	0	0	0	30	39
Finance	1	1	0	0	2	0	0	0	4
Food and Agriculture	12	24	0	0	1	0	0	0	37
Manpower	11	4	0	0	0	0	0	0	15
Legal	1	0	0	0	1	2	1	2	7
Posts & Telecommunications	3	0	1	0	0	0	0	2	6
Education	10	0	0	0	0	0	0	0	10
Public Health	12	2	3	1	0	0	0	1	19
Highways & Highway Transport	2	11	0	0	0	0	0	0	13
Information Control	2	0	0	0	0	0	0	0	2
Forestry	0	1	1	0	0	0	0	0	2
Total	74	45	5	1	4	2	1	36	168

Discretionary removal category	1 mth	2 mth	3 mth	4 mth	5 mth	6 mth	7 mth	8 mth	Total
Police	4	2	7	34	47	10	6	0	110
Administration	8	5	2	0	13	2	0	1	31
Commerce	1	0	0	0	2	5	4	0	12
Industry	161	75	38	1	11	47	15	2	350
Finance	1	1	18	5	25	52	2	0	104
Food and Agriculture	0	1	2	0	0	0	0	0	3
Manpower	31	24	4	1	5	1	3	1	70
Legal	0	1	2	6	20	26	25	11	91
Posts & Telecommunications	0	0	147	315	62	242	110	0	876
Education	20	11	42	58	138	624	2	0	895
Public Health	4	6	3	7	2	5	33	0	60
Highways & Highway Transport	3	0	0	1	0	0	0	0	4
Total	233	126	265	428	325	1,014	200	15	2,606

Source: PRO/FO 1005/1386, Annex II to App A to HQ 06101/10/Sec G, 25 June 1946.

dation of the German denazification panels, 138 were reinstated on appeal in February 1947.[97]

'A horrid, tiresome business':[98] The Pressure to Conclude Denazification

If in the first half of 1946, criticism of British denazification both in Germany itself and in the United Kingdom had been directed chiefly at the failure of the occupying authorities to apply policy with sufficient vigour and comprehensiveness. By the end of 1946, public opinion in Britain was tiring of the manifold complexities of the programme and was increasingly pre-disposed to 'bury the hatchet' and wind up denazification as quickly as possible. This was a view advocated by prominent people with such disparate political opinions as Winston Churchill and Victor Gollancz,[99] and it reinforced the position which officials in Foreign Office's German Department had held virtually from the start of the occupation.[100]

Responding to the change in political climate the London end of the occupation, the Control Office for Germany and Austria (COGA) wrote to the Control Commission in early January 1947 urging the necessity for a quick termination of denazification, preferably by the spring, so as to be able to announce completion of the programme at the forthcoming session of the Council of Foreign Ministers (CFM) in Moscow. The Control Office wished to proclaim the dawning of a new era of reconstruction in Germany and denazification had become a burdensome commitment which they intended to liquidate as soon as was reasonably possible.[101] Increasingly, too, the British began to emphasise the constructive, rehabilitative aspect of categorisation,[102] and the need to concentrate on the 'big Nazis' in preference to the small fry.[103]

---

97. Turner, 'British Occupation', pp. 288–9.
98. Lord Pakenham in a House of Lords debate in November 1947, quoted in Donnison, *Civil Affairs . . . North West Europe*, p. 376.
99. Fürstenau, *Entnazifizierung*, pp. 109–11.
100. Typical of the FO view is Franklin's minute of 10 January 1946 (PRO/FO371/55434/C 315): 'There is the unpleasant odour of fascism and of the Gestapo mind in much of this denazification business . . . We are there to end, not replace, Hitler methods.'
101. PRO/FO371/64352/C223, COGA to CCG Berlin, 3 January 1947.
102. PRO/FO371/64352/C1648, 'Denazification in the British Zone of Germany', draft memorandum by Wilberforce (COGA) for Hynd, n.d. (covering letter dated 29 January 1947). See also the press report of General Bishop's statement on 7 February 1947 (C2278).
103. PRO/FO371/64352/C3828, Berlin to COGA, 5 March 1947.

By the time the Moscow Council came around there was still no end to denazification in sight. In one of the few concrete agreements to be reached at the CFM, the Allies agreed to transfer responsibility for denazification to the Länder governments which had now been established or were about to be established on an elected basis.[104] Subsequently, an attempt was made at ACA to agree a common directive for the hand-over, but proceedings in the Public Safety Committee were slow and marred by periodic slanging matches between the Soviet Union and the western powers over the question of which country's denazification programme had exhibited the most ineptitude and duplicity. When in August 1947, therefore, the Soviet authorities suddenly issued an ordinance transferring denazification unilaterally in their zone, the British heaved a great sigh of relief and prepared to follow suit.[105]

At the same time, however, the CCG were keen to reach a closer coordination of denazification policy with the US Zone, if only for the sake of those Germans employed in Bizonal agencies,[106] so that it was only after these talks had, in turn, proved abortive,[107] that the CCG could proceed with the issue of a zonal ordinance for transferring denazification to the Länder. The ordinance itself was a compromise package: in deference to the Regional Commissioners, ultimate authority for denazification was vested in them and the categorisation of individuals in the two highest categories was reserved to the British authorities.[108] In response to pressure from the Foreign Office's German Section, 1 January 1948 was set as the deadline for removals under denazification and a prohibition was placed upon the reopening of cases already heard unless evidence of falsification of *Fragebogen* could be produced.[109] Table 9.2 gives some figures on the impact of denazification in the British Zone up to this point. As a further limitation on German innovation the Länder laws which the ordinance provided for were still to be bound by the provisions of Directives 24 and 38. The Zonal Advisory Council in Hamburg protested in vain against the draft, which

104. Fürstenau, *Entnazifizierung* p. 111; Krüger, *Entnazifiziert!*, p. 54.
105. PRO/FO 1033/39, Brayne (PS) to Acting Deputy Military Governor 18 August 1947. Public Safety Committee meetings are recorded in PRO/FO1005/625.
106. PRO/FO1033/39, Berlin to FOGS, 2 June 1947.
107. PRO/FO1033/39, Brownjohn (CCG) to Dean (FOGS), 25 August 1947.
108. PRO/FO1033/39, FOGS to Berlin, 19 June 1947.
109. PRO/FO1033/39, Berlin to FOGS, 4 July 1947 and FOGS to Berlin, 12 August 1947.

Table 9.2 Denazification in the British Zone up to November 1947

Date	Compulsory removals	Discretionary removals	Applications for employment	Exclusions	Prosecutions for false answers	Fragebogen evaluated
By 31 December 1945	43,288	28,585	419,492	41,486	928	538,806
By 31 August 1946	91,812	63,844	944,567	86,106	1,634	1,197,621
By 30 April 1947	320,017 (including exclusions)					1,785,507
By November 1947	347,667 (including exclusions)				2,320	2,144,022

Source: *Monthly Statistical Bulletin of the CCG(BE)*, No. 4, Table 68; Friedmann (1947), p. 332; PRO/FO 1033/42, 'Denazification Statistics for the British Zone', PSSB, Berlin, 23 December 1947.

was finally issued on 1 October 1947 as Ordinance 110.[110]

Having handed over the responsibility for denazification to the German Länder, the British authorities came up against the limits of their influence as an occupying power. The German Länder governments proved less than enthusiastic about enacting laws on the basis of a whole set of preconditions laid down by the British of which they disapproved. The insistence on what, to all intents and purposes, was a ban on reopening cases, and the imposition of a set procedure for categorisation were particularly irksome to the Germans. Only in Schleswig-Holstein was a law actually passed and approved by Military Government. In Lower Saxony and North Rhine-Westphalia the Landtage passed acts only after lengthy debate, only to have them rejected as unacceptable by the British authorities.[111] As a result the process had to be continued by parliamentary decree.

Heavy-handed intervention of this nature was not something the Regional Commissioners relished. In this instance they yielded to pressure from London, but successfully resisted attempts by the Foreign Office to apply a deadline for all vetting and a wholesale exoneration of those in categories IV and V.[112] Lord Pakenham, the Foreign Office minister responsible for Germany, also urged that the period after which denazified Germans were to be downgraded automatically should be reduced from two years to one.[113] The original intention of the Foreign Office had been that denazified Germans should be allowed to return to office after a period of exclusion during which they would have foresworn their allegiance to the 'Nazi creed' and embraced the principles of democracy.[114] By late 1949 there was mounting evidence to suggest that reinstatement was preceding conversion, and the Foreign Office became increasingly anxious at the threat this posed to Allied policy in Germany.[115] The promulgation of the Basic Law, which under Article 131 left the way open for the return of denazified Beamte to

110. For the ZAC attitude and its conspicious lack of success, see PRO/FO1033/39, British Liaison (ZAC) to Berlin, 22 August 1947; Fürstenau, *Entnazifizierung*, pp. 122–7 and Parlamentsarchiv, Bonn, Bestand 1, Nr. 193. Ordinance 110 is reprinted in Ruhm von Oppen, *Documents*, pp. 247–50.
111. Fürstenau, *Entnazifizierung*, pp. 129–33.
112. For the CCG attitude see PRO/FO371/64747/CG1269, Berlin to FOGS, 12 March 1948 and PRO/FO371/64747/CG2008, Garran (GOVSC) to RECOs, 23 April 1948. For the FO/Pakenham wish for total exemptions and a rapid conclusion, PRO/FO371/64747/CG1562, Priss, 18 December 1947 and PRO/FO1030/92, Pakenham to Robertson, 23 March 1948.
113. PRO/FO1030/92, Pakenham to Robertson, 23 March 1948.
114. PRO/FO371/77064/CG2405, minute by Tayleur, 12 September 1949.

public service, was further indication of this worrying trend.[116] The Foreign Office blamed the CCG for its 'lackadaisical attitude' and urged intervention.[117] The CCG placed the blame, with some justification, on Foreign Office pressure to transfer responsibility to the Germans in 1947.[118] Whatever the cause, it rapidly became clear that the British no longer had the power to do anything about it.[119]

In Lower Saxony, at least, the gathering tide of reinstatements was held back for a while by Land legislation. The SPD Land government was determined to protect the rights of those individuals who had been installed in official positions by virtue of their democratic credentials. In March 1949 it enacted an ordinance which provided that although officials downgraded on review became eligible for reinstatement they had no automatic right thereto.[120]

Once the Federal Republic was formed, the new government was presented with the unenviable task of sorting out the tattered remnants of a denazification programme which had been designed by the Allies and implemented against German protests. The different practices in the western zones had to be reconciled and the policy wound up with some semblance of dignity. The only practicable way was by announcing amnesties for all but the serious offenders. In October 1950, the Federal government issued guidelines to the Länder and laws were subsequently passed throughout the Federal Republic bringing denazification to a close. The British, concerned as ever about the security implications, retained control over the two most serious categories—war criminals and ardent Nazis. But this was very much a formal power, seldom exercised in practice. In August 1953, concerned at the return of prominent Nazis like Werner Naumann to public life but recognising the limits of their powers as occupiers to prevent it, the British gave up this their final residual responsibility for denazification.[121]

---

115. PRO/FO371/77064/CG2405, minute by O'Grady, 13 September 1949.
116. See Fürstenau, *Entnazifizierung*, p. 216; Niethammer, *Entnazifizierung*, pp. 549–50 and K. Tauber, *Beyond Eagle and Swastika* (Wesleyan University Press, Middletown, Conn., 1967) pp. 937–40.
117. PRO/FO371/77064/CG2405, minute by O'Grady, 13 September 1949.
118. PRO/FO371/77064/CG3155, Robertson to Kirkpatrick, 21 October 1949.
119. Ibid. and PRO/FO371/77064/CG3155, minute by Tayleur, 3 November 1949.
120. PRO/FO371/77064/CG2405, ZEO Lübbecke to FOGS, 31 August 1949. See also: Fürstenau, *Entnazifizierung*, pp. 213–16 and *Monthly Report of the CCG (BE)*, Vol. 4, No. 1, January 1949, pp. 35, 45.
121. Krüger, *Entnazifiziert!*, p. 159.

Ian Turner

Conclusion

Was British denazification policy a fiasco? The process in the British Zone certainly had many negative features. The welter of directives which caused such confusion, the disruption of some industrial and administrative organisations, the resentment of the population at a policy which was seen as punishing the 'small fry' but letting the 'big fish' escape, the scope provided for corruption, hypocrisy and deception—all of these have rightly been seen as hallmarks of British denazification.

Given these drawbacks, the lasting benefits of the process are admittedly limited. The long-term impact of denazification upon West German elites has been studied by a number of scholars.[122] They conclude that the greatest impact was upon the political elites. The civil service was less affected and the industrial elite was barely touched. Of course this reflects the emphasis of Allied and particularly British denazification policy, which in turn implies a value-judgement about the threat posed by each of these elites. In retrospect, however, this assessment may not have been too wide of the mark.

It is certainly arguable that by the limited standards of Britain's own aims of removing 'dangerous' Germans who posed a threat to the purposes of the Allied occupation, denazification was reasonably successful. But like other policies discussed here it suffered from internal conflicts of interests. In the first place, the British had to resolve their desire to remove politically undesirable individuals from positions of influence with the compelling needs of an economy under strain. How this conflict was resolved varied over time but certainly from the start of 1947 onwards denazification in the British Zone was overtaken by developments in the international arena. The need to build up western Germany as a bulwark against communism meant the rehabilitation of former Nazis, who had hopefully recanted their past sins in the meantime, and the integration of the German people into western democratic society. It also meant handing over increasing responsibility to German bodies who, awkwardly from the British point of view, proved less willing to let bygones be bygones. By 1949 the British, too, had started to wonder whether large-scale rehabilitation so soon was quite such a

122. L. J. Edinger, 'Post-Totalitarian Leadership: Elites in the German Federal Republic', *American Political Science Review*, Vol. 54, No. 1, 1960, pp. 58–82.

good idea. This rehabilitative aspect of British denazification has been seen in retrospect as a positive feature, a sign of success in preventing the formation of a pool of disaffected and resentful Germans.[123] In fact, shifting the emphasis onto rehabilitation was essentially a 'Flucht nach vorn' by the British, a means of liquidating a policy which, with the passage of time and the changing international climate, had become an embarrassment to the British government. To describe it as a great success in these circumstances is to make a virtue out of necessity.

123. Krüger, *Entnazifiziert!*, pp. 158–9.

PART IV

Key Groups in Post-War German Society

PART TWO

10

DGB Economic Policy with Particular Reference to the British Zone, 1945–9
Peter Hubsch

Introduction

Attention is focused on the Deutscher Gewerkschaftsbund (DGB) and economic and political developments in the British Zone because of its industrial significance. Located in the north-west of Germany it had the largest population of the three western zones and contained the Ruhr. Deconcentration policies were aimed specifically at the coal and steel cartels of the Ruhr, which had sustained the German armed forces in two world wars. Its future control was of concern to the whole of Europe. This issue was a key factor in the relationship of the unions with the Allies. The trade union concepts of economic democracy bore directly on the question of ownership and control of heavy industry. Subsequently it determined the relationship with German business and the parties which represented them. The British Zone produced the main influential initiatives in the western zones, in both the trade union and political sphere and, in both cases, the first national leaders, Böckler and Adenauer.

The earliest trade union programmes in the British Zone, as in the other zones of occupation in Germany, demanded radical structural reforms. These were closely identified with the socialist planned economy proposed by the Social Democrats (SPD). Extensive public ownership, central planning and industrial controls formed the basis of the anti-capitalist programme.

This policy was modified by the experience of the experiment with codetermination during the deconcentration of the steel industry in the British Zone. It was supported by Böckler and the trade union leaders, who were influenced by the Weimar concepts

271

of economic democracy. Their desire for a highly centralised and unified movement was also influenced by the concentration of industrial power in the Ruhr, and the weakness of the fragmented movement before the war. At the time of the Founding Congress of the Deutscher Gewerkschaftsbund for the British Zone, in April 1947, the DGB began to emphasise self-government and trade union participation at every level of the economy, at the expense of state intervention.

The east–west division led to a further reorientation of DGB economic policy in favour of the Marshall Plan and integration with western Europe. The split with the East German trade unions revealed the fundamental differences between the two sides and the anti-communist sentiments of the DGB leaders. The DGB and the US Zone leaders developed a strong international outlook which distanced them further from the SPD. The DGB rejected the proposals for social partnership with the progressive employers, identified by the US Zone trade union leaders, because of their experiences with the reactionary industrialists of the Ruhr. It opposed the deregulated economy introduced by Erhard, but supported a return to a socially oriented market economy, assisted by the European Recovery Programme, as the best solution for German industry, exports and employment.

The rejection of ideology and dogma was attributable to the principle of strict political and religious neutrality, and the desire of the DGB to be accepted as a force for stability and moderation. This was overlooked by its critics. Böckler reserved the militant potential of the movement to achieve codetermination.

Reconstruction of the Trade Union Movement

The initially restrictive nature of British policy on German trade unions was attributable to a number of different motives, including military security, fear of a National Socialist revival and a growing suspicion of the communists. The concern for economic revival strengthened the position of the trade union leaders, but also accounted for a favourable attitude towards the business sector. All of these factors influenced the development of policy at different stages of the occupation. However, the British authorities openly admitted to the German trade union leaders that their intention to slow down development was a deliberate policy.[1] The same policy applied in the French and US Zones, in contrast with the rapid reconstruction in the Soviet Zone. The explanation for this was the priority given to their concept of democracy, and the aim to democratise all institutions in Germany. Members of the Manpower Division of the Control Commission for Germany (CCG) were aware of the Weimar development of the trade unions, and the majority were convinced of the need to include them in this process. The Allgemeiner Deutscher Gewerkschaftsbund (ADGB) was seen to have provided no resistance in 1933, and to have failed to perceive the nature of National Socialism or to grasp that it was as incompatible as communism with genuine trade unionism.[2] This determined the cautious attitude of members in 1945. It was seen to justify the early policy on slow development at local level.[3]

There was a consensus among trade union leaders on the need to eliminate the ideological rifts and the class divisions of the past, and to create a neutral, unified organisation of all sections of the workforce, including the civil servants and white-collar staff. Members had to decide between the highly centralist organisation, divided into industrial and vocational sub-groups, or autonomous industrial and vocational unions linked within a strong federation. Hans Böckler's proposals for a single, unitary union originally included compulsory membership. Although this was dropped, the concept of a single, highly centralised union remained.[4] On 23 November 1945 a TUC delegation, at the invitation of the Military Government, visited the German trade unionists.[5] Under the chairmanship of Luce, head of Manpower Division, the TUC representatives discussed the organisation issue with Böckler and his trade union colleagues in Düsseldorf. The specific criticism aimed at the German group was that their 'proposed organisation was over-centralised' and that it appeared to the TUC representatives that Böckler and his colleagues were trying to 'build from the top'.[6] In a

1. Deutscher Gewerkschaftsbund, *Die Gewerkschaftsbewegung in der britischen Besatzungszone 1945–1949* (Bund-Verlag, Cologne, 1949), p. 49.
2. E. C. M. Cullingford, *Trade Unions in West Germany* (Wilton House, London, 1976), p. 14.
3. Interview E. C. M. Cullingford, 1 August 1983. For the British attitude to democratisation in general see chapter 7.
4. DGB Archiv, Protokoll der Gewerkschafts-Konferenz der Gewerkschaften der Nord-Rheinprovinz am 7 Dezember 1945 in Düsseldorf.
5. TUC Archive, 943/911; also reprinted in R. Steininger, 'England und die deutsche Gewerkschaftsbewegung 1945–1946', *Archiv für Sozialgeschichte*, Vol. 18, 1978, p. 47.
6. Ibid.

radio broadcast from Hamburg on 24 November 1945, the leader of the delegation, the miners' president, William Lawther, acknowledged the potential role of the trade unions in a future German society, but added a word of 'warning and advice' which clearly illustrated that their position was much closer to that of the Military Government and the Manpower Division than to the German trade unionists.[7] Lawther referred to the continual German threat to world peace and the lack of resistance within Germany to Hitler.

Immediately after the TUC visit Böckler convened a conference of trade unions in North Rhine Province. The specific purpose was to discuss the implications for the structure and aims of their organisation. Böckler linked the proposal for a powerful organisation with the need to have some degree of control over the economy in future.[8] Böckler obtained a majority in favour of accepting the advice of the TUC. Following this agreement the members immediately went on to discuss the principle of organisation of individual trade unions. Members unanimously endorsed the proposal for industrial unions, which Böckler favoured. The miners strongly supported the proposal and also emphasised the importance of absorbing all the workforce in the trade union at each colliery, including non-manual employees. This ensured the principle of the single union plant. The miners formed their industrial union at the end of 1946. The federation for the British Zone was not formed until April 1947.

The Programme for Maximum Influence in the Economy

The trade union demand for maximum influence in the economy after the war was strongly influenced by the programmes of the movement before 1933. The initial demands for planning and public ownership of industry also represented a degree of continuity from the Weimar period. What distinguished the development of economic policy after 1945 was the attitude of the trade unions to the state and to the employers. They not only had a deep suspicion of the employers, they had also lost faith in the ability of the state to guarantee democracy, and emphasised the role of the trade unions in the control of economic life. This was encouraged by the initial

7. Ibid., p. 107.
8. DGB Archiv, Protokoll der Gewerkschaftskonferenz der Gewerkschaften der Nord-Rheinprovinz am 7 Dezember 1945 in Düsseldorf.

absence of democratic elections, and the continuation of strict controls over economic life by Military Government. These factors complicated the development of coherent economic policies. The trade union leaders were also unclear on the aims and method of participation in the future economy, following their limited success after 1918.

A consistent theme at the first conference of trade unions in the British Zone, held in Hanover in March 1946 was the sense of failure of the trade unions between 1918 and 1933. The lesson to be learned from past mistakes was the need to guarantee the rightful place of the workforce in society and to ensure the recognition of trade unions as equal to the employers. It was no longer accepted that real wages could be obtained in traditional wage bargaining procedures alone. The distribution of national wealth was also determined by the activities of local and regional public bodies, including the chambers of commerce, and the policies of government. The trade unions were anxious to develop structures that would enable them to protect themselves from any economic or political threat and to exercise influence on economic policies at every level. They wished to establish the principle of matching the power of the employers, before business had the opportunity to recover and reorganise. The trade union leaders, most of whom had experienced the development of German industry after the First World War, believed that the organisation of trade unions had not kept pace with the intensive concentration of industry.[9] They also believed that the threat was not industrial concentration as such, but the structure of control and ownership. The demand for an effective, centralised trade union movement assumed the continued large-scale organisation of industry.[10] It also implied a revival of the organised economy in which trade unions had begun to play a role during the Weimar Republic. Böckler and the trade union leaders were concerned with the viability of German industry, and its future competitive position in the international economy. It became increasingly difficult to reconcile this fully with the initial demands for a socialist, centrally planned economy with extensive nationalisation of the means of production. No consensus had developed on the control of industry or the form and extent of public ownership. Large-scale nationalisation was regarded as a possibility: 'Welches

9. DGB Archiv, Protokoll der ersten Gewerkschaftskonferenz der britischen Zone, Hannover, März 1946, p. 21.
10. Ibid., p. 18.

Peter Hubsch

aber sollen die Formen sein? Verstaatlichung auf der ganzen Linie?
Genossenschaftliche Betriebsform? Alle diese Dinge beschäftigen
uns. Wir kamen bis jetzt zu keinen Lösungen.'[11]
   An important element in the strategy to create a strong, independent and authoritative movement was the proposal for a research
institute. This was to be capable of providing the information and
statistics to underpin the economic policies of the trade unions.
Böckler had discussed these ideas with Viktor Agartz before the end
of the war.[12] Agartz was to head the institute. When Agartz accepted a senior position in the Zentralamt für Wirtschaft Böckler
turned to Erich Potthoff. The foundations for the development of
the Wirtschaftswissenschaftliches Institut (WWI) were established
immediately after the Hanover Conference. Böckler announced that
Potthoff was to become responsible for the information and research tasks of the trade unions at the first Zone Committee meeting
of the British Zone trade unions.[13]
   The pace of development of economic policy changed from this
point. The work of the Zone Committee and the Secretariat, both of
which were given approval by the British Manpower Division at the
Hanover Conference, illustrated, for the first time, the serious
attempts to provide more practical policy guidelines. The head of
the Secretariat, Werner Hansen, was a close colleague of Böckler,
and, as one of the earliest emigrés allowed to return to Germany,
rejoined him in March 1945.[14] Hansen assisted the return of his
colleague in England, Ludwig Rosenberg, eighteen months later.
Rosenberg also joined the Secretariat and developed the programme
for trade union participation in chambers of commerce and industry.
   At the end of 1946 the trade unions had still not published a
definitive statement on the public ownership of industry, although
the major industrial sectors were gradually being transferred to
German administration. The North German Iron and Steel Control
(NGISC) was established in August 1946 as the controlling authority for the iron and steel industry in the British Zone. The development of the authority was based on an unpublished plan conceived
by the Metallurgy Branch of the CCG's Trade and Industry Divi-

11. Ibid., p. 32.
12. H.–G. Hermann, *Verraten und Verkauft* (Fuldaer Verlaganstalt, Fulda 1958),
    p. 32.
13. DGB Archiv, Protokoll den ersten Tagung des gewerkschaftlichen Zonen-
    ausschusses (BZ), 5–6 April 1946.
14. *British Zone Review*, 1 March 1947, p. 19.

276

sion in Berlin and dated 6 July 1946.[15] The aims of the plan were to break up private ownership of the existing cartels and combines, reduce capacity to the agreed peacetime levels and restructure the industry on the basis of public ownership. The British authorities agreed to a central Allied control body with a German executive organ. The combines were to be broken up and established as financially independent companies which could be transferred rapidly to public ownership whatever their final form. Liquidation of the combines was recognised as being an enormous task, but it was emphasised that there was to be no return to vertical integration under single management.[16] The NGISC established the Stahltreuhandverwaltung on 5 October 1946 to carry out its main tasks. Heinrich Dinkelbach, former executive board member of the Vereinigte Stahlwerke, was appointed its head.

On 4 December Böckler and Potthoff met William Asbury, Regional Commissioner for North Rhine-Westphalia, to discuss public ownership of industry and to present a policy paper on socialisation.[17] The paper criticised the lack of progress and the failure to clarify the future plans for the coal, iron and steel, and chemical industries in the British Zone. On the following day the Executive and Committee met to discuss the constitution of the trade union federation for the British Zone, and the founding congress, which was scheduled for spring 1947. Organisational and constitutional questions were still dominant themes. In the discussion on economic policy members agreed on allocation of RM 150,000 to the recently established research department, with the express purpose of working out practical proposals on the socialisation of the basic industries and trade union participation in the economy.[18]

The policy paper submitted to Asbury represented an initial statement from the trade unions which placed the issue of public ownership in a wider context. It revealed an important change of emphasis in their economic programme, with greater prominence being given to the concept of codetermination. One of the factors

15. Stahltreuhändervereinigung, *Die Neuordnung der Eisen- und Stahlindustrie im Gebiet der Bundesrepublik Deutschland*, (Beck'sche Verlagsbuchhandlung, Munich, 1954) p. 59.
16. Ibid., p. 60.
17. DGB Archiv, Stellungnahme der Gewerkschaften zur Sozialisierung, Gewerkschaftliches Zonensekretariat (BZ) Bielefeld, 4 Dezember 1946. For deconcentration policies in the steel industry see chapter 6.
18. DGB Archiv, Protokoll Zonenvorstand und Zonenausschuss (BZ), 5 Dezember 1946.

Peter Hubsch

contributing to this change was the need to ensure trade union involvement in the management organs of any new industrial units created out of the former combines. It was also seen as essential to be in a position that would enable the direct influence of the trade unions to be brought to bear on any discussions of reform or socialisation of the basic industries.[19] Another factor was the recognition of the growing opposition to nationalisation, and the need to counteract general resistance to public ownership, which was encouraged by the postponement of any final decision. This was being used by their opponents and 'die sich mehrenden Stimmen der Verzögerungstaktiker'.[20] Public ownership was played down. Socialisation was now firmly presented as more than a policy for state control. The concept of codetermination at plant level, and especially beyond the level of the plant, was offered as a solution to the control of industry which mere nationalisation did not provide.[21] Participation at every level of management of large firms or industries in the public sector was seen as a way of socialising the control of industry.

The trade unions were forced to adopt a pragmatic approach to public ownership and control of German industry in the British Zone. The deconcentration of steel was a partial programme which left open the wider issues of economic reform in a future Germany. It was recognised that any British proposals for the future development of the Ruhr industries would have to take account of the demands for international controls discussed in the Allied Control Council (ACC) and the Council of Foreign Ministers meetings. The plan to establish advisory boards for steel and coal, with equal trade union representation, was agreed by the members of the trade union Economic Policy Committee in November 1946.[22] To allay the fears of the workforce about the possible intervention of foreign capital, the British controller for the iron and steel industry, Harris-Burland, arranged a meeting with works councillors in Düsseldorf. The purpose of the meeting was to discuss the unrest of the workforce in the Ruhr, and the concern over the future ownership of the basic industries. Harris-Burland confirmed that the steel industry was to be radically reorganised and eventually returned to

19. DGB Archiv, Stellungnahme der Gewerkschaften zur Sozialisierung, Gewerkschaftliches Zonensekretariat (BZ) Bielefeld, 4 Dezember 1946.
20. Ibid.
21. Ibid.
22. DGB Archiv, Wirtschaftspolitischer Ausschuss der Gewerkschaften (BZ), 8–9 November 1946.

278

the German people.[23] It was made clear that there was no intention to retain the large combines. They were to be broken up into smaller independent units in order to remove the concentration of economic power and eliminate the danger of future rearmament.

The first meeting at which Böckler and trade union representatives officially learnt of the detailed plans for the deconcentration of the steel industry took place on 14 December 1946.[24] Dinkelbach and members of the NGISC explained their proposals. Böckler accepted the Dinkelbach plan and presented the trade union proposals for participation in management, which now formed the central element in their concept of economic democracy. Potthoff believed that the experience of the British with joint consultation and joint production committees during the war made them more sympathetic to these ideas.[25] When the definitive policy of the trade unions on public ownership was eventually published, at the end of January 1947, it was clearly influenced by these exchanges, and integrated with the programme for codetermination.

The demand for public ownership of industry envisaged the retention of the joint stock company. The concept of capitalism as the direct control of the means of production was rejected. In modern industry it was argued that owners had been replaced by managers. Management expertise and initiative had become the main factors in the control of production.[26] The proposals fitted in with the existing British plans for steel. They were also reminiscent of the developments in the Weimar Republic, where the promotion of the joint stock company in the public sector ensured managerial and financial autonomy, as well as independence from public authorities. The trade union leaders accepted the joint stock company as the appropriate form of organisation for capital-intensive industries. Although this model allowed for the public authority to be the effective legal owner, the state was not to be allowed to interfere with the management or independence of firms. Central planning was allowed for in the proposals, but even here the role of the state was seen as setting a planning framework, rather than intervening directly in production decisions. The programme stressed the importance of keeping the representatives of the state, the adminis-

23. E. Potthoff, *Der Kampf um die Mitbestimmung* (Bund-Verlag, Cologne, 1957).
24. Ibid., p. 38.
25. Ibid., p. 40.
26. DGB Archiv, Zonenausschuss der Gewerkschaften der britischen Zone, Leitsätze der Gewerkschaften zur Sozialisierung, 27 Januar 1947.

trative bureaucracies and the political parties out of the socialised industries. The aim of the trade unions was to secure the right to participate in the key management organs of these industries. Codetermination was the precondition for socialisation in the democratised economy.[27]

These guidelines represented a departure from earlier public discussions in the trade union movement after 1945. Although they remained imprecise on the specific role of the state, and on the organisation of management control, it was clear that local management was to have relative freedom to give priority to considerations of productivity and competition.

Economic Democracy Reviewed

The trade union concept of economic democracy began to develop into a more coherent programme after the Bielefeld Conference of trade unions in the British Zone in August 1946. Concrete proposals were not formulated until the beginning of 1947. The *ad hoc* arrangements for economic policy discussions, serviced by the Secretariat in Bielefeld, were superseded by the establishment of an Economic Policy Committee at the end of 1946. The first meetings took place in November and December. Immediately after the initial meeting with Dinkelbach and Harris-Burland the trade union proposals for participation were prepared and presented to the Economic Policy Committee for discussion on the 8 and 9 November.[28] It was a model which provided an advisory board of administration for the sector as a whole, above the level of individual works. It was also intended to apply to the coal sector, and was conceived as a model for any basic industry transferred to the public sector. Potthoff worked out the detail of the proposals for the December meeting. The proposals outlined by Potthoff in the Economic Policy Committee, following briefing meetings with the British on iron and steel, revealed the revised concept of codetermination in the firm,[29] the effective control of the management of the firm through effective participation in the management and super-

27. Ibid.
28. Potthoff, *Der Kampf um die Mitbestimmung*, p. 38.
29. DGB Archiv, Wirtschaftspolitischer Ausschuss der Gewerkschaften (BZ), Bericht über die 2 Sitzung am 13 und 14 Dezember 1946, in Brackwede/ Bielefeld.

visory boards. The trade union leaders now committed themselves to this concept and codetermination in the firm became an integral part of the programme for the public ownership of the basic industries. Although the application of the principle of joint management to the private sector was not defined, it was an implicit element in the programme. It was also to be seen as a parallel development to the proposals for full participation in the local and regional administration of the economy. The official trade unions were to play a central role in the management of industry in partnership with the employers and their representatives. As a consequence the focus moved away from the local workforce at plant level and the elected works councils. It reflected a significant change in the attitudes stated in April, at the time of the publication of the Works Councils Law and explained the reasoning behind the subsequent model works agreement.

The trade union leaders recognised the indispensable contribution of the works councils as the cutting edge of the movement at local level, at a time when the organisation of centralised trade unions was being slowed down. The belated model-works agreement reflected the fear of radicalism at plant level and the gradual shift in the balance of power towards the controlling influence of the trade unions and the central committees in the democratisation of the economy. It was proposed that participation of representatives of the workforce on supervisory boards should be mainly under the control of the official trade unions. The works councils were to be consulted.[30] The trade union leaders were convinced that they would have to regulate the membership of boards to ensure that an appropriate selection of suitably qualified representatives was made. The possession of adequate expertise at this level of activity was now regarded as the main criterion. In effect this proposal removed the political overtones of codetermination and emphasised the technical aspects of management. The trade union leaders believed that the workforce misunderstood the meaning of socialisation and control of the means of production. In their view public ownership would not mean an immediate improvement in social conditions, as was commonly believed. They were also aware of British concern over the shortage of management skills, the loss of senior personnel, and the lack of qualified manpower in the coal and steel industries. The proposals introduced a note of economic

30. Ibid.

and political realism, to take account of this. The same criteria were to be applied to representatives in public bodies. Party political influence was also to be excluded as far as possible. The trade unions were particularly concerned to halt the growth of workforce interests centred on the local plant, which was encouraged by syndicalist thinking, and tended to undermine the influence of trade unions in the plant. It was a further echo from the Weimar works-councils movement, and was rejected as an unacceptable form of *Betriebsegoismus*.[31]

The proposals, if put into practice, meant the virtual exclusion of the works councils from the control of economic policy beyond plant level, although this was denied. An important consultative and participative role was envisaged for them. This only served to confirm the new direction. It represented a fundamental reappraisal of the concept of ownership and control of industry, and a turning point in the economic policy of the trade unions in the British Zone. This was reflected in the increasing concern for practical policies, which avoided dogma, minimised the ideological content of programmes and emphasised economic criteria.

A serious gulf was revealed between grass-roots members, especially the more militant works councillors in the Ruhr industries, and the trade union leadership. Signs of a division became apparent at the end of 1945 when the trade unions were first allowed to reorganise. This grew with the consolidation of works-council influence in 1946, which coincided with the gradual establishment of zonal trade unions, and the preparations for a trade union federation for the British Zone. With the consolidation of trade union influence, and the development of local and central committees, competing spheres of influence became more apparent. The unpopularity of the industrial policies of the occupation authorities contributed to this. The works councils provided a focal point for local opposition to the dismantling of factories and machinery. Their close involvement with local conditions, and their vociferous demands on behalf of the workforce and the community, tended to expose the apparent moderation of the trade union leaders and their increasing concern for longer-term economic objectives. The trade union leaders were faced with the problem of channelling the

31. Ibid. For a more detailed analysis of the relationship between the DGB and the works councils see P. H. Hubsch, 'The Economic Policies of the German Trade Unions in the British Zone of Ocupation 1945–1949', PhD thesis, University of Nottingham, 1988.

hostility of the workforce to Military Government, while attempting to maintain a credible negotiating position.

They were also seriously worried about the food situation at the end of 1946, in view of the approaching winter. There was no sign of any real improvement in supplies in the British Zone, distribution controls remained inadequate and German farmers were evading their quota commitments. A central aim of the proposed federation was to retain the broadest possible solidarity of the workforce, embodied in the concept of the *Einheitsgewerkschaft*, based on religious and political impartiality. The trade union leaders were consistent in their defence of the principle of neutrality, combined with the objective of creating a powerful, unified organisation as quickly as possible. They were also determined to maintain their image as a force for moderation and stability.

The British plans for the reorganisation of steel in separate companies forced the trade unions to devise practical plans for their new role in the economy. It was recognised that a change in company law would be necessary to strengthen the supervisory board, on which trade union representatives would join shareholder representatives. The purpose of this would also be to define the new limitations to the powers of management, without, theoretically, interfering in their ability to manage. It indicated the extent of agreement reached between the trade union leaders and Harris-Burland and other members of the NGISC.

The formation of independent, joint stock companies clearly kept open the option for them to be transferred back to the private sector at a future date. One of the specific conditions of the trade union leaders for their acceptance of the deconcentration plans was that these should not jeopardise the proposals for public ownership. However, the main condition for their cooperation was the agreement to grant codetermination rights in the deconcentrated steel industry.[32]

Management and Control of the Steel Industry

The NGISC informed the public of its detailed measures on 17 January 1947. The plans were to be executed by the Stahltreuhandverwaltung. The new companies were to lose their former names to

32. DGB, *Die Gewerkschaftsbewegung*, p. 109.

Peter Hubsch

emphasise their separate identity, and twenty-five new firms were to be formed.

The experience of public sector enterprises with a high degree of managerial and financial independence already existed in Germany. The trade union leaders did not conceal their support for reconstructed industries being run on commercial lines. The trade unions were also concerned that the reorganisation of industry should not lead to fragmentation, to the point where firms would no longer be viable. Potthoff had stated the position of the trade union leaders at the Bielefeld Conference in August 1946. The basic industries were not to be decentralised or transferred to local or regional authorities. They were essentially the result of organic development determined by technical requirements.[33] Böckler expressed their views more forcefully at the Founding Conference of the DGB in the British Zone in April 1947. In his opinion the steel firms would have to be put back together again for purely economic reasons.[34]

The willingness of industrialists to revive discussions with the trade union leaders, and to make significant concessions on participation in management, was also due to their fear of radical deconcentration. The decartelisation of steel created a special situation in the British Zone. In response to the threat of dismantling and decartelisation entrepreneurs and managers considered an alliance with the trade unions against the occupation authorities as necessary. Certain trade union officials, including Potthoff and Deist, the economics specialists, argued that an alliance with the progressive managers could be the basis of industrial reform and progressive industrial relations.[35]

Potthoff was concerned at the implications of decartelisation for the future competitive position of the integrated Ruhr industries. In a report on the reconstruction of the steel industry he was reflecting the official position of the trade unions when he criticised the technical and commercial weaknesses created by severing links between integrated enterprises.[36] The trade unions also had in mind

33. DGB Archiv, Protokoll der Gewerkschaftskonferenz (BZ) Bielefeld, 21–23 August 1946, p. 12.
34. DGB Archiv, Protokoll des Gründungskongresses des Deutschen Gewerkschaftsbundes für die britische Zone vom 22 bis 25 April 1947 in Bielefeld, p. 79.
35. T. Pirker, Die blinde Macht. Die Gewerkschaftsbewegung in Westdeutschland, Vol. 1, 2nd edn (Olle und Wolter, Berlin, 1979), p. 160.
36. Stahltreuhändervereinigung, Die Neuordnung der Eisen- und Stahlindustrie, p. 698. Stellungnahme des Abgeordneten Dr Erich Potthoff (SPD) namens der Gewerkschaften, 10 Oktober 1947.

the coal industry, and its close integration with chemicals and electricity production, as well as with iron and steel.

In January 1947 the chairman of the supervisory board of Klöckner-Werke, Jarres, wrote to the trade union executive conceding the earlier demands for participation in management. Simultaneously Reusch and Hilbert, directors of Gutehoffnungshütte, wrote on behalf of the management board suggesting that Dinkelbach's plan served neither the workforce nor the general interest. They wished to preserve the integrated works division which linked energy, transport and administration with the production processes of the firm. In their view the implementation of the NGISC proposals would destroy the work of 150 years.[37] Reusch and Hilbert proposed that the employees and trade union representatives, who were familiar with the industry, should work out a more appropriate solution with management. This was suggested as a first step towards establishing a permanent mechanism for participation. The steel companies were also worried about the position of shareholders and creditors. A scheme of mixed ownership was put forward as a way to combine the public interest with the need for profitability. This would allow the trade unions the possibility of participation as public shareholders alongside private shareholders.

The trade union Executive and Committee opposed the idea of share ownership. This was rejected in their guidelines on socialisation, published a week later. However, the paper reflected the change of attitude to the function of management control, now that they were able to build on the substantial concessions guaranteed in the iron and steel industry. They expected management, in partnership with the trade unions, to run industry efficiently, and with a high degree of independence. They also emphasised the need for members to recognise the long-standing separation of ownership from management in large firms. This division was the historical consequence of concentration, and would not, in their view, in any way limit 'the personal initiative or sense of responsibility felt by management'.[38] The exploitation of the opportunity to participate effectively in the management of industry could not be hindered by the deferral of socialisation.

Dinkelbach was aware that a greater number of small companies

---

37. Ibid., p. 610, Gutehoffnungshütte Oberhausen Aktiengesellschaft an die Einheitsgewerkschaft, 18 Januar 1947.
38. DGB Archiv, Zonenausschuss, Leitsätze der Gewerkschaften zur Sozialisierung, 27 Januar 1947.

would be more difficult to nationalise in the long run, but stressed the economic arguments for deconcentration. He was also aware of the concern of the trade unions and the industrialists for the integration of the iron and steel combines with coal, electricity and gas production, into the *Verbundwirtschaft* of the Ruhr. In his view it was important to revive the freedom of contracts between independent firms, and to distribute ownership as widely as possible, while not reducing firms below optimal size. The integrated economy of the Ruhr was not dependent on the existence of large combines.[39] Dinkelbach was forced to adopt a defensive position because of his relationship with the Vereinigte Stahlwerke and the suspicion of some industrialists that he was protecting its interests. He rejected the suggestion that the plan presented a 'perilous amputation' for the firms, and argued against any further delay.[40] Despite this, Reusch organised a joint meeting with the trade unions on 6 February 1947 and attempted to enlist their support.[41] Böckler gave Reusch no grounds for encouraging the idea of an alliance, but the trade union leaders were interested in their views on the future structure and ownership of industry. They regarded the developments in the iron and steel industry as a significant step forward for the trade unions. There was no reason to trust the industrialists, but they adopted a pragmatic approach. They were not prepared to jeopardise their immediate objective, which was to secure and consolidate codetermination rights.

In the negotiations with Harris-Burland and Dinkelbach an important achievement for the unions was the right to appoint a labour director to the management board (Vorstand) in addition to the representatives of the supervisory board (Aufsichtsrat). The labour director was to have equal status with the other two directors, responsible for technical and financial issues, and was to deal with personnel and social policy.[42] The agreement was confirmed in the meeting with Dinkelbach in December 1946. Böckler's efforts to obtain this had important implications for industrial relations. It was partly a response to the wishes of the works councils to have

39. DGB Archiv, Entflechtung, Neuordnung, Sozialisierung 1946–1948, 'Betriebswirtschaftliche Fragen der Konzern—Entflechtung'. Bericht über einen Vortrag von Direktor Heinrich Dinkelbach vor der Schmalenbach-Vereinigung in Köln am 1 März 1948.
40. Stahltreuhändervereinigung, *Die Neuordrung der Eisen- und Stahlindustrie*, p. 611, Dinkelbach an Gutehoffnungshütte, Klöckner-Werke, Otto Wolff 29 Januar 1947.
41. Potthoff, *Der Kampf um die Mitbestimmung*, p. 47.
42. DGB, *Die Gewerkschaftsbewegung*, p. 109.

control over personnel issues.[43] At the NGISC meeting of 8 January 1947 it was confirmed that there would be three equal directors in the management board, including the labour director. Potthoff nominated the labour directors for the first four new steel companies on behalf of the trade unions.

The concept of codetermination that emerged at the beginning of 1947 evolved as a pragmatic response to a combination of factors. Before 1933, codetermination at plant level was regarded as a failure, with works councils participating in supervisory boards in isolation. Trade unions concentrated on codetermination at regional and national level, also with limited success, and revived these demands after 1945. Codetermination in the firm was not an afterthought, following the developments in the iron and steel industry from August 1946. The main impetus, at local level, was given by works councils prior to the promulgation of the Works Council Law. Böckler also linked the different levels of participation in his demand for codetermination at every level of the economy at the first British Zone conference in Hanover in March 1946.[44] Although the trade union leaders initially concentrated on codetermination in the higher levels of the economy the deconcentration policy in the British Zone enabled them to link this directly with the various levels of industrial management. The Economic Policy Committee confirmed this policy in December 1946. The proposed board for the administration of each basic industry represented the intermediate level of control between its component firms and regional and national policy-making bodies.[45] Potthoff regarded the proposed trade union federation, supported by the Economics Research Institute, under his chairmanship, as the most reliable judge of the specific requirements of industry. The importance of local workforce representation was acknowledged, but the vital role of the central organisation was underlined. The participation of the trade unions in the management of industry, and the establishment of representation in the German administration for the steel trust, was also seen as the first step in the socialisation of the industry. Regional and national economic policy constituted the remaining element in an integrated programme. This was to be based on the

43. H. J. Spiro, *The Politics of German Codetermination* (Harvard University Press, Cambridge, Mass, 1958), p. 27.
44. DGB Archiv, Protokoll der Gewerkschaftskonferenz, Hannover, März 1946, p. 33.
45. DGB Archiv, Wirthschaftspolitischer Ausschuss der Gewerkschaften, 13 und 14 Dezember 1946.

model prepared by Rosenberg.[46]

The Rosenberg Model and Participation in the Management of the Economy

Ludwig Rosenberg returned from England in September 1946 and joined Werner Hansen in the Secretariat. He was responsible for the Economics Department within the Secretariat. Rosenberg was immediately involved in the economic policy discussions of the trade unions in the British Zone, and in liaison with Military Government. With the formal establishment of the Economic Policy Committee, Rosenberg became responsible for the trade union proposals for reforming the chambers of commerce and industry. Potthoff assumed responsibility for developing the proposals for codetermination at the level of the firm in private industry and the public sector. The period between the Conference of trade unions in the British Zone in August 1946 and the Founding Congress of the DGB in the British Zone in April 1947 was an intense period of trade union activity in the economic sphere, and marked a turning point in the development of economic policies.

Rosenberg's proposals involved the establishment of chambers of industry (Wirtschaftskammern) based on the industrial unions and the trade associations.[47] The new chambers were to be unified bodies, combining the work of the chambers of industry and commerce and the chambers of craft trades, which would disappear. The trade associations were to be the sole bodies representing business. The notion of interest groups, in the traditional sense, was regarded as irrelevant. The trade association and its counterpart, the industrial union, were to represent specific spheres of economic activity. The role of the chambers in the regulation of industry represented a significant departure from Agartz. They were not to serve as functionaries of the state. Their delegated powers were to be expanded in line with the special needs of post-war Germany. The two sides of industry were seen as the twin pillars of the economy, representing organised labour and organised industry. The chambers were to be directly involved with the public authori-

---

46. Ibid.
47. DGB Archiv, Gewerkschaftliches Zonensekretariat (BZ), L. Rosenberg, 'Wirtschaftsdemokratie: Vorschlag zum Aufbau einer wirtschaftlichen Selbstverwaltung', Januar 1947.

ties in the determination of the plan for the economy. In practice, this would require the nomination of members by the chambers to serve on advisory committees attached to the public authorities. They would in effect be mandated representatives of the chambers, rather than members of interest groups. The system was to operate at every level of public administration, from the commune to central government. The organisation of the proposed regional chambers would reflect this structure.[48]

Rosenberg's original proposals were modified to limit the establishment of chambers to Bezirk, Land and Reich level. They were to have executive functions and wider powers of control. Their responsibilities were to include the familiar areas of supervision, including prices, the issue of licences, and the allocation of quotas. Rosenberg proposed that they should also supervise competition, credit, the stock exchanges, business enterprises, and, where necessary, the closure of uneconomic firms.

Rosenberg emphasised the importance of dispensing with existing institutions and starting from scratch. The traditional craft guilds were a particular case which illustrated that cosmetic changes were insufficient. They were to be reorganized as sub-groups within new chambers. Unlike Agartz, who regarded them as a model of the pre-capitalist system, Rosenberg considered them to be remnants of the middle ages. He wished to prevent any continuity from the past and to remove the power bases of the business community. In his view codetermination in existing institutions could not guarantee this. The control of industry could only effectively be undertaken if parliamentary democracy was augmented by additional control mechanisms. 'Politische Demokratie ist nicht genug—das Prinzip der Demokratie muss auch, ja sogar vor allen Dingen in der Wirtschaft gesichert sein.'[49]

Rosenberg's concepts of economic democracy were reminiscent of trade union discussions during the Weimar Republic. He envisaged a central Reich chamber, the Reichswirtschaftskammer, with consultative and legislative powers comparable to those of the provisional Reichswirtschaftsrat. Although Rosenberg frequently

48. Ibid. For a more detailed examination of the role of the chambers see D. Prowe, 'Wirtschaftsdemokratische Ansätze 1945–1949', *WSI—Mitteilungen* No. 7 1981, pp. 398–405; W. Plumpe, 'Gesellschaftliche Neuordnung oder ökonomische Entwicklungspolitik?', *WSI—Mitteilungen*, No. 7, 1981, pp. 405–14; W. G. Friedmann, *The Allied Military Government of Germany* (Stevens and Sons, London, 1947).
49. DGB Archiv, Gewerkschaftliches Zonensekretariat (BZ), L. Rosenberg, 'Wirtschaftsdemokratie'.

referred to the chambers as a support for the planned economy, the programme pointed to a corporate organisation of industry in which the two sides had considerable independence from the state. It also reflected the influence of the new trade union structure as the culmination of the long-term trend towards concentration and centralisation. It stressed the principle of self-regulation and appeared to have the advantage of reducing public bureaucracies and limiting the powers of the central government.

Rosenberg went to some lengths to acknowledge the sovereignty of the elected parliament in a democratic society, anticipating any possible criticism that the trade unions were attempting to create a state within a state. In the public debate which followed publication of the programme he defended the role of the proposed chambers, and the trade union concept of economic democracy. He stressed the importance of self-regulation in the economy as the only guarantee against 'bureaucratisation of the apparatus of economic controls'.[50] Without labour representatives the current chambers were merely interest groups. Rosenberg also confirmed that their proposals now formed part of an integrated plan for democracy.

At the founding congress of the DGB for the British Zone, in April, Agartz acknowledged the new thinking of the trade unions on the role of the chambers in the economy. The fundamental differences between Rosenberg's concept of the role of the trade unions in the administration of the economy and his own were glossed over.[51] Agartz saw an important role for the proposed chambers at local level. They could carry out those tasks in the controlled economy which were not appropriate for the central parliament. These included the issue of production permits and supervision of rationing and quota allocations. None of the delegates doubted the need for strict controls at local level, and for food rationing, allocation of materials, and detailed planning of production. The background to the congress was the serious food shortage and the worst economic crisis in the British Zone since the end of the war. The talk by Agartz on the trade unions and the economy was preceded by an extended analysis of the food crisis.[52] Agartz tended to diminish the role of the chambers envisaged by Rosen-

50. L. Rosenberg, 'Wirtschaftskammer und Gewerkschaft', *Westfälische Rundschau*, 14 June 1947.
51. DGB Archiv, Protokoll des Gründungskongresses des DGB für die britische Zone, 22–25 April 1947, p. 121.
52. Ibid., p. 97.

berg. He suggested that the extensive controls concerned with local rationing would only be retained while the shortage of goods continued. The implications of the trade union programme for the democratisation of the economy were not examined. Agartz proposed that the new organisations should operate at local level where they would be more effective. As decentralised bodies they would counter the emergence of *Länderegoismus*. It was the view of Agartz that central planning had to remain the prerogative of the government, whereas the trade unions would have a consultative role.

In March 1947, the trade union Executive members from the British and US Zones met in Frankfurt to discuss their policy on participation in the chambers. The talks were combined with a discussion of representation in the advisory and technical committees attached to the departments in the Bizone administration. The trade unions in the US Zone had developed their own programme for participation in the chambers. Willi Richter confirmed that their objectives were the same as those of the British Zone trade unions when he attended the first trade union Conference for the British Zone, in March 1946, as representative of the trade unions of the US Zone.[53] The two groups now agreed to adopt the Rosenberg model as the basis for the trade union programme for participation in management of the economy.

The DGB for the British Zone

The Founding Congress of the DGB in the British Zone, in April 1947, marked the end of an intensive period of programme development which had begun after the Bielefeld Conference in August 1946. The ambitious demands for codetermination at every level of the economy, which now formed the central element of DGB economic policy, met with increasing opposition from the employers. At the first meeting of the new DGB Executive, Hans Böckler, now confirmed in his position as the leader of the trade union movement in the British Zone, assumed responsibility for economic policy and external relations.[54] From this point until the Munich Congress in 1949 the DGB leaders concentrated on defending their

53. DGB Archiv, Protokoll der Gewerkschaftskonferenz März 1946, p. 34.
54. DGB Archiv, Protokoll des Bundesvorstands des DGB (BZ), 19–20 Mai 1947.

economic programme. A strict policy of non-recognition of employers was applied. The pragmatic course of the DGB leaders in their negotiations with Harris-Burland and Dinkelbach exposed the gap between them and the militant grass-roots members, especially the Ruhr workforce. Willi Agatz, the communist deputy leader of the miners, challenged Böckler's course of action, which he saw as a threat to public ownership of the basic industries.[55] The serious economic crisis in the British Zone, following the severe winter and the extended hunger strikes, made it difficult to separate political demands from grievances over material conditions. This threatened to undermine the strategy of the leaders and the neutrality of the DGB.

Böckler also wished to avoid any perceived action which could jeopardise the unification of the trade unions of all zones. The developments in the steel industry made the DGB vulnerable to criticism from the FDGB leaders in the Soviet Zone. Jendretzky, the FDGB Chairman, rejected the concept of joint autonomous, self-regulating chambers as collaboration with private industry. He opposed the concept of codetermination in the supervisory boards of joint stock companies for the same reason.[56] His demand for the transfer of the Ruhr industries to public ownership as a matter of priority could also be seen as an appeal to the workforce in the western zones. Jendretzky identified himself with Viktor Agartz, and not with the DGB leaders. A more perceptible rift emerged at the inter-zone conferences between the trade union representatives of the Soviet Zone and the US Zone over the direction of economic policy. Tarnow, the leading trade unionist in the US Zone, regarded the failure of the Moscow Council of Foreign Ministers on the German question, in spring 1947, as a point of no return. He pressed Böckler to merge the DGB with the federalised unions in the US Zone.[57] Böckler resisted any precipitate move. He also intended maintaining a centralised 'Bund', based on the DGB model, with concentrated industrial unions. This provided the basis of their proposals for participation in the management of the economy. Böckler wished to keep options open, though he was fully aware that a unified trade union movement would be domi-

55. DGB Archiv, 'Gründungskongress des DGB, April 1947', p. 44.
56. DGB Archiv, H. Jendretzky, 'Gewerkschaft und Wirtschaft', Interzone conference, 8 May 1948.
57. DGB Archiv, Zonensekretariat, 'Tagung der Gewerkschaften der Britischen Zone und der Amerikanischen Zone', 5 Juni 1947.

nated by the FDGB, whose claimed membership exceeded that of all three western zones put together. He was under pressure from the World Federation of Trade Unions (WFTU) to start preparations for an all-German trade union movement. This posed a dilemma for the DGB leaders and the development of economic policy in view of the intensifying east–west conflict.

Böckler distanced the DGB from the trade unions in the US Zone by boycotting the joint economics and labour committee with employers organised by Tarnow.[58] Tarnow favoured cooperation with the more progressive employers, and gradual reform agreed within a positive framework by the *Sozialpartner*.[59] Tarnow believed the economic programme of the DGB was unrealistic, particularly the proposals relating to restructured chambers. They lacked the expertise to implement the whole programme which was a recognised weakness and a recurring concern in DGB discussions. However, for the DGB leaders this was not a matter of principle. The more immediate issue was the attitude of the employers in the British Zone. The concept of economic democracy was based on a deep mistrust of the reactionary industrialists in the Zone. Potthoff justified the stance of the DGB to representatives of the US Zone trade unions, and the Military Government, in the context of the special situation in the British Zone. The deteriorating relations were largely due to the fierce resistance of the employers to joint management and to any reform of the chambers.[60] Tarnow experienced the level of opposition to reform in the British Zone when a delegation of employers, led by Vorwerk, joined the joint committee in Frankfurt. The meeting broke down over the technical issue of controlling production which was diverted to barter trade. Because of the controversial nature of this activity a compromise formula was proposed requiring the counter-signature of works councils. Vorwerk rejected this on principle, and reasserted the traditional rights of managers to manage.[61] The statement signalled the opposition of employers to the economic programme of the DGB in the British Zone, and precipitated the abandonment of the joint committee.

58. DGB Archiv, Bundesvordstand und Bundesbeirat des DGB (BZ), 28–9 August 1947.
59. DGB Archiv, DGB Wirtschaftspolitischer Ausschuss (BZ), Besprechung im Gewerkschaftshaus, Frankfurt, 17 Juli 1947.
60. Ibid.
61. DGB Archiv, Gemeinschaftsausschuss für Wirtschaft und Arbeit (BZ), 17 Oktober 1947.

Any impression given by Böckler that he was prepared to compromise with the employers or Military Government, in order to promote a cooperative movement at the expense of adversarial policies, was dispelled in his negotiations with Luce, head of Manpower Division. He rejected Luce's proposals for a consultative and advisory system, which could influence the government and the economy.[62] He believed this to be inapplicable to the British Zone. In an uncompromising statement to Luce and a delegation of British Zone employers Böckler attacked the attitude of the employers and their attempts to confine the DGB to its traditional social role.[63] It was not the threat of the return of entrepreneurial initiative in the future economy that concerned the DGB leaders. The introduction of a social market economy was already anticipated by the beginning of 1948. The central DGB committees reviewed their economic and social policies in the light of political developments, and the expected relaxation of the wage freeze in parallel to a currency reform.[64] The more serious concern was their relationship with the employers and the threat to their proposed role in the economy.

With the increasing economic and political consolidation of the Bizone Böckler reassessed the strategy of the DGB in relation to the issue of reunification. In his view the tensions between east and west were, by August 1947, insuperable.[65] Nevertheless, appearances at the inter-zone conferences were maintained. This was sufficient for the Foreign Office to suspect that Böckler still planned an involvement with the WFTU.[66] Shortly after the Badenweiler Inter-Zone Conference he reported to the Foreign Office in London on his real intentions. Böckler was forced to maintain the demand for unity, but was convinced there could be no merger with the Soviet Zone. He anticipated a breakdown of talks occurring over the issue of democratic principles,[67] but he was not prepared to take responsibility for the break. The maintenance of the relative position of authority of the DGB and the defence of their economic strategy

62. DGB Archiv, Protokoll des Geschäftsführenden Vorstands (BZ), 28 Februar 1948.
63. DGB Archiv, Besprechung der Gewerkschaften der britischen Zone mit den Arbeitgebern, Lemgo, 4 März 1948; DGB Archiv, 'Verschiedene Protokolle'.
64. DGB Archiv, Protokoll der Sitzung der arbeitsrechtlichen, lohnpolitischen, sozialpolitischen und wirtschaftspolitischen Ausschüsse des DGB (Britische Zone), 1–11 März 1948.
65. DGB Archiv, Protokoll des Bundesvorstands und Bundesbeirats (BZ), 28–9 August 1947.
66. PRO/FO371/C11/870, Foreign Office to Luce, 27 August 1947.
67. PRO/FO1051/114/72327, conversation with Hans Böckler, 9 September 1947.

were influenced by Böckler's political realism. This determination
to secure the objectives of the DGB was assessed by Manpower
Division in Germany: 'Let us be quite clear about Böckler and Co.
Böckler is not opposing amalgamation with the FDGB because the
British don't desire that development. If amalgamation suited
Böckler and his colleagues he would go ahead irrespective of British
or Allied interests—or at least he would try to do so.'[68]

Böckler was convinced that an adversarial trade union movement
would confine the DGB to a limited role related to wage-bargaining
and social conditions. Strikes were to be reserved as an ultimate
weapon. There was no question of organising the workforce in
opposition to the proposed Marshall Plan. The DGB Executive
recommended acceptance of the Marshall Plan in August 1947.
They were aware that it would contribute a further threat to public
ownership, but the economic and political conditions would not
necessarily undermine their proposals for participation in economic
management. Above all it offered clear benefits for the industrial
recovery of Germany.[69] The recommendation of the Executive was
accepted by the full DGB Council a fortnight later. It was noted, in
particular, that the resolution required no alteration to their economic programme.[70] The decision committed them to economic
integration within western Europe, and a more neutral position on
the introduction of a mixed economy in western Germany.

British Attitudes to Codetermination

The view among a small group in the Control Commission that the
trade unions should be allowed more scope for free negotiation with
employers and the German administration in pursuit of their economic demands was not initially shared by Bevin. In a special
meeting on German trade unions, Bevin forcefully expressed his
reservations about the works councils and the demands of the trade
unions.[71] He had in mind the British model of industrial relations.
Although he favoured freedom of negotiation between the two sides
of industry in Germany, without British intervention, and also had

68. PRO/FO1051/114/72327, Barber to Luce, 22 September 1947.
69. DGB Archiv, Protokoll des Bundesvorstands des DGB (BZ), 14 August 1947.
70. DGB Archiv, Protokoll des Bundesvorstands und Bundesbeirats des DGB
(BZ), 28–9 August 1947.
71. PRO/FO1051/114/72322 (C9794/7573/180), notes on meeting on German
Trade Unions, 6 August 1947.

no sympathy for the restoration of employer associations, he did not favour structural changes along the lines demanded by the British Zone trade unions. Bevin was not aware of trade union participation in the steel industry under Harris-Burland. He was concerned that the wage freeze should be ended through a financial reform so that the trade unions 'can start functioning properly'.[72] The question of security was also uppermost in his mind. He was opposed to any development which could allow the trade unions to become 'an agency of the Government as in the Soviet Zone'.[73] Despite this, the foundations were laid for the reassessment of trade union participation in the controlling organs of German enterprises as a result of the developments in the steel industry. Harris-Burland's introduction of a labour director on the management board was presented to Bevin as a *fait accompli*. It was justified on the grounds that it compensated for the shortage of skilled staff. Bevin also supported the introduction of labour managers on company boards.[74] The case for appointing managers from the ranks of the workforce was justified by Harris-Burland on the grounds of ability, and not merely because of membership of a trade union: 'There is an acute shortage of managers, proved by the great and increasing difficulty of recruiting suitable members for the boards of our companies.'[75]

The fact remained that Harris-Burland regarded the agreement with the trade unions as a step towards the democratisation of industry. Its application to steel was appropriate because decartelisation reduced the industry to companies based on single works, where involvement of the workforce in management was more meaningful. The Foreign Office expressed a particular interest in Harris-Burland's account: 'A very important document and extremely interesting. This experiment should be watched with great care and results carefully monitored.'[76] Although Bevin's view was that the trade unions should be built up on the British model and restored to their traditional wage-bargaining role, once the currency reform was implemented, his views on codetermination were modified. Böckler visited the Foreign Office in London at the beginning

72. Ibid.
73. Ibid.
74. Ibid.
75. PRO/FO371/64703/72294, 'Workers' Responsibility for Management of Reorganised Iron and Steel Works', memorandum by W. Harris-Burland, Düsseldorf, 11 July 1947.
76. PRO/FO371/164703/C 9797, Governmental Sub-Commision, CCG HQ Berlin to Chaput de Saintonge, 16 August 1947.

of September and discussed DGB policy with Chaput de Saintonge. Although there were still strong reservations about the extent of codetermination in industry and in public bodies, Bevin now accepted the principle of a labour manager on the management board and the possibility of limited representation on the supervisory board.[77]

The view of the Manpower Division was that collective bargaining on wages and conditions, and joint consultation with industry on economic development, should become the main concern of the trade unions. Beyond these spheres of activity they were seen to be encroaching on political areas of concern which obscured their primary role. Luce believed that the claim for codetermination in the public sector of industry contradicted the principle of neutrality since it involved a management role on behalf of the state. What was of particular concern to the Manpower Division and the Foreign Office was the continuing expansion of works-council rights, and the implications of this for transport and communications in the British Zone. Luce expressed his opposition to the DGB concept of codetermination. In his view it obscured the main issues of industrial relations, and prevented the constructions of the negotiating mechanisms which had been developed successfully in Britain: 'When I ask myself which are the things most likely to frustrate our hopes in this connection, my mind is drawn irresistably to the problem of "Mitbestimmungsrecht".'[78]

Böckler rejected this view. While he welcomed the oppotunity to close the gap between prices and wages, the relaxation of the wage freeze was not at issue. He did not accept that industrial relations would improve with goodwill. Böckler was not prepared to trust the employers. He defended the right of the German trade unions to participate in management on the basis of his own personal experiences of the past behaviour of the industrialists. Böckler acknowledged that their priorities had changed. They had now designed a comprehensive plan which broadened the emphasis on participation in the management of the factory to participation in the planning of the economy and of industrial production as a whole.[79]

77. PRO/FO1051/114/72327/C 12107, Chaput de Saintonge to Luce, 16 September 1947.
78. PRO/FO371/64703/72294, address by Luce to trade unionists, 13 November 1947.
79. DGB Archiv, DGB Bundesvorstand und Beirat (BZ) 'Antwort des Kollegen Böckler auf den Vortrag des Chefs der Manpower-Abteilung, Mr Luce, 13 November 1947'. (Translation in PRO/FO 371/64703/72294.)

Peter Hubsch

Integration with Western Europe

Despite the growing opposition of German industrialists, the prospects for trade union participation in the development of Ruhr industries were enhanced by the constructive attitude towards the International Authority for the Ruhr (IAR). The increasingly international outlook of the trade union leaders revealed a gap between them and the SPD leader, Kurt Schumacher. Rosenberg expressed his enthusiasm for the Ruhr Statute establishing the IAR at its outset and criticised those who adopted a negative attitude to the joint reconstruction of Europe.[80] As early as January 1949, Rosenberg organised a meeting with French trade unionists, at the instigation of the American Federation of Labour (AFL), to discuss the future control of Ruhr industries, socialisation and the question of codetermination. The meeting was also attended by Böckler. It formed the basis for subsequent discussions with the Belgian and Luxemburg trade unions. The essential principle established with the French representatives was the support for the organisation of European heavy industry and the avoidance of competition based on national self-interest.[81] Rosenberg subsequently became the West German representative in the international trade union advisory committee for the Marshall Plan.

An important motivating factor in the foreign-policy work of the DGB was the desire to re-create respect for the German trade union movement among the free trade unions of the west.[82] Rosenberg reported directly to Böckler on external affairs. He was in agreement with Max Brauer, a prominent member of the progressive wing of the SPD, that the Germans had little choice other than to integrate with western Europe. Faced with the dilemma of east--west conflict and the threat to the traditional freedom and independence of the labour movement, the DGB made a conscious decision to become an integral part of western Europe and its fundamental ideals.[83]

Böckler emphasised the importance of the DGB's external policy at the movement's British Zone Congress in Hanover in September

80. L. Rosenberg, 'Zum Ruhrstatut', *Der Bund*, 15 January 1949, p. 2.
81. DGB Archiv, Gewerkschaftsrat der Vereinten Zonen, Sekretariat, 'Besuch der Vertreter der französischen Gewerkschaften beim DGB in der Zeit vom 27–8. Januar 1949'.
82. L. Rosenberg, 'Die Weltpolitik der deutschen Gewerkschaften' in U. Borsdorf and H. O. Hemmer (eds.), *Gewerkschaftliche Politik: Reform aus Solidarität* (Bund-Verlag, Cologne, 1978), p. 559.
83. Ibid., p. 564.

1949, which immediately preceded the Founding Congress of the DGB for the Federal Republic. The European Recovery Programme was regarded as vital for German reconstruction and the revival of exports. It was hoped that the pressure of events would lead to a review of the dismantling programme. Böckler was able to provide a positive report on the integration of the DGB in the work of the Marshall Plan without the opposition encountered at the Recklinghausen Congress of the DGB in the British Zone in the previous year. The Hanover Congress confirmed that the political ideologies that had split the Weimar movement had been contained, if not extinguished. The DGB economic programme was based on the social and economic needs of the workforce and the natural interests of West Germany. Böckler regarded himself as a *Realpolitiker*. He was not prepared to remain passive if the interests of the unions were involved, as they were with the IAR.[84] He rejected opposition at the congress to the Ruhr Statute and the recommendation to boycott Law No. 75, concerning the reorganisation of the basic industries. Böckler kept open the option of the DGB to participate fully in the implementation of both.

Böckler left the development of the case for this to Deist, his adviser. Deist was an SPD economist who worked in the WWI with a special interest in the reorganisation of the steel industry. As one of the younger SPD economists his more progressive views did not find acceptance in the party until later. Deist argued for a modern, rationalised, competitive industry, organised within a European framework. He was concerned with the implications for employment of any structural changes, which were still left open in Law No. 75. He confirmed the acceptance by the DGB of the market economy, in which the price mechanism was allowed to adjust factors of production according to supply and demand. He pointed out that dynamic market processes also applied to basic industries, in so far as they could not remain static and ignore the need for continual adjustment. In the case of the *Verbundwirtschaft* of the Ruhr, allowance had to be made for the vulnerability of mass-production processes to sudden market changes. The DGB wished to protect optimum size so that West Germany could become internationally competitive.[85]

84. DGB Archiv, Protokoll des Zweiten ordentlichen Bundeskongresses des Deutschen Gewerkschaftsbundes für die britische Zone vom 7–9 September 1949 in Hannover-Laatzen, p. 36.
85. Ibid., p. 135.

With the election of Böckler as its first chairman, the DGB focused on relations with western Europe and the development of the IAR. The objectives of law No. 75 and the IAR were examined in a positive light. The workforce was made aware of the possible risks to German industry and the significant benefits, provided German interests were protected.

A significant step towards integration was taken with the signing of the Petersberg Agreement in November 1949. This provided for a limitation to dismantling, and was supported by the DGB. The DGB agreed with the policy of gradually freeing the federal Republic from Allied control.[86] The actions of the DGB confirmed the rift with the SPD. Böckler firmly defended the decision of the Executive.[87] In the December meeting of the DGB Executive he reaffirmed the complete independence of the DGB from all parties, and the unanimous support of the Executive for the declaration on German entry into the IAR.[88]

Provision was made for DGB participation in the IAR. The acceptance of the Schuman Plan in 1951 was seen by Rosenberg as a natural development of the external policy of the unions after 1945.[89] In the same year the DGB achieved the implementation of codetermination in coal and steel, based on the steel model. This was Böckler's final major achievement before his death on 16 February 1952. The Munich programme represented an extension of the 1947 Bielefeld programme, in which the DGB in the British Zone had already recognised the need to limit the powers of the state in favour of codetermination and self-government. In place of the early anti-capitalist programmes the DGB for the Federal Republic anticipated a socially oriented market economy which made provision for the organisation of Ruhr heavy industries within a west European framework. The state was expected to provide a macro-economic policy framework in which the safeguarding of effective competition was combined with the protection of employment and the basic needs of all social groups. Codetermination in the key industries of the Ruhr was a priority in the Munich programme, and the first significant step towards establishing economic democracy in German industry.

86. Horst Thum, *Mitbestimmung in der Montanindustrie* (Deutsche Verlags-Anstalt, Stuttgart, 1982), p. 99.
87. W. E. Paterson, *The SPD and European Integration* (Saxon House, Farnborough, 1974), p. 30.
88. DGB Archiv, Geschäftsführender Vorstand des DGB für die Bundesrepublik, 16 und 17 Dezember 1949.
89. L. Rosenberg, 'Zum Ruhrstatus', p. 2.

11

The Refugees and the Currency Reform
Ian Connor

Introduction

In the closing months of the Second World War, German refugees
and expellees began to flood into Central Europe from the eastern
parts of the Reich and by mid-1950 more than 7.8 million had
settled in the newly founded West German state.[1] They included
some 4.4 million 'National Germans' (*Reichsdeutsche*) —the former
inhabitants of those areas east of the Oder–Neisse line which had
formed part of Germany on 31 December 1937. The largest group
of *Reichsdeutsche* were the Silesians (2,053,000), followed by East
Prussians (1,347,000), Pomeranians (891,000) and East Brandenbur-
gers (131,000).[2] In addition, there were 3.4 million refugees of
'Ethnic German' origin (*Volksdeutsche*)—people who had lived as
minority groups in foreign countries. Sudeten Germans (1,912,000)
comprised more than half of the 'Ethnic German' refugee population, while smaller groups of *Volksdeutsche* had previously resided

1. I would like to thank Professor Volker Berghahn, Dr Rainer Schulze and Dr
   Ian Turner for their invaluable comments on an earlier version of this article,
   and Professor Friedrich Kahlenberg for his support and encouragement. I am
   also very grateful to the British Academy and the University of Ulster for the
   generous financial support which enabled me to undertake the research on
   which the article is based.
2. Bundesministerium für Vertriebene (ed.), *Flüchtlinge, Vertriebene, Kriegsgefangene* (Bonn, 1959). For a detailed analysis of the flight and expulsion of the
   refugees, see A. M. de Zayas, *Nemesis at Potsdam. The Anglo-Americans and
   the Expulsion of the Germans. Background, Execution, Consequences* (Routledge and Kegan Paul, London, 1977). For the literature on refugees in the
   British Zone, see the appropriate section in the final chapter of this book. For
   comparative works on Bavaria, see F. Bauer, *Flüchtlinge und Flüchtlingspolitik
   in Bayern 1945–50* (Klett-Cotta, Stuttgart, 1982); M. Kornrumpf, *In Bayern
   angekommen. Die Eingliederung der Vertriebenen. Zahlen-Daten-Namen*
   (Günter Olzog Verlag, Munich, 1979). For a comprehensive study of the
   political party formed by the refugees, see F. Neumann, *Der Block der
   Heimatvertriebenen und Entrechteten 1950–60. Ein Beitrag zur Geschichte und
   Struktur einer politischen Interessenpartei* (A. Hain, Meisenheim, 1968).

Table 11.1 Refugees in the West German States, 1 July 1950

	Total population	Total refugees	Percentage of refugees in population
Schleswig-Holstein	2,667,400	915,957	34.3
Hamburg	1,602,200	102,714	6.4
Lower Saxony	6,914,000	1,842,188	26.6
North Rhine-Westphalia	13,227,100	1,261,391	9.5
Bremen	559,700	41,250	7.4
Hesse	4,369,900	680,022	15.6
Württemberg-Baden	3,918,900	729,101	18.6
Bavaria	9,262,600	1,935,504	20.9
Rhineland-Palatinate	2,976,500	106,093	3.6
Baden	1,327,300	93,098	7.0
Württemberg-Hohenzollern	1,228,500	109,707	8.9
German Federal Republic	48,054,100	7,817,025	16.3

Source: Statistisches Amt des Vereinigten Wirtschaftsgebietes (ed.), *Statistische Unterlagen zum Flüchtlingsproblem*, No. 7, n.p.

in the Baltic States of Latvia, Estonia and Lithuania, the former free city of Danzig, the Soviet Union, Rumania, Hungary, Yugoslavia, Austria and Poland. The majority of *Reichsdeutsche* had fled from their homelands as Soviet troops advanced westwards in the spring and early summer of 1945, while most *Volksdeutsche* had been systematically expelled under the terms of the Potsdam Agreement.

   The integration of these refugees and expellees into the western zones of Germany represented one of the most formidable tasks facing the Allied and German authorities after the Second World War. As a result of the extensive damage to urban housing brought about by the Allies' wartime bombing campaign, the majority of newcomers had to be accommodated in the predominantly rural Länder of Bavaria, Lower Saxony and Schleswig-Holstein (see table 11.1). This led to severe overcrowding in many country areas, and in mid-1948 some 400,000 refugees were still residing in camps. Without connections or the chance to capitalise on the flourishing black market, the newcomers were also seriously affected by the post-war food crisis and in the winter of 1946–7 many died of hunger and starvation. It is clear, then, that the refugees and expellees had to endure appalling material deprivation in the early post-war years, and this chapter will endeavour to assess the effects of the currency reform (*Währungsreform*) of June 1948 on their economic and social position. It will be argued that although historians have tended to concentrate on the positive results of the *Währungsreform*, this measure exacerbated the hardship being suffered by large sections of the refugee population. In fact, there is no doubt that far from improving the plight of the newcomers the adoption of the deutschmark actually led to a decline in their economic circumstances. These developments also had potentially serious implications for the political stability of the new state which was being set up, and, significantly, many leading German politicians feared that the demoralising repercussions of the currency reform of June 1948 would have similar consequences for the Bundesrepublik, as the *Währungsreform* of November 1923 had for the German people in the Weimar period.

The introduction of the deutschmark has been widely regarded as an important factor behind the impressive post-war revival of the West German economy. Indeed, in this volume Wendy Carlin has already outlined its beneficial effects on economic reconstruction: it created the preconditions for business investment, released hoarded goods into the shops, led to the virtual disappearance of the black market and restored the incentive to work.[3] Even though Werner Abelshauser has argued that the origins of the 'Economic Miracle' did not date from the *Währungsreform* of June 1948 but can be traced back to the autumn of 1947,[4] his work has focused renewed attention on the positive economic results of replacing the inflationary reichsmark with the deutschmark. Yet this debate about the contribution of the currency reform to West Germany's remarkable economic recovery has tended to obscure the fact that the adoption of the deutschmark also had negative consequences. While Wendy Carlin rightly states that the partial removal of economic controls accompanying the *Währungsreform* helped to increase industrial output, it must be remembered that this action also led to sharp price increases which hit the poorest population groups with particular severity. Moreover, the introduction of the new currency brought about a dramatic rise in the numbers out of work and by the end of 1950 unemployment figures in the Bundesrepublik had reached almost two million.

These developments gave rise to profound discontent among

3. See chapter 2 in this volume.
4. W. Abelshauser, *Wirtschaft in Westdeutschland, 1945–48. Rekonstruktion und Wachstumsbedingungen in der amerikanischen und britischen Zone* (Deutsche Verlags-Anstalt, Stuttgart, 1975), pp. 167–70.

wide sections of the German people, and, according to a public opinion poll conducted in the western zones of Germany in July 1948, no fewer than 42% of the population believed that their standard of living had deteriorated since the adoption of the deutschmark.[5] There was widespread sympathy with the SPD's demand for the reintroduction of economic controls and the resignation of the Director of the Economic Administration of Bizonia, Ludwig Erhard. The consumer strike coordinated by the trade unions in August 1948 in protest against the steep price increases gained considerable support and in several towns, including Munich, Erlangen and Eckernförde (Schleswig-Holstein), the police were forced to intervene as demonstrators attacked traders and shopkeepers.[6] Trade union leaders also organised a twenty-four-hour general strike on 12 November 1948, and, although it did not prove to be a great success, the danger of social unrest continued to exist well beyond the establishment of the German Federal Republic.

In view of the western Allies' failure to combine the *Währungsreform* with Equalisation of Burdens legislation, the weakest sections of post-war German society received no protection against the harsh economic and social consequences resulting from the replacement of the reichsmark with the deutschmark. Many former prisoners-of-war, victims of war bombing and disabled servicemen suffered acute material distress following the adoption of the new currency. But perhaps the most vulnerable group of all were the refugees and expellees. After all, they had lost their homes, most of their possessions and after their arrival in the west, suffered serious economic distress up to mid-1948. Yet my research would indicate that the currency reform actually worsened the plight of these unfortunate people. The second half of 1948 witnessed a deterioration in the food supplies and housing conditions of many refugees and expellees. The sharp rise in unemployment after the currency reform also hit the newcomers with particular severity, numerous refugee firms being forced to go into liquidation. Moreover, the ecclesiastical relief organisations, which in the early post-war years had assumed responsibility for many areas of the refugee problem, found themselves in such dire financial

---

5. Quoted in G. Stüber, *Der Kampf gegen den Hunger 1945–50. Die Ernährungslage in der Britischen Zone Deutschlands, insbesondere in Schleswig-Holstein und Hamburg* (Karl Wachholtz Verlag, Neumünster, 1984), p. 374.
6. Ibid., p. 398.

difficulties after the *Währungsreform* that they were compelled to reduce the scale of their welfare activities. Refugees in the three major *Flüchtlingsländer* were worst affected by the introduction of the deutschmark and this chapter will therefore focus not only on the British Zone states of Lower Saxony and Schleswig-Holstein, but also on Bavaria, the Land most heavily overburdened with newcomers in the US Occupation Zone.

The Economic Effects of the Currency Reform on the Refugees

The Food Situation

Although there is no doubt that primarily as a result of higher grain imports the general food position in the British and US Zones continued to improve after the currency reform, local reports suggest that this was of little help to the refugees and expellees, some of whom actually had less to eat in the second half of 1948 than in the six months before the introduction of the deutschmark. The increase in official ration levels[7] and the greater variety of foodstuffs available benefited few refugees since they could not afford to buy the extra rations to which their coupons entitled them. This applied particularly to unemployed, disabled or retired newcomers, and the Oberdirektor of the Refugee Office in Burgdorf (Lower Saxony) commented in November 1948 that 'in view of the dizzy heights to which prices have risen, public welfare allowances are insufficient to purchase food'.[8] However, even refugees in gainful employment sometimes encountered this problem and reports from Schleswig-Holstein indicate that a substantial proportion of expellee families were unable to buy more than half of their potato rations in the autumn of 1948.[9] Indeed, it was common for them to sell their fat and sugar coupons in order to obtain basic necessities such as bread,[10] while the Landrat of Traunstein (Upper

7. To take one example, calory rations in Kiel increased from 1,384 per day in May 1948 to 1,958 in August of the same year. Quoted in ibid., p. 379.
8. Niedersächsisches Hauptstaatsarchiv (HStA) Hanover, Nds 120 Lüneburg, Acc. 31/67, 3, Refugee Office of Rural District (RD) of Burgdorf to Regierungspräsident (RP) of Lüneburg, 9 November 1948.
9. Landesarchiv Schleswig-Holstein (LSH), Abt. 605, 1206, Müthling to Lüdemann, 15 September 1948.
10. See, for example, Public Record Office (PRO)/FO1006/72, Monthly Report (MR) of Kreis Resident Officer (KRO) of RD of Norderdithmarschen to Regional Commissioner (RC) of Schleswig-Holstein, 23 November 1948.

Bavaria) noted in June 1949 that refugee women were being 'forced to sell the few personal belongings they had managed to acquire in order to buy urgently needed foodstuffs'.[11]

The introduction of the deutschmark also had serious short-term effects on the diet of refugee schoolchildren. In parts of the British Zone, a school-feeding project had been set up as early as December 1945 to provide needy and undernourished children with a hot midday meal,[12] and after the visit to Germany in 1947 of a fact-finding mission led by the former US President, Herbert Hoover, it was agreed to extend the scheme to the US and French Zones. Although these meals were heavily subsidised, a survey conducted in Nuremberg concluded that, even before the adoption of the new currency, some 18% of parents could not afford their nominal daily contribution of 15–25 pfennings.[13] The *Währungsreform* exacerbated this problem and in some areas up to 60% of children participating in the school-feeding scheme had to be withdrawn during July 1948.[14] As an especially impoverished group, refugee schoolchildren were amongst the worst affected, a fact viewed with grave disquiet by teachers and doctors since *Flüchtlingskinder* were invariably seriously underweight. Even though the Länder governments took steps to reduce the level of parental contributions, thousands of refugee children did not rejoin the school-feeding scheme until it became free in the spring of 1949.[15]

The Housing Problem

It would also be wrong to imagine that the currency reform brought about a general improvement in the housing conditions of the refugees and expellees. On the contrary, it seems that in many parts of Lower Saxony, Schleswig-Holstein and Bavaria, the problem of accommodation actually became more acute after the adoption of

11. Staatsarchiv Munich (StA), LRA 29569, Labour Office (Traunstein) to Labour Office (Southern Bavaria), 27 June 1949.
12. For further details, see I. Turner, 'The British Occupation Policy and its Effects on the Town of Wolfsburg and the Volkswagenwerk 1945–49', PhD thesis, Manchester University, 1984, pp. 149–50.
13. W. Fuhrmann, *Die Bayerische Lagerversorgung 1948–1951. Ein ernährungswirtschaftlicher Beitrag zur Versorgung von Gemeinschaftsverpflegungseinrichtungen und der Schulspeisung* (np, nd), p. 77.
14. Nordrhein-Westfälisches Hauptstaatsarchiv (HStA) Düsseldorf, Reg. Düs. 54328, Oberkreisdirektor (OKD) of RD of Dinslaken to RP of Düsseldorf, 18 July 1948; PRO/FO1006/68, MR of KRO of RD of Plön to RC of Schleswig-Holstein, 24 July 1948.
15. Fuhrmann, *Die Bayerische Lagerversorgung*, p. 77.

the deutschmark. The British Kreis Resident Officer (KRO) in Rendsburg (Schleswig-Holstein), where newcomers made up some 40% of the population, observed in July 1949 'that the housing situation . . . during the past year has deteriorated to quite a marked extent',[16] a view shared by local German officials throughout the major *Flüchtlingsländer*. Millions of refugees were still living in cramped, overcrowded conditions and a government survey carried out in Bavaria in December 1949 showed that 66.7% of newcomers residing in private accommodation or housing camps had only one room at their disposal.[17]

Refugees billeted with private householders were the first to experience the adverse effects of the currency reform. Prior to June 1948, when supplies of inflationary reichsmarks had been plentiful, most newcomers had been in a position to pay for their accommodation, and even those unable to meet the full rent had raised money by selling their cigarette ration or bartering private possessions on the black market. But the introduction of the deutschmark transformed the situation. Many householders simply converted the amount of the original rent from reichsmarks into deutschmarks, even though the purchasing power of the new currency was much greater than the old one. While unemployed refugees could reclaim this money from the state, those in gainful employment had to meet the new rental out of their own resources, and during the summer of 1948 the price-control boards were inundated with requests to settle disputes over rent levels.

This issue proved especially contentious in tourist areas such as the Harz mountains and the East Friesian islands. In view of the acute post-war housing shortage, the Länder governments compelled many hotel and guest-house proprietors to let their rooms to refugees. However, this represented an enormous economic burden to regions heavily dependent on tourism, and in some resorts the number of beds available to guests in mid-1947 totalled less than 20% of the pre-war figure.[18] Faced with this major threat to their livelihood, hotel and guest-house owners often demanded abnor-

16. PRO/FO1006/71, MR of KRO of Rendsburg to RC of Schleswig-Holstein, July 1949.
17. Bayerisches Statistisches Landesamt (BSL) (ed.), *Die Vertriebenen in Bayern. Ihre berufliche und soziale Eingliederung bis Anfang 1950*, Beiträge zur Statistik Bayerns, no. 151, p. 24.
18. For a detailed analysis of the serious shortage of tourist accommodation in Bavaria, see BSL (ed.), *Bayern in Zahlen*, Monatshefte des Bayerischen Statistischen Landesamtes München, no. 5 (May 1948), p. 118.

mally high rents which, after the currency reform, sometimes amounted to more than half of the refugees' total monthly income.[19] In Lower Saxony newcomers already owed more than a million deutschmarks in rent arrears four months after the adoption of the new currency[20] and in Bad Pyrmont, one of its best-known spa towns, 95% of the refugee population had fallen behind with their rent by January 1949.[21]

The sharp increase in the cost of renting private quarters after the currency reform also aggravated the problem of overcrowding in refugee camps. Deeply fearful of 'the social, spiritual, moral . . . and political dangers associated with people constantly living together in a very confined space',[22] the Länder authorities regarded the closure of refugee camps as one of their most important policy objectives. Living conditions in the camps were often appalling and prior to the currency reform most inmates had been anxious to find accommodation in private houses. However, since the occupants of the camps either did not have to pay rent or contributed only a nominal sum, the prospect of leaving the *Flüchtlingslager* became much less attractive after the currency reform. Indeed, some refugees actually refused to move into private quarters on the grounds that they could not afford to pay the rent, and one such incident in Düsseldorf in April 1949 resulted in rental charges being introduced for the inmates of all refugee camps in North Rhine-Westphalia.[23] Moreover, the serious economic repercussions of the currency reform even prompted some newcomers to seek refuge in the camps they had only recently left.[24]

The introduction of the deutschmark also led to a deterioration in the living conditions of refugee camp occupants. In Bavaria, for example, the number of beds, mattresses and blankets placed at the disposal of the camp authorities dropped sharply in the second half

19. According to guidelines laid down in a directive issued by the Bizonal authorities in Frankfurt on 8 October 1948, a family of six occupying two ·rooms of a hotel in a holiday resort would be required to pay rent of DM96 a month, although its income often totalled no more than DM130–50.
20. HStA Hanover, Nds 380, Acc. 62/65,555, Albertz to Kopf, 12 March 1949.
21. HStA Hanover, Nds 380, Acc 62/65,555, Bad Pyrmont Council to Mayor of Hameln, 17 January 1949.
22. Wolfgang Jaenicke (Bavarian State Secretary for Refugees) to George Shuster (US State Commissioner for Bavaria), 2 September 1950. Copy submitted to the Bavarian Landtag's Committee for Refugee Questions, 15 September 1950.
23. HStA Düsseldorf, Reg. Düs., BR 1021/97, MR of RP to Military Government, 1 June 1949.
24. See, for example, StA, LRA 31381, Freisehner to Extraordinary Meeting of Berchtesgaden District Council, 16 April 1949.

of 1948 due to the severe restrictions imposed on government expenditure.[25] The acute shortage of money after the *Währungsreform* also halted the implementation of urgent structural repairs to a number of refugee camps. In Schleswig-Holstein, plans to provide family accommodation by partitioning large barracks in some of the camps had to be postponed,[26] while in September 1949, fifteen months after the currency reform, refugees in Springe (Lower Saxony) were still awaiting the resumption of a project to convert barracks into an old people's home.[27]

In another, even more fundamental respect the adoption of the new currency dashed the refugees' hopes of improving their living conditions. The only long-term solution to the post-war housing crisis was a large-scale building programme, but as a result of the *Währungsreform* the construction of domestic houses practically came to a standstill. While the Catholic Refugee Council (Katholischer Flüchtlingsrat) estimated in 1949 that in addition to repairing damaged housing it would be necessary to construct some 1.8–2 million new dwellings to accommodate satisfactorily the refugees and expellees residing in the German Federal Republic,[28] the total number of houses built in North Rhine-Westphalia in the year after the currency reform was just 18,815.[29] Prior to June 1948 the major obstacle to house building had been the dearth of raw materials; after the introduction of the deutschmark, supplies of lime, cement, glass and tiles were adequate but there was an acute shortage of public and private money for investment in housing projects. Indeed, the scarcity of financial credit brought about by the currency reform continued to hamper the house-building programmes of the Länder governments until 1952–3,[30] and with the continuing influx of refugees from the German Democratic Republic, no fewer than

25. In 1948, the number of beds distributed in the camps was 16,000 (as opposed to 93,000 in 1947), while the number of mattresses totalled 14,000 (compared with 49,000 in 1947) and blankets 104,000 (as opposed to 181,000 in 1947).
26. See, for example, PRO/FO1006/70, MR of KRO of RD of Rendsburg to RC of Schleswig-Holstein, 24 August 1948.
27. HStA Hanover, Nds 120, Acc. 40/78,61, OKD of Springe to Minister of Finance for Lower Saxony, 29 September 1949.
28. Bundesministerium für Vertriebene, *Vertriebene und Flüchtlinge volksdeutschen Ursprungs. Bericht eines Sonder-Unterkomitees des Rechtsausschusses des Abgeordnetenhauses* . . . . (Bonn, 1950), p. 83. (Hereafter known as *Der Walter-Bericht*.)
29. HStA Hanover, Nds 380, Acc 62/65,564, 'Vierteljahresbericht über Wohnverhältnisse und Bautätigkeit im Lande Nordrhein-Westfalen', p. 21.
30. See, for example, S. Schier, *Die Aufnahme und Eingliederung von Flüchtlingen und Vertriebenen in der Hansestadt Lübeck* (Schmidt Römhild, Lübeck, 1982), p. 234.

185,000 newcomers were still being accommodated in camps as late as 1955.[31] It seems clear, then, that the adverse impact of the currency reform on the refugees' housing position was not simply a short-term, transitory phenomenon and the situation did not show a substantial improvement until the second half of the 1950s.

The Unemployment Crisis

The currency reform had even more serious effects on the employment prospects of the refugees and expellees. As table 11.2 shows, the proportion of the total working population in the western zones of Germany without a job trebled from June 1948 to December 1949. Moreover, this rise in unemployment hit the newcomers much more severely than the native inhabitants. For it is clear that the major *Flüchtlingsländer*—Bavaria, Schleswig-Holstein and Lower Saxony—recorded disproportionately high increases in the numbers out of work, and that even within these states refugees and expellees were much more likely to lose their jobs than local people. In Schleswig-Holstein, for example, unemployment figures rose from some 21,000 at the time of the currency reform to more that 221,000 in December 1949; significantly, refugees comprised 58% of this total, even though they made up only 35% of the population (see table 11.3). Newcomers engaged in agriculture and small domestic industries were among the worst affected, and in Eiderstedt (Schleswig-Holstein) the number of refugee women working in the hand-knitting industry fell from 300 to 30 in the first four months after the introduction of the deutschmark.[32]

It should be borne in mind that the currency reform was not the sole cause of the sharp deterioration in the employment situation from mid-1948 onwards. British officials pointed out, with some justification, that the numbers out of work were swollen by returning prisoners-of-war and German refugees entering the western zones illegally from the Soviet Zone and Czechoslovakia (*illegale Grenzgänger*). Meanwhile, German politicians tended to stress the scale of job-losses resulting from Allied dismantling policy. But dismantling created little unemployment in rural areas, where the

---

31. P. Waldmann, 'Die Eingliederung der ostdeutschen Vertriebenen in die westdeutsche Gesellschaft' in J. Becker, T. Stammen and P. Waldmann, (eds.), *Vorgeschichte der Bundesrepublik Deutschland. Zwischen Kapitulation und Grundgesetz* (Wilhelm Fink Verlag, Munich, 1979), p. 177.
32. PRO/FO1006/46, MR of KRO of RD of Eiderstedt to RC of Schleswig-Holstein, 26 October 1948.

Table 11.2 Unemployment in the western zones of Germany after the currency reform

	30 June 1948		30 June 1949		31 December 1949	
	Number of unemployed	Percentage of working population	Number of unemployed	Percentage of working population	Number of unemployed	Percentage of working population
Schleswig-Holstein	21,250	2.7	189,113	22.6	221,184	26.3
Hamburg	14,493	2.5	51,895	8.2	71,874	11.1
Lower Saxony	59,075	2.9	286,750	13.7	367,701	17.3
North Rhine-Westphalia	122,260	3.1	182,710	4.2	196,107	4.5
Bremen	6,923	3.7	16,739	8.3	17,457	8.5
Hesse	41,895	3.4	104,909	7.9	132,977	9.9
Württemberg-Baden	29,972	2.6	57,338	4.7	68,298	5.4
Rhineland-Palatinate	5,144	0.8	33,716	4.6	53,120	7.0
Bavaria	145,727	5.4	348,258	12.6	406,295	14.5
Baden	3,137	1.0	7,093	2.0	11,227	3.0
Württemberg-Hohenzollern	1,215	0.4	4,781	1.5	12,229	3.5
Total	451,091	3.2	1,283,302	8.7	1,558,469	10.3

Source: Bundesministerium für Arbeit (1950), p. 6.

majority of the refugees were living. Moreover, the influx of the *illegale Grenzgänger* cannot obscure the fact that in the period June 1948–December 1949 the major *Flüchtlingsländer* not only registered a sharp rise in the numbers out of work but also a marked decrease in the numbers in employment—as many as 136,000 in Bavaria, 157,000 in Schleswig–Holstein and 211,000 in Lower Saxony.[33] It seems clear, then, that the *Währungsreform* was the most important reason for the dramatic increase in refugee unemployment in the months prior to the establishment of the Bundesrepublik.

Although the western Allies' decision to locate most newcomers in the countryside was unavoidable in view of the acute housing shortage in the towns and cities, it undoubtedly made them especially vulnerable to dismissal after the currency reform. A regional analysis of unemployment trends suggests that the proportion of the population out of work in a particular district was determined less by the number of refugees it accommodated than the capacity of its economy to absorb surplus population elements. Thus, North Rhine-Westphalia, the most prosperous and industrialised Land, recorded the smallest percentage increase in unemployment in the eighteen months following the adoption of the new currency, while Württemberg-Baden, a state with a mixed economy, registered only a moderate rise in the numbers out of work, even though it was severely burdened with refugees. On the other hand, the unemployment crisis after the *Währungsreform* was especially acute in Bavaria, Lower Saxony and Schleswig-Holstein, rural states not only heavily reliant on agriculture and tourism, but also accommodating very large numbers of newcomers. Although the vast majority of refugees in these Länder had managed to secure work of some description by mid-1948, many, unable to obtain employment in the trade or profession for which they had been trained, had taken unskilled jobs,[34] and this made them particularly susceptible to redundancy in the new commercial climate prevailing after the currency reform.

It would also appear that, amid the intensified competition on the

33. Bundesministerium für Arbeit (ed.), *Entwicklung und Ursachen der Arbeitslosigkeit in der Bundesrepublik Deutschland 1946–1950* (Bonn, 1950), p. 13.
34. In Bavaria, for example, the proportion of workers (*Arbeiter*) among the refugee population increased from 40% to 79% between 1939 and 1946, while the number of self-employed fell from 31% to 7% and the proportion of civil servants from 29% to 15%. See Bayerisches Hauptstaatsarchiv (BHStA), MArb 27, *Statistischer Informationsdienst*, no. 148.

Table 11.3 Unemployment among the refugee population in the West German states, 31 December 1949[a]

	Total unemployed	Refugees unemployed	Unemployed refugees as percentage of total	Percentage of refugees in population
Schleswig-Holstein	221,184	129,365	58.5	34.9
Hamburg	71,874	1,441	2.0	5.9
Lower Saxony	367,701	159,514	43.4	26.8
North Rhine-Westphalia	196,107	25,527	13.0	9.1
Bremen	17,457	1,448	8.3	6.9
Hesse	132,977	36,304	27.3	15.4
Württemberg-Baden	68,298	23,818	34.9	18.4
Bavaria	406,295	162,129	39.9	21.0
Baden	11,227	1,691	15.1	5.6
Württemberg-Hohenzollern	12,229	5,426	44.4	8.0
German Federal Republic	1,505,349	546,663	35.1	16.1

[a] Rhineland-Palatinate is excluded, since no figures are available.
The unemployed refugees in Württemberg-Hohenzollern include many who had recently arrived as part of an inter-Länder resettlement scheme.

Source: Calculated from Statistisches Amt des Vereinigten Wirtschaftsgebietes (ed.), *Statistische Unterlagen zum Flüchtlingsproblem*, No. 5 and Bundesministerium für Arbeit (1950), p. 6.

employment market following the introduction of the deutschmark, discrimination against the refugee population increased. Many employers took the view that since the expellees had been most recently recruited they should also be the first to be discharged. In the Regierungsbezirk of Hanover the situation was considered to be so serious in July 1948 that the Regierungspräsident asked to be personally notified of complaints by newcomers against unfair dismissal,[35] while in North Rhine-Westphalia it was felt necessary to remind the employment offices that a member of the indigenous population could not be appointed to a post if there were better-qualified refugee applicants.[36] But these directives were not always followed and in the six months after the *Währungsreform* the proportion of newcomers among secondary school teachers employed in the British Zone fell from 28% to 25%.[37] At local level, more blatant examples of discrimination occurred, and in July 1950 refugees comprised 15.5% of the population in the Urban District of Schwandorf (Upper Palatinate, Bavaria), but only 1.2% of those working for the municipal authorities.[38]

The currency reform had equally disastrous effects on the *Flüchtlingsbetriebe*—commercial undertakings set up by the newcomers after their expulsion to the west. In Lower Saxony, *Reichsdeutsche* had founded a large number of mining and manufacturing enterprises, especially in the Regierungsbezirke of Brunswick, Hildesheim, Hanover and Lüneburg, while refugee clothing and textile firms were of particular importance in Schleswig-Holstein. But many of these concerns collapsed as a result of the currency reform and in Schleswig-Holstein just six out of one-hundred firms established in Lockstedt refugee camp survived.[39] While the failure of some undertakings was inevitable since they had produced goods of inferior quality, many potentially viable businesses also went into liquidation and Fritz Schumacher, Economic Adviser to the British Control Commission in Germany, observed in February 1949 that

35. HStA Hanover, Nds 120 Hanover, Acc.58/65,151, RP of Hanover to District Employment Officer, 31 July 1948.
36. HStA Düsseldorf, Landesarbeitsamt, 32, President of State Labour Office to the Labour Offices, 25 August 1948.
37. HStA Hanover, Nds 380, Acc.62/65,566, Association of War Victims among Language and Literature Teachers to Refugee Minister of Lower Saxony, 23 March 1949.
38. Bayerisches Landtagsarchiv (BLA), Committee for Refugee Questions, minutes of meeting of 10 July 1950, p. 14.
39. G. Ziemer, *Deutscher Exodus. Vertreibung und Eingliederung von 15 Millionen Ostdeutschen* (Seewald Verlag, Stuttgart, 1973), p. 143.

the bankruptcies among *Flüchtlingsbetriebe* included 'productive and enterprising firms that could play a valuable part in recovery'.[40]

While the well-established native businesses were able to hoard their goods in the period before the reform, and sell them for hard currency directly afterwards, the newly founded refugee firms rarely had sufficient capital to follow their example. They were forced to trade for inflationary reichsmarks which had to be exchanged at the unfavourable rate of 10 to 1 on 20 June 1948. Moreover, the cost of renting business premises often rose sharply after the introduction of the deutschmark, and this hit *Flüchtlingsbetriebe* with particular severity. The currency reform also brought to light the unsuitable geographical location of refugee industries established in isolated rural communities. In the unusual economic conditions prevailing until mid-1948, when a buyer could be found for almost every product, many of these enterprises had flourished, but in the tough commercial climate which characterised the period after the reform, they invariably proved uncompetitive.

However, there is no doubt that the most intractable problem facing the refugee industries as a result of the currency reform was a shortage of medium- and long-term financial credit. The Refugee Commissioner in Hesse, Peter Paul Nahm, estimated in September 1949 that DM 750 million would be required to ensure the survival of the *Flüchtlingsbetriebe*,[41] but, in view of the drastic reduction in public expenditure necessitated by the currency reform, the Länder governments were able to release no more than a fraction of this amount. For example, in October 1948, the Finance Ministry in Lower Saxony allocated to each of the state's 76 Kreise just DM 27,000 to help refugee firms finding themselves in financial difficulties. This sum proved woefully inadequate. In the Rural District of Uelzen, 240 *Flüchtlingsbetriebe* applied for loans totalling more than DM 700,000,[42] while the Refugee Office in the Urban District of Celle was able to approve just 26 of the 151 requests for financial assistance.[43] Although government investment in the refu-

40. PRO/FO1036/94, 'Economic Trends in the Bizonal Economy. A Critical Analysis of Inflation and Deflation'. Paper by E. F. Schumacher, discussed at a conference of Regional Commissioners, 15 February 1949.
41. *Der Walter-Bericht*, p. 57.
42. HStA Hanover, Nds 120 Lüneburg, Acc.31/67,3, Refugee Office of RD of Uelzen to RP of Lüneburg, 29 December 1948.
43. D. Brosius, 'Zur Lage der Flüchtlinge im Regierungsbezirk Lüneburg zwischen Kriegsende und Währungsreform' in D. Brosius and A. Hohenstein, *Flüchtlinge im nordöstlichen Niedersachsen 1945–1948* (Verlag August Lax, Hildesheim, 1985), p. 43.

gee industries increased in 1949–50, a study carried out in Bavaria shortly after the formation of the Bundesrepublik concluded that the shortage of credit was responsible for the dismissal of some 30% of newcomers made redundant since the currency reform.[44] It should also be noted that, despite the steady fall in the numbers out of work in West Germany during the 1950s, refugees residing in Bavaria, Lower Saxony and Schleswig-Holstein continued to experience serious difficulties in obtaining a job, since not only was the unemployment rate in these Länder above the national average but newcomers were still less likely to be offered work than members of the indigenous population.[45]

The Plight of Ecclesiastical Welfare Organisations

In other respects, too, the currency reform exacerbated the unfortunate position of the refugees and expellees. In particular, it dealt a severe blow to the work of the ecclesiastical relief agencies which, in the early post-war years, had played a crucial part in integrating the newcomers into German society. Amid the chaotic conditions prevailing directly after the fall of the Third Reich, at a time when there was no German government, either at central or Land level, church welfare organisations ran refugee camps, set up a missing persons' service and established old people's homes as well as distributing gifts and donations from countries such as Sweden, Switzerland and, above all, the United States. But the shortage of money after the currency reform forced many ecclesiastical agencies to reduce the welfare activities they carried out for the refugee population. Even the most important relief bodies, such as the German Caritas Association (Deutscher Caritasverband) and the Protestant Church Welfare Organisation (Hilfswerk der Evangelischen Kirche) found themselves in financial difficulties, while some of the smaller *Wohlfahrtsverbände* never recovered from the introduction of the deutschmark.

The adverse effects of the currency reform on expellee relief organisations were immediately apparent, and on 22 July 1948 Pastor Wolff, chairman of the Arbeitsgemeinschaft der freien Wohlfahrtsverbände in Hanover, reported that while he needed DM 7.7 million a month to maintain Lower Saxony's 1,456 private

---

44. *Der Walter-Bericht*, p. 57.
45. Neumann, *Der Block der Heimatvertriebenen und Entrechteten*, pp. 6–7.

welfare institutions, just DM 350,000 were available.[46] In Schleswig-Holstein the situation was equally serious and the KRO of Rendsburg commented in December 1948 that 'all welfare organisations are fighting a losing battle'.[47] As a result of higher staff costs and a sharp increase in the price of rented housing, the German Red Cross was forced to shut down old people's homes accommodating large numbers of needy refugees. Many children's holiday camps also fell victim to the *Währungsreform* and in Malente (near Eutin, Schleswig-Holstein) a health farm where sick youngsters from Lübeck had been able to recuperate was closed in August 1948.[48]

Despite the grave financial predicament facing ecclesiastical relief agencies after the adoption of the new currency, the western Allies refused to grant them special treatment on the grounds that this would 'prejudice the reform as a whole and . . . delay the recovery of general economnic stability'.[49] At the same time, the state governments found themselves compelled to reduce their level of financial support to the welfare organisations.[50] In addition, public contributions to church funds fell drastically in the aftermath of the currency reform. Wolff estimated that the first collection in Lower Saxony after 20 June 1948 would yield no more than DM 180,000, as opposed to a monthly average of RM 1.5 million during 1947,[51] and local examples confirmed his worst fears.[52] However, while ecclesiastical dignitaries had anticipated these developments, they did not foresee that the currency reform would in another crucial respect hamper their efforts to integrate the refugees and expellees

---

46. Niedersächsisches Landtagsarchiv (NdsLA), minutes of meeting of Committee of Public Safety, 22 July 1948, p. 2.
47. PRO/FO1006/70, MR of KRO of RD of Rendsburg to RC of Schleswig-Holstein, nd.
48. PRO/FO1006/54, MR of KRO of RD of Eutin to RC of Schleswig-Holstein, 21 August 1948.
49. PRO/FO1013/381, Regional Governmental Officer (RGO) of North Rhine-Westphalia to *Arbeitsgemeinschaft der Spitzenverbände der Freien Wohlfahrtspflege* (Freiburg Breisgau), 2 December 1948.
50. See, for example, PRO/FO1006/72, H. Dauge (German Red Cross), 'Die Wohlfahrtsarbeit in Norderdithmarschen vor Weihnachten 1948', 16 December 1948. In Schleswig-Holstein, for example, the Landesregierung could afford to make no more than a small loan at an interest rate of 5%. Only in Bavaria did the state authorities manage to give substantial aid to the *Wohlfahrtsverbände*. For details, see Kornrumpf, *In Bayern angekommen*, p. 205.
51. NdsLA, minutes of meeting of committee of Public Safety, 22 July 1948, p. 2.
52. HStA Hanover, Nds 120 Lüneburg, Acc.31/67,3, OKD of RD of Soltau to RP of Lüneburg, 20 October 1948: 'As collections by the welfare organisations have produced nothing worth speaking of since the currency reform, only 4,654 deutschmarks could be distributed'.

into post-war Germany.

In the months following the introduction of the new money, leading members of refugee welfare organisations noted with concern a sharp fall in the quantity of aid they received from abroad. For example, the value of packages donated by the Swiss Caritas Association decreased from 4,691,677 Swiss francs in 1947–8 to 2,283,729 in 1948–9 and just 707, 317 in 1949–50,[53] while some of the less prosperous South American countries discontinued their assistance to Germany altogether. Local reports indicate that these cutbacks involved considerable hardship for the newcomers, and an official from the *Flüchtlingsamt* in Celle (Lower Saxony) remarked that 'the extraordinarily small number of foreign donations severely restrict the ability of the relief associations to provide help'.[54]

This reduction in foreign aid reflected the way in which world public opinion had been misinformed about the economic impact of the currency reform on the western zones of Germany. Observing the variety and quality of goods displayed in shop windows in the towns and cities, as well as the construction of cinemas, theatres and restaurants, foreign journalists wrote about the remarkable recovery of the German economy in the second half of 1948, and such reports undoubtedly made readers less responsive to the appeals of welfare organisations for financial aid to alleviate the refugees' proverty.[55] Significantly, few newspaper correspondents ventured beyond the main commercial centres and they would certainly have gained a very different impression of conditions after the currency reform if they had visited the rural areas where, as we have seen, many refugees and expellees were living in more abject squalor than before the adoption of the new money.

The Social Inequities of the Currency Reform

While we have so far focused on the adverse economic effects of the *Währungsreform* on the newcomers, the introduction of the deutschmark also had profound social consequences. Prior to June 1948, the social differences between the refugees and the native population

53. H.-J. Wollasch, *Humanitäre Auslandshilfe für Deutschland nach dem Zweiten Weltkrieg. Darstellung und Dokumentation kirchlicher und nichtkirchlicher Hilfen* (Deutscher Caritasverband, Freiburg, 1976), p. 328.
54. HStA Hanover, Nds 120 Lüneburg, Acc.31/67,3, Refugee Office of Urban District of Celle to RP of Lüneburg, 5 April 1949.
55. See, for example, *Daily Express*, 29 November 1948.

had been partially blurred by the 'barter economy', in which material wealth depended heavily on one's opportunity and inclination to participate in the flourishing black market. But the normalisation of economic conditions after the currency reform emphasised the wide gap between the newcomers and large sections of the indigenous inhabitants. The refugees found it particularly difficult to accept the decline in their own material position since it coincided with an improvement in the standard of living of the native population. This aroused deep resentment among the newcomers, and both Allied and German observers commented on the growing hostility of many refugees towards the original inhabitants in the second half of 1948.

Until the currency reform, all sections of the population had suffered to some degree from the general food shortage, but the adoption of the deutschmark produced wide discrepancies in the dietary patterns of the rich and poor. While, as we have seen, many refugees could not afford to buy their full food rations in the period immediately after the *Währungsreform*, the wealthy were able to eat luxurious meals at extravagant prices. A leading restaurant in Hamburg sold more lobster in the month following the currency reform than in the whole of the previous year,[56] while in Oldenburg (Schleswig-Holstein), a district accommodating a large number of unemployed refugees, the KRO noted in May 1949 that cafés specialising in expensive cream cakes and strawberries were doing excellent business.[57] Developments in the building industry also focused attention on the social divisions the currency reform had created between the newcomers and the more affluent sections of the native population. Although the cutbacks in public expenditure in the second half of 1948 forced Länder governments to reduce the scope of their housing programmes and postpone repairs to refugee camps, private individuals evidently had plentiful funds to finance the construction of business premises, restaurants and cinemas. Indeed, in the holiday resort of Travemünde (near Lübeck), two casinos were opened during the first half of 1949, while plans to build flats for the local refugee population could not proceed due to a shortage of money.[58]

56. PRO/FO1014/46, MR of KRO of West Hamburg to RGO of Hamburg, 28 July 1948.
57. PRO/FO1006/59, MR of KRO of RD of Oldenburg to RC of Schleswig-Holstein, 24 May 1949.
58. *Norddeutsche Zeitung*, 28 June 1949, in HStA Hanover, Bestand 200, Acc.53/83, 707.

The newcomers' awareness of the social inequalities produced by the *Währungsreform* was heightened by the availability of high-quality consumer goods for those rich enough to be able to buy them. The relaxation of economic controls after the introduction of the deutschmark encouraged profit-conscious industrialists to manufacture luxury goods at the expense of cheap simple items, and this, too, helped to widen the gap between the 'haves' and 'have-nots' in German society. While the KRO in the Rural District of Steinburg (Schleswig-Holstein) commented in July 1948 that 'as elsewhere the currency reform has resulted in shop windows being full with such things as watches, clocks, radios, leather goods, china and glassware',[59] it was equally commonplace to see newcomers gazing at basic necessities they could not afford to purchase.

It is clear, then, that the *Währungsreform* dealt a severe blow to the refugees and expellees residing in the western zones of Germany. In view of the material deprivation they had endured in the early post-war years, the newcomers were unable to reconcile themselves to a further decline in their quality of life, particularly as this coincided with a visible improvement in the economic position of the native population. Indeed, the failure of the western Allies to combine the currency reform with Equalisation of Burdens legislation convinced many refugees that they alone were having to atone for the evils of National Socialism. At the same time, the newcomers' indignation at the consequences of the currency reform can be partly explained by their *expectation* that this measure, far from worsening their unhappy plight, would have a positive effect on their own economic position.

Local reports from the major *Flüchtlingsländer* during the first half of 1948 reveal that many expellees viewed the approaching *Währungsreform* with confidence. The Mayor of Kirchweidach (Altötting, Upper Bavaria) noted in February 1948 that 'the population is preoccupied with the issue of currency reform and the refugees, in particular, are expecting an improvement in their living conditions'.[60] Similar optimism was expressed in northern Germany and the KRO of Stormarn, a district heavily populated with newcomers, remarked on 22 May 1948 that 'people seem to place great hopes in the forthcoming currency reform'.[61] Even the minority of

59. PRO/FO1006/78, MR of KRO of RD of Steinburg to RC of Schleswig-Holstein, 22 July 1948.
60. StA, LRA 65849, Mayor of Kirchweidach to Landrat of Altötting, 17 February 1948.
61. PRO/FO1006/60, MR of KRO of RD of Stormarn to RC of Schleswig-

expellees who believed that the adoption of the deutschmark would involve economic hardship expected to receive special treatment from the western Allies.[62] Certainly, very few anticipated the sudden deterioration in their material position,[63] and, as we shall see now, this was undoubtedly a major factor in the growing unrest among the refugee population during the second half of 1948.

The Political Radicalisation of the Refugees

At the beginning of this chapter, it was noted that leading German politicians pointed to ominous parallels between the economic and social consequences of the currency reform introduced on 15 November 1923 and that implemented on 20 June 1948. It was feared that, just as the measure of November 1923 had estranged large sections of the German people from the Weimar Republic, the harsh impact of this latest reform on the dispossessed refugees and expellees might transform them into a radical force likely to endanger the political stability of the new state which was being established. Germany's post-war political elites were, then, most concerned that history would repeat itself, a view summed up by the Bavarian Social Democrat, Hans Kramer, when he argued on 2 July 1948 that disaffected groups such as the refugees 'will, just like twenty-five years ago, lend support to those parties which represent a threat to democracy. This is the enormous political danger we cannot ignore in drawing comparisons with 1923.'[64]

An examination of developments at local level would appear to bear out the authorities' fears that the mood of the newcomers was becoming increasingly radical as a result of the *Währungsreform*. In Hesse, for example, Nahm detected in September 1948 'a growing radicalisation among the refugees . . . since the currency reform',[65] while the Flüchtlingsminister in Lower Saxony, Heinrich Albertz, received numerous petitions deploring the failure to combine the

---

Holstein, 22 May 1948.

62. PRO/FO1013/381, memorandum outlining 'German Views on Currency Reform', sent by Regional Intelligence Officer (North Rhine-Westphalia) to RGO, 7 June 1948.

63. See, for example, Schier, *Die Aufnahme und Eingliederung von Flüchtlingen in Lübeck*, p. 188.

64. BLA, minutes of Landtag Debate, vol. 2/2 (2 July 1948), p. 1610.

65. BHStA, MArb 822, Nahm to US Military Government (Hesse), 20 September 1948.

introduction of the new currency with Equalisation of Burdens legislation.[66] Indeed, such was the desperation of the newcomers in Schleswig-Holstein that, at a time of mounting international tension, some even advocated war between the United States and the Soviet Union as a means of regaining their homelands.[67]

Another indication of the newcomers' increasing radicalisation was the emergence of refugee associations pursuing political objectives. Although the western Allies' ban on the formation of a *Flüchtlingspartei* was not lifted until after the establishment of the German Federal Republic, the events of 20 June 1948 undoubtedly convinced many newcomers that their economic grievances would be remedied only by united, organised opposition to the policies of the western Allies and Länderregierungen. Shortly after the adoption of the new currency, a British official in North Rhine-Westphalia noticed 'very definite signs that the refugees are getting together in a big way',[68] while a leading Bavarian politician, Hans Schütz of the conservative CSU, observed that 'among the consequences of the currency reform is the desire of expellees everywhere to mobilise themselves'.[69] Indeed, according to one estimate, the membership of refugee organisations in the western zones of Germany increased from about 100,000 in September 1948 to 1,250,000 in March 1949.[70]

The second half of 1948 also witnessed close cooperation between the newcomers and other groups disappointed with the outcome of the currency reform. On 17 July 1948, a mass meeting in the Rural District of Ochsenfurt (Lower Franconia), attended not only by refugees and expellees but also wartime evacuees and victims of war bombing, drew up a resolution calling for 'an immediate and just Equalisation of Burdens Bill',[71] while at a rally held in Coburg (Upper Franconia) on 7 August 1948 more than 5,000 refugees, war victims, disabled people and victims of National Socialism unanimously agreed on a series of wide-ranging demands to the Bavarian

66. See, for example, HStA Hanover, Nds 380, Acc.62/65, 612, Refugee Association of Gemeinde Hoysinghausen to Albertz, 30 October 1948.
67. See, for example, PRO/FO1006/58, MR of KRO of RD of Oldenburg (Holstein) to RC of Schleswig-Holstein, 22 July 1948.
68. PRO/FO1013/368, Matheson (RGO) to Chief Manpower Officer, 27 September 1948.
69. BHStA, MArb 8005 1751, meeting of the Main Committee of Refugees and Expellees in Bavaria, 14 October 1948.
70. *Der Walter-Bericht*, p. 66.
71. BHStA, MArb 822, resolution from refugees and evacuees of Ochsenfurt to Bavarian State Secretary for Refugees, 20 July 1948.

Interior Ministry.[72] Thus, the currency reform unified the different groups of 'have-nots' in post-war German society, and, as we shall see now, it was also an important factor in the radicalisation of the refugees' voting behaviour from mid-1948 onwards.

The newcomers' vulnerability to nationalist agitation after the *Währungsreform* was graphically illustrated in the local elections in Lower Saxony held on 28 November 1948. To the consternation of political observers throughout the western zones of Germany, the radical right-wing Deutsche Rechtspartei, under the leadership of Adolf von Thadden and Leonard Schlüter, won no less than 64.3% of the vote in the Urban District of Wolfsburg, and it would appear that much of its support came from dispossessed refugees dissatisfied at the outcome of the currency reform.[73] The expellees' growing susceptibility to nationalist slogans was reaffirmed at the Federal election held on 14 August 1949. In Schleswig-Holstein, British officials were convinced that the newcomers had contributed significantly to the success of the right-wing Deutsche Partei which captured 12.1% of the vote even though it had been granted a Land licence only a month before polling day.[74] Meanwhile, in Bavaria the Wirtschaftliche Aufbau-Vereinigung (WAV), led by Alfred Loritz, a deeply controversial figure who was thought to have modelled himself on Adolf Hitler, collected no fewer than 14.4% of the votes cast, and, as I have shown elsewhere,[75] there is no doubt that the refugees were largely responsible for this impressive result. The newcomers' move to the right was reinforced by the outcome of the Landtag election in Schleswig-Holstein on 9 July 1950 when the newly formed refugee party, Der Block der Heimatvertriebenen und Entrechteten under Waldemar Kraft, a former captain in the SS, polled 23.4% of the vote.

Conclusion

In my introduction, I noted that historical research on the currency reform of June 1948 has focused primarily on its role in bringing

72. BHStA, MArb 822, Association for Promoting the Integration of Refugees in Coburg to Bavarian Interior Ministry, 13 August 1948.
73. For further details, see Turner, 'British Occupation Policy', pp. 698–705.
74. PRO/FO371/76738, MR of RC of Schleswig-Holstein to GB Military Governor, August 1949.
75. I. Connor, 'The Bavarian Government and the Refugee Problem', *European History Quarterly*, vol. 16 (1986), pp. 144–6.

about the impressive revival of the West German economy after the Second World War. However, there was also a less positive side to the *Währungsreform* and this chapter has endeavoured to analyse its harsh impact on one of the most vulnerable groups in post-war Germany, the refugees and expellees. It seems clear that the introduction of the deutschmark led to a deterioration in the newcomers' economic position, a view summed up by Heinrich Albertz when he commented that 'the poverty of the refugees is greater than ever since the currency reform'.[76] Local reports indicate that, in spite of the greater availability of food in the second half of 1948, some newcomers had so little money that the quality of their diet was even worse than prior to the currency reform. Similarly, the increase in the cost of rented accommodation caused great hardship to many refugees. But it was, above all, the striking increase in unemployment and the collapse of numerous refugee firms after the *Währungsreform* which resulted in many newcomers having to endure more severe economic distress from mid-1948 to the end of 1949 than at any stage since the end of the war.

The decline in the refugees' material position following the currency reform also had important political consequences. Although it has generally been assumed that the adoption of the deutschmark created political stability by laying the foundations of West Germany's 'Economic Miracle', my research would suggest that the demoralising repercussions of this measure on the newcomers made them an increasingly radical and volatile force, capable of posing a major threat to the new state which was being established. The currency reform not only prompted the refugees to unite with other disadvantaged groups to campaign for Equalisation of Burdens legislation but also made them determined to establish their own political party. Moreover, the Federal election of August 1949 demonstrated the newcomers' vulnerability to the slogans of right-wing, nationalist parties in the aftermath of the currency reform. It would appear, then, that the 'traditional' view of the *Währungsreform* of June 1948 as a measure promoting the political stability of the Bundesrepublik requires some modification in view of its damaging economic and social effects on the refugee population.

---

76. HStA Hanover, Nds. 380, Acc.62/65,577, Aufbau-Selbsthilfe der Flüchtlinge in Niedersachsen, n.d.

PART V

The Occupation as a Field of Research

12

Research on the British Occupation of Germany
Ian Turner

Introduction

This book presents the results of recent research into the immediate post-war period in Germany and in particular into the British role in the occupation. As will have become apparent, over the last five years much has been achieved in the way of charting previously unexplored terrain. It is no longer possible to claim that British policy and actions are 'virgin territory' and we are now in a much better position to judge both the scope and the limitations of British influence. However, the burgeoning bibliography on this topic notwithstanding, the period still has a high research potential. The impact of the occupation period on future developments in Germany and hence the value of research on the subject are self-evident. The availability of material is unparalleled: German and Allied official documents and records from private sources can be constructively combined with purposeful interviewing of former protagonists to yield fresh insights. Much remains to be done. Important subjects await research. Established assumptions need testing. New techniques and perspectives can be applied.

One of the purposes of this book is to encourage further exploration in this area. However, to stretch the analogy, researchers need to be acquainted with the landmarks of the existing literature, they must know how to locate material and have to be aware of the blank spots on the map. Only thus can we hope to push back the boundaries and avoid rediscovering the same terrain through ignorance.

The aim of this chapter, then, is to provide an overview of the existing literature on the British occupation, to point out the most

327

important primary sources, to record what work is at present in progress and to indicate where the opportunity for research is greatest. I have restricted myself in the main to works dealing with British policy and the British Zone but have included literature on other zones and Germany as a whole where I deem it relevant.[1]

Primary Sources

British Sources

The main archival sources for information on British policy are the official records housed at the Public Record Office in Kew. Perhaps the most important and certainly the most accessible class of records is the General Correspondence of the Foreign Office (FO 371), which is provided with a detailed and extremely useful catalogue. Researchers interested in the international aspects of policy towards Germany should consult this class as well as the Cabinet papers (CAB), the Prime Minister's Office papers (PREM) and the private office papers of Ernest Bevin (FO 800) and General Robertson (FO 1030). For further information consult Foschepoth and Steininger (1985) and Bullock (1982).

Information on how policy was formulated and implemented in Germany can be gleaned from the records of the Control Office for Germany and Austria (COGA) (FO 935–946), the London end of the occupation until 1947. A collection of reports, minutes and other papers, including the records of the various Control Council committees in Berlin, is contained in the Records Library collection (FO 1005). The files of the Control Commission for Germany (British Element) constitute the largest collection of records. Between 1949 and 1956 some 240 tons of CCG material was repatriated, a large part of this was 'weeded out' subsequently but most of what remains is now accessible to researchers.[2] Despite its size the CCG collection has proved to be something of a disappointment. No official guidelines were apparently issued to CCG officials on the preservation or disposal of official records. As a result

1. The editor would like to thank all those who took the trouble to reply to a questionnaire on research in this area. Particular thanks are due to Wolfgang Benz for permitting me to see a pre-publication copy of his excellent review article (Benz, 1987).
2. Letter from A. W. Mabbs, Keeper of Public Records to Mr Paul Dean MP, 30 July 1981.

the process was very haphazard. Many important classes were not preserved and important functions like the Intelligence Division were almost completely destroyed for security reasons. Other classes such as the Maintenance Branch were repatriated intact. The deficiencies are particularly apparent at regional level. The Länder are disproportionately represented—North Rhine-Westphalia comes off best and the amount of material available for Hamburg and Berlin is not negligible given their size. But the records for Schleswig-Holstein, and above all Lower Saxony, are very sparse. Perhaps most disappointingly, hardly any records have survived for Military Government functions at Regierungsbezirk (RB) or Kreis level. Despite the frustrations and efforts involved, however, the CCG collection remains an indispensable source of material on the occupation, particularly as regards the operations of individual divisions.

There are a number of other PRO classes which also deserve mention. WO 171 contains the war diaries of the Military Government units which crossed Europe with the Allied advance in 1944–5 and ended up assuming responsibility for the day-to-day administration of British occupied Germany. The diaries include weekly reports for Military Government units at Land (or rather Provinz), RB and Kreis level for 1945 and part of 1946 but the quantity of information declines appreciably the lower the level of government. Back in Whitehall, other British departments were also interested in occupation policy. Relevant material can be found in the Treasury papers (T 230 and T 236), on such subjects as the currency reform and occupation costs. The Board of Trade, particularly its German Division (BT 211), and the Ministry of Supply (SUPP 14 and AVIA 49), were also closely involved in attempts to protect British commercial and economic interests. The Ministry of Food records (MAF 83) contain material on the international food crisis in 1946 and its repercussions for Germany. In the nature of things, many of the documents contained in these classes are duplicates of minutes, memoranda and correspondence contained in FO 371 and in the COGA records. These records do, however, also provide a valuable insight into the *intra*departmental discussions on German policy.

As with all official British records, the thirty-year rule for releasing documents applies, at least in principle, and after some delay all the available material relating to the occupation has now been made public. Exceptions to the rule are documents retained by the department under Section 3(4) of the Official Secrets Act. The main justification for retention of material is that it may impinge on national security. It is also understood that records are retained if it is thought that they might damage or embarrass persons still alive who rendered assistance to the occupying authorities or if they might cause embarrassment to the British Royal Family. Obviously such retentions are largely arbitrary and retained documents can often be found in other files or classes.

The FO 371, COGA and CCG files are currently being catalogued by a team of archivists/historians as part of a cooperative project funded by the Bundesarchiv, the Länder archives of the former British Zone and the Stiftung Volkswagenwerk. The finished product will be a multi-volumed catalogue which will include a rough description in English of each file's contents and a subject index. This valuable aid to research is to be completed by 1991.[3] Researchers on the British occupation should not confine themselves to the PRO files, however. A number of non-governmental and quasi-governmental organisations also played a role and have kept records from the period documenting their interest in Germany. These include the Labour Party archives and the TUC library which cover respectively relations with the SPD and the German trade union movement.[4] On the business side little material has as yet been identified despite the close commercial connections between the two countries. A comprehensive inventory could only be made following exploration of the myriad company archives.[5] Business associations in Britain are generally wary of betraying the commercial confidences of their members, but some material on the attitude of the Federation of British Industry (FBI) to German industry and British occupation policy can be discerned from the FBI's records located in the Modern Record Centre at the University of Warwick. Still on the subject of industrial interests, the Imperial War Museum[6] has a full collection of the reports on German industry produced for the British Intelligence Objectives Sub-Committee (BIOS) and its Anglo-American counterpart, the Combined Intelligence Objectives Sub-Committee (CIOS). It also houses a collection of captured German material relating to military/ industrial processes. The British Broadcasting Corporation's archives[7]

3. Information kindly supplied by Rainer Schulze.
4. Labour Party Archive, 150 Walworth Road, London TUC Library Congress House, Great Russell Street, London.
5. A first attempt at a catalogue is Richmond and Stockford (1986).
6. Imperial War Museum, Lambeth Road, London.
7. BBC Written Archives Centre, Peppard Road, Caversham Park, Reading.

have interesting material on German attitudes to the occupation and the University of London has the archive of the refugee organisation 'German Educational Reconstruction'.[8]

There is no catalogue available of personal papers relating to the occupation and the German Historical Institute in London has not seen fit to undertake the task. A number of papers are deposited in the PRO.

The papers of John B. Hynd, the minister responsible for the British Zone from 1945–7, can now be seen at Churchill College, Cambridge, but they reportedly contain little of significance on policy to Germany. Harold Ingrams, the former head of Administration and Local Government Branch, also deposited his papers at Churchill College. Two political figures who took a vigorous interest in occupied Germany, Victor Gollancz and Richard Crossman, deposited their papers at the Modern Record Centre in Warwick.[9] As is the custom in Britain, many officials took papers with them on leaving government service and many are still in private possession. Austen Albu, a political appointee to the CCG's Governmental Sub-Commission, has some papers in his possession including correspondence and a very illuminating diary of his time in Berlin.[10] Lady Edith Chambers, the widow of Sir Paul Chambers (head of Finance Division 1945–7) and herself an ex-CCG official, has a small collection of papers which include a manuscript by her husband on the currency reform.[11] Barbara Wood, daughter of E. F. Schumacher, former economic adviser to the Military Governor, has access to a collection of papers relating to economic policy in Germany which was drawn upon in Wood (1984). Mr George Foggon, a former official in Manpower Division has a collection of material bequeathed to him by his friend Barber, formerly head of the CCG's Industrial Relations Branch.[12]

German Sources

As the British occupation affected virtually every aspect of German life in the Zone in some way, the list of potential archival sources is almost limitless. Obvious starting points are the main state archives. Government records in the Federal Republic are also governed by a

8. GER-Archiv, Institute of Education, University of London.
9. Modern Record Centre, University of Warwick.
10. Austen Albu, 17 The Crescent, Keymer, Hassocks, Sussex.
11. Lady Edith Chambers, 1A Frognal Gardens, Hampstead, London.
12. George Foggon, 8 Churton Place, London.

thirty-year rule and in general this is applied with fewer exceptions than in Britain. The Bundesarchiv[13] has the records of the main bizonal and trizonal organisations for the 1947–9 period. After some difficulty in the early 1980s (Schwarz, 1982), the files of the Federal ministries from 1949 onwards are also now accessible, at least in principle.[14] The records of British Zone institutions like the Zonenbeirat are housed in the Parlamentsarchiv in Bonn.[15] More important for the period of direct occupation, however, are the archives of the British Zone Länder. They contain the records of the Minister-Präsidenten and of the various Land ministries. In North Rhine-Westphalia[16] and now also in Lower Saxony[17] all surviving records for the period are accessible. This is also true for Hamburg[18] and Berlin.[19] In Schleswig-Holstein,[20] however, only the records of the Staatskanzlei and the Economics Ministry have been transferred in any quantity to the Land archive.[21] The cataloguing of the Länder records is as yet rather rudimentary so that some effort is required to find the right material. The Länder archives and the Bundesarchiv also contain a number of *Nachlässe* of prominent German politicians. Amongst the most notable are those of Hinrich Wilhelm Kopf (Lower Saxony, closed until 1992), Ernst Reuter (Berlin), Theodor Steltzer (Schleswig-Holstein) and Hans Schlange-Schöningen and Hermann Pünder (Bundesarchiv). In this context, see also Benz (1984a, pp. 191–200).

A wealth of material is also available on the political parties in the British Zone. Local and regional branches will often either have their own records or will have deposited them with public archives but the important head-office records are to be found in the archives of the party foundations.[22] This applies equally to the DGB which has an important collection of material, including the *Nachlass* of Hans Böckler and some of Agartz's papers, at its archive in

13. Bundesarchiv, Koblenz.
14. Information from Dr Werner, Bundesarchiv, 2 March 1988.
15. Parlamentsarchiv des Deutschen Bundestags, Bonn.
16. Nordrhein-Westfälisches Hauptstaatsarchiv, Düsseldorf.
17. Niedersächsiches Hauptstaatsarchiv, Hanover.
18. Staatsarchiv, Hamburg.
19. Landesarchiv Berlin, West Berlin.
20. Landesarchiv Schleswig-Holstein, Schleswig.
21. Letter to the author, 21 August 1987.
22. Archiv für christlich-demokratische Politik, Konrad-Adenauer-Stiftung, Sankt Augustin; Archiv der sozialen Demokratie der Friedrich-Ebert-Stiftung, Bonn; Archiv des deutschen Liberalismus, Friedrich-Naumann-Stiftung, Gummersbach.

Düsseldorf,[23] and to individual trade unions like the IG Metall.[24] The papers of two prominent post-war leaders, Adenauer and Erhard, are preserved by separate foundations.[25] The records of two defunct parties, the Deutsche Partei and the Deutsche Rechtspartei (*Nachlass* of Von Thadden) are located in the main archive in Lower Saxony. Material relating to the Bund der Heimatvertriebenen und Entrechteten (BHE) covering the early 1950s is located in the Institut für Zeitgeschichte in Munich.

The main industrial organisations, the Bundesverband der Deutschen Industrie (BDI) and the Bundesvereinigung deutscher Arbeitgeber Verbände (BDA), were not permitted to form until quite late but much information can be gleaned from trade associations like the Verband der Automobilindustrie[26] or the archives of companies prominent in associations.[27] A multi-volumed catalogue of company archives has been published in part (Klarmann and Wessell, 1983).

Other Countries

The most important source is the OMGUS collection of files relating to the US occupation of Germany (Weiss, 1984). Approximately one-third of the total collection has been microfilmed and the headquarters files can be viewed in the Bundesarchiv and the Institut für Zeitgeschichte. The records of the French Military Government are stored in Colmar, but access is reportedly not easy (Hudemann, 1986). The Colmar archive apparently also contains the surviving records of the Joint Export and Import Agency (JEIA). It goes without saying that the files of the Soviet Military Administration in Germany are not accessible but records of the dealings between Soviet officials and German politicians in the Soviet Zone are apparently preserved in various state archives in the GDR (Badstübner, 1987).

Published Documents

A number of collections of documents on this subject have been published. In English, Ruhm von Oppen (1955) and HMSO (1972)

---

23. DGB Bundesvorstand Archiv, Düsseldorf.
24. IG Metall, Vorstand, Zentralbibliothek, Frankfurt on Main.
25. Stiftung Bundeskanzler-Adenauer-Haus, Bad Honnef; Ludwig Erhard Stiftung, Bonn.
26. Verband der Automobilindustrie, Westendstr. 61, Frankfurt on Main.
27. See, for example, Bührer (1986).

cover the key international events. Butler and Pelly (1984) contains reprints and microfiches of the most important documents on the Potsdam Conference and is the first volume of the official series on post-war British foreign policy. A second volume on the Schuman Plan has recently been published (Bullen, 1986). Ross (1984) is a collection of Foreign Office correspondence on policy towards the Soviet Union up to the end of the war. By far the most useful source, however, is the series of US diplomatic papers, *Foreign Relations of the United States* (US Dept of State, 1960ff.) The relevant sections should be read alongside Clay's papers (Smith, 1974) and *The Forrestal Diaries* (Millis, 1951).

In German, the major collection to consult are the five volumes of *Akten zur Vorgeschichte der Bundesrepublik* (Bundesarchiv/Institut für Zeitgeschichte, 1976–83), now available in a low-priced version, and the six volumes of bizonal and trizonal records (Bundesarchiv/Institut für Zeitgeschichte, 1977). An official edition of the full minutes of the Zonal Advisory Council for the British Zone is being prepared by Kurt Jürgensen and Gabriele Stüber. On party-political developments, there is a seven-volume collection edited by Flechtheim of which volume 1 (1962) is the most relevant. The evolution of the Basic Law is covered in several volumes, of which three are already published, edited by Wernicke and Booms (1975, 1981, 1986). The minutes of Cabinet meetings for the first two years of the Federal Republic have been published (Booms, 1982, 1984), but are less interesting than anticipated. The same cannot be said for the *Rhöndorfer Ausgabe* of Adenauer's papers including the three volumes of his letters (Morsey and Schwarz, 1983–85) and the two volumes of *Teegespräche* with journalists (Morsey and Schwarz, 1984, 1986).

A recent trend has been towards the publication of documentations with short commentaries on particular issues. Thus we have a documentation on codetermination. (Müller-List, 1985) and on the Petersberg Agreement (Lademacher, 1985). We also have useful collections of documents from North Rhine-Westphalia on denazification (I. Lange, 1976) and dismantling (Scriverius, 1981). 'King of the documenters' is Rolf Steininger who has published collections on international labour (1979b), Foreign Office attitudes to the German question in 1946 (1985e), the Robertson Plan for a neutral Germany in 1948 (1983b), the Stalin Note controversy (1985d), Churchill's ideas on German reunification in 1953 (1984), and the Ruhr question (1988). Steininger has also provided a two-

334

volume history of the 1945–61 period in documents, many from British sources (1983a). In the same genre are the useful collections by Ruhl (1982, 1985).

Newspapers and Contemporary Journals

Much useful information can be gleaned from reading newspaper reports. The best British dailies are *The Times, Daily Telegraph, Financial Times* and *Manchester Guardian*. Also useful are *The Economist*, the *New Statesman* and the *Board of Trade Journal*. German papers are also valuable sources: there are numerous regional and local publications but *Die Welt* and *Die Zeit* are perhaps the most accessible. Back numbers of these and other newspaper material can be viewed at the Pressearchiv des Presse und Informationsamtes der Bundesregierung in Bonn. Perhaps most helpful for British-based researchers are the bound facsimile editions of *Der Spiegel* (1979–) which now cover the years 1947–54.

The zonal authorities also had their own publications: the *British Zone Review*, which has short snappy articles by CCG members, and the authoritative *Monthly Report of the CCG* (BE), which has regular standardised sections on all aspects of the occupation. For facts and figures there is also the *Monthly Statistical Bulletin of the CCG* (BE).

Bibliographical Aids

Apart from the usual bibliographical aids (*Historical Abstracts, Dissertation Abstracts*) a number of journals give periodic information on newly published work and reviews of the literature. The most important are the relevant sections in the rear of *Vierteljahreshefte für Zeitgeschichte* and the regular reviews in *Geschichte in Wissenschaft und Unterricht*. Other useful general sources are *Recently Published Articles* and *Das Politische Buch*. With regard to the history of the labour movement, the journal *Internationale Wissenschaftliche Korrespondenz zur Geschichte der Arbeiterbewegung* has literature reviews and information regarding ongoing research on the labour movement, as does *Militärgeschichtliche Mitteilungen* for international relations. The journal of the *Ludwig-Erhard-Stiftung, Orientierungen zur Wirtschafts- und Gesellschaftspolitik* has an annual bibliographical supplement, the *Bibliographie zur Sozialen Marktwirtschaft,* which has a useful section on the occupation period. Good audits of the available literature are provided by Uffelmann (1982) and more recently by Benz (1987). The best single work with a bibliography specifically on the British occupation is Foschepoth and Steininger (1985).

Biographical Sources

Memoirs, Autobiographies and Diaries

Two older works which are still essential are the memoirs of the US Military Governor (Clay, 1950) and the first West German Chancellor (Adenauer, Vol. 1, 1965–8). Clay's were written immediately after his period in office with the aid of official papers and the first volume of Adenauer's memoirs is both a useful history of the period and a reflection of his views on Allied policy.

Unfortunately, few works have been published by leading British figures. Neither Attlee, Bevin, nor Hynd left memoirs. Dalton's autobiography (1957, 1962), and his recently published diaries (Pimlott, 1987) upon which it was based, give an insight into his wartime role as Labour's arch-Vansittartist and his concern as Chancellor of the Exchequer for the costs of the occupation. Lord Pakenham (now Lord Longford), who succeeded the hapless Hynd as minister for the British Zone, devotes a section of his autobiography to his time in Germany but his account reveals little beyond his evident disapproval of dismantling and his preference for left-wing Christian Democrats like Karl Arnold (Pakenham, 1953). He has also recounted his recollections in Blumenwitz *et al.* (1976) and Wuermeling (1981). Gladwyn Jebb was a leading Foreign Office official and his memoirs (1972) contain much that is interesting on British plans for the post-war world. Otherwise only Lord Strang (1956, 1981), the political adviser to the Military Governor, and Sir Ivone Kirkpatrick (1959), Foreign Office official turned High Commissioner, appear to have committed their recollections to paper. In both cases their experiences in Germany in the post-war period appear as just another episode in long and successful foreign service careers.

Senior members of the Control Commission, despite the fact that in many cases they went on to attain considerable distinction in their respective fields, have left little in the way of reminiscences of their period in Germany. Montgomery's memoirs (1958) are notable for the lack of political sophistication he exhibits and for the pragmatic approach which he adopted to his duties in Germany. Sholto Douglas, who succeeded Montgomery as Military Governor in early 1946, seems to have played mainly a figure-head role in Germany. His memoirs (Douglas and Wright, 1966) convey his evident lack of enthusiasm for the job and in particular his distress at being required to act as a court of last appeal for convicted war criminals. Recent writings have portrayed Douglas as a Germano-phobe who was not averse to exploiting his position for gain (Thomas, 1984). The key figure in the Control Commission, General Robertson, has left no memoir, but some revealing reminiscences are contained in a talk which he gave at Chatham House (Robertson, 1965). General Macready, who was successively Regional Commissioner, British head of BICO and Economic Adviser to the UK High Commissioner, has written his memoirs (Macready, 1965). At the operational level there is an article and a published autobiography by the former President of the Economics Sub-Commission (Weir, 1949, 1953), a memoir by the former head of NGCC (Collins, 1985) and a retrospective contribution by the Educational Adviser (Birley, 1978). Sir Alec Cairncross, who was an economic adviser to the British team on the Berlin Level of Industry talks has recently published a slim volume based on an earlier memoir, which confirms existing accounts and gives some highly evocative background information (Cairncross, 1987). Also a good read but 'mit Vorsicht zu geniessen' is Michael Thomas's autobiography (Thomas, 1984).

Thomas was an émigré German who returned as a Military Government officer and became by turns an intermediary between General Templer and leading German politicians, a liaison officer in Bremen and an official of the CCG's Public Relations and Information Services Commission. A colourful personal account of life in the Zone is also provided by Melrose (1983). The first head of the Nord-West Deutscher Rundfunk (NWDR) has written of his struggle to change prevailing German attitudes to broadcasting (Greene, 1969), and Airey Neave records his disgust at viewing the Villa Hügel in his book on Nuremberg (Neave, 1978). There are unpublished memoirs in the papers of Austen Albu and Sir Paul Chambers. Chambers also wrote a short article on post-war West German finances (Chambers, 1948). Interestingly, there appear to be no direct equivalent on the British side of the revelatory accounts of US and Soviet occupation policy published at the height of the Cold

War by disaffected former officials (Kahn, 1950, 1964; Wheeler, 1958; Martin, 1950; Klimov, 1953).

A German industrialist who worked closely with the British authorities on the economy was Frowein (1968). Also prominent in the zonal and bizonal bureaucracies was Hermann Pünder (1968). Less than reliable as a source but indicative of a particular type of German mentality is Ahrens' work (1982) on dismantling. The Institut für Zeitgeschichte has published some diaries of the post-war period to accompany the *Akten zur Vorgeschichte*. Troeger (1985) gives a rather unflattering view of German Bizonal politicians. By contrast, British officials are regarded almost with adulation. Vaubel (1984), on the other hand, had factories in both the British and US Zones and writes scathingly of the British predilection for bureaucracy and interference. American observers of British rule in Germany include two eminent economists. W. W. Rostow has published an interesting monograph which includes impressions written at the time of Anglo-American relations in Berlin at the start of 1946 (Rostow, 1982). J. K. Galbraith's memoirs (1983) also have details of the Potter-Hyndley talks and other economic aspects of the occupation.

Also worth mentioning are some examples of contemporary reportage. Brockway (1946) is an account of a trip to the British Zone, which has revealing impressions of Control Commission figures. A more celebrated journey is documented in Gollancz (1947), which includes some graphic photographs. A biased and unreliable book, but often quoted in German critiques of Allied occupation policy, is Utley (1949).

Biographies

The most useful biographical source is Bullock's account of Bevin's period as Foreign Secretary (Bullock, 1983). Also of interest is Harris (1982) on Attlee, and Pimlott (1985) on Dalton. J. B. Hynd's reputation as a 'minnow among whales' has recently received a reassessment by Reusch (1986). There is unfortunately no biography of Robertson—a sad contrast with his American counterpart General Clay who has an excellent biography by Backer (1983), and a recently published provocative study of his time in Germany by Wolfgang Krieger (1987). Because of the fame which he subsequently gained in Malaya, General Templer has fared rather better. Cloake's biography (1985) has a chapter on his time in Germany where, if other accounts are to be believed (Thomas, 1984; Trees, Whiting and Omansen, 1978), he was the dominant figure in the zonal administration. Two other members of the Control Commission who later attained distinction in their respective fields were E. F. Schumacher and Robert Birley. Barbara Wood has written a biography which covers her father's period in Germany (Wood, 1984) and Birley's life is written by an ex-Education Branch official (Hearnden, 1984). Also of interest is the recent biography of the Duke of Portland (Howarth, 1986) whose colourful and distinguished career included a spell as head of an organisation of British industrialists with interests in Germany. Victor Gollancz has already been mentioned: a biography by Edwards (1987) includes detailed coverage of his campaign on behalf of the German people. A study of Gollancz's German activities has also been written by John Farquharson (1987). A biography of another larger-than-life character, Robert Maxwell, has been written by Tom Bower.[28] Maxwell was a press officer in Berlin during the occupation.

On the German side, there are the well-known biographies of Adenauer by Prittie (1972) and Schwarz (1986), both of which cover his bumpy relations with the British. Less informative in this respect are the biographies of Arnold (Hüwel, 1980), Kopf (Vogelsang, 1963) and Hellwege (Ehrich, 1977). A study of a leading post-war CDU politician, Hans Schlange-Schöningen has been written by Günter Trittel (Trittel, 1987). The standard work on Schumacher, who like Adenauer began his post-war political career in the British Zone, is Edinger (1965). There is also a recent set of papers on Schumacher (Friedrich Ebert Shiftung, 1988) and a new biography is being written by Wolfgang Benz.[29] As yet we have no study of Böckler, who was generally regarded as a British protégé. There are, however, some works on other trade unionists including Richter (Beier, 1978), Bleicher (K. Benz *et al.*, 1983) and Freitag (Herberts, 1954). A life of the trade union leader in the US Zone, Fritz Tarnow, is reportedly being commissioned by the Hans-Böckler-Stiftung. On the business side, Volker Berghahn is preparing a biography of the influential industrialist Otto A. Friedrich.[30]

28. Tom Bower, BBC Documentaries, London.
29. Wolfgang Benz, Institut für Zeitgeschichte, Munich.
30. Volker Berghahn, Brown University, Providence, Rhode Island, USA.

Oral History

There appears to have been no systematic attempt to record the recollections of the main protagonists in this area, either on the British or the German side. Many, of course, have already passed on and with each year that passes fewer remain. The German Historical Institute in London which is well placed to coordinate such a programme in Britain evidently has other priorities. Ulrich Reusch interviewed several officials on the British side for his book on Civil Service reform (1985a), and reportedly has transcripts of the interviews. Projects involving interviews with 'ordinary people' include the work carried out on the Ruhr by Niethammer *et al.* (Niethammer, 1983 a and b; von Plato, 1985). In Lower Saxony, the Arbeitskreis für die Geschichte Niedersachsens has a number of oral-history projects running.[31]

Biographical Aids

A large number of British officials involved in policy towards Germany went on to greater things and have attracted official honours. They thus qualify for inclusion in biographical compendia like *Who's Who* and *Who was Who*, from which much interesting information can be gleaned. Indispensable for work on the British records are the *Imperial Calendars*, the forerunner of today's *Civil Service Lists*. They cover COGA, FOGS and other Whitehall personnel, but not the CCG itself. Details of CCG positions can be pieced together from the official records, particularly FO 936, and from the minutes of evidence to the House of Commons Committee of Estimates (1946, 1947). A number of scholars give full biographical details including Reusch (1980), Schneider (1980) and Turner (1984). On the German side a post-war edition of *Wer ist Wer* was published in 1948 but the full version was not forthcoming until three years later (Habel, 1951). A fascinating collection of potted biographies of post-war German politicians, prepared by the CCG's Intelligence Staff in Lower Saxony, has been edited by Röpcke (1985).

Chronology

Apart from standard works like *Keesings Contemporary Archives*,

---

31. Prof. Helga Grebing, Arbeitskreis 'Geschichte des Landes Niedersachsens nach 1945', Ruhr-Univesität Bochum.

there is one recent noteworthy addition to the chronologies of this period: Overesch (1987) has produced a detailed day-by-day account of the 1945–49 period in two volumes. A shorter chronology is in Overesch (1979).

Histories of the Occupation Period

Academic studies of the Allied occupation of Germany started to appear within a couple of years after the end of the war. This reflects the large number of professional historians and social scientists who were involved in Military Government, particularly on the US side (Holborn, 1947; Friedrich, 1948). Balfour and Mair (1956) and Ebsworth (1960) have both become standard works, but Friedmann (1947) and Litchfield *et al.* (1953) are also worth reading. All these works were written by former participants, and only in the 1960s did non-participants tackle the area. Hymans (1960), Watt (1965) and later Balshaw (1972) had little more to go on than the few published sources and newspapers. Neither did Schwarz, but this did not prevent him from producing what is arguably still the best single volume history of the 1945–9 period (2nd edn, 1980).

The preoccupation of historians with the Cold War and the early availability of US records has produced a number of studies of the US occupation. These start with John Gimbel's remarkable case study of Marburg (Gimbel, 1961a). Gimbel subsequently produced the first history of the US occupation (1968) which was followed by the works of Latour and Vogelsang (1973), Ziemke (1975) and Peterson (1977). A recent research project by the Institut für Zeitgeschichte in Munich has produced two further studies of the US Zone (Woller, 1986; Henke, 1988). The stream of monographs and articles called for fresh syntheses and these have been provided by, amongst others, Overesch (1979) and Klessmann (1982). The two volumes by the indefatigable Wolfgang Benz (1984 a and b), and the work by Graml (1985) not only reflect the state of current research but also contain a great deal of new material in their own right. Authoritative but less accessible are the two volumes by Schwarz (1981) and Eschenburg (1983) respectively in the excessively opulent 'History of the Federal Republic'. Adolf Birke is writing the comparable volume in the rival series on the 'Germans and their Nation'.

A lot of excellent work is also contained in the many anthologies on the period. Institut für Zeitgeschichte (1976), Winkler (1979) and Becker *et al.* (1979) are recommended, as are Scharf and Schröder (1977), Foschepoth (1985b), Becker and Knipping (1986), Herbst (1986) and Broszat *et al.* (1987).

By comparison work on the French Zone is still at an early stage. The flavour of French occupation policies can nevertheless be gleaned from Willis (1967), Manz (1968), Scharf and Schröder (1983) and Hudemann (1986). Information on the Soviet Zone is even harder to come by. There is the early work by Nettl (1951), based on a journey through Eastern Germany, and later studies by von Buttlar (1980) and Mastny (1979) on policy towards Germany and the Soviet road to 'Cold War' respectively. Recent contributions by Zank (1984, 1987) deal with the economy of the Soviet Zone.

There is no overall history of the British occupation although Falk Pingel is reportedly engaged in writing one.[32] Anthologies by Scharf and Schröder (1979) and Foschepoth and Steininger (1985) deal exclusively with the British involvement in Germany and present the fruits of archival research in an accessible manner. There are also histories of the British Zone Länder in this period. For North Rhine-Westphalia there is the excellent study by Peter Hüttenberger (1973b) and the general history by Först (1970). Jürgensen (1969) is a history of Schleswig-Holstein. No comparable work for Lower Saxony yet exists but Ullrich Schneider is currently working on a political history of the period.[33] It is fair to say, however, that the full impact of the availability of British records has still to be felt.

Diplomatic History

Research on the occupation period must inevitably be placed within the context of the great changes which occurred in the international order. Cold War history is a well-developed field in its own right, which can only be briefly mentioned here. An outstanding representative of the genre, however, is Yergin (1977). Of those works which bear especially upon Germany, mention should be made of Gimbel (1968), Backer (1978) and Kuklick (1972).

32. Falk Pingel, Georg Eckert Institut für Internationale Schulbuchforschung, Brunswick.
33. Ullrich Schneider, Weissdornstr. 24, OT Harderberg, Georgsmarienhütte, West Germany.

British foreign policy from 1945 to 1950 has provided the material for several substantial studies. The early part is covered by Woodward in the official history (1976). R. Douglas (1981), Rothwell (1982), Backer (1983), Bullock (1984) and Ovendale (1985), all deal to a greater or lesser extent with the division of Germany. More details on the British *Deutschlandpolitik* are provided by Foschepoth (1982), for the first half of 1945, Schneider (1981, 1982), for the second half of that year, and by Steininger (1982a) and Pingel (1982), for the so-called *Wende* in early 1946. British policy in 1946-7 is analysed by Foschepoth (1985a) and a full account of policy up to the end of 1947 is given in Deighton (1987 a and b). The year 1948 saw the currency reform whose international implications are discussed in Turner (1987), and also the Berlin blockade. For two contrasting accounts see Shlaim (1984) and Bell (1985). Robertson's 1948 plan for a neutralised Germany is presented by Steininger (1983) and Churchill's abortive efforts in the same direction during 1953 are described in Steininger (1984) and Foschepoth (1984). No full account exists at the time of writing of British plans for the founding of the Federal Republic, but Eric Hahn is doing research in the area.[34]

An important aspect of British foreign policy during this period was the Anglo-American relationship. Apart from the older work by McNeill (1953), there are a number of monographs including Hathaway (1981), Anderson (1981), Edmunds (1986) and Harbutt (1986). A much broader account is Watt (1984). Also of interest is British policy towards western Europe and European integration (Warner, 1980, 1986; Ovendale, 1984)

Wartime Planning for Occupation Policy

The wartime discussions within Whitehall on the future direction of policy in occupied Germany is one of the best-researched topics in this area. The early study by Penrose (1953) and the official histories by Donnison (1961, 1966) and Woodward (1976) outlined the contours of British thinking. Disproportionate academic interest has been focused on the Morgenthau Plan and the dismemberment issue, both of which have generated minor bibliographies in their own right (see Turner, 1984 pp. 32 and 41). A detailed account of

34. Eric Hahn, Social Science Center, University of Western Ontario, London, Canada.

Ian Turner

the allocation of zones and a more-or-less definitive treatment of
dismemberment are provided by Sharp (1975) and Webb (1979).

Disarmament and reparations plans are dealt with in Cairncross
(1986) and the progress of British directives for the occupation is
traced in Schneider (1980, 1981). The fullest accounts yet of wartime
planning have been produced by Kettenacker (1981, 1985 a and b)
and Tyrell (1985 a and b). Both authors stress the primacy of
security in British plans.

The Institutions of the Occupation

This is an area which deserves far greater attention than it has
obtained to date. There is no monograph on the Allied Control
Council and an assessment of its activities and output is long
overdue. A research project run by the Institut für Zeitgeschichte
should remedy this situation. With the exception of Plischke (1955)
there is also no study of the Allied High Commission after 1949.

On the British side, there is very little on the structure of Military
Government in the Zone. Balfour and Mair (1956), Thies (1979),
Schneider (1980) and Turner (1984) each have some details. The
London end of the occupation is comprehensively covered by
Reusch (1980).

As far as the German institutions are concerned, Dorendorf
(1953) is an account of the activities (and frustrations) of the Zonal
Advisory Council in the British Zone. Frowein (1968) has recollections of the German administrative organisations in the British
Zone. T. Pünder (1966) and Vogel (1956, 1964, 1983) deal with the
bizonal institutions, and can be complemented by Troeger (1985).
Foelz-Schroeter (1974) covers relations between the zonal administrative organisations and the Länder governments.

The Economy

Economic Policy

The standard accounts of the German post-war recovery are Wallich
(1955) and Stolper, Häuser and Borchardt (1967). A very thorough
contemporary analysis of pre-currency reform Germany is Deutsches Institut für Wirtschaftsforschung (1948). Economic analyses of

344

Allied policy, but focusing mainly on the US side, were first provided by Balabkins (1964) and Backer (1971). Undoubtedly the landmark work in this area, however, is Abelshauser's 1975 study of the economy of the western zones, upon which he drew heavily for his later short history (Abelshauser, 1983). Since the early 1980s Abelshauser's revisionist view of the period has been fleshed out in a number of respects, but also subjected to challenge. A most useful collection of papers on the economy of the British Zone which presents the results of much of this new research is Petzina and Euchner (1984). A provocative and highly critical re-evaluation of Abelshauser's thesis has recently been furnished by Klemm and Trittel (1987).

On trade policy there are two German studies: Jerchow (1978) and Knapp (1984). Both works rely heavily on German primary sources and accept too readily the thesis that British policy was aimed at suppressing German competition. Turner (1988a) is an attempt to refute this thesis. A better picture of this whole area should emerge as a result of a research project currently being conducted by a team at the Institut für Zeitgeschichte on Germany's return to the world market. Alan Milward is also researching into Anglo-German trade competition in the 1950s.[35] Quite properly, a good deal of attention has been directed at the heavy industries of the Ruhr. As far as the coal industry is concerned, there is a contribution by Milert (1984) on British policy and a history of the sector by Abelshauser (1984). Collins (1985) has a section in his memoirs on the subject. Roseman (1987, 1988 and forthcoming) deals with British attempts to manage the manpower problems of the industry and Lynch (1981) analyses the crucial role played by France. Bührer (1986) has material on developments in the steel industry during this period and Adamsen (1981) shows how state subsidies provided the essential investment funds for the Ruhr industries whose prices remained controlled even after the currency reform. The socialisation question has been subject to saturation coverage with contributions from Rudzio (1978, 1985), Steininger (1979, c and d, 1982b, 1985b and 1988), Lademacher (1979 a and b, Lüders (1984), Greenwood (1986) and Post (1986). Decartelisation and deconcentration, by contrast have received less attention. Martin (1950) is a highly coloured account by a disaffected former OMGUS official. Forthcoming theses by Isabel Warner[36] and Al-

---

35. Alan Milward, London School of Economics and Political Science, London, England.

bert Diegmann[37] cover the deconcentration of the steel industry and the decartelisation of the coal industry respectively. A recent doctoral dissertation by Raymond Stokes (1986) deals with the breaking up of IG Farben as does an article by Kreikamp (1977). A useful overview of these deconcentration measures based on secondary sources is given in Berghahn (1986, pp. 84–110). A partial resolution of the Allied–German conflict over the deconcentration of the steel industry was of course achieved by the Schuman Plan for a European Coal and Steel Community. Details of this subject can be found in Milward (1984), Gillingham (1986) and, specifically for the German side, in Bührer (1986), Berghahn (1986) and Gillingham (forthcoming).

Allied reparations policy is a central theme of many of the works which deal with wartime planning and the onset of the Cold War. The best single study of British reparations policy is Cairncross (1986) which deals with the whole occupation period. An early study of the negotiations over the Allied Level of Industry Plan by the American participants is Ratchford and Ross (1947), now supplemented by Müller (1984) and Cairncross (1987). A more specialised but nonetheless fascinating aspect of reparations is the exploitation of industrial secrets and technological know-how. Beyerchen (1984) is mainly concerned with the US Zone. Some information on British efforts, particularly as related to the VW works, is contained in Turner (1984). The best general account to date is the relevant chapter in Bower (1987) which is a searing condemnation of British arrogance and incompetence. A fuller account of British attempts in this direction which reportedly paints a more positive view is being prepared by Karl Glatt.[38] A publication on Allied technological exploitation of German industry can also be expected shortly from the distinguished American historian, John Gimbel.[39] Gimbel has recently produced an article on the subject (1986).

Within the overall subject of reparations, a massive area still as yet barely touched is the issue of dismantling and disarmament. Several contemporary German studies were produced and these can be quite informative. However, they were written for the most part with the specific aim of exposing Allied (and especially British) dismantling policy. Good examples of this genre are the Harmssen

36. Isabel Warner, Institut für Europäische Geschichte, Mainz.
37. Albert Diegmann, Gerberstr. 12, 5138 Heinsberg.
38. Karl Glatt, European University Institute, Florence.
39. John Gimbel, Humboldt State University, Arcata, Cal., USA.

studies (1948, 1951) the works by Hasenack (1949, 1951), and the report prepared on behalf of the Minister-Präsidenten of the western zones (Büro der Ministerpräsidenten, 1948). Much of the subsequent German research on the subject echoes the attitudes of resentment and self-righteousness which dismantling evoked in Germany at the time. Treue (1967) is the earliest historical account and concentrates on Lower Saxony. The most controversial case of dismantling within that Land was the former Reichswerke in Salzgitter. A detailed and critical account based on German sources is Riedel (1967), summarised in Riedel (1983). For North Rhine-Westphalia there is a valuable collection of documents and an article by Scriverius (1979, 1981). A study of dismantling in Hamburg based on the ideal combination of German and British sources has been conducted by Alan Kramer, resulting in an article (1985) and a monograph (1989). The diplomatic conclusion to dismantling was the Petersberg Agreement, covered in depth by Lademacher (1982, 1985 a and b). Ship-building because of its obvious military applications was a major target of British dismantling and disarmament programmes. Stödter (1982) is a study of how the industry overcame these problems. Kramer (1986) has also written on the reconstruction of Hamburg docks. Grieser (1979) is a well documented local study of the demilitarisation of the port of Kiel which shows that despite massive destruction of the naval dockyards, carried out on British orders as late as 1950–1, Kiel had regained its position as a centre of ship-building by 1954. Grieser's is the only substantial study of demilitarisation, although some details of how the policy was applied in the VW works can be gleaned from Turner (1984). This also has some information on restitution: the restoration of goods seized by German companies during the Nazi occupation of Germany. Büttner (1986) has written on restitution as it related in particular to Jews.

Economic Planning

Whether or not the British and Allied plans for the German economy actually resulted in a planned economy or merely 'vegetative control', the economic plans are important for understanding the motives and priorities of British policy. Apart from Abelshauser (1975), there is a contribution by Drexler *et al.* (1985) on the aptly named Sparta Plan and an article by Ambrosius (1979) on the Bizonal economic plans. More specifically, there is an article (1984)

347

and a monograph (1985) by Drexler which look at planning in the textile industry and a contribution (1984) and book-length study (1987) by Stratmann on the chemical industry. An important aspect of the ecnomic planning system was the role played by business associates and chambers of commerce, for which see the section below on 'Capital and Labour'.

Food and Agriculture

This is an area which is well covered by the literature. Still useful as an overview is the volume prepared by Rohrbach (1955) from official German sources. Günter Trittel has written a monograph on the land reform in the British Zone (1975), which he has subsequently complemented with a study based on British material (1985a). The same author, as already mentioned, has published an article (1987) on Hans Schlange-Schöningen and two articles on the politics of hunger (1985b, 1986). John Farquharson has published widely on food and agriculture in this period (1985a and b, 1988), stressing the link between the food situation and the decline of British influence in Germany and has recently brought out an article on land reform. Gabriele Stüber (1984) has written a massive account of the food problem in the British Zone and Schleswig-Holstein in particular, relying chiefly on German sources.

The Currency Reform, Financial Policy and the Social Market Economy

The currency reform is an important and controversial issue with respect to its economic impact, its international political significance and also its consequences for the development of German society. Abelshauser's (1975) devaluation of the economic significance of the currency reform and the associated measures of liberalisation touched a chord amongst German historians in the 1970s and for a time became, often in exaggerated form, (see e.g. Ambrosius, 1977) the new conventional wisdom. A backlash was inevitable. Ritschl (1985) challenges the statistical basis of Abelshauser's thesis and Buchheim (1987, 1988) argues that the measures had a profound effect on labour productivity and distribution. Klemm and Trittel (1987) sustain this attack. The preparations for the currency reform are described, not always reliably, by Wandel (1980). The process is also analysed from a British perspective by Turner (1987). A dissertation specifically on the currency reform is being prepared by Craig Scott.[40]

British and Allied reform plans for the banking system have been analysed in a thesis by Theo Horstmann (1986). Horstmann has also published widely on this topic (1985), as well as on financial and credit policy in the British Zone (1984 a and b). Public finance in the British Zone has also been studied in some depth by Scherpenberg (1984, 1985).

The negative social effects of the currency reform were supposed to be mitigated by the *Lastenausgleich* or Equalisation of Burdens law. Schillinger (1985) is the best article on the subject. Michael Hughes is working on a study of it.[41] The Equalisation of Burdens constituted part of the social component of what became known as the 'social market economy'. Ambrosius (1979) discusses its origins from a critical standpoint. A more positive appraisal may be expected from Anthony Nicholl's forthcoming study.[42]

The Marshall Plan

There are many books which deal with the Marshall Plan, including Gimbel (1976) and more recently Mee (1984), Haberl and Niethammer (1986) and Carew (1987). To my knowledge there is nothing specifically written on the British attitude towards German participation in the European Recovery Programme (ERP). The role of Bevin in shaping the European response to Marshall's offer is a prominent theme in Bullock (1984), however. A major point of controversy is the economic impact of the ERP. Abelshauser (1975, 1986) argues that there was little effect on Germany before the end of 1948, but Knapp (1977), Hardach (1987) and, taking the textile industry as a case study, Borchardt and Buchheim (1987), attribute greater importance to the ERP. For Europe as whole, of course, there is the pathbreaking work by Alan Milward (1984), to which a new challenge has been launched by Michael Hogan (1987).

Capital and Labour

Industrialists after 1945 complained bitterly that British policy

40. Craig Scott, Department of History, University of Wisconsin, Madison, Wisconsin, USA.
41. Michael Hughes, Wake Forest University, Winston-Salem, NC, USA.
42. Anthony Nicholls, St Antony's College, Oxford University.

impeded their efforts to reorganise politically. Such complaints have found their echo in the work of Hüttenberger (1973b) and Rudzio (1981). This version has recently been challenged by Werner Plumpe (1984, 1986, 1987) who emphasises the essential *Industriefreundlichkeit* of CCG officials and the reliance of the British upon the expertise and personnel of business associations. For Schleswig-Holstein, by contrast, Menne-Haritz (1987) documents a strong antipathy amongst British officials to corporatist models of planning involving business associations as intermediaries and a clear preference for central bureaucratic control exercised via the Landeswirtschaftsämter. In Lower Saxony, at least, the Verbände seem to have been less influential during the occupation than the Industrie und Handelskammer (IHK). Rainer Schulze has uncovered some fascinating information on the operations of the IHK in that Land (Schulze, 1987 a and b) The attempts by the trade unions to attain parity of representation in the IHK are described in Pollmann (1977), Prowe (1981, 1984b) and Schneider (1984b). There is no study of the links between British industry, the CCG and German industrialists, *à la* Berghahn (1986).

The development of trade unions in the British Zone deserves greater attention. Apart from the general works by Pirker (1979) and Grebing (1966), there is the long article by Steininger (1978) which relates how under British pressure the German trade unions relinquished their favoured model of *Einheitsgewerkschaft*. This organisational principle lingered longest in Lower Saxony, which as Hartmann (1972) shows, was a bastion of the single union concept. There is no history of the British Zone Deutscher Gewerkschaftsbund (DGB) which emerged in its stead, but Peter Hubsch (1988) has written a thesis on the DGB's economic policy which describes in some detail the internal politics of the organisation. Individual trade unions are also badly served. Apart from documentations like IG Metall (1979), and local studies like Wannöffel (1984) there is little, for instance, on the metal workers', miners' or chemical workers' unions. For the public sector, however, there is a forthcoming thesis on the ÖTV by Curt Garner.[43]

A major area of interest is the origins of codetermination. Spiro (1958) had unparalleled access to material for his time. Turner (1984, 1988) has written on the British aversion to codetermination, as has C. Müller (1987). Hubsch (1988) also touches the subject. A thesis

43. Curt Garner, Technische Universität, West Berlin.

by Christoph Dartmann which covers this and related issues is also in preparation.[44] For works councils and the influence of the KPD there is the article by Klessmann (1983). The tension between works councils and unions is explored by Fichter (1987). The achievement of parity codetermination in the coal and steel industry and its connections with Adenauer's policy of European integration have been documented by Müller-List (1982, 1984, 1985) and Thum (1982).

Social Policy

A post-war German phenomenon which in its way is every bit as remarkable as the 'economic miracle' is the integration of the refugees and expellees into West German society. The last few years has seen increasing interest in this subject amongst German historians, reflected, for example, in anthologies on the subject, like Benz (1985) and works by Bauer (1982) and Becker (1987a). As far as the British Zone is concerned the concentration has been very much on the individual Länder. Thus the refugee problem in North Rhine-Westphalia is being studied by Falk Wiesemann who has written a number of contributions on the subject (Wiesemann and Kleinert, 1984; Wiesemann, 1985 a and b). In addition, a thesis by Steinert (1985) deals with refugee associations in that Land. For Lower Saxony a major research initiative on refugees has commenced under the direction of Helga Grebing.[45] The first fruits are the book by Brosius and Hohenstein (1985) on the integration of refugees in north-eastern Lower Saxony, the article by Schulze and von der Brelie-Lewien (1987) and the anthology by Schulze et al. (1987). Other projects in the initiative deal with specific localities, (e.g. Krug and Mundhenke, 1988) with the political activity of the refugees, the refugee policy of the Lower Saxony governments, the electoral behaviour of refugees and the experiences of individual refugees. For Schleswig-Holstein, the *Flüchtlingsland* par excellence, there is apparently no comprehensive history as yet. Two case studies have been published, however, one of refugees in Lübeck by Schier (1982) and one on the lack of political radicalisation of refugees in the Kiel camps (Grieser, 1980). Work has also begun on disaggregating the refugee problem by origin as well as destination:

44. Christoph Dartmann, European University Institute, Florence.
45. See above n. 31.

Karen Gatz is working on a thesis comparing the integration of East Prussian and Sudeten expellees.[46]

The refugees were not the only people on the move at the end of the war, of course. The millions of *Fremdarbeiter* who had been forced to work for the German war-effort suddenly became 'displaced persons'. Their fate is described in Jacobmeyer (1985). The same author has written too (1983) on Jewish survivors as DPs. The problem of German Jews in the British Zone is addressed by Ursula Büttner (1986). Jewish life in post-war West Germany is covered in the volume by Brumlik (1986). The re-establishment of Jewish communities in North Rhine-Westphalia is also being researched by Reynold Koppel.[47] A study of the integration into society of those persecuted under the Nazis is also underway.[48] Another sizeable group in German society during this period was made up of demobbed soldiers: James Diehl is doing a study of the integration of veterans in West Germany.[49]

A further feature of the immediate post-war period in Germany is the absence of epidemics of disease on a really large scale. Some information on the health of the population in the British Zone is contained in the book by Farquharson (1985b). The controversial issue of the prevalence of tuberculosis is discussed by two contemporary experts (Daniels and Hart, 1948, 1949). Further information on the health of the population in Lower Saxony can be found in Schneider (1980) and Turner (1984), and, in Schleswig-Holstein, in Stüber (1984). The most comprehensive treatment so far is the work by Sons (1983) on health care in North Rhine-Westphalia. The health system of course is something of a test case for the nature of British occupation policy. Given that the Labour government had staked its prestige on the creation of a National Health Service at home, surely they would press for a similar system in Germany? In fact, the British authorities, as Hockerts (1980, 1981) shows, evinced little enthusiasm for such a reform and the system of separate sickness funds was retained by default.

A further area as yet not fully explored is the impact of the social upheaval on the family as an institution. There are contributions by Wirth (1979) and Willenbacher (1987) on this subject. Closely

46. Karen Gatz, Indiana University, Bloomington, Indiana, USA.
47. Reynold Koppel, Millersville University of Pennsylvania, Millersville, Pennsylvania, USA.
48. Ursula Büttner, Forschungsstelle für die Geschichte des Nationalsozialismus in Hamburg, Hamburg.
49. James Diehl, Indiana University, Bloomington, Indiana, USA.

related is the development of the role of women in a period when men were often absent or incapacitated in one way or another. Nori Möding (1987) looks at middle-class women and their organisations. Robert Moller is researching the position of women as workers and mothers during this period,[50] and Eva Kolinsky has done work on the *Trümmerfrauen*.[51] The deprivations of post-war life also placed great strain on public morality. The Germans are usually seen as inherently law-abiding but Alan Kramer (1988) shows that the incidence of theft during the period was high and continued even after the currency reform.

Political Life

Apart from the classic works by Ebsworth, Litchfield *et al.*, Friedmann, and Balfour and Mair already cited, a number of regional and local studies deal with the recommencement of political life in the British Zone. For Lower Saxony as a whole there is the work of Ullrich Schneider (1980), which concentrates in the main on 1945, and the contribution by Karl-Heinz Nassmacher (1983). Barbara Marshall has done a study of Hanover which has given rise to an article (1986) and a book (1988). Also of interest for Hanover is the book by Grabe *et al.* (1985). Case studies also exist for Göttingen (Feselfeldt, 1962) and Wolfsburg (Turner, 1984). North Rhine-Westphalia has the general work by Hüttenberger (1973b), but also an excellent study of the Ruhr towns by Hartmut Pietsch (1978), which amongst other things brings out the conservative *Personalpolitik* of local military government officers. For Cologne there is a volume of essays based on local sources (Dann, 1981). There are apparently no comparable works for Schleswig-Holstein or Hamburg. Robert Eriksen is currently studying the political impact of the British occupation in Germany.[52]

The development of political parties in West Germany has unleashed prodigious energy amongst historians and political scientists alike. As Wolfgang Benz notes in a recent review (Benz, 1987), a bibliographical survey of the post-war history of the CDU (Hahn, 1982) alone, lists nearly 12,000 titles. A good starting point is the two-volume *Parteien-Handbuch* (Stöss, 1983, 1984). Other recent works on the political parties include Becker (1987b) for the CDU,

50. Robert Moller, University of California, Santa Cruz, USA.
51. Eva Kolinsky, Aston University, Birmingham, England.
52. Robert Eriksen, Olympic College, Bremerton, USA.

Klotzbach (1982) for the SPD and two books on the FDP: Hein (1985) and K. Schröder (1985). A new study by Horstwalter Heitzer on the CDU in the British Zone is reportedly now complete. Lower Saxony has attracted a number of *Parteiengeschichten*: von Petzold (1983) and Franke (1980) cover aspects of the SPD, Marten (1978) deals with the FDP and two contributions address the formation and activities of the NLP/DP (Rode, 1981, Schulze, 1985). A fascinating aspect of party history is the relationship between the SPD and the Labour Party. The tensions between the two parties go back to when the SPD leadership was in exile in London as Anthony Glees shows (1982). As Burridge (1976) and Grantham (1979) point out, there were strong Germanophobic tendencies in the Labour leadership. The best study of relations in the immediate post-war period is Steininger (1979a). Paterson (1988) reassesses the relationship in the light of recent evidence on the attitudes of Labour politicians.

The type of party system which the British hoped would emerge in West Germany was, of course, influenced by the choice of electoral system. The British were wary of proportional representation and introduced a modified majority system for the local elections of 1946. The genesis of this voting system and its eventual fate is described in Turner (1983). The discussions on the electoral system to be adopted for the Landtag elections of 1947 are outlined in Brautmeier (1987). By far the most comprehensive treatment of how electoral systems evolved out of the interplay of Allied intentions and German politics is Lange (1975).

Equally distinctive was the British approach to local government. The standard work on this important subject is Rudzio (1968). For the influence of Allied policy on Länder constitutions there are contributions by Pfetsch (1985, 1986) and for the genesis of the *Grundgesetz* there is the article by Grabbe (1978), a dissertation by Zimmermann (1983) and books by Benz (1984 a and b) and Pfetsch (forthcoming). After Potsdam the British announced radical plans to alter the position in German society of the state officials, the Beamte. Ulrich Reusch (1985 a and b) documents how these intentions come to nought.

In order to ensure the democratic reconstruction of Germany, former Nazis and other anti-democratic elements were to be removed from positions of authority or denazified. The British denazification programme has received a good deal less attention than the measures in the US Zone. Nevertheless there is the standard work by Fürstenau (1969), an important collection of documents by I. Lange (1976) and a study by Krüger (1982) of denazification in North-Rhine Westphalia.

Empirical evidence of denazification is presented in Schneider (1980), which deals notably with the purging of the police, and Turner (1984). Schneider has also written a study of the denazification of university teachers in Lower Saxony (forthcoming). Tom Bower's passionate but overdrawn account of British failures to prosecute war criminals (1981), also has some material on denazification. Jill Jones is writing a dissertation on the genesis of British denazification policy.[53]

Cultural Life and Political Culture

There has been a revival of interest of late in the cultural life and everyday aspects of the 1945–48 period in Germany. Perhaps this trend was inevitable given the enormous interest generated in the Federal Republic by historical descriptions of life under National Socialism. As Wolfgang Benz reports (1987), a new genre of *Trümmerlyrik* has emerged in response to recent historical anniversaries, which, chiefly through the medium of photographs, portrays a romantic vision of life among the ruins. If the motive behind such publications is the shrewd exploitation of nostalgia, the generally positive view of the pre-1948 period which they convey also features in the more serious literature, such as the works of Hermann Glaser (1985 a and b, 1986). Glaser documents the post-war revival of literary and dramatic activity in Germany and its abrupt decline after the currency reform. His researches lead him to the conclusion that after 1948 West Germans largely turned their backs on culture in headlong pursuit of material wealth. How accurate a picture this is, remains to be seen. One suspects that the pre-currency-reform period was atypical of German history. At least if the findings of a recent oral history project are to be believed, the average Ruhr worker viewed the decade of the 1940s *in toto* as a period of disruption and upheaval squeezed between periods of normality in the 1930s and 1950s (Niethammer 1983 a and b, von Plato, 1985). Studies of cultural activities during the period at the local level have reportedly been prepared by Wolfgang Horn (Düsseldorf) and

53. Jill Jones, Department of History, Manchester University.

Gudrun Ramthun (Krefeld).

If, as Glaser and others like Reulecke (1987) seem to imply, there was a cultural restoration after 1948, to what extent did British policy contribute towards it? Most of the literature which addresses this question does so under the rubric of re-education. Much has already been written on this subject. The standard works include an article by Koszyk (1978), the study of British re-education policy by Pakschies (1979), and the anthology edited by Hearnden (1978), all published before the official British files had become available. More recently we have conference volumes by Pronay and Wilson (1985) and Heinemann (1981). The doyen of writing on British re-education policy is Kurt Jürgensen (1979, 1981, 1983). Arguably Jürgensen attributes greater importance to British efforts in this direction than they deserve, given the overall allocation of resources to re-education within the Control Commission. Moreover, whilst British scholars like Welch (1987) and Turner (1984) are sceptical of the long-term impact of British policy on German political culture, Jürgensen maintains that the impact of the British example on individual members of the elite, although unquantifiable, was nevertheless significant. The findings of a major research project on re-education 1945–55 directed by David Welch at the Polytechnic of Central London should enliven this debate once more. On German political culture in general a good starting point is a recent anthology edited by Berg-Schlösser and Schissler (1987). The impact of the British occupation on German public opinion is discussed in Marshall (1980). A forthcoming article from Ian Connor takes issue with Marshall's assertion that attitudes towards the occupiers improved after the Berlin blockade.[54]

Re-education, of course, is a portmanteau word which can be interpreted in a number of ways. Clearly an important theme of re-education is the reform, of rather lack of reform, of the educational system. On this there is a monograph by Halbritter (1979) and contributions in the volumes by Hearnden (1978) and Heinemann (1981), but no study as yet using British records. Higher education also resisted British reform attempts as is shown by David Phillips (1980, 1981, 1983 a and b) and Falk Pingel (1985). There appear to be no comparable studies on adult education.

A subject almost totally neglected to date is British policy towards German youth. German historians seem more interested in the

54. Ian Connor, University of Ulster, Coleraine, Northern Ireland.

Wandervögel than the *Edelweisspiraten*. There is a chapter on youth
groups in Turner (1984) and, happily, a study of youth in Lower
Saxony is being conducted by Friedhelm Boll.[55] Also worthy of
mention is the chapter on youth by Ulrich Chaussy in Benz (1983)
and the paper on the socialisation of youth in the Ruhr mining
towns by Roseman (1987). Another interesting but apparently
unresearched subject is the twinning of German and British towns
from 1947 onwards and the contribution which it made to overcoming the international isolation of West Germany after the war.

Although not generally considered part of re-education, British
policy towards the German churches is an important but little-
known aspect of the occupation. Ian Connor has done research on
the strained relations between Military Government and the Roman
Catholic Church in North Rhine-Westphalia and Fionualla Corry
is preparing a thesis on the subject which underlines the suspicions
which policy-makers in Whitehall harboured towards the churches
as a consequence of their role in the Third Reich.[56] The standard
work on church–state relations, Spotts (1973), also covers the
occupation period in some detail. More recently Conway (1986) has
looked at the involvement, or lack of involvement, of the churches
in re-education. A bibliography on the Catholic Church in the
post-war period is Von Hehl and Hürtem (1983).

The other main topic encompassed by the term re-education is
policy towards what we now call the media. Here the most notable
contribution is the work of Kurt Koszyk (1983, 1986), which is
based on both British and German sources. Also useful are the
studies by Norbert Frei (1983), on press in the Federal Republic,
and Arnulf Kutsch (1987), on the *Lizenzpresse* in the British Zone.
As the main organ of British policy in Germany, the newspaper *Die
Welt* has rightly attracted scholarly attention, notably by Harenberg
(1976) and Fischer (1978). At the other end of the spectrum,
communist publications were soon at loggerheads with the British
authorities as Perk (1979) recalls. Many of West Germany's most
successful and influential journals first saw the light of day in the
British Zone. There is nothing apparently on *Stern* or *Die Zeit*, but
a recent memoir by Brawand (1987) provides an interesting insight
into the early days of *Der Spiegel*. In the area of broadcasting,
British hopes were set on establishing the Nordwestdeutscher-

55. See n. 31.
56. Fionualla Corry, c/o St Antony's College, Oxford University.

rundfunk as a German version of the British Broadcasting Corporation. Greene (1969) and Tracey (1983) show why Hugh Greene's efforts failed to overcome German resistance. There is nothing on the theatre, but Brennan (1987) deals with the question of which films the Germans were to be permitted to see.

Appendix

The Apparatus of Occupational Rule

Any attempt to outline the apparatus of government for the occupation of Germany must of course recognise that the system was constantly evolving in response to international political developments and the more practical demands of administration.[1] This brief and oversimplified description is intended simply as a guide for readers of this volume.

Establishing Occupational Rule in Germany

Military Government units had followed the advancing Allied forces through western Europe after the Normandy landings. From the start of 1945 these units were allocated to specific geographical areas within the British Zone and assumed total responsibility for administering the Zone following the redeployment of Allied forces to the agreed areas in June 1945. A hierarchy of regional Military Government was formed with P Detachments at Province headquarters, L/R Detachments at the smaller Länder and the Regierungsbezirk, and K Detachments at Kreis level.

The Control Commission for Germany (British Element)—known as the Control Commission or CCG—took over the administration of the British Zone in late August 1945. The existing Military Government detachments were subsumed within the CCG, and acted as the Control Commission's executive arm on the ground. At the top the direction of the Control Commission was split initially between Advanced Headquarters situated in Berlin and the Main Headquarters or Zonal Executive Offices (ZEO) in the Zone. The ZEO were dispersed along functional lines amongst a

---

1. This appendix does not deal with the machinery of wartime planning which is covered in Donnison (1961, 1964). The editor is indebted to Rainer Schulze for his comments on a first draft of this outline.

number of small but relatively intact towns in Westphalia: Lubbecke, Minden, Herford and Bad Oeynhausen. Overall operational responsibility for the British Zone was vested in the Commander-in-Chief who was also Military Governor. Field Marshal Montgomery, the first incumbent, was replaced by Marshal of the Royal Air Force Sir Sholto Douglas in early 1946. However, Douglas, who later became a Labour Peer, was mainly a figurehead; the principal figure in the British administration in Germany was Lieutenant General (later General) Sir Brian Robertson who was Deputy Military Governor (DMG) under both Montgomery and Douglas before taking over from the latter in November 1947. Robertson and his close advisers were based in Berlin for the most part, essentially because the capital city was the seat of the machinery for Allied rule in Germany: the Allied Control Authority (ACA). Administration of policy in the Zone in the first phase of the occupation was the responsibility of Robertson's Chief of Staff, General Templer. The DMG attended two weekly meetings of representatives from the Divisions in Berlin (referred to as BERCOS) and a further meeting each week in Lubbecke (ZONCOS). In addition, there were periodic meetings with the P Detachment commanders (later Regional Commissioners) referred to as RECOS.

The British End of the Occupation of Germany

Back in London a number of government departments were interested in the conduct of British policy in Germany. For the first months of its existence the Control Commission was formally responsible to the War Office, but took its lead from the Foreign Office and its German Department. In October 1945, however, a separate body was set up to oversee occupation policy. This was the Control Office for Germany and Austria (COGA) located in Norfolk House in London. Its political head was the Chancellor of the Duchy of Lancaster, John B. Hynd. Hynd was a junior member of the Labour government, and COGA was often referred to disparagingly as the 'Hyndquarters'. The organisational structure of COGA in 1946 is shown in fig. 1 (p. 364). The detachment of responsibility for Germany from the Foreign Office was to prove dysfunctional. The Foreign Office had far greater status in Whitehall and key policy decisions affecting international politics were reserved to Ernest Bevin, the Foreign Secretary and a dominant figure in Cabinet. COGA was starved of information from the British Zone and Control Office officials were often regarded by the CCG in Germany as meddling bureaucrats. Robertson also insisted that communication from COGA to the Control Commission had to be channelled through his office. At the same time, Robertson himself maintained direct contacts with Bevin and the Foreign Office. In mid-1947 this unsatisfactory situation was recognised by the absorption of COGA into the FO. The Foreign Office German Section (FOGS), as it was called, comprised COGA and the old German Department of the FO, now renamed the German Political Department (see fig. 2, p. 365). FOGS was placed under the political direction of Lord Pakenham, but as before Bevin's shadow loomed large.

Other departments in Whitehall also sought to influence occupation policy. The Treasury was interested in reducing the costs of occupation, the Board of Trade's German Division and the Ministry of Supply hoped for machinery and know-how from German industry, the Ministry of Food competed with the CCG for scarce food supplies, the defence ministries were interested in security matters, and so on. Interdepartmental committees therefore sprang up to resolve conflicts of interest and CCG representatives flew over regularly from Germany to participate. Ultimately, policy decisions of significance were taken in Cabinet or in Cabinet committee, notably the Overseas Reconstruction Committee. But by this stage in the proceedings, of course, most of the differences had already been ironed out.

In theory, the administration of the British Zone was subject to parliamentary scrutiny. In practice, debates on German affairs were infrequent and interest tended to be confined to a few MPs with a special knowledge or concern for Germany like Richard Crossman, Ashley Bramall and Richard Stokes. A more significant control organ was the House of Commons Committee on Estimates which investigated the occupation of Germany on two occasions, travelling widely in Germany to collect evidence and producing two penetrating reports.

Policy, of course, was not just determined by government departments. British pressure groups with a vested interest or a moral concern for development in Germany were frequently involved. From the Bank of England to the Boy Scouts they all sought to influence British policy.

Appendix

The Apparatus of Four-Power Rule

In Berlin, the highest level within the ACA was the Allied Control Council (ACC). All Allied legislation had to be agreed unanimously in the ACC. Before any legislation could reach the Military Governors, however, it had first to negotiate the sub-structure of the quadripartite bureaucracy. Beneath the Control Council was the important Co-ordinating Committee upon which the DMGs or equivalent were represented. In practice a great deal of the 'nitty-gritty' political questions were resolved at this level, possibly because of the calibre of the DMGs (e.g. Robertson for the UK and Clay for the US), but presumably also because agreement at that level could in an emergency always be revoked in the ACC. Beneath the Co-ordinating Committee there were twelve Directorates each with a separate function (see fig. 3, p. 366). The Directorates were originally intended to shadow the central German administrations, but these failed to materialise. The Directorates corresponded to the Divisions within the CCG responsible for administration in the Zone and the Chiefs of the Divisions were the British representatives at the monthly meetings of the Directorates. Within each Directorate the various policy aspects of the function were apportioned to specialist committees, sub-committees and working parties.

Zonal, Bizonal and Trizonal Rule

In the British Zone the shape of Military Government was constantly changing. The size of the CCG peaked in early 1947 at just under 26,000 civilian and military employees (see fig. 4). The breakdown of personnel by functions is depicted in fig. 5. The evolution of the CCG's formal structure between 1945 and 1949 is shown in fig. 6 (a–f). Note the combination of regional and functional organisations. It should also be recognised that the personalities involved and the personal relationships which developed were often as or more important than the official structure of the Control Commission. After 1945 the term Military Government was officially reserved for the regional detachments. Following the *Gebietsreform* these were located at Land, Regierungsbezirk (RB) and Kreis level. At Land level the detachments were divided into branches corresponding to the various CCG divisions. Some of

362

these divisions were also represented in the 'functions' at RB level. At Kreis level the staff limitations for the most part precluded formal demarcation by divisions.

Over time this regional structure inevitably changed. For a time in 1946 an intermediate coordinating stage between RB and Kreis level was introduced, the so-called 'Kreis Group'. This was quickly dropped as the pressure from Britain to reduce staff forced cutbacks in the number of officers, particularly at local level. Closely associated with this was the less interventionist stance adopted by the occupying authorities. Military commanders at Land level became Regional Commissioners, Kreis Detachments became Kreis Resident Officers and so on.

In addition to the official Control Commission apparatus, there were a number of other British control organisations, nominally independent of the CCG, which had responsibility for key economic sectors. The North German Coal Control (NGCC), the North German Iron and Steel Control (NGISC) and the North German Timber Control (NGTC) are prime examples. Following fusion, these became bipartite organisations, so that for example the NGCC became the UK/US Coal Control Group. Fusion also produced new offices like the Joint Export and Import Agency (JEIA) in Frankfurt. With the linking up of the French Zone in 1949 these bodies became tripartite.

By 1946 the British had become disillusioned with four-power rule, and the focus of occupation policy shifted for a short time back to the Zone. A massive new headquarters complex was planned in Hamburg but local protest and parliamentary criticism in Britain put an end to the project. In any case, economic fusion with the US Zone meant the new emphasis was on bizonal (German) and bipartite (US–British) structures . The first bizonal German administration was set up in early 1947 and the functions were dispersed initially in five different locations. Above each department an Anglo-American Bipartite Group was established, responsible to separate Bipartite Panels of divisional heads and ultimately to the Bipartite Board, consisting of the Military Governors in Berlin. In June 1947 the Bizone was reorganized and the administration centralised in Frankfurt. Allied supervision was now exercised through Bipartite Panels in the Bipartite Control Office (BICO) located in the old IG Farben building in Frankfurt and headed jointly by Generals Adcock (US) and Macready (UK). In early 1948 the British and American staffs in BICO were merged to form joint

Appendix

Fig. 1 The Control Office for Germany and Austria

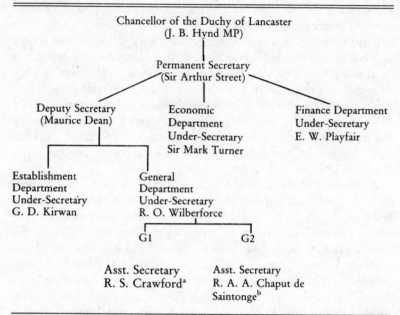

[a] Communications; Service questions; legal questions; civil aviation, refugees, distressed and displaced persons and prisoners-of-war; public health; censorship.
[b] German and Austrian political, central and local government questions; religious affairs; trade unions; social insurance; labour; police.
Source: Reusch (1980), pp. 437–8.

Bipartite Groups shadowing the German administration.

With the founding of the Federal Republic in May 1949, the occupation entered a new phase. In September BICO was dissolved. The western Allies, however, retained substantial powers by virtue of the Occupation Statute and these were exercised via the Allied High Commission which was located in the Petersberg near Bonn. The British element was the office of the UK High Commissioner (see fig. 6e). Two other bodies were also supposed to control West Germany: the Military Security Board, about which little is yet known, and the International Authority for the Ruhr, which turned out to be something of a paper tiger.

Fig. 2 The Foreign Office General Section, October 1947

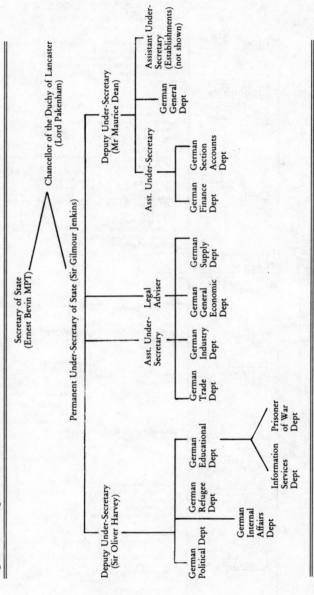

Secretary of State
(Ernest Bevin MPT)

Chancellor of the Duchy of Lancaster
(Lord Pakenham)

Permanent Under-Secretary of State (Sir Gilmour Jenkins)

Deputy Under-Secretary
(Sir Oliver Harvey)

German Political Dept

German Internal Affairs Dept

German Refugee Dept

German Educational Dept

Information Services Dept

Prisoner of War Dept

Asst. Under-Secretary

German Trade Dept

German Industry Dept

German General Economic Dept

German Supply Dept

Legal Adviser

Deputy Under-Secretary
(Mr Maurice Dean)

Asst. Under-Secretary

German Finance Dept

German Section Accounts Dept

German General Dept

Assistant Under-Secretary (Establishments) (not shown)

Source: Reusch (1980), p. 443.

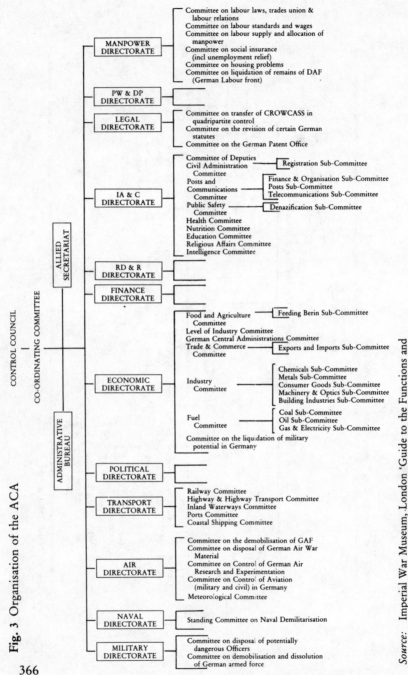

Fig. 3 Organisation of the ACA

366

CONTROL COUNCIL

CO-ORDINATING COMMITTEE

ALLIED SECRETARIAT

ADMINISTRATIVE BUREAU

MANPOWER DIRECTORATE
- Committee on labour laws, trades union & labour relations
- Committee on labour standards and wages
- Committee on labour supply and allocation of manpower
- Committee on social insurance (incl unemployment relief)
- Committee on housing problems
- Committee on liquidation of remains of DAF (German Labour front)

PW & DP DIRECTORATE

LEGAL DIRECTORATE
- Committee on transfer of CROWCASS in quadripartite control
- Committee on the revision of certain German statutes
- Committee on the German Patent Office

IA & C DIRECTORATE
- Committee of Deputies
- Civil Administration Committee — Registration Sub-Committee
- Posts and Communications Committee — Finance & Organisation Sub-Committee / Posts Sub-Committee / Telecommunications Sub-Committee
- Public Safety Committee — Denazification Sub-Committee
- Health Committee
- Nutrition Committee
- Education Committee
- Religious Affairs Committee
- Intelligence Committee

RD & R DIRECTORATE

FINANCE DIRECTORATE

ECONOMIC DIRECTORATE
- Food and Agriculture Committee — Feeding Berin Sub-Committee
- Level of Industry Committee
- German Central Administrations Committee
- Trade & Commerce Committee — Exports and Imports Sub-Committee
- Industry Committee — Chemicals Sub-Committee / Metals Sub-Committee / Consumer Goods Sub-Committee / Machinery & Optics Sub-Committee / Building Industries Sub-Committee
- Fuel Committee — Coal Sub-Committee / Oil Sub-Committee / Gas & Electricity Sub-Committee
- Committee on the liquidation of military potential in Germany

POLITICAL DIRECTORATE

TRANSPORT DIRECTORATE
- Railway Committee
- Highway & Highway Transport Committee
- Inland Waterways Committee
- Ports Committee
- Coastal Shipping Committee

AIR DIRECTORATE
- Committee on the demobilisation of GAF
- Committee on disposal of German Air War Material
- Committee on Control of German Air Research and Experimentation
- Committee on Control of Aviation (military and civil) in Germany
- Meteorological Committee

NAVAL DIRECTORATE
- Standing Committee on Naval Demilitarisation

MILITARY DIRECTORATE
- Committee on disposal of potentially dangerous Officers
- Committee on demobilisation and dissolution of German armed force

Source: Imperial War Museum, London 'Guide to the Functions and Organisation of the Allied Control Authority and the Control Commission for Germany (British Element) Provisional)' British Saone

Fig. 4 Control Commission Personnel

The graph below shows the run-down in strengths of military and civilian staffs of the Control Commission (British Element)

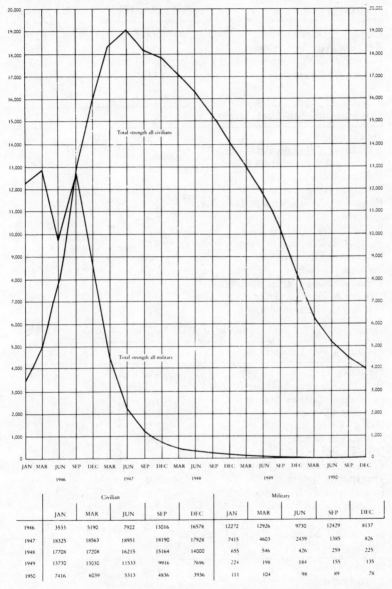

	Civilian					Military				
	JAN	MAR	JUN	SEP	DEC	JAN	MAR	JUN	SEP	DEC
1946	3533	5190	7922	13016	16578	12272	12926	9730	12429	8137
1947	18325	18563	18951	18190	17928	7415	4603	2439	1385	826
1948	17708	17208	16215	15164	14000	655	546	426	259	225
1949	13730	13030	11533	9916	7696	224	198	184	155	135
1950	7416	6039	5313	4836	3936	111	104	98	89	78

Source: Quarterly Report of the UK High Commissioner for Germany, No. 1, 1951.

367

Fig. 5 Establishment of the Control Commission as at 1 April 1947, and as planned for 1 April 1948

Headquarters & Quadripartite Organisation	1 April 1947	1 April 1948
Central Administration	1,481	1,219
Regional Administration	1,249	968
Local Administration Services	2,656	2,629
Car Organisation	2,411	2,200
Totals	7,797	7,016

Governmental Sub-Commission		
Headquarters	56	
Education, Religious Affairs & Health Administration Section	20	
Public Health	88	
Religious Affairs	33	1,767	1,360
Education, Monuments & Fine Arts	234	
Education Adviser	—	
Public Safety	725	
Posts & Telecommunications	611	
Manpower Division	300	315
Political Division	60	60
Public Relations & Information Services Control Group	374	250
PW & DP Division	126	—
Totals	2,627	1,985

Economic Sub-Commission		
Headquarters	140	
Bipartite Economic Group	67	
Building Industries Branch	187	
Industry Division	1,081	1,951	1,391
Fuel & Power Division	338	
Commerce Division	138	
Joint Export/Import Agency	—	
Food & Agriculture Division	354	190
Transport Division	586	335
Reparations, Deliveries & Restitutions Division	354	361
Totals	3,245	2,277

Other Units		
Finance Division	691	540
Legal Division	746	669
Intelligence Division	3,913	2,826

Combined Services Division	48	
Civil Aviation Branch	—	236
Interpreters Group	579	350
British Families Education Services (CCG)	100	101
Totals	6,077	4,722
Total staff within the manpower ceiling of 20,000	19,746	16,000

Staff Engaged on functions other than for the purpose of the Control of Germany	1 April 1947	1 April 1948
North German Timber Control	466	466
Political Division (British Interests Branch)	105	40
British Families Education Service (Forces element)	199	201
'T' Force (including 'T' Force Car Units)	2,246	1,175
RD & R Division (Dismantling & Packing)	130	120
Ministry of Supply Disposals Branch	291	200
PW & DP Division Detachments	892	892
Demolition Units	275	300
Totals	4,604	3,394

Source: House of Commons (1947), pp. xxxiv–xxxv.

369

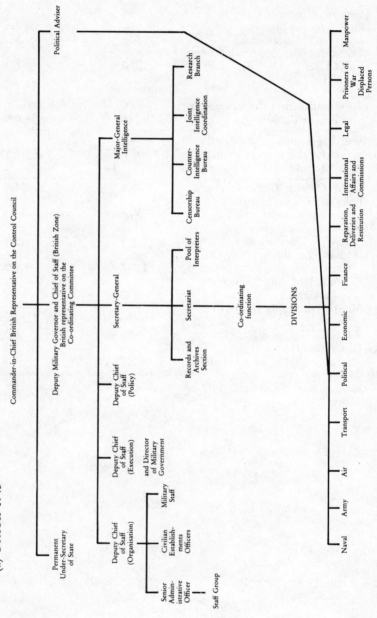

Fig. 6 The Evolution of the Structure of the CCG(BE) 1945–9

(a) October 1945

(b) June 1946

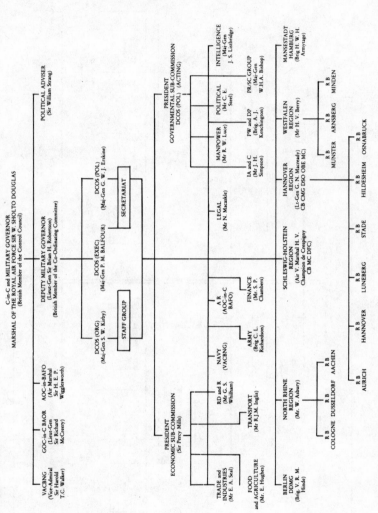

C-in-C and MILITARY GOVERNOR
MARSHAL OF THE ROYAL AIR FORCE SIR W. SHOLTO DOUGLAS
(British Member of the Control Council)

POLITICAL ADVISER
(Sir William Strang)

VACIGNG
(Vice-Admiral
Sir Harold
T.C. Walker)

GOC-in-C BAOR
(Lieut-Gen
Sir Richard
McCreery)

AOC-in-BAFO
(Air Marshal
Sir H. E. P.
Wigglesworth)

DEPUTY MILITARY GOVERNOR
(Lieut-Gen Sir Brian H. Robertson)
(British Member of the Co-Ordinating Committee)

DCOS (ORG)
(Maj-Gen S. W. Kirby)

DCOS (EXEC)
(Maj-Gen P. M. BALFOUR)

DCOS (POL)
(Maj-Gen G. W. J. Erskine)

STAFF GROUP

SECRETARIAT

PRESIDENT
ECONOMIC SUB-COMMISSION
(Sir Percy Mills)

PRESIDENT
GOVERNMENTAL SUB-COMMISSION
DCOS (POL) (ACTING)

TRADE and
INDUSTRIES
(Mr E. A. Seal)

FOOD
and AGRICULTURE
(Mr. E. Hughes)

RD and R
(Mr G. S.
Whitham)

TRANSPORT
(Mr R.J.M. Inglis)

NAVY
(VACIGNG)

ARMY
(Brig C. L.
Richardson)

A R
(AOC-in-C
BAFO)

FINANCE
(Mr S. P.
Chambers)

LEGAL
(Mr N. Macaskie)

IA and C
(Mr J. H.
Simpson)

MANPOWER
(Mr R. W. Luce)

PW and DP
(Brig. A. J.
Kenchington)

POLITICAL
(Mr C. E.
Steel)

PR/SC GROUP
(Maj-Gen
W.H.A. Bishop)

INTELLIGENCE
(Maj-Gen
J. S. Lithbridge)

BERLIN
DDMG
(Brig. V. R. M.
Hinde)

NORTH RHINE
REGION
(Mr. W. Asbury)

SCHLESWIG-HOLSTEIN
REGION
(Air V. Marshal H. V.
Champion de Crespigny
CB MC DFC)

HANNOVER
REGION
(Lt-Gen G. N. Macready)
CB CMG DSO OBE MC)

WESTFALEN
REGION
(Mr H. V. Berry)

MANSESTADT
HAMBURG
(Brig H. W. H.
Armytage)

R B
COLOGNE

R B
DUSSELDORF

R B
AACHEN

R B
AURICH

R B
HANNOVER

R B
LUNEBERG

R B
STADE

R B
HILDESHEIM

R B
MUNSTER

R B
ARNSBERG

R B
MINDEN

R B
OSNABRUCK

(c) March 1947

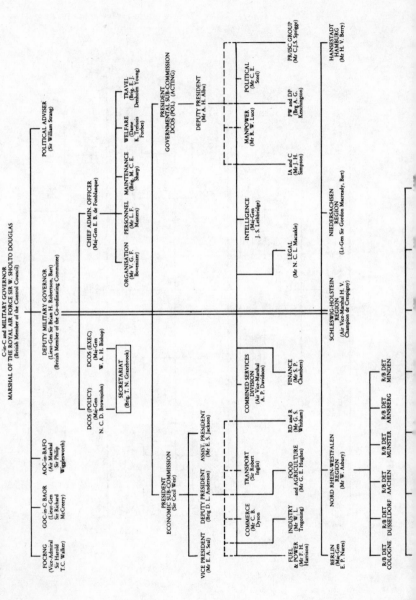

C-in-C and MILITARY GOVERNOR
MARSHAL OF THE ROYAL AIR FORCE SIR W. SHOLTO DOUGLAS
(British Member of the Control Council)

FOCBNG
(Vice-Admiral Sir Harold T.C. Walker)

GOC-in-C BAOR
(Lieut-Gen Sir Richard McCreery)

AOC-in-BAFO
(Air Marshal Sir Philip Wigglesworth)

POLITICAL ADVISER
(Sir William Strang)

DEPUTY MILITARY GOVERNOR
(Lieut-Gen Sir Brian H. Robertson, Bart)
(British Member of the Co-ordinating Committee)

DCOS (POLICY)
(Maj-Gen N. C. D. Brownjohn)

DCOS (EXEC)
(Maj-Gen W. A. H. Bishop)

SECRETARIAT
(Brig. T. N. Grazebrook)

CHIEF ADMIN. OFFICER
(Maj-Gen E. B. de Fonblanque)

ORGANISATION
(Mr V. G. F. Bovenizer)

PERSONNEL
(Mr L. F. Masters)

MAINTENANCE
(Brig. M. C. E. Sharp)

WELFARE
(Dame K. Trefusis Forbes)

TRAVEL
(Brig. E. J. Denholm Young)

PRESIDENT
ECONOMIC SUB-COMMISSION
(Sir Cecil Weir)

DEPUTY PRESIDENT
(Brig. D. L. Anderson)

ASSIST. PRESIDENT
(Mr E. S. Jackson)

VICE PRESIDENT
(Mr E. A. Seal)

COMMERCE
(Mr C. B. Dyson)

TRANSPORT
(Sir Rupert Inglis)

COMBINED SERVICES
DIVISION
(Air Vice-Marshal A. P. Davidson)

FINANCE
(Mr S. P. Chambers)

PRESIDENT
GOVERNMENTAL SUB-COMMISSION
DCOS (POL.) (ACTING)

DEPUTY PRESIDENT
(Mr A. H. Albu)

FUEL
& POWER
(Mr F. H. Harrison)

INDUSTRY
(Mr W. L. Tregoning)

FOOD
and AGRICULTURE
(Mr G. E. Hughes)

RD and R
(Mr G. S. Whitham)

INTELLIGENCE
(Mr J. S. Lethbridge)

LEGAL
(Mr N. C. L. Macackie)

IA and C
(Mr J. H. Simpson)

MANPOWER
(Mr R. W. Luce)

PW and DP
(Brig. A. G. Ketchingman)

POLITICAL
(Mr C. E. Steel)

PR/ISC GROUP
(Mr C. J. S. Sprigge)

BERLIN
(Maj-Gen E. P. Nares)

NORD RHEIN-WESTFALEN
REGION
(Mr W. Asbury)

SCHLESWIG-HOLSTEIN
REGION
(Air Vice-Marshal H. V. Champion de Crespigny)

NIEDERSACHSEN
REGION
(Lt-Gen Sir Gordon Macready, Bart)

HANSESTADT
HAMBURG
(Mr H. V. Berry)

R/B DET
COLOGNE

R/B DET
DUSSELDORF

R/B DET
AACHEN

R/B DET
MÜNSTER

R/B DET
ARNSBERG

R/B DET
MINDEN

(d) October 1948

HEADQUARTERS OF THE MILITARY GOVERNOR AND COMMANDER-IN-CHIEF, ORGANIZATION

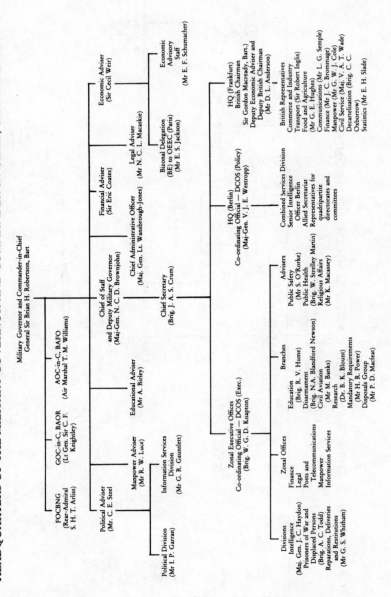

(e) November 1949

ORGANISATION OF THE OFFICE OF THE UNITED KINGDOM HIGH COMMISSIONER

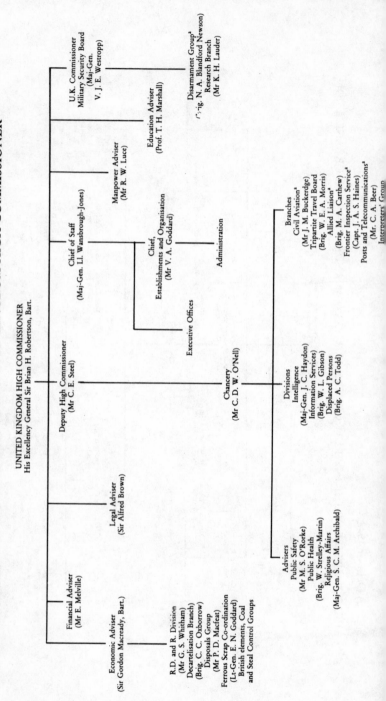

UNITED KINGDOM HIGH COMMISSIONER
His Excellency General Sir Brian H. Robertson, Bart.

Deputy High Commissioner
(Mr C. E. Steel)

Financial Adviser
(Mr E. Melville)

Economic Adviser
(Sir Gordon Macready, Bart.)

R.D. and R. Division
(Mr G. S. Whitham)
Decartelisation Branch
(Brig. C. C. Oxborrow)
Disposals Group
(Mr P. D. Macfeat)
Ferrous Scrap Co-ordination
(Lt.-Gen. E. N. Goddard)
British elements, Coal
and Steel Control Groups

Legal Adviser
(Sir Alfred Brown)

Chief of Staff
(Maj.-Gen. Ll. Wansbrough-Jones)

Manpower Adviser
(Mr R. W. Luce)

Chief,
Establishments and Organisation
(Mr V. A. Goddard)

Executive Offices

Administration

U.K. Commissioner
Military Security Board
(Maj.-Gen.
V. J. E. Westropp)

Education Adviser
(Prof. T. H. Marshall)

Disarmament Group*
(Brig. N. A. Blandford Newson
Research Branch
(Mr K. H. Lauder)

Chancery
(Mr C. D. W. O'Nell)

Advisers
Public Safety
(Mr M. S. O'Rorke)
Public Health
(Brig. W. Strelley-Martin)
Religious Affairs
(Maj.-Gen. S. C. M. Archibald)

Divisions
Intelligence
(Maj.-Gen. J. C. Haydon)
Information Services
(Brig. W. L. Gibson)
Displaced Persons
(Brig. A. C. Todd)

Branches
Civil Aviation*
(Mr J. M. Buckcrdge)
Tripartite Travel Board
Allied Liaison*
(Brig. W. E. A. Morris)
Frontier Inspection Service*
(Capt. J. A. S. Haines)
Posts and Telecommunications*
(Mr. C. A. Beer)
Interpreters' Group

LAND ORGANISATION

(f) September 1949

HIGH COMMISSIONER
General Sir Brian H. Robertson, Bart

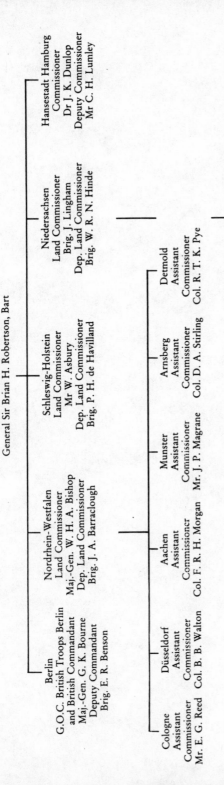

Berlin
G.O.C. British Troops Berlin and British Commandant
Maj.-Gen. G. K. Bourne
Deputy Commandant
Brig. E. R. Benson

Nordrhein-Westfalen
Land Commissioner
Maj.-Gen. W. H. A. Bishop
Dep. Land Commissioner
Brig. J. A. Barraclough

Schleswig-Holstein
Land Commissioner
Mr W. Asbury
Dep. Land Commissioner
Brig. P. H. de Havilland

Niedersachsen
Land Commissioner
Brig. J. Lingham
Dep. Land Commissioner
Brig. W. R. N. Hinde

Hansestadt Hamburg
Commissioner
Dr J. K. Dunlop
Deputy Commissioner
Mr C. H. Lumley

Cologne
Assistant Commissioner
Mr. E. G. Reed

Düsseldorf
Assistant Commissioner
Col. B. B. Walton

Aachen
Assistant Commissioner
Col. F. R. H. Morgan

Munster
Assistant Commissioner
Mr. J. P. Magrane

Arnsberg
Assistant Commissioner
Col. D. A. Stirling

Detmold
Assistant Commissioner
Col. R. T. K. Pye

Oldenburg
Assistant Commissioner
Brig. C. F. Blackden

Brunswick
Assistant Commissioner
Col. T. A. Dillon

Hanover
Assistant Commissioner
Rear-Admiral W. L. Jackson

Luneburg
Assistant Commissioner
Mr. H. F. Piper

Stade
Assistant Commissioner
Brig. C. H. V. Cox

Osnabruck
Assistant Commissioner
Capt F. C. Flynn, R.N.

Source (Fig. 6 (*a*)-(*f*)): Imperial War Museum, 'Guide to the Functions and Organisation of the ACA', *Monthly Reports of the CCG (BE)* 1946–50.

Notes on the Contributors

Dr Wendy Carlin is Lecturer in Economics at University College London. She has recently completed a PhD thesis on the economic development of post-war Germany.

Dr Ian Connor is Lecturer in European Studies and Modern Languages at the University of Ulster at Coleraine. He is author of several articles on the refugee problem and is currently making a study of German attitudes towards British Military Government in the period 1948–50.

Dr Anne Deighton is lecturer in International Relations at Reading University and has recently completed a study of British policy on the German question from 1945 to 1947.

Dr Peter Hubsch is head of the Department of Modern Languages, Newcastle-on-Tyne Polytechnic, and lectures on aspects of the West German economy. He has recently completed a doctoral thesis on the economic policy of the Deutscher Gewerkschaftsbund in the British Zone.

Dr Alan Kramer is Lecturer in History at Trinity College, Dublin. His research interests are in the social and economic history of western Germany 1945–55 and his thesis on dismantling in Hamburg is due to be published in 1989.

Dr Barbara Marshall is Senior Lecturer for European History and European Studies at the Polytechnic of North London. Her research interests cover the rise of National Socialism, German reactions to military defeat and occupation, and post-war British occupation policy.

Dr Mark Roseman is Lecturer in the Modern Languages Department at Aston University. He has recently completed a doctorate at Warwick University on 'New Miners in the Ruhr' and has written a number of articles and papers on the history of the Ruhr and on Germany's reconstruction after 1945.

Dr Ian Turner is Lecturer at Henley The Management College. His research interests include the British occupation of Germany and contemporary government–industry relations.

Isabel Warner is Research Fellow at the Institut für Europäische Geschichte in Mainz. She was previously Research Student at the European University Institute in Florence and is working on a doctoral thesis which examines both the evolution of Allied policy on the deconcentration of the West German steel industry and its effects.

Dr David Welch is Senior Lecturer in Modern History at the Polytechnic of Central London. He is the author of *Propaganda and the German Cinema, 1933–45* (Clarendon Press, Oxford, 1983) and a forthcoming book on *German Society and the Impact of Total War, 1914–18: The Sins of Omission*. He is currently working on a research project on 'The Political Re-Education of Germany after World War II: 1945–55'.

Bibliography

Main Archives

Public Record Office, Kew
Archives Nationales, Paris
Bundesarchiv, Koblenz
Parlamentsarchiv des Deutschen Bundestags, Bonn
Landesarchiv Schleswig-Holstein, Kiel
Niedersächsisches Hauptstaatsarchiv, Hanover
Nordrheinwestfälisches Haupstaatsarchiv, Düsseldorf
Staatsarchiv, Harmburg
Staatsarchiv, Munich
Niedersächsisches Landtagsarchiv, Hanover
Bayerisches Landtagsarchiv, Munich
Westfälisches Wirschaftsarchiv
Stadtarchiv Hanover
DGB Archiv, Düsseldorf
BBC Archive, Caversham

Published Documents

In addition to those included in the bibliography, there are the standard US and German official documents:

United States Department of State (ed.) (1958–), *Foreign Relations of the United States 1941–* (Government Publications, Washington) (FRUS)
Bundesarchiv and Institut für Zeitgeschichte, (1976–83), *Akten zur Vorge-schichte der Bundesrepublik Deutschland 1945–1949*, 5 volumes (Oldenbourg Verlag, Munich) (AVB)

Institut für Zeitgeschichte and Bundestag (1977), *Wörtliche Berichte und Drucksachen des Wirtschaftsrats des Vereingten Wirtschaftsgebietes 1947–49*, 6 volumes (Oldenbourg Verlag, Munich)

Bibliography

Journals and Newspapers

Keesings Contemporary Archives
Monthly Report of the CCG(BE)
British Zone Review
Der Spiegel
The Times
The Economist
Board of Trade Journal
Westfälische Rundschau

Books and Articles

Abelshauser, W. (1975), *Wirtschaft in Westdeutschland, 1945–1948. Rekonstruktion und Wachstumsbedingungen in der amerikanischen und britischen Zone*, Deutsche Verlags-Anstalt, Stuttgart
—— (1981), 'Korea, die Ruhr und Erhards Marktwirtschaft: die Energiekrise von 1950–51', *Rheinische Vierteljahrsblätter*, Vol. 45, No. 3, pp. 287–316
—— (1982), 'Ansätze korporativer Marktwirtschaft in der Koreakrise der frühen fünfziger Jahre', *Vierteljahrshefte für Zeitgeschichte*, Vol. 30, No. 4, pp. 715–56
—— (1983), *Wirtschaftsgeschichte der Bundesrepublik 1945–1980*, Suhrkamp, Frankfurt
—— (1984), *Der Ruhrkohlenbergbau seit 1945. Wiederaufbau, Krise, Anpassung*, C. H. Beck, Munich
—— (1985), 'Schopenhauer's Gesetz und die Währungsreform', *Vierteljahrshefte für Zeitgeschichte*, Vol. 33, No. 1, pp. 214–18
—— (1986), 'Ein deutsches Entwicklungsmodell? Zur Rolle des Marshall-Plans beim Wiederaufstieg der westdeutschen Wirtschaft nach dem Zweiten Weltkrieg', *Aus Politik und Zeitgeschichte*, B49/86, pp. 8–14
Adamsen, H. R. (1981), *Investitionshilfe für die Ruhr: Wiederaufbau, Verbände und Soziale Marktwirtschaft 1948–1952*, Peter Hammer Verlag, Wuppertal
Adenauer, K. (1965), *Erinnerungen 1945–1953*, Deutsche Verlags-Anstalt, Stuttgart
Ahrens, A. D. (1982), *Demontage. Nachkriegspolitik der Alliierten*, Universitas, Munich
Ambrosius, G. (1977), *Die Durchsetzung der Sozialen Marktwirtschaft in Westdeutschland*, Deutsche Verlags-Anstalt, Stuttgart
—— (1979), 'Marktwirtschaft oder Planwirtschaft? Planwirtschaftliche Ansätze der bizonalen deutschen Selbstverwaltung 1946–1949', *Vierteljahrschrift für Sozial und Wirtschaftsgeschichte*, Vol. 66, No. 1, pp. 74–110

Anderson, T. H. (1981), *The United States, Great Britain and the Cold War 1944–1947*, University of Missouri Press, Columbia, Miss.

Arndt, K.-D. (1955), 'Wohnungsversorgung und Mieteniveau in der Bundesrepublik', *DIW Sonderheft*, No. 35

Arnold, C. (1948), 'Der Arbeitsmarkt in den Besatzungszonen' in Deutsches Institut für Wirtschaft (ed.), *Wirtschaftsprobleme der Besatzungszonen*, DIW, Berlin

Backer, J. (1971), *Priming the German Economy. American Occupational Policies 1945–1948*, Duke University Press, Durham, NC

—— (1978), *The Decision to Divide Germany. American Foreign Policy in Transition*, Duke University Press, Durham

—— (1983), *The Winds of History. The German Years of Lucius DuBignon Clay*, Von Nostrand Rheinhold, New York

Badstübner, R. (1987), 'Die alliierte Viermächteverwaltung und die gesellschaftlich-staatliche Entwicklung in Deutschland nach dem Zweiten Weltkrieg', unpublished paper given at a symposium on 'Continuity and change: German society in transition to the new German States 1945–55', University of Liverpool, September–October

Balabkins, N. (1964), *Germany under Direct Controls*, Rutgers University Press, New Brunswick

Balfour, M. (1987), 'Re-education in Germany after 1945: Some Further Considerations' *German History*, No. 5, pp. 25–34

Balfour, M. and Mair, J. (1956), *Four Power Control in Germany and Austria 1945–1946*, Oxford University Press, London

Balogh, T. (1950), 'Germany: An Experiment in Planning by the "Free" Price Mechanism', *Banca Nazionale del Lavoro Quarterly Review*, Vol. 13, No. 3, pp. 71–102

Balshaw, H. (1972), 'The British Occupation of Germany 1945–1949. With Special Reference to Hamburg', PhD thesis, Oxford University

Barker, E. (1984), *The British Between the Superpowers, 1945–50*, Macmillan, London

Bartholomäi, R. *et al.* (eds.) (1977), *Sozialpolitik nach 1945, Geschichte und Analysen*, Verlag Neue Gesellschaft, Bonn

Bauer, F. J. (1982), *Flüchtlinge und Flüchtlingspolitik in Bayern 1945–50*, Klett-Cotta, Stuttgart

Bauer, W. (1948), 'Der allgemeine wirtschaftliche Charakter der Zonen' in Deutsches Institut für Wirtschaft (ed.), *Wirtschaftsprobleme der Besatzungszonen*, DIW, Berlin

Baumgart, E. (1961), 'Investitionen und ERP Finanzierung', *DIW Sonderhefte* No. 56, Berlin

—— Krengel, R., Moritz, W. (1960), *Die Finanzierung der industriellen Expansion in der BRD während der Jahre des Wiederaufbaus*, Duncker & Humblot, Berlin

Bayerisches Statistisches Landesamt (ed.) (1948), *Bayern in Zahlen*, Monatshefte des Bayerischen Statistischen Landesamtes, No. 5

Bibliography

—— (ed.) (1950), *Die Vertriebenen in Bayern. Ihre berufliche und soziale Eingliederung bis Anfang 1950*, Beiträge zur Statistik Bayerns, No. 151

Baylis, J. (1983), 'British Wartime Thinking About a Post-War European Security Group' *Review of International Studies*, Vol. 9, pp. 265–81

—— (1984), 'Britain, the Brussels Pact and the Continental Commitment', *International Affairs*, Vol. 60, No. 4, pp. 615–29

Becker, J., Stammen T., and Waldmann P. (eds.) (1979), *Vorgeschichte der Bundesrepublik Deutschland. Zwischen Kapitulation und Grundgesetz*, Wilhelm Fink Verlag, Munich

Becker, J. and Knipping F. (eds.) (1986), *Power in Europe? Great Britain, France, Italy and Germany in a Post-war World, 1945–1950*, Walter de Gruyter, Berlin and New York

Becker, W. (ed.) (1987a), *Die Kapitulation von 1945 und der Neubeginn in Deutschland*, Böhlau Verlag, Cologne

—— (ed.) (1987b), *CDU und CSU. Vorläufer, Gründung und regionale Entwicklung bis zum Entstehen der CDU–Bundespartei*, von Hase & Koehler Verlag, Mainz

Bedell Smith, W. (1950), *Moscow Mission, 1946–49*, Heinemann, London

Beier, G. (1978), *Willi Richter. Ein Leben für die Neuordnung*, Bund-Verlag, Cologne

Bell, M. (1985), 'Die Blockade Berlins—Konfrontationen der Alliierten in Deutschland' in J. Foschepoth (ed.), *Kalter Krieg und deutsche Frage*, Vandenhoeck & Ruprecht, Göttingen and Zurich, pp. 217–39

Benz, K. *et al.* (1983), *Willi Bleicher. Ein Leben für die Gewerkschaften*, Nachrichten-Verlags Gesellschaft, Frankfurt on Main

Benz, W. (1981), 'Versuche zur Reform des öffentlichen Dienstes in Deutschland 1945–52',*Vierteljahreshefte für Zeitgeschichte*, Vol. 29, No. 2, pp. 216–45

—— (1984a), *Die Gründung der Bundesrepublik. Von der Bizone zum souveränen Staat*, Deutscher Taschenbuch Verlag, Munich

—— (1984b), *Von der Besatzungsherrschaft zur Bundesrepublik*, Fischer, Frankfurt on Main

—— (1984c), 'Zwangswirtschaft und Industrie. Der Kasseler Spinnfaser-Prozess von 1947', *Vierteljahreshefte für Zeitgeschichte*, Vol. 34, No. 3, pp. 422–40

—— (1987), 'Deutsche Geschichte nach dem Zweiten Weltkrieg: Probleme und Tendenzen zeitgeschichtlicher Forschung in der Bundesrepublik', *Tel Aviver Jahrbuch für deutsche Geschichte*, pp. 398–420

Benz, W. (ed.) (1985), *Die Vertreibung der Deutschen aus dem Osten*, Fischer, Frankfurt on Main

—— (ed.) (1986), *Potsdam 1945*, Deutscher Taschenbuch Verlag, Munich

Berg-Schlösser, D. and Schissler, J. (eds.) (1987), *Politische Kultur in Deutschland. Facetten einer dramatischen Entwicklung*, Politische Vierteljahreschrift-Sonderheft, Westdeutscher Verlag, Opladen

Berghahn, V. (1985), *Unternehmer und Politik in der Bundesrepublik*,

Suhrkamp, Frankfurt on Main
—— (1986), *The Americanisation of West German Industry 1945–1973*, Berg, Leamington Spa
Bericht der Stahltreuhändervereinigung (1954), *Die Neuordnung der Eisen und Stahlindustrie im Gebiet der Bundesrepublik Deutschland*, C. H. Beck, Berlin and Munich
Besatzungskosten—ein Verteidigungsbeitrag? (1950), Institut für Besatzungsfragen, Tübingen
Beyerchen, A. (1984), 'German Scientists and Research Institutions in Allied Occupation Policy', *History of Education Quarterly*, Vol. 22, No. 3, pp. 289–99
Birke, A. M. (1984), 'Geschichtsauffassung und Deutschlandbild im Foreign Office Research Department', *Historisches Jahrbuch*, Vol. 104, pp. 372–91
Birley, R. (1978), 'British Policy in Retrospect' in A. Hearnden (ed.), *The British in Germany: Educational Reconstruction after 1945*, Hamish Hamilton, London, pp. 46–63
Bischoff, H. H. (1951), 'Arbeiterzahl und Förderanstieg', *Glückauf*, Vol. 87, No. 23–4, pp. 565–7.
Blum, J. M. (1970), *Roosevelt and Morgenthau*, Houghton, Boston, Mass.
Blumenwitz, D. *et al.* (eds.) (1976), *Konrad Adenauer und seine Zeit*, Vol. 1, Deutsche Verlags-Anstalt, Stuttgart
Boons, H. (1982, 1984), *Die Kabinettsprotokolle der Bundesregierung*, Vols. 1 and 2, Boldt Verlag, Boppard
Borchardt, K. and Buchheim, C. (1987), 'Die Wirkung der Marshallplan-Hilfe in Schlüsselbranchen der deutschen Wirtschaft', *Vierteljahreshefte für Zeitgeschichte*, Vol. 35, No. 3, pp. 317–48
Borsdorf, U. (1979), 'Speck oder Sozialisierung. Produktionssteigerungskampagnen im Ruhrbergbau 1945–1947' in H. Mommsen and U. Borsdorf (eds.), *Glückauf Kamaraden! Die Bergarbeiter und ihre Organisationen in Deutschland*, Bund Verlag, Cologne, pp. 345–66
Borsdorf, U. *et al* (eds.) (1977), *Gewerkschaftliche Politik: Reform aus Solidarität*, Bund-Verlag, Cologne
Botting, D. (1985), *In the Ruins of the Reich*, Allen & Unwin, London
Bower, T. (1981), *Blind Eye to Murder*, Deutsch, London
—— (1987), *The Paperclip Conspiracy*, Michael Joseph, London
Brautmeier, J. (1987), 'Wahlrecht zwischen Militärregierung und Parteipolitik. Dokumente zur Landtagwahl 1947', *Geschichte im Westen*, Vol. 2, No. 1, pp. 90–9
Brawand, L. (1987), *Die Spiegel Story*, Econ Verlag, Düsseldorf
Breder, P. (1979), *Geschichten vor Ort. Erinnerungen eines Bergmanns*, Glückauf Verlag, Essen
Brennan, G. (1987), 'Re-educating Germany: Film Censorship in the Post-war Period', *Politics*, Vol. 7, No. 1, pp. 40–7
Brockway, F. (1946), *German Diary*, Gollancz, London

Bibliography

Brosius, D. (1985), 'Zur Lage der Flüchtlinge im Regierungsbezirk Lüneburg zwischen Kriegsende und Währungsreform' in D. Brosius and A. Hohenstein (eds.), *Flüchtlinge im nordöstlichen Niedersachsen 1945–1948*, Verlag August Lax, Hildesheim

Brosius, D. and Hohenstein, A. (eds.) (1985), *Flüchtlinge im nordöstlichen Niedersachsen 1945–1948*, Verlag August Lax, Hildesheim

Broszat, M. *et al.* (eds.) (1987), *Von Stalingrad zur Währungsreform*, Oldenbourg Verlag, Munich

Brumlik, M. (ed.) (1986), *Judisches Leben in Deutschland seit 1945*, Jüdischer Verlag bei Athenäeum, Frankfurt on Main

Buchheim, C. (1987), 'Bemerkungen zur Währungs- und Bewirtschaftungsreform', unpublished manuscript, Institut für Zeitgeschichte, Munich

—— (1988), 'Die Währungsreform 1948 in Westdeutschland', *Vierteljahrshefte für Zeitgeschichte*, Vol. 36, No. 2, pp. 189–231

Bührer, W. (1986), *Ruhrstahl und Europa. Die Wirtschaftsvereinigung Eisen- und Stahlindustrie und die Anfänge der europäischen Integration 1945–52*, Oldenbourg Verlag, Munich

Bullen, R. (ed.) (1986), *Documents on British Policy Overseas: The Schuman Plan, The Council of Europe and Western European Integration. May 1950–December 1952*, HMSO, London

Bullock, A. (1983), *Ernest Bevin: Foreign Secretary 1945–1951*, Heinemann, London

Bundesministerium für Arbeit (ed.) (1950), *Entwicklung und Ursachen der Arbeitslosigkeit in der Bundesrepublik Deutschland 1956–1950*, Bonn

Bundesministerium für Vertriebene (1950), *Vertriebene und Flüchtlinge volksdeutschen Ursprungs. Bericht eines Sonder-Unterkomitees des Rechtsausschusses des Abgeordnetenhauses . . .* , Bonn

Bundesministerium für Vertriebene (ed.) (1959), *Flüchtlinge, Vertriebene, Kriegsgefangene*, Bonn

Burchardt, F. A. and Martin, K. (1947), 'West Germany and Reconstruction', *Bulletin of Oxford Institute of Statistics*, Vol. 9, No. 12, pp. 405–16.

Burmeister, W. (1978), 'Were the British too Neutral?', *Adult Education*, July, pp. 98–100

Burn, D. (1961), *The Steel Industry 1939–1959*, Cambridge University Press, Cambridge

Büro der Ministerpräsidenten des amerikanischen, britischen und französischen Besatzungsgebietes (1948), *Report on the Effect of Envisaged Dismantling on Germany's Economic Situation and her Role in European Reconstruction*, Verwaltung für Wirtschaft, Frankfurt on Main

Burridge, T. D. (1976), *British Labour and Hitler's War*, Deutsch, London

Butler, R. and Pelly, M. E. (eds.) (1984), *Documents on British Policy Overseas. The Potsdam Conference*, Series 1, Vol. 1, HMSO, London

Buttlar, W. von (1980), *Ziele und Zielkonflikte in der sowjetischen Deutschlandpolitik*, Klett-Cotta, Stuttgart

Büttner, U. (1986), 'Not nach der Befreiung: die Situation der deutschen Juden in der britischen Besatzungszone 1945–1948' in U. Büttner (ed.), *Das Unrechtsregime*, Vol. 2, Christians Verlag, Hamburg, pp. 373–406.

Cairncross, A. (1986), *The Price of War. British Policy on German Reparations 1941 to 1949*, Basil Blackwell, Oxford

—— (1987), *A Country to Play With. Level of Industry Negotiations in Berlin 1945–1946*, Colin Smythe, Gerrards Cross

Carew, A. (1987), *Labour under the Marshall Plan*, Manchester University Press, Manchester

Carlin, W. (1987), 'The Development of the Factor Distribution of Income and Profitability in West Germany, 1945–1973', D. Phil. thesis, Oxford University

Cave, M. and Hare, P. (1981), *Alternative Approaches to Economic Planning*, Macmillan, London

Chambers, S. P. (1948), 'Post-War German Finances' in *International Affairs*, Vol. 24, No. 3, pp. 364–76

Clarke, M. (1984), 'Die Gewerkschaftspolitik der KPD 1945–1951, dargestellt am Beispiel des "Industrieverbandes Bergbau/Industriegewerkschaft Bergbau" im Ruhrgebiet', unpublished dissertation, University of Bochum

Clay, L. D. (1950), *Decision in Germany*, Doubleday, Garden City, NY

Cloake, J. (1985), *Templer, Tiger of Malaya: The Life of Field Marshall Sir Gerald Templer*, Harrap, London

Collins, H. E. (1985), *Mining Memories and Musings*, Ashire Publishing, London

Connor, I. (1985), 'The Churches and the Refugee Problem in Bavaria 1945–49', Journal of Contemporay History, Vol. 20, pp. 399–421

—— (1986), 'The Bavarian Government and the Refugee Problem', *European History Quarterly*, Vol. 16, pp. 131–53.

Conway, J. S. (1986), 'Die Rolle der Kirchen bei der Umerziehung in Deutschland' in U. Büttner (ed.), *Das Unrechtsregime*, Vol. 2, Christians Verlag, Hamburg, pp. 360–72

Conze, W. and Lepsius M. R. (eds.) (1983) *Sozialgeschichte der Bundesrepublik. Beiträge zum Kontinuitätsproblem*, Klett-Cotta, Stuttgart

Cromwell, W. C. (1982), 'The Marshall Plan, Britain and the Cold War' *Review of International Studies*, Vol. 8, No. 4, pp. 233–50

Cullingford, E. C. M. (1976), *Trade Unions in West Germany*, Wilton House, London

Dalton, H. (1957), *The Fateful Years: Memoirs 1931–1945*, Muller, London

—— (1962), *High Tide and After: Memoirs 1945–1960*, Muller, London

Daniels, M. and Hart, P. D. A. (1948), *Tuberculosis in the British Zone*, HMSO, London

Dann, O. (ed.) (1981), *Köln nach dem Nationalsozialismus*, Peter Hammer Verlag, Wuppertal

Deighton, A. (1987a), 'Britain, the German Problem and the Origins of the

Cold War in Europe: A Study of the Council of Foreign Ministers 1945–1947' PhD thesis, University of Reading

—— (1987b), "The frozen front": the Labour Government, the Division of Germany and the Origins of the Cold War, 1945–1947', *International Affairs*, Vol. 63, No. 3, pp. 449–65

Der Spiegel (1979–87), several volumes 1947–54 (Athenäeum Verlag, Königstein

Deutscher Gewerkschaftsbund (1949), *Die Gewerkschaftsbewegung in der britischen Besatzungszone 1945–1949*, Bund-Verlag, Cologne

Deutsches Institut für Wirtschaftsforschung (ed.) (1948), *Wirtschaftsprobleme der Besatzungszonen*, Duncker & Humblot, Berlin

Diebold, W. (1959), *The Schuman Plan. A Study in Economic Cooperation 1950–59*, Frederick A. Praeger, New York

Domes, J. and Wolffsohn, M. (1979), 'Setting the Course for the FRG: Major Policy Decisions in the Bizonal Economic Council and Party Images, 1947–49', *Zeitschrift für die gesamte Staatswissenschaft*, Vol. 135, No. 3, pp. 332–51

Donnison, F. S. V. (1961), *Civil Affairs and Military Government. North West Europe, 1944–46*, HMSO, London

—— (1966), *Civil Affairs and Military Government. Central Organisation and Planning*, HMSO, London

Dorendorf, A. (1953), *Der Zonenbeirat der britisch-besetzten Zone. Ein Rückblick auf seine Tätigkeit*, Schwartz, Göttingen

Dotterwich, V. (1970), 'Die Entnazifizierung' in J. Becker, T. Stammen and P. Waldmann (eds.), *Vorgeschichte der Bundesrepublik Deutschland. Zwischen Kapitulation und Grundgesetz*, Wilhelm Fink Verlag, Munich, pp. 123–62.

Douglas, R. (1981), *From War to Cold War 1942–48*, Macmillan, London

Douglas, S. and Wright, R. (1966), *Years of Command*, Collins, London

Drexler, A. (1984), 'Wirtschaftsplanung nach 1945. Das Beispiel der Textilwirtschaft' in D. Petzina and W. Euchner (eds.), *Wirtschaftspolitik im britischen Besatzungsgebiet 1945–1949*, Schwann, Düsseldorf, pp. 121–52

—— (1985), *Planwirtschaft in Westdeutschland*, Steiner, Stuttgart and Wiesbaden

Drexler, A., Krumbein, W. and Stratmann, F. (1985), 'Die britischen "Sparta-Pläne" 1946' in J. Foschepoth and R. Steininger (eds.), *Britische Deutschland- und Besatzungspolitik 1945–1949*, Schöningh, Paderborn, pp. 245–63

Ebsworth, R. (1960), *Restoring Democracy in Germany. The British Contribution*, Stevens & Son, London

Edinger, L. J. (1960), 'Post-Totalitarian Leadership: Elites in the German Federal Republic', *American Political Science Review*, Vol. 54, No. 1, pp. 58–82

—— (1965), *Kurt Schumacher. A Study in Personality and Political Behav-*

iour, Stanford University Press, Stanford, Cal.

Edmonds, R. (1986a), *'Setting the Mould'. The United States and Britain 1945–50*, Clarendon, Oxford

—— (1986b), 'Yalta and Potsdam, Forty Years Afterwards', *International Affairs*, Vol. 62, No. 2, pp. 197–296.

Edwards, R. D. (1987), *Victor Gollancz. A Biography*, Gollancz, London

Eggebrecht, A. (1979), *Zornige alte Männer*, Rowohlt, Hamburg

Ehrich, E. (1977), *Heinrich Hellwege*, Niedersächsische Landeszentrale für Politische Bildung, Hannover

Eisenberg, C. (1983), 'Working Class Politics and the Cold War: American Intervention in the German Labour Movement 1945–9' *Diplomatic History*, Vol. 7, No. 4, pp. 283–306

Emminger, O. (1948), 'Wirtschaftsplanung in der Bizone' in Deutsches Institut für Wirtschaftsforschung, *Wirtschaftsprobleme der Besatzungszonen*, Duncker & Humblot, Berlin, pp. 143–78

Enders, U. and Reiser, K. (eds.) (1982 and 1984), *Die Kabinettsprotokolle der Bundesregierung*, 2 vols. (1949 and 1950), Boldt Verlag, Boppard

Eschenburg, T. (1983), *Geschichte der Bundesrepublik Deutschland*, Vol. 1, *Jahre der Besatzung 1945–1949*, Deutsche Verlags-Anstalt, Stuttgart

Farquharson, J. E. (1985a), 'Landwirtschaft und Ernährung in der Politik der Alliierten 1945–48' in J. Foschepoth (ed.), *Kalter Krieg und Deutsche Frage*, Vandenhoeck & Ruprecht, Göttingen and Zurich pp. 147–74

—— (1985b), *The Western Allies and the Politics of Food*, Berg, Leamington Spa

—— (1987), ' "Emotional but Influential" Victor Gollancz, Richard Stokes and the British Zone of Germany, 1945–9', *Journal of Contemporary History*, Vol. 22, No. 3, pp. 501–20

—— (1988), 'Land Reform in the British Zone 1945–1947', *German History*, Vol. 6, No. 1, pp. 35–56

Faulk, H. (1970), *Die deutschen Kriegsgefangenen in Grossbritannien: Re-education*, Gieseking, Munich and Bielefeld

Feselfeldt, W. (1962), *Der Wiederaufbau des kommunalen Lebens in Göttingen*, Vandenhoeck & Ruprecht, Göttingen and Zurich

Fichter, M. (1987), 'Aufbau und Neuordnung: Betriebsräte zwischen Klassensolidarität und Betriebsloyalität' in M. Broszat *et al.* (eds.), *Von Stalingrad zur Währungsreform*, Oldenbourg Verlag, Munich

Fischer, H. D. (1978), *Re-educations und Pressepolitik unter britischem Besatzungsstatus. Die Zonenzeitung 'Die Welt' 1946–50*, Droste, Düsseldorf

Fitzgibbon, C. (1969), *Denazification*, Michael Joseph, London

Flechtheim, O. K. (ed.) (1962), *Dokumente zur parteipolitischer Entwicklung in Deutschland seit 1945*, Vol. 1, Dokumenten Verlag Wendler, Berlin

Foelz-Schroeter, M. E. (1974), *Föderalistische Politik und nationale Repräsentation 1945–1947*, Deutscher Verlags-Anstalt, Stuttgart

Föllmer-Edling, A. (1977), 'Die Politik des IVB im Ruhrgebiet 1945–1948 (Die Anstrengung um die Erhöhung der Kohlenförderung im Ruhrbergbau)', unpublished dissertation, University of Bochum

Först, W. (1970), *Geschichte Nordrhein-Westfalens*, Vol. 1, *1945–1949*, Grote, Cologne

—— (1979), 'Die Politik der Demotage' in W. Först (ed.), *Entscheidungen im Westen*, Grote, Cologne and Berlin

—— (1982), *Zwischen Ruhrkontrolle und Mitbestimmung*, Kohlhammer, Cologne and Stutgart

Foschepoth, J. (1982), 'Britische Deutschlandpolitik zwischen Yalta und Potsdam', *Vierteljahreshefte für Zeitgeschichte*, Vol. 30, No. 4, pp. 676–704

—— (1984), 'Churchill, Adenauer und die Neutralisierung Deutschlands', *Deutschland Archiv*, Vol. 17, No. 11, pp. 1286–301

—— (1985a), 'Grossbritannien und die Deutschlandfrage auf den Aussenministerkonferenzen 1946/47' in J. Foschepoth and R. Steininger (eds.), *Britische Deutschland- und Besatzungspolitik 1945–49*, Schöningh, Paderborn, pp. 65–86

—— (1985b), *Kalter Krieg und Deutsche Frage*, Vandenhoeck & Ruprecht, Göttingen and Zurich

—— (1985c), 'Konflikte in der Reparationspolitik der Alliierten' in J. Foschepoth (ed.), *Kalter Krieg und Deutsche Frage*, Vandenhoeck & Ruprecht, Göttingen and Zurich, pp. 175–97.

—— (1985d), 'Potsdam und danach—die Westmächte, Adenauer und die Vertriebenen' in W. Benz (ed.), *Die Vertreibung der Deutschen aus dem Osten*, Fischer Verlag, Frankfurt, pp. 70–90

—— (1986a), 'British Interest in the Division of Germany after the Second World War', *Journal of Contemporary History*, Vol. 21, No. 3, pp. 391–411

—— (1986b), 'Zur deutschen Reaktion auf Niederlage und Besatzung' in L. Herbst (ed.), *Westdeutschland 1945–1955*, Oldenbourg Verlag, Munich, pp. 151–66

Foschepoth, J. and Steininger, R. (eds.) (1985), *Britische Deutschland- und Besatzungspolitik 1945–49*, Schöningh, Paderborn

Franke, K. (1980), *Die niedersächsische SPD—Führung im Wandel der Partei nach 1945*, Verlag August Lax, Hildesheim

Frei, N. (1983), 'Presse' and 'Hörfunk und Fernsehen' in W. Benz (ed.), *Die Bundesrepublik Deutschland*, Vol. 3, *Kultur*, Fischer, Frankfurt on Main, pp. 275–357

Friedmann, W. G. (1947), *The Allied Military Government of Germany*, Stevens & Sons, London

Friedrich, C. J. (1948), *American Experiences in Military Government in World War Two*, Rinehart, New York

Friedrich Ebert Stiftung (1988), *Kurt Schumacher als deutscher und europäischer Sozialist*, Bonn

Fromm, H. (1982), *Deutschland in der öffentlichen Kriegszieldiskussion Grossbritanniens 1939–1945*, Lang, Frankfurt on Main

Frowein, A. (1968), *Erinnerungen an seine Tätigkeit im Deutschen Wirtschaftsrat bei der britischen Kontrollkommission in Minden*, Boldt Verlag Boppard on Rhein

Fuhrmann, W. (nd), *Die Bayerische Lagerversorgung 1948–1951. Ein ernährungswirtschaftlicher Beitrag zur Versorgung von Gemeinschaftsverpflegungseinrichtungen und der Schulspeisung* (np)

Fürstenau, J. (1969), *Entnazifizierung*, Lüchterhand, Neuwied and Berlin

Galbraith, J. K. (1983), *A Life in Our Times*, Deutsch, London

Gillingham, J. (1986), 'Zur Vorgeschichte der Montanunion. Westeuropas Kohle und Stahl in Depression und Krieg', *Vierteljahreshefte für Zeitgeschichte*, Vol. 34, No. 3, pp. 382–404

—— (1987), 'Die französische Ruhrpolitik und die Ursprünge des Schuman Plans', *Vierteljahreshefte für Zeitgeschichte*, Vol. 35, No. 1, pp. 1–24

—— 'German Heavy Industry and the Schuman Plan' in forthcoming volume of 'European Community Historians Group' on Schuman Plan, edited by K. Schwabe

Gimbel, J. (1960), 'American Denazification and German Local Politics, 1945–1949. A Case Study in Marburg', *The American Political Science Review*, Vol. 54, pp. 83–105

—— (1961a), *A German Community under American Occupation, Marburg 1945–1952*, Stanford University Press, Stanford, Cal.

—— (1961b), 'The Artificial Revolution in Germany. A Case Study', *Political Science Quarterly*, Vol. 76, No. 1, pp. 88ff.

—— (1968), *The American Occupation of Germany. Politics and the Military 1945–49*, Stanford University Press, Stanford, Cal.

—— (1976), *The Origins of the Marshall Plan*, Stanford University Press, Stanford, Cal.

—— (1986), 'US Policy and German Scientists: The Early Cold War', *Political Science Quarterly*, Vol. 101, No. 3, pp. 433–51

Glaser, H. (1985a), 'Kultur der Trümmerzeit', *Aus Politik und Zeitgeschichte*, B40–185 October, pp. 3–31

—— (1985b), *Kulturgeschichte der Bundesrepublik*, Vol. 1, *Zwischen Kapitulation und Währungsreform 1945–1948*, Hanser, Munich

—— (1986), *Kulturgeschichte der Bundesrepublik*, Vol. 2, *Zwischen Grundgesetz und Grosse Koalition*, Hanser, Munich

Glees, A. (1982), *Exile Politics During the Second World War. The German Social Democrats in Britain*, Oxford University Press, Oxford

Gollancz, V. (1947), *In Darkest Germany*, Gollancz, London

Grabbe, H.-J. (1978), 'Die deutsch-alliierte Kontroverse um den Grundgesetzentwurf im Frühjahr 1949', *Vierteljahreshefte für Zeitgeschichte*, Vol. 26, No. 3, pp. 398–418

Grabe, T., Hollmann, R. and Mlynek, K. (1985), *Wege aus dem Chaos. Hannover 1945–1949*, Ernst Kabel Verlag, Hamburg

Bibliography

Graml, H. (1985), *Die Alliierten und die Teilung Deutschlands*, Fischer, Frankfurt on Main

Grantham, J. T. (1979), 'Hugh Dalton and the International Post-War Settlement: Labour Party Foreign Policy Formulation 1943–44', *Journal of Contemporary History*, Vol. 14, No. 4, pp. 713–29

Grebing, H. (1966), *Geschichte der deutschen Arbeiterbewegung*, Nymphenburger Verlagshandlung, Munich (English edn: *The History of the German Labour Movement: A Survey*, abridged by Mary Saran, trans. by Edith Körner, Berg, Leamington Spa, 1985)

Grebing, H. and Klemm, B. (1983), *Lehrstücke in Solidarität. Briefe und Biographien deutscher Sozialisten, 1945–49*, Deutsche Verlags-Anstalt, Stuttgart

Grebing, H. *et al.* (1980), *Die Nachkriegsentwicklungen in Westdeutschland*, Metzler & Poeschener, Stuttgart

Greene, H. C. (1969), *The Third Floor Front*, Bodley Head, London

Greenwood, S. (1986), 'Bevin, the Ruhr and the Division of Germany: August 1945–December 1946', *Historical Journal*, Vol. 29, No. 1, pp. 203–12

Grieser, H. (1979), *Reichsbesitz, Entmilitärisierung und Friedensindustrie in Kiel nach dem Zweiten Weltkrieg*, Gesellschaft für Kieler Stadtgeschichte, Kiel

Griffith, W. E. (1950), 'Denazification in the United States Zone of Germany', *Annals of the American Academy of Political and Social Science*, Vol. 267, No. 1, pp. 68–76

Guldin, H. (1987), 'Aussenwirtschaftspolitische und aussenpolitische Einflussfaktoren im Prozess der Staatswerdung der Bundesrepublik Deutschland 1947–52', *Aus Politik und Zeitgeschichte*, B32/87, pp. 3–20

Habel, W. (ed.) (1951), *Wer ist Wer?*, 11th edn Societäts Verlag, Frankfurt

Haberl, O. N. and Niethammer, L. (eds.) (1986), *Der Marshallplan und die europäische Linke*, Europäische Verlagsanstalt, Frankfurt on Main

Hahn, G. (1982), *Bibliographie zur Geschichte der CDU and CSU 1945–1980*, Klett-Cotta, Stuttgart

Halbritter, M. (1979), *Schulreformpolitik in der britischen Zone 1945–49*, Beltz, Weinheim

Hammond, P. Y. (1963), 'Directives for the Occupation of Germany: The Washington Controversy' in H. Stein (ed.), *American Civil–Military Decisions*, University of Alabama Press, Birmingham Ala., pp. 335ff.

Harbutt, F. J. (1986), *The Iron Curtain. Churchill, America and the Origins of the Cold War*, Oxford University Press, New York

Hardach, G. (1987), 'The Marshall Plan in Germany, 1948–1952', *Journal of European Economic History*, Vol. 16, No. 3, pp. 433–87

Harenberg, K.–H. (1976), 'Die Welt 1946–1953: eine deutsche oder eine britische Zeitung?', PhD thesis, Federal University, Berlin

Harmssen, G. W. (1948), *Reparationen, Sozialprodukt, Lebensstandard. Versuch einer Wirtschaftsbilanz*, Trüjen Verlag, Bremen

—— (1951), *Am Abend der Demontage—6 Jahre Reparationspolitik*, Trüjen Verlag, Bremen

Harris, K. (1982), *Attlee* (Weidenfeld and Nicolson, London).

Hartmann, F. (1972), *Geschichte der Gewerkschaftsbewegung nach 1945 in Niedersachsen*, Niedersächsische Landeszentrale für politische Bildung, Hanover

Hasenack, W. (1949), *Dismantling in the Ruhr Valley*, Westdeutscher Verlag, Cologne and Opladen

—— (1951), *Bilanz der Demontage*, Vandenhoeck & Ruprecht Göttingen

Hathaway, R. M. (1981), *Ambiguous Partnership: Britain and America, 1944–47*, Columbia University Press, New York

Häuser, K. (1967), 'The Partition of Germany' in W. Stolper, K. Häuser and K. Borchardt, *The German Economy 1870 to the Present*, Weidenfeld & Nicholson, London

Hearnden, A. (1984), *Red Robert: A Life of Robert Birley*, Hamish Hamilton, London

—— (ed.) (1978), *The British in Germany: Educational Reconstruction after 1945*, Hamish Hamilton, London

Hehl, U. von and Hürten, H. (1983), *Der Katholizismus in der Bundesrepublik Deutschland 1945–1960. Eine Bibliographie*, Grünewald Verlag, Mainz

Hein, D. (1985), *Zwischen liberaler Milieupartei und nationaler Sammlungsbewegung—Gründung, Entwicklung und Struktur der Freien Demokratischen Partei 1945–1949*, Droste, Düsseldorf

Heinemann, M. (ed.) (1981), *Umerziehung und Wiederaufbau*, Klett-Cotta, Stuttgart

Heller, W. W. (1950), 'The Role of Fiscal-Monetary Policy in the German Economic Recovery', *American Economic Review Papers and Proceedings*, Vol. 40, No. 2, pp. 531–47

Henke, J. (1982), 'Das amerikanische–deutsche OMGUS Projekt. Erschliessung und Verfilmung der Akten der amerikanischen Militärregierung in Deutschland 1945–9', *Der Archivar*, Vol. 35, cols. 149–58

Henke, K.-D. (1981), *Politische Säuberung unter französischer Besatzung*, Deutsche Verlags-Anstalt, Stuttgart

—— (1986), 'Die Grenzen der politischen Säuberung in Deutschland nach 1945' in L. Herbst (ed.), *Westdeutschland 1945–1955*, Oldenbourg Verlag, Munich, pp. 127–34

—— (1988), *Die amerikanische Besetzung Deutschlands*, Oldenbourg Verlag, Munich

Herberts, H. (1954), *Walter Freitag. Weg und Wollen eines deutschen Gewerkschafters*, Arani Verlags GmbH, Berlin-Grünewald

Herbst, L. (ed.) (1986), *Westdeutschland 1945–1955*, Oldenbourg Verlag, Munich

Hermann, H.-G. (1958), *Verraten und Verkauft*, Fuldaer Verlagsanstalt, Fulda

Herz, J. H. (1948), 'The Fiasco of Denazification in Germany', *Political Science Quarterly*, Vol. 63, No. 4, pp. 569–94

HMSO (1955), *Overseas Economic Surveys: The Federal Republic of Germany: Economic and Commercial Conditions in the Federal Republic of Germany and West Berlin*, HMSO, London

HMSO (1972), *Selected Documents on Germany and the Question of Berlin 1944–1961*, HMSO, London

Hockerts, H. G. (1980), *Sozialpolitische Entscheidungen in Nachkriegsdeutschland. Alliierte und deutsche Sozialversicherungspolitik 1945 bis 1947*, Klett-Cotta, Stuttgart

—— (1981), 'German Post-War Social Policy Against the Background of the Beveridge Plan' in W. J. Mommsen (ed.), *The Emergence of the Welfare State in Britain and Germany*, Croom Helm, London, pp. 315–39

Hogan, M. J. (1987), *The Marshall Plan, America, Britain and the Reconstruction of Western Europe 1947–52*, Cambridge University Press, Cambridge

Holborn, H. (1947), *American Military Government*, Infantry Journal, Washington

Horstmann, T. (1984a), 'Die Angst vor dem finanziellen Kollaps. Banken und Kreditpolitik in der britischen Zone zwischen 1945 und 1948' in D. Petzina and W. Euchner (eds.), *Wirtschaftspolitik im britischen Besatzungsgebiet 1945–1949*, Schwann, Düsseldorf, pp. 121–52

—— (1984b), 'Financing the Reconstruction of the German Iron and Steel Industry 1945–1951', unpublished conference paper

—— (1985), 'Um das "schlechteste Bankensystem der Welt". Die Interalliierten Auseinandersetzungen über amerikanische Pläne zur Reform des deutschen Bankwesens 1945–46', *Bankhistorisches Archiv*, Vol. 11, No. 1, pp. 3–27

—— (1986), 'Alliierte Bankenpolitik nach dem Zweiten Weltkrieg in Westdeutschland. Neuordnung und Rekonzentration der deutschen Grossbanken 1945–56', Phd thesis, Ruhr Universität Bochum

—— (1987), '"The Worst Banking Practice in the World". Inter-Allied Discussion over American Plans to Reform the German Banking System in 1945/46', *German Yearbook on Business History 1986*, Springer Verlag, Berlin, pp. 93–115

House of Commons (1946), *Second Report from the Select Committee on Estimates. The Control Office for Germany and Austria (Expenditure in Germany)*, HMSO, London, 23 July 1946

—— (1947), *8th Report from the Select Committee on Estimates together with the Minutes of Evidence taken before Sub-committee F. Session 1946–47. British Expenditure in Germany*, HMSO, London

Howarth, P. (1986), *Intelligence Chief Extraordinary: Life of the Ninth Duke of Portland*, Bodley Head, London

Hubsch, P. H. (1988), 'The Economic Policies of the German Trade

Unions in the British Zone of Occupation 1945–1949', PhD thesis, University of Nottingham

Hudemann, R. (1986), 'Wirkungen französischer Besatzungspolitik: Forschungsprobleme und Ansätze zu einer Bilanz' in L. Herbst (ed.), *Westdeutschland 1945–1955*, Oldenbourg Verlag, Munich, pp. 167–82

Hüttenberger, P. (1973a), 'Die Anfänge der Gesellschaftspolitik in der britischen Zone', *Vierteljahreshefte für Zeitgeschichte*, Vol. 21, No. 2, pp. 171–6

—— (1973b), *Nordrhein-Westfalen und die Entstehung seiner parlamentarischen Demokratie*, Respublica Verlag, Siegburg

Hüwel, D. (1980), *Karl Arnold. Eine politische Biographie*, Peter Hammer Verlag, Wuppertal

Hymans, H. H. E. (1960), 'Anglo-American Policies in Occupied Germany 1945–52', Ph.D. thesis, London School of Economics

IG Metall (1979), *IG Metall—30 Jahre Soziale Gegenmacht*, Frankfurt

Institut für Zeitgeschichte (1976), *Westdeutschlands Weg zur Bundesrepublik 1945–1949*, C. H. Beck, Munich

Inter-Allied Reparation Agency (1952), *Report of the Secretary-General for the Year 1951*, Brussels

Jacobmeyer, W. (1983), 'Jüdische Überlebende als "Displaced Persons". Untersuchungen zur Besatzungspolitik in den deutschen Westzonen und zur Zuwanderung osteuropäischer Juden 1945–1947', *Geschichte und Gesellschaft*, Vol. 9, No. 4, pp. 421–52

—— (1985), *Vom Zwangsarbeiter zum Heimatlosen Ausländer. Die Displaced Persons in Westdeutschland 1945–1951*, Vandenhoeck & Ruprecht, Göttingen

Jaffe, L. S. (1985), *The Decision to Disarm Germany. British Policy towards Postwar German Disarmament 1914–1919*, Allen & Unwin, London and Boston

Jebb, G. (1972), *The Memoirs of Lord Gladwyn*, Weidenfeld & Nicholson, London and New York

Jerchow, F. (1978), *Deutschland in der Weltwirtschaft 1944–1947. Alliierte Deutschland- und Reparationspolitik und die Anfänge der westdeutschen Aussenwirtschaft*, Droste, Düsseldorf

Jürgensen, K. (1969), *Die Gründung des Landes Schleswig-Holstein nach dem Zweiten Weltkrieg*, Wachholtz, Neumünster

—— (1979), 'Elemente britischer Deutschlandpolitik' in C. Scharf and H.–J. Schröder (eds.), *Die Deutschlandpolitik Grossbritanniens und die Britische Zone*, Franz Steiner, Wiesbaden, pp. 103–27

—— (1981), 'Zum Problem der "Political Re-education"' in M. Heinemann (ed.), *Umerziehung und Wiederaufbau. Die Bildungspolitik der Bestazungsmächte in Deutschland und Österreich*, Klett-Cotta, Stuttgart

—— (1983), 'British Occupation Policy after 1945 and the Problem of Re-educating Germany', *History*, Vol. 68, No. 223, pp. 225–44

Kahn, A. D. (1950), *Betrayal. Our Occupation in Germany*, Ksiazka-i-

Wiedza, Warsaw
—— (1964), *Offiziere, Kardinäle und Konzerne. Ein Amerikaner über Deutschland*, Kongress Verlag, East Berlin
Kaldor, N. (1945–46), 'The German War Economy', *Review of Economic Studies*, Vol. 13, No. 2, pp. 33–52
Kennan, F. (1968), *Memoirs 1925–50*, Hutchinson, London
Kettenacker, L. (1977), 'Die britische Haltung zum deutschen Widerstand während des Zweiten Weltkriegs' in L. Kettenacker (ed.), *Das 'Andere Deutschland' im Zweiten Weltkrieg*, Klett, Stuttgart, pp. 49–76
—— (1981), 'Preussen in der alliierten Kriegszielplanung 1939–1947' in L. Kettenacker, M. Schlenke and H. Seier (eds.), *Studien zur Geschichte Englands und der deutsch-britischen Beziehungen. Festschrift für Paul Kluke*, Wilhelm Fink Verlag, Munich, pp. 322–33
—— (1982), 'The Anglo–Soviet Alliance and the Problem of Germany', *Journal of Contemporary History*, Vol. 17, pp. 435–58
—— (1985a), 'Die anglo-amerikanischen Planungen für die Kontrolle Deutschlands' in J. Foschepoth (ed.), *Kalter Krieg und Deutsche Frage*, Vandenhoeck & Ruprecht, Göttingen, pp. 66–87
—— (1985b), 'Grossbritannien und die zukünftige Kontrolle Deutschlands' in J. Foschepoth and R. Steininger (eds.), *Britische Deutschland- und Besatzungspolitik 1945–49*, Schöningh, Paderborn, pp. 27–46
—— (1986), 'Die alliierte Kontrolle Deutschlands als Exempel britischer Herrschaftsausübung' in L. Herbst (ed.), *Westdeutschland 1945–1955*, Oldenbourg Verlag, Munich, pp. 51–64
—— *Friedenssicherung als Kriegsziel. Die britische Nachkriegsplanung für Deutschland während des Zweiten Weltkriegs* (forthcoming)
Keynes, J. M. (1977), *Collected Writings*, Vol. 2, *The Economic Consequences of the Peace*, Macmillan and Cambridge University Press, Cambridge
—— (1980), *Collected Writings*, Vol. 26, *Activities 1942–46. Shaping the Post-War World: Bretton Woods and Reparations*, edited by D. Moggridge, Macmillan and Cambridge University Press, Cambridge
Kirkpatrick, I. (1959), *The Inner Circle*, Macmillan, London
Klarmann, N. and Wessel, H. A. (eds.) (1983), *Verzeichnis deutscher Wirtschaftsarchive*, Institut für bankhistorische Forschung/Gesellschaft für Unternehmensgeschichte, Wiesbaden
Klemm, B. and Trittel G. J. (1987), 'Vor dem "Wirtschaftswunder": Durchbruch zum Wachstum oder Lähmungskrise? Eine Auseinandersetzung mit Werner Abelshausers Interpretation der Wirtschaftsentwicklung 1945–1948', *Vierteljahrshefte für Zeitgeschichte*, Vol. 35, No. 4, pp. 571–624
Klessman, C. (1979), 'Betriebsräte und Gewerkschaften in Deutschland 1945–1952' in H. Winkler (ed.), *Politische Weichenstellungen in Nachkriegsdeutschland 1945–1952*, Vandenhoeck & Ruprecht, Göttingen, pp. 44–73

—— (1982), *Die doppelte Staatsgründung. Deutsche Geschichte 1945–1955*, Vandenhoeck & Ruprecht, Göttingen

—— (1983), 'Betriebsparteigruppen und Einheitsgewerkschaft', *Vierteljahreshefte für Zeitgeschichte*, Vol. 31, No. 2, pp. 272–307

Klessmann, C. and Friedmann, P. (1977), *Streiks und Hungermärsche im Ruhrgebiet 1946–1948*, Campus Verlag, Frankfurt.

Klimov, G. (1953), *The Terror Machine. The Inside Story of the Soviet Administration in Germany*, Praeger, New York

Klopstock, F. H. (1949), 'Monetary Reform in Western Germany', *Journal of Political Economy*, Vol. 57, No. 4, pp. 277–92

Klotzbach, K. (1982), *Der Weg zur Staatspartei. Programmatik, praktische Politik und Organisation der deutschen Sozialdemokratie 1945 bis 1965*, Dietz, Berlin and Bonn

Knapp, M. (1977), 'Deutschland und der Marshallplan' in C. Scharf and H.–J. Schröder, *Politische und ökonomische Stabilisierung Westdeutschlands 1945–1949*, Franz Steiner, Wiesbaden, pp. 19–43

—— (1984), 'Die Anfänge westdeutscher Aussenwirtschafts- und Aussenpolitik im bizonalen Vereinigten Wirtschaftsgebiet (1947–1949)' in M. Knapp (ed.), *Von der Bizonengründung zur ökonomisch-politischen Westintegration*, Haag & Herchen Verlag, Frankfurt on Main, pp. 13–94

Knapp, M. (ed.) (1984), *Von der Bizonengründung zur ökonomisch-politischen Westintegration*, Haag & Herchen Verlag, Frankfurt on Main

Knipping, F. and Le Rider, J. (eds.) (1987), *Frankreichs Kulturpolitik in Deutschland 1945–1950*, Attempto Verlag, Tübingen

Köchling, M. (1986), 'Demontagepolitik in Nordrhein-Westfalen 1945–48. Zur Rolle der Industrie- und Handelskammer', MA thesis, University of Bochum

Kogon, E. (1948), 'Der entscheidende Schritt', *Frankfurter Hefte*, Vol. 3, pp. 586–91

Kornai, J. (1971), *Anti-Equilibrium: On Economic Systems Theory and the Tasks of Research*, North Holland, Amsterdam

—— (1980), *The Economics of Shortage*, Vols. A and B, North Holland, Amsterdam

Kornai, J. and Martos, B. (1973), 'Autonomous Control of the Economic System', *Econometrica*, Vol. 41, No. 3, pp. 509–28

Kornrumpf, M. (1979), *In Bayern angekommen. Die Eingliederung der Vertriebenen. Zahlen—Daten—Namen*, Günter Olzog Verlag, Munich

Koszyk, K. (1978), '"Umerziehung" der Deutschen aus britischer Sicht', *Aus Politik und Zeitgeschichte* B29//78, pp. 3–12

—— (1983), *The German Press under British Occupation*, Neue Gesellschaft, Siegen

—— (1986), *Pressepolitik für Deutsche 1945–1949*, Colloquium Verlag, Berlin

Kramer, A. (1985), 'Demontagepolitik in Hamburg' in J. Foschepoth and R. Steininger (eds.), *Britische Deutschland- und Besatzungspolitik*

1945–49, Schöningh, Paderborn, pp. 265–80

—— (1986), 'Demontage der Industrie und Wiederaufbau des Hafens: Die Hamburger Wirtschaft im Zeichen der britischen Besatzungspolitik' in J. Ellermeyer and R. Postel (eds.), *Stadt und Hafen. Hamburger Beiträge zur Geschichte von Handel und Schiffahrt*, Arbeitshefte zur Denkmalpflege in Hamburg, No. 8, Christians Verlag, Hamburg, pp. 142–53

—— (1988), '"Law-abiding Germans"? Social Disintegration, Crime and the Re-imposition of Order in Post-War Germany 1945–1949' in J. Evans (ed.), *The German Underworld*, Croom Helm, London

—— (1989), 'Die britische Demontagepolitik am Beispiel Hamburgs 1945–1950', PhD thesis, Hamburg University 1987; forthcoming, Christians Verlag, Hamburg, 1989

Kreikamp, H.–D. (1977), 'Die Entflechtung der IG Farbenindustrie AG und die Gründung der Nachfolgegesellschaften', *Vierteljahreshefte für Zeitgeschichte*, Vol. 25, No. 2, pp. 220–51

—— (1981), 'Die amerikanische Deutschlandpolitik im Herbst 1946 und die Byrnes-Rede in Stuttgart', *Vierteljahrshefte für Zeitgeschichte*, Vol. 29, No. 2, pp. 269–85

Krengel, R. (1957), 'Die Investitionstätigkeit der westdeutschen Industrie seit Mitte 1948 im konjunkturellen Verlauf', *Vierteljahrshefte zur Wirtschaftsforschung*, Vol. 1, pp. 49–68

—— (1958), *Anlagevermögen, Produktion und Beschäftigung der Industrie im Gebiet der Bundesrepublik Deutschland von 1924 zu 1956*, DIW, Berlin

Krieger, W. (1987), *General Lucius D. Clay und die amerikanische Deutschlandpolitik 1945–1949*, Klett-Cotta, Stuttgart

Krug, M. and Mundhenke, K. (1988), *Flüchtlinge in der Stadt Hameln und in der Region Hannover 1945–1952*, Verlag August Lax, Hildesheim

Kruger, W. (1982), *Entnazifiziert!*, Hammer, Wuppertal

Krumbein, W. (1984), 'Wirtschaftsteuerung zwischen den Organisationsformen "Staat" und "Selbstverwaltung". Das Beispiel des Verwaltungsamtes für Stahl und Eisen 1945–1950' in D. Petzina and W. Euchner (eds.), *Wirtschaftspolitik im britischen Besatzungsgebiet 1945–1949*, Schwann, Düsseldorf, pp. 197–214

Kuklick, B. (1972), *American Policy and the Division of Germany. The Clash with Russia over Reparations*, Cornell University Press, Ithaca, New York

Kutsch, A. (1987), 'Zur Geschichte der Lizenzpresse in der Britischen Besatzungszone', *Geschichte im Westen*, Vol. 2, No. 2

Lademacher, H. (1979a), 'Die britische Sozialisierungspolitik im Rhein–Ruhr-Raum 1945 bis 1948' in C. Scharf and H.–J. Schröder (eds.), *Die Deutschlandpolitik Grossbritanniens und die britische Zone 1945–49*, Franz Steiner Verlag, Wiesbaden, pp. 51–92

—— (1979b), 'Grossbritannien und die Rhein–Ruhr-Frage' in W. Först (ed.), *Entscheidungen im Westen*, Grote, Cologne and Berlin, pp. 83–143

—— (1982), 'Das Petersberger Abkommen' in W. Först (ed.), *Zwischen Ruhrkontrolle und Mitbestimming*, Kohlhammer/Grote, Cologne, pp. 67–90

—— (1985), 'Zur Bedeutung des Petersberger Abkommens vom 22 November 1949' in J. Foschepoth (ed.), *Kalter Krieg und Deutsche Frage*, Vandenhoeck & Ruprecht, Göttingen, pp. 240–68

—— (1986), 'Sozialökonomische Weichenstellungen: Sozialisierung und Mitbestimmung', *Aus Politik und Zeitgeschichte*, B49/86, pp. 15–23

Lademacher, H. and Mühlhausen, W. (eds.) (1985), *Sicherheit, Kontrolle, Souveränität. Das Petersberger Abkommen vom 22 November 1949. Eine Dokumentation*, Verlag Kasseler Forschungen zur Zeitgeschichte, Melsungen

LaFeber, W. (1976), *America, Russia and the Cold War 1945–1975*, John Wiley, New York

Lange, E. H. (1975), *Wahlrecht und Innenpolitik*, Hain, Meisenheim on Glam

Lange, I. (ed.) (1976), *Die Entnazifizierung in Nordrheinwestfalen*, Respublica Verlag, Sieburg

Latour, C. F. and Vogelsang, T. (1973), *Okkupation und Wiederaufbau*, Deutsche Verlags-Anstalt, Stuttgart

Link, W. (1978), *Deutsche und amerikanische Gewerkschaften und Geschäftsleute 1945–75: Eine Studie über transnationale Beziehungen*, Droste, Düsseldorf

Litchfield, E. H. *et al.* (1953), *Governing Post-War Germany*, Cornell University Press, Ithaca, New York

Lüders, C. (1984), 'Die Regelung der Ruhrfrage in den Verhandlungen über die politische und ökonomische Stabilisierung Westdeutschlands 1945–1949' in D. Petzina and W. Euchner (eds.), *Wirtschaftspolitik im britischen Besatzungsgebiet 1945–1949*, Schwann, Düsseldorf, pp. 87–105

Lynch, F. M. B. (1981), 'The Political and Economic Reconstruction of France 1944–1947 in the International Context', PhD thesis, Manchester University

Macready, G. (1965), *In the Wake of the Great*, William Clowes & Sons, London

Malinvaud, E. (1977), *The Theory of Unemployment Reconsidered*, Blackwell, Oxford

Manz, M. (1968), 'Stagnation und Aufschwung in der französischen Besatzungszone von 1945 bis 1948', PhD thesis, University of Mannheim

Marshall, B. (1980), 'German Attitudes to British Military Government 1945–47', *Journal of Contemporary History*, Vol. 15, No. 4, pp. 655–84

—— (1986), 'The Democratisation of Local Politics in the British Zone of Germany: Hanover 1945–7', *Journal of Contemporary History*, Vol. 21, No. 3, pp. 413–51

—— (1988), *Origins of West German Politics*, Croom Helm, London

Marten, H. G. (1978), *Die unterwanderte FDP*, Musterschmidt, Göttingen

Martin, J. S. (1950), *All Honourable Men*, Little Brown, Boston, Mass.

Mastny, V. (1979), *Russia's Road to the Cold War*, Columbia University Press, New York

McNeil, W. H. (1953), *America, Britain and Russia: Their Cooperation and Conflict 1941–1946*, Oxford University Press, London

Mee, C. L. (1975), *Meeting at Potsdam*, Deutsch, London

—— (1984), *The Marshall Plan*, Simon & Schuster, New York

Meinicke, W. (1984), 'Die Entnazifizierung in der sowjetischen Besatzungszone 1945 bis 1948', *Zeitschrift für Geschichtswissenschaft*, Vol. 32, No. 10, pp. 969–79

Melissen, J. and Zeeman, B. (1986–7), 'Britain and Western Europe, 1945–51: Opportunities Lost?,' *International Affairs*, Vol. 63, No. 1, pp. 81–95

Melrose, G. (1983), *A Strange Occupation*, New Horizon, Bognor Regis

Mendershausen, H. (1949), 'Prices, Money and the Distribution of Goods in Post-War Germany', *American Economic Review*, Vol. 39, No. 4, pp. 646–72

Menne-Haritz, A. (1987), 'Wirtschaftsverwaltung in der Nachkriegszeit. Der Einfluss der britischen Besatzungsbehörden auf den Wiederaufbau der Wirtschaftsverwaltung in Schleswig-Holstein', *Zeitschrift der Gesellschaft für Schleswig-Holsteinische Geschichte*, Vol. 112, pp. 245–65

Merkl, P. H. (1963), *The Origins of the West German Republic*, Oxford University Press, Oxford

Merritt, A. J. and Merritt, R. L. (1970), *Public Opinion in Occupied Germany: the OMGUS Surveys 1945–49*, University of Illinois, Chicago, Ill.

—— (1980), *Public Opinion in Semisovereign Germany*, University of Illinois Press, Chicago, Ill.

Milert, W. (1984), 'Die verschenkte Kontrolle. Bestimmungsgründe und Grundzüge der britischen Kohlenpolitik im Ruhrbergbau 1945–1948', in D. Petzina and W. Euchner (eds.), *Wirtschaftspolitik im britischen Besatzungsgebiet 1945–1949*, Schwann, Düsseldorf, pp. 105–20

Millis, W. (1951), *The Forrestal Diaries*, The Viking Press, New York

Milward, A. S. (1984a), *The Reconstruction of Western Europe 1945–51*, Methuen, London

—— (1984b), 'Grossbritannien, Deutschland und der Wiederaufbau Westeuropas' in D. Petzina and W. Euchner (eds.), *Wirtschaftspolitik im britischen Besatzungsgebiet 1945–1949*, Schwann, Düsseldorf, pp. 25–40

Möding, N. (1987), 'Die Stunde der Frauen? Frauen und Frauenorganisationen des bürgerlichen Lagers' in M. Broszat *et al.* (eds.), *Von Stalingrad zur Währungsreform*, Oldenbourg Verlag, Munich

Monnet, J. (1976), *Memoirs*, Fayard, Paris

Montgomery, B. (1958), *The Memoirs of Field Marshal Montgomery*, Collins, London

Montgomery, J. D. (1957), *Forced to be Free. The Artificial Revolution in Germany and Japan*, Chicago University Press, Chicago, Ill.

Morgenthau, H. (1945), *Germany is Our Problem*, Harper, New York

Morsey, R. (1977), 'Personal- und Beamtenpolitik im Übergang von der Bizonen- zur -Bundesverwaltung (1947–1950)' in R. Morsey (ed.), *Verwaltungsgeschichte: Aufgaben, Zielsetzungen, Beispiele*, Duncker & Humblot, Berlin, pp. 191–238

Morsey, R. and Schwarz, H.–P. (eds.) (1984 and 1986), *Adenauer Rhöndorfer Ausgabe*, including *Briefe 1945–1951*, 3 volumes, prepared by H.–P. Mensing and *Teegespräche 1950–1958*, 2 volumes, prepared by H.–J. Kusters, Siedler Verlag, Berlin

Müller, C. (1987), *Mitbestimmung in der Nachkriegszeit. Britische Besatzungsmacht, Unternehmer, Gewerkschaften*, Schwann, Düsseldorf

Müller, G. (1984), 'Sicherheit durch wirtschaftliche Stabilität? Die Rolle der Briten bei der Auseinandersetzung der Alliierten um die Stahlquote des I. Industrieniveauplans vom 26 März 1946' in D. Petzina and W. Euchner (eds.), *Wirtschaftspolitik im britischen Besatzungsgebiet 1945–1949*, Schwann, Düsseldorf, pp. 65–86

Müller-List, G. (1982), 'Die Enstehung der Montanmitbestimmung' in W. Först (ed.), *Ruhrkontrolle und Mitbestimmung*, Kohlhammer/Grote, Cologne, pp. 121–44

—— (1984), (ed.), *Montanmitbestimmung*, Droste, Düsseldorf

—— (1985), 'Adenauer, Unternehmer und Gewerkschaften. Zur Einigung über die Montanmitbestimmung 1950/1', *Vierteljahreshefte für Zeitgeschichte*, Vol. 35, No. 2, pp. 288–309

Nassmacher, K. H. (1983), 'Der Wiederbeginn des politischen Lebens in Niedersachsen', *Niedersächsisches Jahrbuh für Landesgeschichte*, Vol. 55, pp. 71–97

Neave, A. (1978), *Nüremberg*, Hodder and Stoughton, London

Nettl, J. P. (1951), *The Eastern Zone and Soviet Policy in Germany 1945–1950*, Oxford University Press, London

Neumann, F. (1968), *Der Block der Heimatvertriebenen und Entrechteten 1950–60. Ein Beitrag zur Geschichte und Struktur einer politischen Interessenpartei*, A. Hain, Meisenheim

Newton, S. (1983), 'How successful was the Marshall Plan?', *History Today*, Vol. 33, pp. 11–15

Niehues, A. (1947), 'Ruhrbergbau und Arbeitsvermittlung', *Arbeitsblatt für die britische Zone*, Vol. 1, No. 3, pp. 88–90

Niethammer, L. (1972), *Entnazifizierung in Bayern*, S. Fischer, Frankfurt on Main

—— et al. (eds.) (1976), *Arbeiterinitiative 1945*, Hammer, Wuppertal

Niethammer, L. (ed.) (1983a), '*Die Jahre weiss man nicht, wo man sie heute hinsetzen soll'. Faschismuserfahrungen im Ruhrgebiet*, Dietz, Berlin and Bonn

—— (1983b), '*Hinterher merkt man, dass es richtig war, dass es schiefge-*

gangen ist!' Nachkriegserfahrungen im Ruhrgebiet, Dietz, Berlin and Bonn

Nübel, O. (1980), *Die amerikanische Reparationspolitik gegenüber Deutschland 1941–1945*, Metzner, Frankfurt, pp. 78–113

OECD (1970), *National Accounts 1950–68*, Paris

Ovendale, R. (1985), *The English-Speaking Alliance. Britain, the United States, the Dominions and the Cold War 1945–1951*, Allen and Unwin, London

—— (ed.) (1984), *The Foreign Policy of the British Labour Governments 1945–1951*, Leicester University Press, Leicester

Overesch, M. (1979), *Deutschland 1945–1949*, Athenäum Droste, Düsseldorf

—— (1987), *Chronik deutscher Zeitgeschichte. Das besetzte Deutschland 1945–1947, 1948–1949*, 2 vols., Droste, Düsseldorf

Pakenham, F. (1953), *Born to Believe*, Jonathan Cape, London

Pakschies, G. (1979), *Umerziehung in der britischen Zone 1945–1949*, Beltz, Weinheim and Basel

—— (1981), 'Re-education und die Vorbereitung der britischen Bildungs-politik während des zweiten Weltkriegs' in M. Heinemann (ed.), *Umerziehung und Wiederaufbau. Die Bildungspolitik der Besatzungsmächte in Deutschland und Österreich*, Klett-Cotta, Stuttgart, pp. 103–13

Paterson, W. E. (1974), *The SPD and European Integration*, Saxon House, Farnborough

—— (1988), 'The British Labour Party and the SPD 1945–52' in Friedrich Ebert Stiftung, *Kurt Schumacher als deutscher und europäischer Sozialist*, Bonn

Penrose, E. F. (1953), *Economic Planning for Peace*, University Press, Princeton, NY

Perk, W. (1979), *Besatzungsmacht gegen Pressefreiheit*, Verlag Marxistische Blätter, Frankfurt on Main

Peterson, E. N. (1977), *Retreat from Victory. The American Occupation of Germany 1945–1952*, Wayne State University Press, Detroit, Mich.

Petzina, D. and Euchner, W. (eds.) (1984), *Wirtschaftspolitik im britischen Besatzungsgebiet 1945–49*, Schwann, Düsseldorf

Petzold, J. D. von (1983), *Sozialdemokraten in Niedersachsen 1945/46*, Verlag August Lax, Hildesheim

Pfetsch, F. R. (1985), *Verfassungspolitik der Nachkriegszeit. Theorie und Praxis des bundesdeutschen Konstitutionalismus*, Wissenschaftliche Buchgesellschaft, Darmstadt

—— (1986), 'Die Verfassungspolitik der westlichen Besatzungsmächte in den Ländern nach 1945', *Aus Politik und Zeitgeschichte*, B22/86, 31 May, pp. 3–17

—— *Ursprünge der Zweiten Republik*, Westdeutscher Verlag, Opladen, forthcoming

Phillips, D. (1980), 'Lindsay and the German Universities: An Oxford

Contribution to the Post-War Reform Debate', *Oxford Review of Education*, Vol. 6, pp. 91–105

—— (1981), 'Britische Initiativen zur Hochschulreform in Deutschland. Zur Vorgeschichte und Entstehung des "Gutachtens zur Hochschulreform" von 1948' in M. Heinemann (ed.) *Umerziehung und Wiederaufbau. Die Bildungspolitik der Besatzungsmächte in Deutschland und Österreich*, Klett-Cotta, Stuttgart, pp. 172–89

—— (1983a), 'Die Wiedereröffnung der Universitäten in der britischen Zone: Das Problem Nationalsozialismus und Zulassung zum Studium', *Bildung und Erziehung*, Part 1

—— (1983b), *German Universities after the Surrender: British Occupation Policy and the Control of Higher Education*, University of Oxford, Dept of Educational Studies, Oxford

Pietsch, H. (1978), *Militärregierung, Bürokratie und Sozialisierung. Entwicklung des politischen Systems in den Städten des Ruhrgebiets, 1945–48*, Walter Braun, Duisburg

Pimlott, B. (1985), *Hugh Dalton*, Cape, London

—— (ed.) (1987), *The Political Diary of Hugh Dalton 1918–40, 1945–60*, Weidenfeld and Nicholson, London

Pingel, F. (1982), '"Die Russen am Rhein?" Zur Wende der britischen Besatzungspolitik im Frühjahr 1946', *Vierteljahrshefte für Zeitgeschichte*, Vol. 30, No. 1, pp. 98–116

—— (1984), 'Der aufhaltsame Aufschwung. Die Wirtschaftsplanung für die britische Zone im Rahmen der aussenpolitischen Interessen der Besatzungsmacht' in D. Petzina und W. Euchner (eds.) *Wirtschaftspolitik im britischen Besatzungsgebiet 1945–1949*, Schwann, Düsseldorf, pp. 41–64

—— (1985), 'Wissenschaft, Bildung und Demokratie—der gescheiterte Versuch einer Universitätsreform' in J. Foschepoth and R. Steininger (eds.), *Britische Deutschland- und Besatzungspolitik 1945–1949*, Schöningh, Paderborn, pp. 183–209

Pirker, T. (1979), *Die blinde Macht. Die Gewerkschaftsbewegung in Westdeutschland*, Vol. 1, Olle und Wolter, Berlin

Plato, A. von (ed.) (1985), '*Wir kriegen jetzt andere Zeiten*'. *Auf der Suche nach der Erfahrung des Volkes in nach-faschistischen Ländern*, Dietz, Berlin and Bonn

Plischke, E. (1955), *History of the Allied High Commission for Germany. Its Establishment, Structure and Procedures*, Historical Division, Office of Executive Secretary, Office of the US High Commission for Germany, Berlin

Plumpe, W. (1981), 'Gesellschaftliche Neuordnung oder ökonomische Entwicklungspolitik?' *WSI-Mitteilungen*, No. 7, pp. 405–14

—— (1984), 'Wirtschaftsverwaltung und Kapitalinteresse im Britischen Besatzungsgebiet 1945/46' in D. Petzina and W. Euchner (eds.), *Wirtschaftspolitik im britischen Besatzungsgebiet 1945–49*, Schwann, Düsseldorf, pp. 121–52

—— (1986), 'Auf dem Weg in die Marktwirtschaft: Organisierte Industrieinteressen, Wirtschaftsverwaltung und Besatzungsmacht in Nordrhein-Westfalen 1945–1947' in G. Brunn (ed.), *Neuland, Nordrhein-Westfalen und seine Anfänge nach 1945/46*, Hobbing, Essen, pp. 67–84

—— (1987), '*Vom Plan zum Markt*'. *Wirtschaftsverwaltung und Unternehmerverbände in der britischen Zone*, Schwann, Düsseldorf

Poidevin, R. (1983), 'Frankreich und die deutsche Frage 1943–49' in J. Becker and A. Hillgruber (eds.), *Die deutsche Frage im 19. und 20. Jahrhundert*, Vogel, Munich, pp. 405–20

Pollmann, B. (1977), *Reformansätze in Niedersachsen 1945–1949*, Niedersächsische Landeszentrale für politische Bildung, Brunswick

Post, O. (1986), 'Zwischen Sicherheit und Wiederaufbau. Die Ruhrfrage in der alliierten Diskussion 1945–1949', PhD thesis, University of Giessen

Potthoff, E. (1957), *Der Kampf um die Mitbestimmung*, Bund-Verlag, Cologne

Potthoff, H. and Wenzel, R. (1983), *Handbuch politischer Institutionen und Organisationen 1945–49*, Droste, Düsseldorf

Prais, S. J. (1981), *Productivity and Industrial Structure*, Cambridge University Press, Cambridge

Prittie, T. (1972), *Adenauer*, Stacey, London

Pritzkoleit, K. (1963), *Gott erhält die Mächtigen. Rück- und Rundblick auf den deutschen Wohlstand*, Karl Rauch, Düsseldorf

Pronay, N. and Wilson, K. (eds.) (1985), *The Political Re-education of Germany and Her Allies after World War II*, Croom Helm, London

Prowe, D. (1981), 'Wirtschaftsdemokratische Ansätze 1945–1949: Die Auseinandersetzung um die paritätische Mitbestimmung der Arbeitnehmer in den Industrie- und Handelskammern', *WSI-Mitteilungen*, No. 7, pp. 398–405

—— (1984a), *Führer zu den Archiven und Bibliotheken und Forschungseinrichtungen zur Geschichte der europäischen Arbeiterbewegung*, Verlag Neue Gesellschaft, Bonn

—— (1984b), 'Unternehmer, Gewerkschaften und Staat in der Kammerneuordnung in der britischen Besatzungszone bis 1950' in D. Petzina and W. Euchner (eds.), *Wirtschaftspolitik im britischen Besatzungsgebiet 1945–49*, Schwann, Düsseldorf, pp. 235–54

—— (1985), 'Economic Democracy in Post World War II Germany: Corporatist Crisis and Response 1945–8', *Journal of Modern History*, Vol. 57, No. 3, pp. 461–82

—— 'Im Sturmzentrum: Die Industrie- und Handelskammern in den Nachkriegsjahren 1945–1949', *DIHT-Materialien zur Geschichte*, Vol. 4, forthcoming

Pünder, H. (1968), *Von Preussen nach Europa*, Deutsche Verlags-Anstalt, Stuttgart

Pünder, T. (1966), *Das Bizonale Interregnum*, Grote, Waiblingen

Ratchford, B. U. and Ross, W. D. (1947), *Berlin Reparations Assignment.*

Round One of the German Peace Settlement, University of North Carolina Press, Chapel Hill, NC

Reidegeld, E. (1984), 'Die klassische Sozialversicherung in der Entscheidung: deutsche und alliierte Kräfte und Interessen vor und nach 1945', *Zeitschrift für Sozialreform*, Vol. 30, No. 11, pp. 649–75

Reulecke, J. (1987), 'Probleme einer Sozial- und Mentalitätsgeschichte der Nachkriegszeit', *Geschichte im Westen*, Vol. 2, No. 1, pp. 7–25

Reusch, U. (1980), 'Die Londoner Institutionen der britischen Deutschlandpolitik 1943–1949', *Historisches Jahrbuch*, Vol. 100, pp. 318–423

—— (1985a), *Deutsches Berufsbeamtentum und britische Reformpolitik: Planung und Politik 1943–1947*, Klett-Cotta, Stuttgart

—— (1985b), 'Versuche zur Neuordung des Berufsbeamtentums' in J. Foschepoth and R. Steininger (eds.), *Britische Deutschland- und Besatzungspolitik 1945–49*, Schöningh, Paderborn, pp. 171–82

—— (1986), 'Das Porträt: John Burns Hynd (1902–1971)', *Geschichte im Westen*, Vol. 1, No. 1, pp. 53–80

—— (1987), 'Briten und Deutsche in der Besatzungszeit', *Geschichte im Westen*, Vol. 2, No. 1, pp. 145–58

Reynolds, D. (1985), 'Origins of the Cold War: The European Dimension 1945–51', *Historical Journal*, Vol. 28, No. 2, pp. 497–515

Richmond, L. and Stockford, B. (1986), *Company Archives*, Gower, Aldershot

Riedel, M. (1967), *Vorgeschichte, Entstehung und Demontage der Reichswerke im Salzgittergebiet*, Technikgeschichte in Einzeldarstellungen, No. 4, Düsseldorf

—— (1983), 'Die wirtschaftliche Entwicklung in Niedersachsen 1945–50', *Niedersächsisches Jahrbuch für Landesgeschichte*, Vol. 57, pp. 115–38

Ritschl, A. (1985), 'Die Währungsreform von 1948 und der Wiederaufstieg der westdeutschen Industrie', *Vierteljahrshefte für Zeitgeschichte*, Vol. 33, No. 1, pp. 136–65

Robertson, Lord (1965), 'A Miracle? Potsdam 1945—Western Germany 1965', *International Affairs*, Vol. 41, No. 3, July, pp. 401–10

Robinson, S. B. and Kuhlmann, J. C. (1967), 'Two Decades of Non-Reform in West German Education', *Comparative Education Review*, Vol. 11, No. 3, pp. 311–30

Rode, N. (1981), 'Zur Entstehungsgeschichte der NLP/DP', *Niedersächsisches Jahrbuch für Landesgeschichte*, Vol. 53, pp. 290ff

Rohrbach, J. (1955), *Im Schatten des Hungers*, Parey, Hamburg and Berlin

Röpcke, A. (1985), 'Who's Who in Lower Saxony. Ein politisch–biographischer Leitfaden der britischen Besatzungsmacht 1948/49', *Niedersächsiches Jahrbuch für Landesgeschichte*, Vol. 57, pp. 243ff

Roseman, M. (1987), 'Recasting the Labour Force: Employers, New Labour and Mining Hostels 1945–1958', unpublished paper given at a symposium on 'Continuity and Change: German Society in Transition in the New German States 1945–55', University of Liverpool, September–October.

—— (1988), 'New Miners in the Ruhr 1945–1958', PhD thesis, Warwick University.

—— (1989), 'Delayed Recovery. British Manpower Policy in the Ruhr Mines 1945–1947' in R. Lee (ed.), *Industrialisation and Industrial Development in Germany*, Croom Helm, London,

Rosenberg, L. (1947), 'Wirtschaftskammer und Gewerkschaft', *Westfälische Rundschau*, 14 June

—— (1949), 'Zum Ruhrstatut', *Der Bund*, Vol. 3, 15 January, p. 2

—— (1978), 'Die Weltpolitik der deutschen Gewerkschaften' in U. Börsdorf and H. O. Hemmer (eds.), *Gewerkschaftliche Politik: Reform aus Solidarität*, Bund-Verlag, Cologne

Roskamp, K. W. (1965), *Capital Formation in West Germany*, Wayne State University Press, Detroit, Mich.

Ross, G. (1981), 'Foreign Office Attitudes to the Soviet Union 1941–45', *Journal of Contemporary History*, Vol. 16, No. 3, pp. 521–40

Ross, G. (ed.) (1984), *The Foreign Office and the Kremlin, British Documents on Anglo-Soviet Relations, 1941–45*, Cambridge University Press, Cambridge

Rostow W. W. (1982), *The Division of Europe after World War II: 1946*, Gower, Aldershot

Rothwell, V. (1982), *Britain and the Cold War 1941–1947*, Cape, London

Rudzio, W. (1968), *Die Neordnung des Kommunalwesens in der Britischen Zone. Zur Demokratisierung und Dezentralisierung der politischen Struktur: eine britische Reform und ihr Ausgang*, Deutsche Verlags-Anstalt, Stuttgart

—— (1969), 'Export englischer Demokratie?', *Vierteljahreshefte für Zeitgeschichte*, Vol. 17, No. 2, pp. 219–36

—— (1978), 'Die ausgebliebene Sozialisierung am Rhein und Ruhr. Zur Sozialisierungspolitik von Labour Regierung und SPD 1945–1948', *Archiv für Sozialgeschichte*, Vol. 18, pp. 1–39

—— (1981), 'Grossbritannien als sozialistische Besatzungsmacht in Deutschland—Aspekte des deutsch–britischen Verhältnisses 1945–1948' in L. Kettenacker, M. Schlenke and H. Seier (eds.), *Studien zur Geschichte Englands und der deutsch-britischen Beziehungen. Festschrift für Paul Kluke*, Wilhelm Fink Verlag, Munich, pp. 341–52

—— (1985), 'Das Sozialisierungskonzept der SPD und seine internationalen Realisierungsbedingungen' in J. Foschepoth and R. Steininger (eds.), *Britische Deutschland- und Besatzungspolitik 1945–1949*, Schöningh, Paderborn, pp. 119–34

Ruhl, H.-J. (ed.) (1982), *Neubeginn und Restauration. Dokumente zur Vorgeschichte der Bundesrepublik Deutschland 1945–1949*, Deutscher Taschenbuch Verlag, Munich

—— (1985), *'Mein Gott was soll aus Deutschland werden?' Die Adenauer-Ära 1949–1963*, Deutscher Taschenbuch Verlag, Munich

Ruhm von Oppen, B. (1955), *Documents on Germany under Occupation*

1945–1954, Oxford University Press, London

Sainsbury, K. (1979), 'British Policy and German Unity at the End of the Second World War', *English Historical Review*, Vol. 94, No. 373, pp. 786–804

Scharf, C. and Schröder, H. J. (eds.) (1977), *Politische und ökonomische Stabilisierung Westdeutschlands*, Franz Steiner Verlag, Wiesbaden

—— (1979), *Die Deutschlandpolitik Grossbritanniens und die britische Zone 1945–49*, Franz Steiner Verlag, Wiesbaden

—— (1983), *Die Deutschlandpolitik Frankreichs und die französische Zone 1945–49*, Franz Steiner Verlag, Wiesbaden

Scherpenberg, J. van (1984), *Öffentliche Finanzwirtschaft in Westdeutschland 1944–1948. Steuer- und Haushaltswesen in der Schlussphase des Krieges und den unmittelbaren Nachkriegsjahren, dargestellt unter besonderer Berücksichtigung der Entwicklung in der britischen Zone*, Fischer, Frankfurt on Main

—— (1985), 'Die Rekonstruktion der öffentlichen Finanzwirtschaft' in J. Foschepoth and R. Steininger (eds.), *Britische Deutschland- und Besatzungspolitik 1945–1949*, Schöningh, Paderborn, pp. 213–44

Schier, S. (1982), *Die Aufnahme und Eingliederung von Flüchtlingen und Vertriebenen in der Hansestadt Lübeck*, Schmidt Römhild, Lübeck

Schillinger, R. (1985), 'Der Lastenausgleich' in W. Benz (ed.), *Die Vertreibung der Deutschen aus dem Osten*, Fischer, Frankfurt on Main, pp. 183–92

Schmidt, E. (1970), *Die verhinderte Neuordnung 1945–52*, Europäische Verlagsanstalt, Cologne

Schmidt, G. (1986), *The Politics and Economics of Appeasement*, Berg, Leamington Spa

Schmidt, H. G. (1952), 'The Reorganisation of the West German Coal and Iron and Steel Industries under the Allied High Commission for Germany 1949–52', Office of the US High Commissioner, Historical Division, September

Schneider, U. (1980), 'Britische Besatzungspolitik 1945', PhD thesis, University of Hanover.

—— (1981), 'Grundzüge britischer Deutschland- und Besatzungspolitik', *Zeitgeschichte*, Vol. 9, No. 3, pp. 73–89

—— (1982), 'Zur Deutschland- und Besatzungspolitik Grossbritanniens im Rahmen der Vier-mächte Kontrolle Deutschlands von Kriegsende bis Herbst 1945', *Militärgeschichtliche Mitteilungen*, Vol. 34, No. 2, pp. 77–112

—— (1984), *Niedersachsen 1945/46. Kontinuität und Wandel unter britischer Besatzung*, Niedersächsische Landeszentrale für politische Bildung, Hanover

—— (1984), 'Wirtschaftsausschüsse als Mittel praktizierter Wirtschaftsdemokratie? Überbetriebliche Mitbestimmung und die Versuche zur "Demokratisierung der Wirtschaft" in der britischen Besatzungszone' in

B. Rebe *et al.* (eds.), *Idee und Pragmatik in der politischen Entscheidung. Alfred Kubel zum 75 Geburtstag*, Neue Gesellschaft, Bonn and Bad Godesberg, pp. 317–32

—— (1985), *Niedersachsen 1945. Kriegsende, Wiederaufbau, Landesgründung*, Schlütersche Verlangsanstalt, Hanover

—— *Die Entnazifizierung der Hochschullehrer in Niedersachsen 1945–1949. Unter besonderer Berüchsichtigung der T. H. Hannover* (forthcoming)

Schröder, H.-J. (1987), 'The Economic Reconstruction of West Germany in the Context of International Relations 1945–1949' in J. Becker and F. Knipping (eds.), *Power in Europe? Great Britain, France, Italy and Germany in a Post-War World, 1945–1950*, Walter de Gruyter, Berlin and New York, pp. 302–22

Schröder, K. (1985), *Die FDP in der britischen Besatzungszone 1946–1948*, Droste, Düsseldorf

Schulze, R. (1985), 'Bürgerliche Sammlung oder Welfenpartei? Ergänzungen zur Enstehungsgeschichte der Niedersächsischen Landespartei 1945/46: Die Konzeption Wolfgang Bodes', *Niedersächsisches Jahrbuch für Landesgeschichte*, Vol. 57, pp. 207–36

—— (1987a), 'Interessenvertretung und Eliterekrutierung. Zur Rolle der Industrie- und Handelskammern in der Politik nach dem Ende des Zweiten Weltkrieges', unpublished paper given at a symposium on 'Continuity and Change: German Society in Transition to the New German States 1945–55', University of Liverpool, September–October

—— (1987b), *Unternehmerische Selbstverwaltung und Politik. Die Rolle der Industrie und Handelskammern in Niedersachsen und Bremen als Vertretungen der Unternehmerinteressen nach dem Ende des Zweiten Weltkrieges*, Verlag August Lax, Hildesheim

—— (1988), *Unrühige Zeiten. Erlebnisberichte aus dem Landkreis Celle 1945–1949*, Oldenbourg Verlag, Munich

Schulze, R. and von der Brelie-Lewien, D. (1987), 'Flucht und Vertreibung—Aufnahme und Sesshaftwerdung. Neue Fragen und Ansätze für einen alten Themenbereich der deutschen Nachkriegsgeschichte', *Jahrbuch für ostdeutsche Volkskunde*, Vol. 30

Schulze, R. *et al.* (eds.) (1987), *Flüchtlinge und Vertriebene in der westdeutschen Nachkriegsgeschichte*, Verlag August Lax, Hildesheim

Schwarz, H.-P. (1980), *Vom Reich zur Bundesrepublik: Deutschland im Widerstreit der aussenpolitischen Konzeptionen in den Jahren der Besatzungsherrschaft 1945–49*, Klett-Cotta, Stuttgart, 1965, 2nd edn

—— (1981), *Geschichte der Bundesrepublik Deutschland*, Vol. 2, *Die Ära Adenauer. Gründerjahre der Republik 1949–1957*, Deutsche Verlags-Anstalt, Stuttgart

—— (1982), 'Geschichtsschreibung und politisches Selbstverständnis. Die Geschichte der Bundesrepublik Deutschland—Herausforderung für die Forschung', *Aus Politik und Zeitgeschichte*, B36/82, pp. 3–26

—— (1986), *Adenauer. Der Aufstieg: 1876–1952*, Deutsche Verlags-Anstalt, Stuttgart

Scriverius, D. (1979), 'Die britische Demontagepolitik im Spiegel der Überlieferung des Hauptstaatsarchivs Düsseldorf' in C. Scharf and H.-J. Schröder (eds.), *Die Deutschlandpolitik Grossbritanniens und die britische Zone 1945–1949*, Steiner, Wiesbaden, pp. 93–101

Scriverius (ed.) (1981), *Demontage in Land Nordrhein-Westfalen 1946 bis 1951*, Republica Verlag, Siegburg

Sharp, T. (1975), *The Wartime Alliance and the Zonal Division of Germany*, Clarendon Press, Oxford

Shlaim, A. (1983), *The United States and the Berlin Blockade 1948–1949*, University of California Press, Berkeley, Ca.

—— (1984), 'Britain, the Berlin Blockade and the Cold War', *International Affairs*, Vol. 60, No. 1, pp. 1–14

Smith, J. E. (ed.) (1974), *The Papers of General Lucius D. Clay. Germany 1945–1949*, 2 vols., Indiana University Press, Bloomington, Ind.

Sons, H.-V. (1983), *Gesundheitspolitik während der Besatzungszeit*, Hammer, Wuppertal

Spiro, H. (1958), *The Politics of German Codetermination*, Harvard University Press, Cambridge, Mass.

Spotts, F. (1973), *Churches and Politics in Germany*, Wesleyan University Press, Middletown, Conn.

Stahltreuhändervereinigung (1954), *Die Neuordnung der Eisen- und Stahlindustrie im Gebiet der Bundesrepublik Deutschland*, Beck'sche Verlagsbuchhandlung, Munich

Stamp, A. M. (1947), 'Germany Without Incentive', *Lloyds Bank Review*, Vol. 5, pp. 14–28

Steinert, J. D. (1985), 'Vertriebenenverbände in Nordrheinwestfalen 1945–54', PhD thesis, University of Düsseldorf

Steininger, R. (1978), 'England und die deutsche Gewerkschaftsbewegung 1945/1946', *Archiv für Sozialgeschichte*, Vol. 18, pp. 41–118

—— (1979a), 'British Labour, Deutschland und die SPD 1945–1946', *Internationale Wissenschaftliche Korrespondenz*, Vol. 15, No. 2, pp. 182–226

—— (1979b), 'Deutschland und die Sozialistische Internationale nach dem Zweiten Weltkrieg', *Archiv für Sozialgeschichte*, Vol. 7, Neue Gesellschaft, Bonn

—— (1979c), 'Die Rhein–Ruhr-Frage im Kontext britischer Deutschlandpolitik 1945/46' in H. A. Winkler (ed.), *Politische Weichenstellungen in Nachkriegsdeutschland 1945–53*, Vandenhoeck & Ruprecht, Göttingen, pp. 41–166

—— (1979d), 'Reform und Realität. Ruhrfrage und Sozialisierung in der anglo-amerikanischen Deutschlandpolitik 1947/48', *Vierteljahreshefte für Zeitgeschichte*, Vol. 27, No. 2, pp. 167–240

—— (1982a), 'Die britische Deutschlandpolitik 1945/6', *Aus Politik und*

Zeitgeschichte, B1–2/82, pp. 28–47

—— (1982b), 'Grossbritannien und die Ruhr' in W. Först (ed.), *Ruhrkontrolle und Mitbestimmung*, Kohlhammer/Grote, Cologne, pp. 11–66

—— (1983a), *Deutsche Geschichte 1945–1961. Darstellung und Dokumente in zwei Bänden*, Fischer, Frankfurt on Main

—— (1983b), 'Wie die Teilung Deutschlands verhindert werden sollte. Der Robertson-Plan aus dem Jahre 1948', *Militärgeschichtliche Mitteilungen*, Vol. 33, No. 1, pp. 49–90

—— (1984), 'Ein vereintes, unabhängiges Deutschland? Winston Churchill, der Kalte Krieg und die deutsche Frage im Jahre 1953', *Militärgeschichtliche Mitteilungen*, Vol. 34, 1984, pp. 105–44

—— (1985a), 'Das Scheitern der EVG und der Beitritt der BRD zur NATO', *Aus Politik und Zeitgeschichte*, B17/85, pp. 3–18

—— (1985b), 'Die Sozialisierung fand nicht statt' in J. Foschepoth and R. Steininger (eds.), *Britische Deutschland- und Bezatzungspolitik 1945–1949*, Schöningh, Paderborn, pp. 135–50

—— (1985c), 'Die Stalin Note vom März 1952—eine Chance zur Wiedervereinigung Deutschlands?' in J. Foschepoth (ed.), *Kalter Krieg und Deutsche Frage*, Vandenhoeck & Ruprecht, Göttingen, pp. 362–79

—— (1985d), *Eine Chance zur Wiedervereinigung? Die Stalin-Note vom 10 März 1952*, Neue Gesellschaft, Bonn

—— (1985e), 'Westdeutschland ein "Bollwerk gegen den Kommunismus"? Grossbritannien und die deutsche Frage im Fruhjahr 1946', *Militärgeschichtliche Mitteilungen*, Vol. 35, No. 2, pp. 163–207

—— (1988), *Die Ruhrfrage 1945/46 und die Entstehung Nordrhein-Westfalens*, Droste, Düsseldorf

Stiefel, D. (1981), *Entnazifizierung in Österreich*, Europaverlag, Vienna

Stödter, R. (1982), *Schicksalsjahre deutscher Seeschiffahrt 1945–1955*, Mittler, Herford

Stokes, R. (1986), 'Recovery and Resurgence in the West German Chemical Industry: Allied Policy and the IG Farben Successor Companies 1945–51', PhD thesis, Ohio State University

Stolper, G., Häuser, K. and Borchardt, K. (1967), *The German Economy, 1870 to the Present* Weidenfeld and Nicolson, London

Stolper, W. and Roskamp, K. (1979), 'Planning a Free Economy: Germany 1945–60', *Zeitschrift für die gesamte Staatswissenschaft*, Vol. 135, No. 3, pp. 374–404

Stöss, R. (1983 and 1984), *Parteien-Handbuch. Die Parteien der Bundesrepublik Deutschland 1945–1980*, Vols. 1 and 2, Westdeutscher Verlag, Opladen

Strang, W. (1956), *Home and Abroad*, Deutsch, London

—— (1981), 'War and Foreign Policy 1933–45' in D. Dilks (ed.), *Retreat from Power. Studies in Britain's Foreign Policy of the Twentieth Century*, Vol. 2, *After 1939*, Macmillan, London, pp. 66–100

Stratmann, F. (1984), 'Strukturen der Bewirtschaftung in der Nachkriegszeit' in D. Petzina and W. Euchner (eds.), *Wirtschaftspolitik im britischen Besatzungsgebiet 1945–1949*, Schwann, Düsseldorf, pp. 153–72

—— (1987), *Chemische Industrie unter Zwang? Staatliche Einflussnahme am Beispiel der chemischen Industrie Deutschlands 1933–1949*, Steiner, Wiesbaden and Stuttgart

Stüber, G. (1984), *Der Kampf gegen den Hunger 1945–1950. Die Ernährungslage in der Britischen Zone Deutschlands, insbesondere in Schleswig-Holstein und Hamburg*, Karl Wachholtz Verlag, Neumünster

Sutton, A. C. (1973), *Western Technology and Soviet Economic Development*, Vol. 3, *1945–1965*, Stanford University Press, Stanford, Cal.

Tauber, K. (1967), *Beyond Eagle and Swastika*, Wesleyan University Press, Middletown, Conn.

Thies, J. (1979), 'What is going on in Germany? Britische Militärverwaltung in Deutschland 1945–46' in C. Scharf and H.–J. Schröder (eds.), *Die Deutschlandpolitik Grossbritanniens und die britische Zone 1945–49*, Franz Steiner, Wiesbaden, pp. 29–50

Thomas, M. (1984), *Deutschland, England über alles. Rückkehr als Besatzungsoffizier*, Siedler Verlag, Berlin

Thum, H. (1982), *Mitbestimmung in der Montanindustrie. Der Mythos vom Sieg der Gewerkschaften*, Deutsche Verlags-Anstalt, Stuttgart

Tracey, M. (1983), *Das unerreichbare Wunschbild. Ein Versuch über Hugh Greene und die Neugründung des Rundfunks in Nordwestdeutschland nach 1945*, Kohlhammer-Grote, Cologne

Trees, W., Whiting C. and Omansen T. (1978), *Drei Jahre nach Null. Geschichte der britischen Besatzungszone 1945–1948*, Droste, Düsseldorf

Treue, W. (1956), *Zehn Jahre Land Niedersachsen*, Niedersächsische Landeszentrale für Heimatdienst, Hanover

—— (1967), *Die Demontagepolitik der Westmächte nach dem Zweiten Weltkrieg. Unter besonderer Berücksichtigung ihrer Wirkung auf die Wirtschaft in Niedersachsen*, Niedersächsische Landeszentrale für politische Bildung, Hanover

Trittel, G. J. (1975), *Die Bodenreform in der Britischen Zone 1945–1949*, Klett-Cotta, Stuttgart

—— (1985a), 'Das Scheitern der Bodenreform "im Schatten des Hungers"' in J. Foschepoth and R. Steininger (eds.), *Die britische Deutschland- und Besatzungspolitik 1945–1949*, Schöningh, Paderborn, pp. 153–170

—— (1985b), 'Hunger und Politik in Westdeutschland, 1945–1948, Umrisse eines zentralen Nachkriegsphänomens', *Sozialwissenschaftliche Information für Unterricht und Studium*, Vol. 14, pp. 126ff

—— (1986), 'Die westlichen Besatzungsmächte und der Kampf gegen den Mangel 1945–1949', *Aus Politik und Zeitgeschichte*, B22/86, pp. 18–29

—— (1987), 'Hans Schlange-Schöningen: ein vergessener Politiker der "ersten Stunde"', *Vierteljahreshefte für Zeitgeschichte*, Vol. 35, No. 1, pp. 25–63

—— *Hunger und Politik in Westdeutschland, 1945–1950. Zum Einfluss der*

Ernährungskrise auf die politische und ökonomische Entwicklung in Westdeutschland (forthcoming)

Troeger, H. (1985), *Interregnum*, Oldenbourg Verlag, Munich

Turner, I. D. (1983), 'Electoral System Innovation: A Comparison of the Lower Saxony Electoral Laws of 1946 and 1977, Their Origins and Effects', *Electoral Studies*, Vol. 2, no. 2, pp. 131–49

—— (1984), 'British Occupation Policy and Its Effects on the Town of Wolfsburg and the Volkswagenwerk 1945–1949', PhD thesis, Manchester University

—— (1985), 'Das Volkswagenwerk—ein deutsches Unternehmen unter britischer Kontrolle' in J. Foschepoth and R. Steininger (eds.), *Britische Deutschland- und Besatzungspolitik 1945–1949*, Schöningh, Paderborn, pp. 281–302

—— (1987), 'Great Britain and the Post-War German Currency Reform', *Historical Journal*, Vol. 30, No. 3, pp. 685–708

—— (1988a), 'Being Beastly to the Germans? British Policy on Direct Imports of German Goods from the British Zone of Occupation to the UK, 1946–1948', *Journal of European Economic History*, forthcoming

—— (1989), 'Codetermination in British Occupied Germany 1945–1949' in C. J. Lammers and G. Szell (eds.), *International Handbook of Participation in Organisations*, Vol. 1, Oxford University Press, Oxford, forthcoming

Turnow, I. (1979), 'Die deutschen Unternehmerverbände 1945–50. Kontinuität oder Diskontinuität?' in J. Becker *et al.* (eds.), *Vorgeschichte der Bundesrepublik*, Wilhelm Fink Verlag, Munich, pp. 235–60

Tyrell, A. (1985a), 'Die deutschlandpolitische Hauptziele der Siegermächte im Zweiten Weltkrieg', *Aus Politik und Zeitgeschichte*, B13/85, pp. 23–39

—— (1985b), *Grossbritannien und die Deutschlandplanung der Alliierten 1941–45*, Alfred Metzner Verlag, Frankfurt

Uffelmann, U. (1982), 'Wirtschaft und Gesellschaft in der Gründungsphase der Bundesrepublik Deutschland. Eine Bestandsaufnahme in didaktischer Absicht', *Aus Politik und Zeitgeschichte*, B1–2/82, pp. 3–27

United Nations Economic Commission for Europe (UNECE) (1949), *Europe in 1948*, UN, Geneva

—— (1950), *Economic Survey of Europe in 1949*, UN, Geneva

—— (1953), *Economic Survey of Europe Since the War: A Reappraisal of Problems and Prospects*, UN, Geneva

—— (1954), *Economic Survey of Europe in 1953*, UN, Geneva

Utley, F. (1949), *The High Cost of Vengeance*, Regnery, Chicago Ill.

Vansittart, R. (1941), *Black Record: Germans Past and Present*, Hamish Hamilton, London

Vaubel, L. (1984), *Zusammenbruch und Wiederaufbau*, Oldenbourg Verlag, Munich

Vogel, W. (1956, 1964, 1983), *Westdeutschland 1945–1950. Der Aufbau von*

Verfassungs- und Verwaltungseinrichtungen über den Ländern der drei westlichen Besatzungszonen, Vols. 1–3 Bundesarchiv Koblenz and Boppard on Rhein

Vogelsang, T. (1963), *Hinrich Wilhelm Kopf und Niedersachsen*, Verlag für Literatur und Zeitgeschehen, Hanover

Volle, A. (1976), 'Deutsch–britische Beziehungen. Eine Untersuchung des bilateralen Verhältnisses auf der staatlichen und nichtstaatlichen Ebene seit dem Zweiten Weltkrieg', PhD thesis, University of Bonn

Waldmann, P. (1979), 'Die Eingliederung der ostdeutschen Vertriebenen in die westdeutsche Gesellschaft' in J. Becker, T. Stammen and P. Waldmann (eds.), *Vorgeschichte der Bundesrepublik Deutschland. Zwischen Kapitulation und Grundgesetz*, Wilhelm Fink Verlag, Munich, pp. 163–92

Wallich, H. C. (1955), *Mainsprings of the German Revival*, Yale University Press, New Haven, Conn.

Wandel, E. (1972), 'Adenauer und der Schuman Plan. Protokoll eines Gesprächs zwischen Konrad Adenauer und Hans Schäffer vom 3 Juni 1950', *Vierteljahreshefte für Zeitgeschichte*, Vol. 20, No. 2, pp. 192–203

—— (1980), *Die Entstehung der Bank der deutschen Länder und die deutsche Währungsreform 1948*, Knapp, Frankfurt

Wannöffel, M. (1984), 'Soziale und ökonomische Bedingungen gewerkschaftlichen Neuanfangs. Das Beispiel des Industrieverbandes Metall in Bochum 1945 bis 1947' in D. Petzina and W. Euchner (eds.) *Wirtschaftspolitik im britischen Besatzungsgebiet 1945–1949*, Schwann, Düsseldorf, pp. 277–96

Ward, P. D. (1979), *The Threat of Peace*, Kent State University Press, Kent City, Ohio

Warner, G. (1980), 'Die britische Labour-Regierung und die Einheit Westeuropas 1949–1951', *Vierteljahreshefte für Zeitgeschichte*, Vol. 28, No. 3, pp. 310–30

—— (1986), 'Britain and Europe in 1948: The View from the Cabinet' in J. Becker and F. Knipping (eds.), *Power in Europe? Great Britain, France, Italy and Germany in a Post-war World, 1945–1950*, Walter de Gruyter, Berlin and New York, pp. 27–46

Watt, D. C. (1965), *Britain Looks to Germany. British Opinion and Policy Towards Germany Since 1945*, Wolff, London

—— (1984), *Succeeding John Bull: America in Britain's Place 1900–75*, Cambridge University Press, Cambridge

Webb, R. G. (1979), 'Britain and the Future of Germany: British Planning for German Dismemberment and Reparations 1942–1945', PhD thesis, University of New York at Buffalo

Weir, C. (1949), 'Economic Developments in Western Germany', *International Affairs*, Vol. 25, No. 3, pp. 249–56

—— (1953), *Civilian Assignment*, Methuen, London

Weiss, H. (1984), 'Abschlussbericht über das OMGUS-Projekt (1976–1983)', *Vierteljahrshefte für Zeitgeschichte*, Vol. 32, No. 2, pp. 318–26

Welch, D. (1987), 'The Political Re-education of Germany after World War II: A Need for a Reappraisal?' *German History*, No. 4, pp. 23–35

Wendt, B.–J. (1971), *Economic Appeasement. Handel und Finanz in der britischen Deutschlandpolitik 1933–1939*, Bertelsmann, Düsseldorf

Wer ist Wer? (1948), Arani Verlags-GmbH, Berlin-Grünewald

Wernicke, K. G. and Booms, H. (eds.) (1975, 1981, 1986), *Der Parlamentarische Rat 1948–1949. Akten und Protokolle*, of which the following have appeared: *Vorgeschichte*, prepared by J. V. Wagner, *Der Verfassungskonvent auf Herrenchiemsee*, prepared by P. Bucher, and *Ausschuss für Zuständigkeitsabgrenzung*, prepared by W. Werner, Boldt, Boppard

Wheeler, G. S. (1958), *Die amerikanische Politik in Deutschland 1945–50*, Kongress-Verlag, East Berlin

Wiesemann, F. (1976), 'Die Gründung des deutschen Weststaats' in Institut für Zeitgeschichte (ed.), *Westdeutschlands Weg zur Bundesrepublik 1945–49*, Beck, Munich, pp. 118–34

—— (1985a), 'Flüchtlingspolitik in Nordrheinwestfalen' in W. Benz, *Die Vertreibung der Deutschen aus dem Osten*, Fischer, Frankfurt, pp. 183–92

—— (1985b), 'Flüchtlingspolitik und Flüchtlingsintegration in Westdeutschland', *Aus Politik und Zeitgeschichte*, B23/85, June pp. 35–44

Wiesemann, F. and Kleinert, U. (1984), 'Flüchtlinge und wirtschaftlicher Wiederaufbau im britischen Besatzungsgebiet' in D. Petzina and W. Euchner (eds.), *Wirtschaftspolitik im britischen Besatzungsgebiet 1945–49*, Schwann, Düsseldorf, pp. 297–326

Willenbacher, B. (1987), 'Zerrüttung und Bewährung der Nachkriegsfamilie' in M. Broszat *et al.* (eds.), *Von Stalingrad zur Währungsreform*, Oldenbourg Verlag, Munich

Williams, F. (1952), *Ernest Bevin*, Hutchinson, London

Willis, F. R. (1962), *The French in Germany 1945–49*, Stanford University Press, Stanford, Cal.

—— (1967), *France, Germany and the New Europe*, Stanford University Press, Stanford, Cal.

Windsor, P. (1969), *German Reunification*, Elek Books, London

Winkler, H. A. (ed.) (1979), *Politische Weichenstellungen in Nachkriegsdeutschland 1945–53*, Vandenhoeck & Ruprecht, Göttingen

Wirth, D. (1979), 'Die Familie in der Nachkriegszeit. Desorganisation oder Stabilität?' in J. Becker *et al.* (eds.), *Vorgeschichte der Bundesrepublik*, Wilhelm Fink Verlag, Munich, pp. 193–216

Wisotzky, K. (1983), *Der Ruhrbergbau im Dritten Reich*, Schwann, Düsseldorf

Wolf, E. (1948), 'Aufwendungen für die Besatzungsmächte, öffentliche Haushalte und Sozialprodukt in den einzelnen Zonen' in Deutsches Institut für Wirtschaftsforschung, *Wirtschaftsprobleme der Besatzungs-*

zonen, Duncker & Humblot, Berlin, pp. 116–42

Wolfe, R. (ed.) (1984), *Americans as Proconsuls. United States Military Government in Germany and Japan 1944–1952*, Southern Illinois University Press, Carbondale and Edwardsville, Ill.

Wolff, G. (1977), 'Behörden- und verbandsgeschichtliche Dokumentation der Vor- und Frühgeschichte der Bundesrepublik', *Vierteljahreshefte für Zeitgeschichte*, Vol. 25, No. 4, pp. 931–2

Wollasch, H.–J. (1976), *Humanitäre Auslandshilfe für Deutschland nach dem Zweiten Weltkrieg. Darstellung und Dokumentation kirchlicher und nichtkirchlicher Hilfen*, Deutscher Caritasverband, Freiburg

Woller, H. (1986), *Gesellschaft und Politik in der amerikanischen Besatzungszone*, Oldenbourg Verlag, Munich

Wood, B. (1984), *Alias Papa: A Life of Fritz Schumacher*, Cape, London

Woodward, E. L. (1976), *British Foreign Policy in the Second World War*, Vol. 5, HMSO, London

Wuermeling, H. (1981), *Die Weisse Liste*, Ullstein, Berlin, Frankfurt and Vienna

Yergin, D. (1977), *Shattered Peace: The Origins of the Cold War and the National Security State*, Houghton Mifflin, Boston, Mass.

Young, J. W. (1986), 'The Foreign Office, the French and the Post War Division of Germany, 1945–46', *Review of International Studies*, Vol. 12, pp. 223–34

Zank, W. (1984), 'Wirtschaftsplanung und Bewirtschaftung in der Sowjetischen Besatzungszone—Besonderheiten und Parallelen im Vergleich zum Westlichen Besatzungsgebiet', *Vierteljahrschrift für Sozial- und Wirtschaftsgeschichte*, Vol. 71, No. 4, pp. 485–504

—— (1987), *Wirtschaft und Arbeit in Ostdeutschland 1945–1949*, Oldenbourg Verlag, Munich

Zayas, A. M. de (1977), *Nemesis at Potsdam. The Anglo-Americans and the Expulsion of the Germans. Background, Execution, Consequences*, Routledge and Kegan Paul, London

Zelinsky, U. (1979), 'Bedingungen und Probleme der Neubildung von Führungsgruppen in Deutschland 1945–1949' in J. Becker *et al.* (eds.), *Vorgeschichte der Bundesrepublik*, Wilhelm Fink Verlag, Munich, pp. 217–34

Ziebura, G. (1970), *Die deutsch–französischen Beziehungen seit 1945. Mythen und Realitäten*, Neske, Pfullingen

Ziemer, G. (1973), *Deutscher Exodus. Vertreibung und Eingliederung von 15 Millionen Ostdeutschen*, Seewald Verlag, Stuttgart

Ziemke, E. (1975), *The US Army in the Occupation of Germany 1944–1946*, Center of Military History, US Army, Washington

Zimmerman, E. P. (1983), 'Germany's Defeat and the Creation of the West German Basic Law 1945–49', PhD thesis, University of California (Riverside)

Index

415

Index